Contemporary Views on Architecture a

Current Studies in Linguistics
Samuel Jay Keyser, general editor

A complete list of books published in the Current Studies in Linguistics series appears at the back of this book.

Contemporary Views on Architecture and Representations in Phonology

edited by Eric Raimy and Charles E. Cairns

A Bradford Book
The MIT Press
Cambridge, Massachusetts
London, England

MIT Press books may be purchased at special quantity discounts for business or sales promotional use. For information, please e-mail special_sales@mitpress.mit.edu or write to Special Sales Department, The MIT Press, 55 Hayward Street, Cambridge, MA 02142.

This book was set in Times New Roman and Syntax on 3B2 by Asco Typesetters, Hong Kong and was printed and bound in the United States of America.

Library of Congress Cataloging-in-Publication Data

Contemporary views on architecture and representations in phonology / edited by Eric Raimy and Charles E. Cairns.
    p.   cm. — (Current studies in linguistics)
Includes bibliographical references and index.
ISBN 978-0-262-18270-6 (hardcover : alk. paper) — ISBN 978-0-262-68172-8 (pbk. : alk. paper)
1. Grammar, Comparative and general—Phonology—Methodology. I. Raimy, Eric.
II. Cairns, Charles E.
P217.C667   2009
414—dc22   2008029816

10 9 8 7 6 5 4 3 2 1

Contents

Contributors

Juliette Blevins   Department of Linguistics, Max Planck Institute for Evolutionary Anthropology

Charles E. Cairns   MA/PhD Program in Linguistics, City University of New York

Andrea Calabrese   Department of Linguistics, University of Connecticut

G. N. Clements   Laboratoire de Phonétique et Phonologie, CNRS/Sorbonne-Nouvelle

B. Elan Dresher   Department of Linguistics, University of Toronto

Morris Halle   Department of Linguistics and Philosophy, MIT

Harry van der Hulst   Department of Linguistics, University of Connecticut

William J. Idsardi   Department of Linguistics, University of Maryland

Ellen M. Kaisse   Department of Linguistics, University of Washington

Andrew Nevins   Department of Linguistics, Harvard University

Thomas Purnell   Department of Linguistics, University of Wisconsin–Madison

Eric Raimy   Department of English, University of Wisconsin–Madison

Charles Reiss   Linguistics Program, Concordia University

Keren Rice   Department of Linguistics, University of Toronto

Bert Vaux   Department of Linguistics, University of Cambridge

Andrew Wolfe

Acknowledgments

This volume is the result of the City University of New York (CUNY) Phonology Forum Symposium on Architecture and Representation in Phonology that was held in Manhattan on 20–21 February 2004. At this conference, the initial forms of the chapters contained here were presented, followed by comments from the symposium participants. All of the authors then revised their work, taking the symposium discussion into account.

We want to thank all the members of the organizing committee who helped put the symposium together. We especially want to thank the cosponsors of the symposium, the CUNY Phonology Forum, and the CUNY MA/PhD Program in Linguistics.

1 Architecture and Representations in Phonology

Charles E. Cairns and Eric Raimy

1.1 Introduction

The essays in this volume address foundational questions in phonology: What sorts of phenomena comprise the explananda of the field? How should phonological objects be represented? What is the optimal architecture for phonological theory? These questions cut across different schools of thought within the discipline, and they remain largely open after a half century of research.

A main theme is that to study phonology productively, one must ask what modules are necessary, how these modules interact with each other and with other components of linguistic theory, and what the representational and computational resources of each module are. Computation and representation are inherently linked; as John McCarthy sagely remarked, "Simply put, if the representations are right, then the rules will follow" (1988:84).

The modular approach seems natural simply because phonology is a component of human cognition, ultimately a biological object; all biological entities more complex than viruses are arguably best understood in a modular framework. The modular approach also enables us to break the larger questions of phonology into smaller ones. We can ask of apparently bewildering arrays of complex surface phenomena: What components are responsible for the facts at hand? Which aspects of the behavior are directly due to operations within components and which emerge from interactions between components? Rough answers to these questions help develop more precise questions about the individual components and the architecture that houses them.

The following sections introduce three examples showing how the modular approach advances our understanding of phonology. The first example (section 1.2) illustrates the benefits of a modular perspective by showing that advances in the understanding of phonetic modules allow us to remove from phonology's purview a classic and formerly vexing problem, the North American English vowel length alternations before voiced and voiceless obstruents. The efficacy of modularity within the phonology proper is shown in the next example (section 1.3), where we argue that the interaction among stress, syllabification, and vowel devoicing in Southern Paiute suggests distinct internal modules, one for stress and another for syllable structure. The third example (section 1.4) shows that positing three distinct modules for morphology, syllable structure, and "segmental" phonological processes (e.g., assimilation, vowel reduction) resolves the challenging problem of an apparent lexical syllabic contrast in Sinhala. The organization of the volume is described in section 1.5.

1.2 Phonetics and Phonology as Distinct Components

Keyser and Stevens (2001, 2006; KS) propose a theory of the phonetic component consisting of an interacting set of devices that transform representations produced by the phonology into articulatory instructions. Some of these phonetic modules are sensitive to language-particular information.

In his famous 1941 paper "Phonemic Overlapping," Bloch introduced the theoretical problem of the North American English vowel length alternations that occur before voiced and voiceless consonants. He pointed out that "the pairs of words *bit bid*, *bet bed*, *bat bad*, *but bud*, *bite bide*, *beat bead*, etc., have respectively the same vowel phoneme, but exhibit a regular and fairly constant difference in the length of the vowel allophones" (1941:283). He went on to identify the vowel in *pot* as the same phoneme in *bomb*; the vowel in *balm* is phonemically longer, but identical in quality. So, except for *bomb balm*, all the length alternations are allophonic.

The length alternations cited above would lead the rational phonologist to conclude that *pot* should have the same phoneme as in *pod*, just as the vowel pairs in *bit bid*, *bet bed*, *but bud* all share respectively the same phoneme. However, Bloch objected that "in the sentence *Pa'd go (if he could)*, the utterance fraction *pa'd* must be analyzed... as containing the phoneme of *balm*. In the sentence *The pod grows*, the utterance fraction *pod* must be analyzed... as containing the phoneme of *pot*" (1941:283–284). But if *Pa'd* has the long phoneme, homophonous *pod* cannot have the short phoneme because there would be no taxonomic procedure that could reliably assign the vowel of *Pa'd* to the long phoneme and of *pod* to the short one. Therefore, *pod*, *Pa'd*, and *balm* all have the same vowel, which is different from the vowel in *pot*, which of course has the same vowel phoneme as *bomb*. The insistence on taxonomic procedures destroys the parallelism between *pot pod* and *bit bid*, *bet bed*, *but bud*. Bloch admits that "the resulting system is lopsided; but the classes it sets up are such that if we start from the actual utterances of the dialect we can never be in doubt of the class to which any particular fraction of utterance must be assigned" (1941:284).

Chomsky (1964:90ff.), mentioning Bloch's forfeiture of a linguistically significant generalization, proposed to capture the length alternations with a rule of generative phonology that lengthens vowels before voiced obstruents. Although this rule is descriptively adequate, it lacks any explanatory force. The rule seems to somehow reflect a phonetically "natural" process of some kind, yet an otherwise identical rule that had just the opposite effect would be as easy to formulate in his system. So the generative solution is as unsatisfactory as was the taxonomic one, albeit for different reasons.

According to KS, it turns out that the length alternations are not handled in the phonology at all. They are due to a phonetic effect known as enhancement (a topic also discussed in Clements's chapter 2 in this volume). *Enhancement* refers to a set of phonetic processes that add salience to phonological contrasts. For example, the perceptibility of the contrast between [ʃ] and [s] is enhanced by rounding the lips for the former; lip rounding produces resonance in the frequency region typical of nonanterior sounds (KS 2006:50). This rounding is a phonetic phenomenon, not a phonological one, as shown by its variable nature and its inertness with respect to any purely phonological process. It is handled by a distinct *phonetic* module responsible for enhancement.

KS (2001) say that the length alternation at the heart of the Bloch-Chomsky dispute is also an example of phonetic enhancement. A glottal constriction gesture accents the salience of the voicelessness of the final obstruent, which results in a shortening of the vowel. The length reductions produced by this phonetic process never serve as focus, trigger, or blocker of any known phonological rule or constraint. Chomsky's rule becomes unproblematic because it ceases to exist.

We have sketched how the development of an explicit, modular theory of the phonetic component has enabled phonologists to get on with building a phonological theory with one niggling problem safely withdrawn from its domain of explananda. As KS recognize and address, any theory of the phonetic component raises the same questions as does a theory of phonology in Universal Grammar (UG): What modules are involved? What are their computational and representational resources? How do they interact? We now turn to a discussion of these questions within phonology.

1.3 Modularity within Phonology: The Syllable and the Foot

What is the modular structure of the phonology proper? This topic is illuminated at length in chapters 13–15, but here we demonstrate the efficacy of the modular approach by asking whether all prosodic categories are generated by the same mechanism, or whether some categories may require unique mechanisms. We will focus in particular on the categories "syllable" and "foot" and on whether each has its own dedicated module or whether they are both produced by one. (We will not deal with the internal structure of the syllable in this chapter, as that is discussed in chapters 5–8.)

At least some sort of syllable structure is apparently present at a variety of phonetic, phonological, and morphological levels. Phonetically, KS have shown that the glottalization typical of syllable-final coronal consonants in American English is an enhancement phenomenon (KS 2006:54–55), so phonetic theory must define at least "syllable-final." The syllable is well known to be active in the phonology, where it is crucial for understanding constraints on sequences of segments, a variety of epenthesis and deletion facts, and a host of other phenomena. As illustrated in chapters 8 and 19, the morphology also needs syllable structure in order to spell out morphemes. Therefore, syllables appear to be formed in some module that interacts with phonetic, phonological, and morphological components in interesting ways.

Are syllables produced by a unique mechanism, or are they part of something larger? The theory of the prosodic hierarchy (e.g., Selkirk 1980, Selkirk and Shen 1990) claims that syllables are part of a larger hierarchical plane, the prosodic plane, (1), that contains prosodic feet, prosodic words, and higher-level constituents (Blevins 1995:210). "Prosodic foot" is a key prosodic hierarchy notion in accounting for word stress.

(1) *The prosodic plane showing the universal prosodic hierarchy*

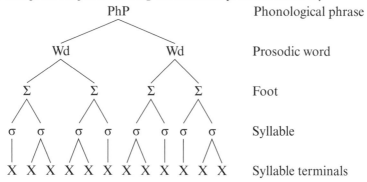

PhP	Phonological phrase
Wd	Prosodic word
Σ	Foot
σ	Syllable
X	Syllable terminals

To restate the hypothesis of the prosodic hierarchy theory in modular terms, it asserts that one module is responsible for producing representations like those in (1) on the prosodic plane. Stress, sequential constraints, deletion, and epenthesis—in fact, all foot-based and syllable-based generalizations—can be deduced from a single two-dimensional plane as in (1), the output of a single module of UG.

The one-module versus two-module question is an empirical one. Are there cases where the constituents needed for stress phenomena conflict with those needed for syllable-based facts? The nub of the issue is whether or not the syllable is the inviolable unit for bearing stress (e.g., Hayes 1995 and much recent work). If it were, one would expect syllables to nest neatly within feet; but if some languages were to employ vowels as the stress-bearing unit, then the possibility would exist that the constituents needed for stress might conflict with those needed for syllabic facts.

Recall the hypothesis that syllables and feet are the responsibility of different modules, each drawing graphs on distinct planes. These planes intersect along a line, known as the segmental tier; because such representations require three dimensions to be depicted, they are known as three-dimensional theories (Halle and Vergnaud 1980, 1987; see chapter 6). We will comment briefly at the end of this section on the alignment among the planes of 3-D phonology. Chapters 10–12 present theories of a module responsible for stress, all of which assume that syllables are generated by a mechanism distinct from the one that produces metrical feet. Such theories are typically known as metrical theories of stress, and the constituents corresponding to word stress are known as metrical feet. Metrical and prosodic feet result from conflicting theories, so they are difficult to compare. Nevertheless, they are very different, as we will show below and as Cairns shows in chapter 6.

The prosodic hierarchy and 3-D theories make contrasting predictions about how the edges of feet and of syllables align. A prosodic foot cannot split a syllable, for the straightforward reason that syllables are constituents of feet. No such restriction applies to metrical feet, however; syllables and metrical feet are created in independent modules and their alignment is orthogonal to their generation. This raises the issue of Syllable Integrity (Everett 1998), the principle that supposedly prevents a foot from bisecting a syllable; see (2). Violations of Syllable Integrity are formally prohibited in prosodic hierarchy theory but freely predicted in 3-D phonology.

(2) Syllable Integrity prohibits . . . (v][v)(v][v) . . . , where syllable boundaries are shown by square brackets and foot boundaries by parentheses. Equivalently: no language may make a contrast between tautosyllabic v̀v and vv̀.

Southern Paiute, a Shoshonean language, provides compelling evidence of violations of Syllable Integrity. The feet required to account for stress clearly bisect the syllables required to account for distributional and other phonological phenomena. Cairns (2002) uses a version of metrical theory known as the simplified bracketed grid model of prosody (Idsardi 1992, this volume, Halle and Idsardi 1995) to show that Southern Paiute may assign adjacent, tautosyllabic vowels to separate feet, a clear violation of Syllable Integrity. Southern Paiute counts vowels, not syllables, in its stress system, yet syllables are necessary to account for phonotactics and some morpheme alternations. Cairns demonstrates that the syllables needed to account for these phenomena do not always respect the foot structure that is part of the stress system, resulting in violations of Syllable Integrity.

The strongest evidence that Southern Paiute violates Syllable Integrity is the interaction between stress and a vowel-devoicing rule. Even-numbered, nonfinal vowels, counting from the left edge of a word, are stressed; in metrical terms, the grammar constructs iambic feet from left to right, and the word-final vowel is extrametrical. Unstressed vowels that immediately precede a geminate obstruent are devoiced (as are final vowels). Tautosyllabic long vowels and diphthongs behave like a sequence of two vowels for calculating stress and for devoicing; the second half is subject to devoicing if in the proper environment, and the first half retains its voicing.

The key example involves a lexical stem of the form /papapaa/, where the last two vowels are demonstrably tautosyllabic (we are using Sapir's (1949) designation of /p/ for obstruent and /a/ for vowel; for actual examples, arguments about the tautosyllabicity of the relevant vowel sequences, and an account of the phonetic details, see Sapir 1949 and Cairns 2002). In our example, this stem is followed by a suffix of the shape /−ppapaa/, where the first two *p*'s refer to a geminate obstruent. In a word consisting of just this stem and suffix (i.e., /papapaa + ppapaa/), stress falls on the second of the adjacent vowels in the stem (we have underlined the vowel of interest): /papàpaa̲ppapàa/. The vowel we are interested in is stressed, and therefore not susceptible to devoicing, even though it precedes a geminate obstruent.

If we now add a prefix that contains one vowel (so the word becomes /nam + papapaa + ppapaa/), the vowel count in the stem is shifted to the left by one, and stress now falls on the first of the adjacent vowels: /nampàpapàappàpaa/. The vowel we are watching (still underlined) is now the weak member of the foot headed by the vowel that follows it in the next syllable; our vowel devoices, because it precedes a geminate obstruent (voiceless vowels are represented as A, and the first half of the geminate becomes [h]): [nampàpapàA̲hpàpaA]. This is a clear violation of Syllable Integrity: the behavior of the tautosyllabic v̀v differs dramatically from that of tautosyllabic vv̀.

Recall that we are interested in whether stress and syllable structure must be represented on one or two planes. The 3-D model of phonology accounts for the facts of Southern Paiute as in (3).

(3) *3-D model showing violation of Syllable Integrity*

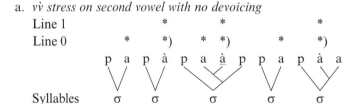

    a. *v̀v stress on second vowel with no devoicing*

    b. *v̀V stress on first vowel with devoicing of second vowel*

(3a) and (3b) show the metrical and syllabic analysis of /papàpaàppapàa/ and /nampàpapàappàpaa/, respectively. Syllable structures are depicted below the strings of phonemes, which represent the segmental tier. The syllable structures for (3a) and (3b) are identical, except that (3b) has the added syllable from the prefix.

The metrical planes are above the strings of phonemes. Line 0 of the metrical plane has an asterisk for every potentially stress-bearing unit, which is every nonfinal vowel in Southern Paiute. The brackets on line 0, which define metrical feet, are inserted by a rule of a form described in greater detail in chapters 9–12. The marks on line 1 (also inserted by rule) represent the heads of the iambic feet defined on line 0. Notice that the metrical structure in (3b) is similar to that in (3a) (except for an extra asterisk on the right in (3b)), but it is shifted over one vowel because of the prefix /nam/.

Observe that the second metrical bracket in (3a) is immediately to the right of the asterisk that is projected from the underlined /a/, which is the final vowel of the syllable in which it resides. This bracket conforms to Syllable Integrity, because it does not bisect a syllable. In (3b), however, the second metrical foot is terminated by a bracket that occurs between the first and second vowels of a tautosyllabic vowel sequence. This is a violation of Syllable Integrity.

(4) presents two possible representations for (3b) in a prosodic hierarchy–type model.

(4) *Violations of Syllable Integrity in a prosodic hierarchy–type model*

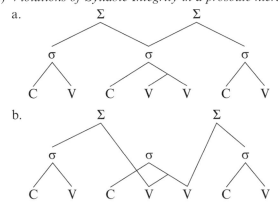

Since the prosodic hierarchy theory produces syllables as constituents of feet, it may be mathematically impossible for it to produce objects like those presented in (4). One might propose an "ambifooted syllable" analysis, as shown in (4a). The problem with (4a) is that it does not clearly specify that the left vowel of the shared syllable is the head of the left foot and that the right vowel in the same syllable is the weak member of the right foot. (4b) overcomes these infelicities of (4a) but has other serious problems. For example, each of the two feet directly dominates one syllable and one vowel, and they do so just when there is a syllable not parsed into a foot also dominating those same vowels. While this representation does not have the problems associated with the ambifooted syllables in (4a), the syllable in (4b) that requires stress is not contained in a foot and thus cannot be stressed in the prosodic hierarchy theory.

One possible response to this problem for the prosodic hierarchy theory is the derivational approach adopted by Hayes (1995:121–122), who posits a level of representation where long vowels are syllabified into two distinct syllables. This early syllabification makes each vowel a syllable so stress can be calculated on syllables alone. The vowel-devoicing rule also applies at this stage. A second syllabification rule then converts CV.V sequences into a single syllable. This solution to the mismatch between syllables and feet is ad hoc and should be rejected.

One might alternatively try to turn Syllable Integrity into a violable constraint as in Optimality Theory (Prince and Smolensky 2004), as Everett (1998) suggests. This would license the incoherent representations shown in (4) as possibly optimal outputs. However, these presumably cannot be generated in a prosodic hierarchy–based theory of representation. A 3-D model of representation must be assumed by any theory that tolerates violation of Syllable Integrity.

The Southern Paiute facts show that phonology contains at least two modules, one for syllables and the other for metrical feet. These modules operate independently of each other, and each has its own computational and representational resources, as discussed later in this volume. Each creates graphs on its own two-dimensional plane. The 3-D proposal is that these planes intersect at the segmental tier. What constraints there are on how representations from these two planes may align with respect to each other on the segmental tier remains an open and important question. Whatever these constraints are, they clearly do not preclude violations of Syllable Integrity.

1.4   Modularity Producing Emergent Phenomena

If syllabification and stress are calculated in separate modules, what is the role of phonological rules of the sort that account for assimilation, vowel reduction, and other segmental phenomena? Do such rules inhabit a distinct module that interacts with the stress and syllabification modules? And what about morphological rules that situate affixes with respect to roots and are responsible for true allomorphy? Are they also in a dedicated module?

An example from Sinhala throws some light on these questions.

(5) *A Sinhala contrast (syllable boundaries supplied)*
    a. ka.^{n}də   'trunk, sg. def.'
    b. kan.də   'hill, sg. def.'

These examples appear to show a lexical contrast between a prenasalized stop and a heterosyllabic nasal-stop sequence. If this were valid, it would be the only such contrast attested in the world. Cairns and Feinstein (1982) and Feinstein (1979) show that this is a surface contrast between a tautosyllabic and a heterosyllabic nasal-stop sequence, also unattested as a lexical contrast. As we will show, this contrast emerges from the interaction among three modules: one for morphology, one for syllable structure, and one dedicated to phonological rules.

We first digress into a brief examination of the data in (6) (from Cairns and Feinstein 1982:217), illustrating causative formation in Sinhala.

(6) *Some Sinhala verbs, all in the present indicative*

	Noncausative		Causative		Root	Gloss
	Phonetic	*Lexical*	*Phonetic*	*Lexical*		
a.	yanəwa	ya na waa	yawənəwa	ya wa na waa	ya	'go'
b.	kapənəwa	kapa na waa	kappənəwa	kap wa na waa	kapa	'cut'
c.	aⁿdənəwa	anda na waa	andənəwa	and wa na waa	anda	'put on'

Note the alternation between the supposedly prenasalized stop and the heterosyllabic nasal-stop sequence in (6c); this is parallel to the alternation between the singleton and geminate stops in (6b). Because such parallel alternations are common in Sinhala paradigms, a single set of generalizations must be responsible for both of these alternations. Note that we are in fact dealing with an alternation between a tautosyllabic and a heterosyllabic sequence, as in (7).

(7) *Geminates and prenasalized stops in Sinhala*
    a. ka.pə... kap.pə...
    b. a.ndə... an.də...

To understand these facts, we must delve into the morphological structure of the forms in (6). To quote Cairns and Feinstein (1982:217), "The morphological structure of these forms is *Root (+ Causative) + Present + Indicative.*" The underlying form of the causative is /wa/ for the forms in (6) (Feinstein 1979). The causative suffix is added after the last consonant of the root, entailing deletion of any stem-final vowel; however, if the stem is monosyllabic, the suffix is added after the final vowel. The present tense, indicated by the morpheme /na/, is added after the last segment of the stem. The indicative suffix is /waa/. These morphological rules, coupled with the syllabification process mentioned below, produce the structures in (8).

(8) *Structure of Sinhala present indicative verbs in (6)*
    Noncausative   *Causative*

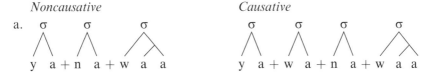

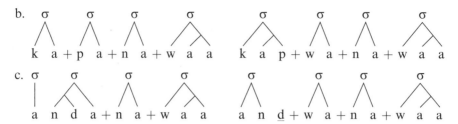

b.

k a + p a + n a + w a a   k a p + w a + n a + w a a

c.

a n d a + n a + w a a   a n d̲ + w a + n a + w a a

Sinhala analyzes an intervocalic nasal-stop sequence as a tautosyllabic onset; see the noncausative in (8c). Observe that Sinhala also allows nasals in coda position, as the causative of (8c) indicates; this will prove crucial in our analysis. Sinhala does not allow complex codas, nor may onsets consist of a /dw-/ sequence. Therefore, the /d/ in the causative of (8c) ends up being unsyllabified, which we indicate both by underlining it and by representing it as unaffiliated with a syllabic node. These brief comments about Sinhala syllabification suffice for present needs.

The morphological and syllabification modules interact to produce the representations in (8), which are in turn handed over to a module that contains phonological rules. One such rule reduces all occurrences of the vowel /a/ to [ə] in open, nonstressed (= noninitial) syllables in Sinhala. Feinstein (1977) argues that long vowels in unstressed, word-final position in Sinhala are shortened and unreduced, so /waa/ always surfaces as [wa]. (Shortening and reduction are counterfeeding.) Note that the surface forms of the noncausative examples are all generated simply by the rules of Vowel Reduction and Vowel Shortening, applied in that order. Sinhala also has a productive rule of Glide Assimilation, which renders a glide identical to a consonant to its left (Feinstein 1977, 1979, Cairns and Feinstein 1982); it is unordered with respect to Vowel Reduction and Vowel Shortening. The three rules are shown in (9).

(9) *Some Sinhala phonological rules*
    a. *Vowel Reduction*
       /a/ → [ə] / open, nonstressed (noninitial) syllables
    b. *Vowel Shortening*

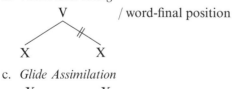

/ word-final position

    c. *Glide Assimilation*

Obs   Glide

The rules of Glide Assimilation, Vowel Reduction, and Vowel Shortening apply to the forms in (8) to produce the surface forms in (6). (10) shows the derivations of the causative forms of (8b) and (8c).

(10) *Derivations for* kappənəwa *and* andənəwa

   a. *Underlying representation*

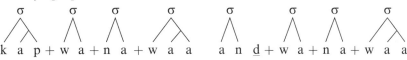

   b. *Vowel Reduction*

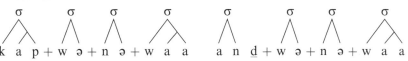

   c. *Vowel Shortening*

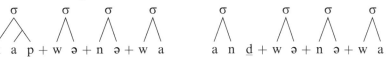

   d. *Glide Assimilation*

   e. *Unsyllabified Consonant Deletion*

Glide Assimilation assimilates the underlying /w/ to the consonant to its left, /p/ in the causative of (8b) and /d/ in the causative of (8c). The root-final /d/ then deletes because it is unsyllabified. (Note that the /p/ and /d/ become root-final as a result of the morphological rule adding the causative suffix.) Without making a firm theoretical statement regarding how the unsyllabified segment is eliminated, it is commonplace in phonology to invoke deletion as one of the strategies for handling unsyllabified segments. (The examples in (5) are treated in a way similar to those in (6): Cairns and Feinstein (1982) argue that *kaⁿdə* and *kandə* (better, *ka.ndə* and *kan.də*) are underlyingly /kand + a/ and /kand + wa/.)

It can now be seen that the heterosyllabic nasal-obstruent sequence is the result of Glide Assimilation followed by the deletion of unsyllabified consonants. Both the heterosyllabic and the tautosyllabic nasal-obstruent sequences are licit in Sinhala, so there is no need for resyllabification to apply. Therefore, the derivations in (10) are complete. The parallelism between the geminate/singleton and the heterosyllabic/tautosyllabic alternations is explained, and there is no question of a lexical contrast based on syllabification.

Note that this problem is easily understood with minimal and uncontroversial assumptions about the nature of each of the three relevant modules, as well as of their mode of interaction. These facts are troubling to most other perspectives in phonology because they appear to demonstrate contrastive syllabification in the lexicon.

1.5   Organization of the Volume

This volume has five main parts, four dealing with core aspects of phonology and the fifth dealing with interactions within and among modules. Parts I–IV each consist of a main chapter followed by two or three shorter commentaries; part V contains four freestanding chapters.

1.5.1   Phonological Features

Part I deals with the status of phonological features. In the lead chapter of this part (chapter 2), Clements argues for general principles underlying phonological features that make up the segmental inventory of specific languages. He describes several principles governing segment inventories, including Feature Bounding, which determines an upper bound on how many segments and contrasts may occur in an inventory. Another principle is Feature Economy, which favors the maximum use of feature combinations. A distinct theory of markedness can be developed from these principles. Clements uses the expanded UPSID (UCLA Phonological Segment Inventory Database) as his source of data.

Two commentaries follow, both agreeing with Clements on the primacy of distinctive features in phonological theory. In chapter 3, Halle stresses the importance of the details of distinctive feature theory; he points out that the distinctive feature [±palatalized] is profitably replaced with [±back], and that [±slack vocal cords] should substitute for [±voiced]. He questions the validity of conclusions based on an outmoded theory of features. Halle's chapter also contains an important cautionary tale based on the history of feature theory.

Vaux, in chapter 4, asks exactly where Clements's principle of Feature Economy resides in the overall cognitive capacities of human beings. Is this principle unique to the language component of the human brain? Is it a general property of the human brain and not specific to human language? Are this and other principles merely the result of the interaction of other cognitive functions? Vaux also questions those of Clements's conclusions that are based on faulty data from UPSID.

1.5.2   The Syllable

Part II focuses on contemporary theories of syllabification in phonology. Chapter 5 by Vaux and Wolfe is the lead chapter of this part. In Vaux and Wolfe's view, all segments must be prosodically licensed by association with some syllable, foot, prosodic word, or other level of the prosodic hierarchy, as in (1). Segments are typically associated with syllables, in strict conformity with the Sonority-Sequencing Principle (SSP). An appendix is any segment that cannot be associated with a syllable in accordance with the SSP. Such segments are instead associated with some higher prosodic structure.

In the first commentary on syllables, chapter 6, Cairns suggests that prosodic licensing has no content, because all possible responses to prosodically unlicensed segments (epenthesis, deletion, no action) are attested. He also argues that the SSP is not useful in understanding syllabification. Cairns splits Vaux and Wolfe's appendices into either plain stray segments (i.e., not associated to any prosodic structure) or members of more richly conceived syllables.

In the second commentary on syllables, chapter 7, Clements argues that the main phonetic correlate of phonological sonority is resonance within the phonetic signal, consistent with a salient formant structure. This explains why low vowels are the most sonorous (have the strongest formant structures) and obstruent stops are the least sonorous (completely lack formant structures). Clements also explains what sonority is and is not supposed to account for, and differs from Cairns regarding the utility of the SSP.

In the final commentary on syllables, chapter 8, Raimy seeks to demonstrate that many of the distributional arguments based on reduplication and infixation to support Vaux and Wolfe's idea of an appendix are actually irrelevant. He also presents a case of reduplication from Thao that requires an abstract syllabification that Vaux and Wolfe deny.

1.5.3 Metrical Structure

Part III deals with metrical structure and begins with chapter 9, Idsardi's revision of the simplified bracketed grid (SBG) approach to stress patterns using finite state automata as the computational basis of the formalism. This revision of the SBG approach abandons avoidance constraints and adds ternary counting as a parameter. The previous distinction between edge marking and iterative constituent construction is replaced with a parameter governing whether or not a rule is iterative. These new parameters, plus an account of the finite state automata that constitute the mathematical underpinning of the rules, produce an exhaustive listing of the basic metrical rules.

Dresher's comments on Idsardi's proposals, in chapter 10, are based on an SBG analysis of "metrical incoherence" found in Tiberian Hebrew. Dresher argues in favor of a well-known feature of the SBG approach, that constituents are defined with unmatched brackets. This allows the analytical possibility of building part of the stressed foot with a rule that inserts an unmatched bracket and then completing it later in the derivation with a rule that inserts a bracket delimiting the original constituent. Dresher suggests that the derivational approach and the possibility of unmatched brackets renders the SBG approach unique among theories of stress in its ability to provide a satisfactory analysis of the Tiberian Hebrew facts.

In chapter II, van der Hulst presents an alternative view of the nature of stress systems by discussing the main-stress-first model. This contribution provides the opportunity to evaluate current understanding of metrical systems. Van der Hulst also questions the utility of attention to formalisms and finite state automata, as does Reiss in chapter 12.

Reiss attempts to simplify representational aspects of the SBG approach by his *Separator Theory*, where left and right brackets are replaced by a single symbol, the separator symbol "|." This approach is conceptually simpler than the SBG approach because it reduces the number of primitives, but it requires empirical argumentation, as Reiss discusses.

1.5.4 Architecture

Part IV addresses the overall architecture of the phonological component. Calabrese, in chapter 13, argues that a model of phonology must account for both natural and conventional aspects of phonology. By "natural," Calabrese means those aspects accounted for more or less directly by the phonological components of UG, which include various aspects of markedness, constraints, repairs, and natural rules. "Conventional" aspects of phonology are those that require idiosyncratic rules and extrinsic ordering; these are frequently vestiges of diachronic processes. Calabrese's theory of the overall architecture attempts to capture the ways in which the natural and the conventional aspects of phonology interact. As is consistent with the theme of this volume, Calabrese proposes a concrete and detailed theory of the modules within phonology, the representations appropriate for and the computations within each module, and the interaction among these modules.

Calabrese also suggests that language change occurs primarily through lexical and social diffusion. This point is disputed by Kaisse, who in chapter 14 points out that roughly 30 years of Labovian sociolinguistics provide evidence against the view that lexical diffusion is the main vector of language change. She suggests that gradient phonetic changes are part of language change.

Rice, in chapter 15, who along with Kaisse generally agrees with Calabrese's approach, compares her view of markedness as a substantive part of UG with Hale and Reiss's (2000) model of substance-free phonology. She suggests that the presence or absence of phonological contrast is a key factor in sorting out these issues. Markedness appears to be "substance-free" in the absence of contrast, but it is productive to apply contentful markedness principles in the presence of contrast.

1.5.5 Interactions

Part V contains four chapters about various sorts of interaction among components of phonology. Blevins, in chapter 16, begins this part by discussing the relationship between phonological and phonetic knowledge; she argues against models of phonology that incorporate strong models of phonetic knowledge (such as Hayes, Kirchner, and Steriade's (2004)) because an adequate theory of language change would remove any explanatory role for phonetic knowledge in a phonological grammar.

In chapter 17, Purnell also makes the case that phonetic knowledge has no predictive power in phonology. He argues that the lack of any universal one-to-one mapping of acoustic characteristics to or from phonological features shows that phonetic knowledge does not perform any work in phonology.

Halle and Nevins, in chapter 18, investigate the interaction among individual rules. They invoke the Principle of Morphological Consistency, which states that all the surface representations of a given morpheme are derived by means of phonological rules from a single underlying form. This principle severely limits possible mappings between surface forms and underlying representations. Halle and Nevins's proposal for marking exceptionality, coupled with the Principle of Morphological Consistency, provides the basis for an analysis of verbal forms in Russian, Czech, and Serbo-Croatian that have eluded successful explanation in frameworks that do not accept these proposals.

Raimy, in chapter 19, argues that the principles of modularity lead to a new understanding of reduplicative templates. The interaction between the morphology and phonology components, a theory of computation in the phonology component, and a theory of language acquisition all interact in ways that remove the need for any explicit constraint requiring reduplicative templates to be an authentic unit of prosody. Because of this result, Raimy suggests that surface-oriented, prosodically based analyses of reduplicative templates should be abandoned.

1.5.6 Conclusion

In conclusion, each chapter in this volume can be profitably viewed within a modular view of phonology. Each either directly investigates interactions among distinct modules or develops specific aspects of representation within a particular module. It is evident that there are many places where understanding of phonology can be improved by considering points of disagreement in this volume. On the whole, this lack of unanimity is positive because of the questions that it raises. Understanding progresses when the field comes up with better questions.

References

Blevins, Juliette. 1995. The syllable in phonological theory. In *The handbook of phonological theory*, ed. by John Goldsmith, 206–244. Cambridge, Mass.: Blackwell.

Bloch, Bernard. 1941. Phonemic overlapping. *American Speech* 16:278–284.

Cairns, Charles. 2002. Foot and syllable in Southern Paiute. Ms., City University of New York. http://www.cunyphonologyforum.net/papers/20Sopai.pdf.

Cairns, Charles, and Mark Feinstein. 1982. Markedness and the theory of syllable structure. *Linguistic Inquiry* 13:193–226.

Chomsky, Noam. 1964. *Current issues in linguistic theory*. The Hague: Mouton.

Everett, Daniel. 1998. Syllable integrity. In *Proceedings of the Sixteenth West Coast Conference on Formal Linguistics*, ed. by Emily Curtis, James Lyle, and Gabriel Webster. Stanford, Calif.: CSLI Publications.

Feinstein, Mark. 1977. The linguistic nature of prenasalization. Doctoral dissertation, City University of New York.

Feinstein, Mark. 1979. Prenasalization and syllable structure. *Linguistic Inquiry* 10:245–278.

Hale, Mark, and Charles Reiss. 2000. "Substance abuse" and "dysfunctionalism": Current trends in phonology. *Linguistic Inquiry* 31:157–169.

Halle, Morris, and William J. Idsardi. 1995. General properties of stress and metrical structure. In *The handbook of phonological theory*, ed. by John Goldsmith, 403–443. Cambridge, Mass.: Blackwell.

Halle, Morris, and Jean-Roger Vergnaud. 1980. Three-dimensional phonology. *Journal of Linguistic Research* 1:83–105.

Halle, Morris, and Jean-Roger Vergnaud. 1987. *An essay on stress*. Cambridge, Mass.: MIT Press.

Hayes, Bruce. 1995. *Metrical stress theory: Principles and case studies*. Chicago: University of Chicago Press.

Hayes, Bruce, Robert Kirchner, and Donca Steriade. 2004. *Phonetically based phonology*. New York: Cambridge University Press.

Idsardi, William J. 1992. The computation of prosody. Doctoral dissertation, MIT.

Keyser, Samuel Jay, and Kenneth N. Stevens. 2001. Enhancement revisited. In *Ken Hale: A life in language*, ed. by Michael Kenstowicz, 271–291. Cambridge, Mass.: MIT Press.

Keyser, Samuel Jay, and Kenneth N. Stevens. 2006. Enhancement and overlap in the speech chain. *Language* 82:33–63.

McCarthy, John. 1988. Feature geometry and dependency: A review. *Phonetica* 43:84–108.

Prince, Alan, and Paul Smolensky. 2004. *Optimality Theory: Constraint interaction in generative grammar*. Malden, Mass.: Blackwell.

Sapir, Edward. 1949. The psychological reality of phonemes. In *Language, culture, and personality*, ed. by David G. Mandelbaum, 46–72. Berkeley and Los Angeles: University of California Press.

Selkirk, Elisabeth. 1980. The role of prosodic categories in English word stress. *Linguistic Inquiry* 11:563–605.

Selkirk, Elisabeth, and Tong Shen. 1990. Prosodic domains in Shanghai Chinese. In *The phonology-syntax connection*, ed. by Sharon Inkelas and Draga Zec, 313–336. Chicago: University of Chicago Press.

Phonological Features

2 The Role of Features in Phonological Inventories

G. N. Clements

2.1 Introduction

As linguists have long noted, not just any set of consonants and vowels can make up a phonological inventory.[1] A central finding of the earliest work in phonology was that speech sound systems are structured in terms of recurrent elementary components known as features (e.g., Trubetzkoy 1969 [1939], Hockett 1955, Martinet 1955).

More recently, however, the study of inventory structure has been subject to some neglect. The intensive effort devoted within the generative tradition to discovering the architecture of rule systems (or more recently, constraint systems) has not been matched by similar efforts in the area of phonological inventories. This may be due to the belief that inventories have no existence independent of the lexicon and that generalizations regarding their structure are external to the grammar as such. Although this was not the position of Chomsky and Halle, their remarks on the subject (1968:chap. 9) focused almost exclusively on markedness and barely touched on such issues as economy and feature hierarchy.

For these and other reasons, in recent years the nature of inventory structure has been more vigorously debated among phoneticians than among phonologists (see, e.g., Maddieson 1984). Two general approaches have emerged, based on the role they assign to features. In one, which we might term a *feature-mediated* theory of inventory structure, sound systems are viewed as constrained by the fact that speech is perceived and produced in terms of distinctive features. In this approach, features are viewed as biologically grounded in that they correspond to articulatory regions that have relatively stable, distinctive acoustic properties. Inventory-based generalizations are typically formulated over natural classes of sounds as defined by features. This approach has been exemplified notably in the work of Kenneth N. Stevens and his colleagues.

In an alternative approach, features play little or no role. In this approach, which we might term a *direct-access* theory of phonological explanation, generalizations about speech sound inventories—including surface-phonemic inventories in the classical sense—refer directly to the finer-grained categories provided by phonetic theory. These categories may include

• the minute and in some cases infinitely divisible articulatory categories postulated by descriptive phonetics (e.g., Maddieson 1984, Ladefoged and Maddieson 1996);
• the auditory and articulatory variables employed in a model that views phonological inventories as emerging from the interplay of auditory dispersion and articulatory ease (e.g., Lindblom 1986, 1992, Lindblom and Maddieson 1988);
• the articulator sets and quantitative parameter settings employed in gesture-based phonetics, which models phonological systems in terms of gestures and their interactions (e.g., Browman and Goldstein 1989, 1992, 2000).

These trends of research have been salutary in bringing to light many respects in which phonological patterning is shaped by constraints imposed by the medium of speech itself, and they have introduced a necessary corrective to the "overly formal" approach to inventory structure (Chomsky and Halle 1968:400) taken by classical generative phonology. However, by neglecting features, these approaches appear to make phonetic explanation incommensurable with phonological structure. They raise the following question: if features are the principal categories in terms of which phonological systems are structured, why should they be irrelevant to universals of phonological inventories?

While there has been valuable work on inventory structure by generative phonologists, this work has tended to emphasize descriptive formalisms over system-level principles. Because constraint systems usually evaluate individual forms rather than system-wide generalizations, work in mainstream Optimality Theory has reinforced the neglect of inventory structure. More recently, however, some Optimality Theory–oriented phonologists have proposed incorporating system-level principles into the theory (e.g., Boersma 1997, Flemming 2002). Even in this work a tendency to reduce or eliminate the role of features can be observed, to the point that a contemporary linguist can maintain that the study of contrast "does not require a restrictive inventory of distinctive features" but that "phonological representation can include the entire sea of predictable or freely varying phonetic detail" (Kirchner 2001:112).

This chapter reviews a range of evidence showing that distinctive features play a central role in structuring inventories of contrastive speech sounds. It examines a number of general principles that appear to be most straightforwardly stated in terms of features. These principles heavily constrain the shape of preferred sound inventories and make strong and testable predictions regarding the trends we may expect to find as we examine as yet undescribed languages.

The discussion proceeds as follows. Section 2.2 outlines the general view of features that will be assumed here. Section 2.3 presents the database used in this study.

The next sections review five feature-based principles that significantly constrain the structure of sound systems: Feature Bounding (section 2.4), Feature Economy (section 2.5), Marked Feature Avoidance (section 2.6), Robustness (section 2.7), and Phonological Enhancement (section 2.8). Section 2.9 applies these principles to illustrative cases, and section 2.10 discusses some implications of these results for phonological theory.

2.2 Features: Their Nature and Cognitive Status

I first review some fundamental aspects of feature theory, stressing its phonetic and cognitive grounding.

Features have been defined from the very beginning in concrete physical terms, though linguists have hesitated between auditory, acoustic, and articulatory definitions. Trubetzkoy suggested that though acoustics is basic to the definition of speech units, articulatory definitions must still be used for most practical purposes as "acoustic terminology unfortunately is still very sparse" (1969 [1939]:92). The acoustic study of speech was greatly advanced by the work of Jakobson and his collaborators in the 1950s, who were able to draw upon technological advances in the study of speech such as the use of the Sonograph (sound spectrograph). They believed, however, that the most relevant definitions of speech units lay in the perceptual and auditory domains:

> The closer we are in our investigation to the destination of the message (i.e. its perception by the receiver), the more accurately can we gage the information conveyed by its sound shape. This determines the operational hierarchy of levels of decreasing pertinence: perceptual, aural, acoustical and articulatory (the latter carrying no direct information to the receiver). The systematic exploration of the first two of these levels belongs to the future and is an urgent duty. (Jakobson, Fant, and Halle 1952:12)

Though the auditory and perceptual domains are somewhat better understood a half century later, there is still nothing approaching a consensus on how the properties of speech sounds are to be defined in these terms. Subsequent work on feature theory, inspired in part by the motor theory of speech perception (Liberman et al. 1967), has given new prominence to articulatory definitions (Chomsky and Halle 1968), though it is usually agreed that features have acoustic correlates as well (Lieberman 1970, Halle 1983).

More recently, a new integration of articulatory, acoustic, and perceptual approaches to feature definition has been achieved within the context of quantal theory (Stevens 1972, 1989). This approach is based on the observation that there are continuous articulatory regions within which moderate changes in the positioning of an articulator have essentially negligible acoustic and perceptual effects, while at the boundaries between such regions small articulatory movements have significant effects. The stable regions typically define distinctive features. Thus, for example, as the tongue blade is retracted from the dental to the alveopalatal region in the production of fricatives, the acoustic spectrum undergoes abrupt, perceptually salient changes as the constriction passes through the unstable region corresponding to the boundary separating anterior sounds such as [s] from posterior sounds such as [ʃ]. This boundary, then, separates [+anterior] sounds from [−anterior] sounds. Within the class of [+anterior] sounds or [−anterior] sounds, in contrast, acoustic differences are too small (all else being equal) to be used in defining distinctive contrasts. In this approach, features are grounded in objectively observable discontinuities between production and perception.[2]

Quantal theory provides a new basis for understanding fundamental aspects of speech processing. One of the more robust results emanating from psycholinguistic work in recent years is that speech is processed in categorical terms. In discrimination and identification tasks, adult speakers of a language have been found to identify and distinguish speech stimuli more accurately *across* the phoneme boundaries of their language than within them (Liberman et al. 1957, Repp 1984, Harnad 1987). In contrast, perception of nonnative contrasts falling within these boundaries is rather poor. Though other studies have shown that perception of nonnative contrasts can be improved by explicit training or prolonged exposure to a second language, adult speech perception remains relatively inflexible in comparison to the plasticity shown by very young learners (Pallier, Bosch, and Sebastián-Gallés 1997). The phonetic dimensions for which categorical perception has been confirmed, including voicing and major place-of-articulation contrasts, correspond closely to those used by distinctive features.[3]

There is much evidence that categorical perception is present even at birth and that infants abstract phoneme-like categories from irrelevant "noise" in the signal (such as differences among speakers). For example, full-term newborn babies (aged from 2 to 6 days) have been shown to discriminate between the syllables *pa* and *ta*, regardless of whether the stimuli were uttered by the same speaker or by any of four different speakers (Dehaene-Lambertz and Pena 2001). Moreover, categorical perception in infants is not restricted to the features of the mother tongue. Babies born into an English-speaking environment have been found to discriminate non-English place-of-articulation contrasts that exist in Hindi (Werker et al. 1981) and non-English vowel contrasts that exist in French (Trehub 1976), while infants 6 to 8 months old discriminate non-English contrasts found in Hindi and the Interior Salish language Thompson (Werker and Tees 1984).

Such findings suggest that the ability to distinguish major phonetic categories—typically corresponding to quantally defined features—exists in early infancy. In later infancy, the ability to discriminate speech sounds becomes "fine-tuned" to the categories of the native language. By 6 months of age, infants have established prototypes for the vowels used in their language (Kuhl et al. 1992) and start to lose sensitivity to nonnative vowels (Polka and Werker 1994). By 12 months, they seem to have lost the capacity to discriminate nonnative consonantal contrasts that can be assigned to a single native category (Werker and Tees 1984). After that, the capacity to perceive foreign contrasts remains generally poor, although it is still fairly good if the foreign contrasts can be assimilated to native contrasts, or if they are perceived as nonspeech sounds (Best, McRoberts, and Sithole 1988, Best, McRoberts, and Goodell 2001).

It appears, then, that there is a continuity in speech processing from early infancy to adulthood and that the predisposition for categorical perception and speaker normalization shown by infants carries over to a large extent to adult speech processing. If this is so, one might naturally expect phonological inventories to be structured in terms of the same broad feature-based categories that appear in the course of language acquisition. This hypothesis will be explored in the rest of this chapter.

2.3   Data and Method

This chapter examines crosslinguistic trends in the structure of sound inventories. Evidence is drawn primarily from the expanded UCLA Phonological Segment Inventory Database (UPSID), as described in Maddieson and Precoda 1989. This database presents several advantages. First, it contains phoneme inventories drawn from 451 languages, representing about 7% of the world's languages, according to current estimates. Second, it was constructed by selecting just one language from each moderately distant genetic grouping, ensuring a minimum of genetic balance. Third, its electronic format facilitates rapid searches, eliminating the need for the laborious and time-consuming scrutiny of printed materials such as Maddieson 1984. Fourth, since the database is publicly available from the Web site of the UCLA Phonetics Laboratory where it was compiled, results obtained from it can be independently verified by others.

However, even the best available database is necessarily imperfect. A number of problems in UPSID have been discussed by Basbøll (1985), Maddieson (1991), Simpson (1999), and myself (Clements 2003b), among others (see also Vaux, this volume). These include

- an inevitable skewing toward the properties of larger genetic units (e.g., the Niger-Congo unit is represented by 55 languages, Basque by only 1);
- the heterogeneity of the primary sources and disagreements in analyses;
- the inclusion of some allophonic details but not others (e.g., the dental vs. alveolar stop distinction is registered even when noncontrastive, while the apical vs. laminal stop distinction is rarely noted);
- the occasionally inconsistent choice of basic allophones for each phoneme;
- the presence of a fair number of coding errors.

To a considerable extent, these problems are alleviated by the sheer size of the sample. Generalizations supported at a high level of significance by large numbers of genetically diverse languages are unlikely to be far off the mark, and most generalizations discussed in the present chapter are of this type. However, caution must be taken in interpreting results, especially when there is a likelihood of error or oversight in the primary sources. Many of the sources used in compiling UPSID are outdated or less than fully reliable, and in such cases other sources should be consulted as well.

"Inventories" such as one finds in UPSID are abstractions over sounds that are contrastive in a language and typically include consonants that may appear in different positions in the syllable and word. Most consonants of a language, however, can appear word-initially, and consonants that appear elsewhere are usually a subset of these. A consonant inventory usually approximates an inventory of word onsets, and the sounds selected as the basic allophone or variant of a consonant phoneme in UPSID are typically those that appear in strong positions such as the onset. The rationale for this choice is that consonants that appear elsewhere can often be regarded as reduced or lenited realizations of this basic variant. (For fuller discussion of the criteria used in selecting basic allophones in UPSID, see Maddieson 1984:62–63, 1991:196.) For the purposes of the ongoing research of which this chapter is a part, the phoneme systems of UPSID have been recompiled in terms of phonological features. A fairly conservative feature system has been used, containing widely familiar features similar to those proposed in Halle and Clements 1983, to which the articulator features [labial] and [dorsal] of Sagey 1990 have been added. While further revisions of this system have been suggested (see, e.g., Halle 1992, Clements and Hume 1995), for present purposes these more familiar features will be adequate.

Most results reported in this chapter have been evaluated for statistical significance with the chi-square test, which is typically used to find out whether two independent characteristics are associated in such a way that high frequencies of one tend to be coupled with high frequencies of the other. The .01 level of probability is taken as criterial. See Clements 2003b for further discussion of the statistical method.

2.4   Feature Bounding

Let us now review a number of feature-based principles that appear to govern the structure of speech sound inventories. The first is one I will call *Feature Bounding*. This principle involves two claims. One is that features set an upper limit on how many *sounds* a language may have. More exactly, given a set of n features, a language may have at most 2^n distinctive sounds. For example, a language using 3 features may have up to 8 sounds (2^3), one using 4 features may have up to 16 sounds (2^4), and so forth. No more are possible.[4]

Second, features also set an upper limit on the number of *contrasts* that may appear in a language. The number of possible contrasts (C) in a language is a function of the total number of its sounds (S) and is given by the expression $C = (S * (S - 1))/2$. Given that the maximum number of possible sounds is 2^n, the maximum number of contrasts for a system with n features is $(2^n * (2^n - 1))/2$. By this calculation, for example, a language with 2 features may have up to 4 sounds and 6 contrasts.

Coronal consonants provide an illustration. Feature theory proposes 2 features distinguishing "major place of articulation" in coronal sounds, defined in terms of the location and form of the front-of-the-tongue constriction along the midline of the oral cavity. These are [anterior/posterior] and [distributed/nondistributed] (i.e., nonapical/apical). These 2 features define 4 classes of sounds, as shown in (1).[5]

(1)	*Apical* *anterior*	*Nonapical* *anterior*	*Retroflex*	*Postalveolar/* *Palatal*
[posterior]	−	−	+	+
[distributed]	−	+	−	+

"Major place" as just defined is a broader notion than "place of articulation" in traditional phonetic theory, which recognizes many more place categories within the coronal region. By providing a larger set of distinctions, phonetic theory admits a greater number of potential contrasts. Table 2.1 makes this point by comparing the maximum number of sounds and contrasts predicted by a feature theory making use of the 4 categories shown in (1) and those predicted by a phonetic theory recognizing the 7 categories "apicodental," "apicoalveolar," "laminodental," "laminoalveolar," "palatoalveolar," "retroflex," and "palatal." As row (a) shows, a feature theory providing just 2 features and 4 major coronal categories predicts up to 6 potential contrasts. In contrast, as row (b) shows, a traditional phonetic theory recognizing 7 coronal categories predicts up to 21 potential contrasts, more than three times the number predicted by feature theory.

The predictions of feature theory appear to be correct in this case. I have elsewhere (Clements 1999) reported plausible attestations for all 6 predicted contrasts, not only

Table 2.1
Maximum number of distinct coronal sounds and maximum number of coronal contrasts predicted by a feature system recognizing 4 coronal categories (row a) and a phonetic theory recognizing 7 coronal categories (row b).

	Max. no. of coronal sounds	Max. no. of coronal contrasts
a. Feature theory	4	6
b. Traditional phonetic theory	7	21

among simple stops but also among strident stops (affricates). Examples of the 6 predicted contrasts for simple plosives are listed in (2), with illustrative languages drawn from Ladefoged and Maddieson 1996.

(2) *Contrast*   *Example*   *Found in (e.g.)*

Apical anterior vs.   Apical /t/ vs. nonapical /t/   Temne
nonapical anterior

Apical anterior vs.   Apical /t/ vs. retroflex /ʈ/   Yanyuwa
retroflex

Apical anterior vs.   Apical /t/ vs. palatal /c/   Arrernte
postalveolar/palatal

Nonapical anterior vs.   Nonapical /t/ vs. retroflex /ʈ/   Toda
retroflex

Nonapical anterior vs.   Nonapical /t/ vs. palatal /c/   Ngwo
postalveolar/palatal

Retroflex vs.   Retroflex /ʈ/ vs. palatal /c/   Sindhi
postalveolar/palatal

Most strikingly, *no other primary coronal contrasts* were found in either plosives or affricates in a survey of several hundred languages. (The sample comprised all 451 languages of the expanded UPSID and several other languages known for their rich coronal inventories.) In particular, no reliable example was found of a minimal contrast, unaccompanied by any other feature difference, between dental and alveolar stops or between palatoalveolar and palatal stops such as the traditional International Phonetic Association (IPA) categories predict.[6]

Proposed contrasts beyond the six predicted by the features [±posterior] and [±distributed] have not been substantiated. I have elsewhere discussed several alleged cases of this type (Clements 1999) and have shown that they do not require additional coronal categories. Beyond the cases discussed there, Ladefoged and Maddieson (1996:42) cite two allegedly minimal contrasts between apicodental and apicoalveolar sounds that prove, on closer examination, to be accompanied by other featural differences. First, Albanian is said to contrast apicodental and apicoalveolar laterals. Such sounds cannot be distinguished by the features assumed here since both are [−posterior] and [−distributed]. However, a study of the source, Bothorel 1969–70, shows that the distinction between the two apical sounds transcribed *l* and *ll* is accompanied by a further distinction involving the position of the tongue body. As Bothorel describes it (p. 135), the essential difference between the two laterals comes from the lowering of the entire body of the tongue for *ll*, with consequent retraction of the tongue root, narrowing of the pharyngeal passage, and opening of the lateral passages, a configuration distinct from the conic form and gradual lowering found in *l*. Examination of Bothorel's X-ray figures confirms that *ll* is indeed strongly backed with respect to *l*, a difference that can be expressed by the secondary articulation feature [dorsal] or [pharyngeal]. Second, Ladefoged and Maddieson (1996:42) state that in many Khoisan languages such as !Xóõ, some speakers have an apicodental contact for the dental click /ǁ/ and an apicoalveolar contact for the alveolar click /!/. However, as they point out elsewhere in the same work (1996:257–259), these sounds have a prominent difference that is far more regular across speakers: /!/ is produced with an abrupt release while /ǁ/ is produced with an affricated release, making the first plosive-like and the second affricate-like. This difference parallels similar differences between nonclick stop types in these languages and can be described with the feature [±strident].

It appears, then, that the features [±posterior] and [±distributed] successfully characterize the set of primary coronal contrasts that are actually attested across languages. It is not obvious how a feature-free account of phonetic structure could predict this set of contrasts.[7] It might be thought, perhaps, that phonetic theory could exclude unattested contrasts on the basis of a principle of "sufficient dispersion" according to which sounds must meet a minimum criterion of auditory distinctness in order to contrast in a phonemic system. In such a view, the fact that few if any languages have minimal contrasts between apicodental and apicoalveolar stops would be explained by the observation that these two sounds are auditorily very similar. It appears, however, that the contrasts overgenerated by traditional phonetic categories—such as dental versus alveolar stops—*are just those that cannot be described in terms of phonological features*. Once we eliminate such contrasts by assigning them to the appropriate feature categories, we obtain the attested number of distinctive sounds and contrasts. There is no need to appeal to a special theory of sufficient dispersion for this purpose since auditory dispersion is built into feature theory itself, through its requirement that features be specified for quantally distinct attributes.

2.5   Feature Economy

Feature Economy is the tendency to maximize feature combinations (see Clements 2003a,b, after sources in de Groot 1931, Martinet 1955, 1968). This principle can be observed in most speech sound inventories, regardless of size. Let us consider, by way of illustration, the surface-distinctive consonants of a standard variety of English as shown in (3), focusing attention on the sounds in the box.

(3)

p^h	t^h		$tʃ^h$	k^h
b	d		dʒ	g
f	θ	s	ʃ	
v	ð	z	ʒ	
m	n			ŋ

w   l, r   j   h

It can be seen that voicing cross-classifies stops and fricatives to double the number of obstruents; this feature is used with maximum efficiency in the obstruent sub-system. Though the feature [+continuant] is used with less efficiency (since English lacks the fricatives /x/ and /ɣ/), it nevertheless creates two full fricative series. The feature [+nasal] creates nasal stops at three places of articulation. At the other extreme, the feature [+lateral] is used with minimal efficiency, as it only distinguishes the pair /l/ and /r/.[8]

Though the vast majority of languages exhibit Feature Economy to some degree, no language makes use of all theoretically possible feature combinations. For example, English fails to combine nasality with obstruence to create a series of nasal fricatives. As observed by Martinet (1955), such gaps often correspond to functionally inefficient feature combinations and tend to be widely avoided across languages. Thus, to take one of Martinet's examples, nasality is inefficient in fricatives because it is difficult to achieve the air pressure buildup required in the production of fricative noise while allowing air to pass through the nasal cavity. (I will discuss markedness considerations further in the next section.)

Feature Economy can be quantified in terms of a measure called the *economy index* (Clements 2003b). Given a system using F features to characterize S sounds, its economy index E can be expressed, to a first approximation, by the equation in (4).

(4) $E = S/F$

The higher the value of E, the greater the economy. For example, if we use the 9 features in (5) to distinguish the 24 English consonants, the economy index of the English consonant system is 24/9, or 2.7.[9]

(5) [labial], [dorsal], [glottal], [posterior], [continuant], [voiced], [strident], [nasal], [lateral]

Feature Economy can be defined as the tendency to maximize E. This goal can be accomplished either by

• increasing the number of sounds,
• decreasing the number of features

(or eventually both). Both strategies are exemplified in phonological systems. First, increasing the number of sounds while holding the number of features constant is reflected in historical changes that create new phonemes by recombining existing features (Martinet 1955). A familiar example is the historical creation of a new series of [+nasal] vowels in French following the deletion of syllable-final [+nasal] consonants. Second, decreasing the number of features while holding the number of sounds constant is reflected in the frequent historical elimination of "isolated" sounds that do not fall into regular patterns of correlation with other sounds; after such sounds are eliminated, the feature that previously characterized them becomes redundant. The latter process is exemplified by two stages of Zulu, as described in Clements 2003b.

(6) *Stage 1*   *Stage 2*
   p' t' k'   p' t' k'
   pʰ tʰ kʰ   pʰ tʰ kʰ
   b   d   g   p   t   k
           k   b   g
   ɓ

In stage 1, reflecting the usage of a century ago, we find two isolated stops, the implosive /ɓ/ and the plain voiceless /k/, both of which are the sole members of their series. Through a subsequent evolution whose end product is shown in stage 2, the two isolated sounds shifted into a single voiced series, as shown in the last row. Stage 2 differs from stage 1 in its increased economy, since the feature that previously distinguished the implosive from its plain voiced counterpart has been eliminated.[10]

Feature Economy must be distinguished from the more familiar criterion of *parsimony*, which requires the use of the fewest units possible in any given analysis. Like economy, parsimony favors reducing the number of features, but it also militates against increasing the number of sounds and thus fails to predict historical trends in which existing features recombine to yield new sounds (as in the evolution of French nasal vowels). Feature Economy is also different from *symmetry*. Symmetry, like Feature Economy, requires the number of gaps in a system to be minimized, but it would not usually be viewed as penalizing a 3 × 3 system such as that in (7).

(7) p   t   k
    b   d   g
    f   s   x

Feature Economy would penalize this system, though, as it is missing a voiced fricative series /v, z, ɣ/ combining the existing features [+voiced] and [+continuant]. Feature Economy predicts that a voiced fricative series should tend to be present if the three series shown in (7) are present as well. (This prediction is correct, as we will see below.)

How can such predictions be tested? Earlier work examined the predictions of Feature Economy in the historical domain (Martinet 1955). In a recent publication (Clements 2003b), I outline a method for testing this principle at the synchronic level and apply it to the phoneme systems of the expanded UPSID inventories. One prediction of Feature Economy is *Mutual Attraction*, which can be stated as follows:

(8) A given speech sound will be more frequent than expected in inventories in which all of its features are distinctively present in other sounds.

Table 2.2
Observed frequencies of voiced labial fricatives (V) across UPSID languages, according to whether the language does ("Yes" column) or does not ("No" column) have another labial, another voiced obstruent, and another fricative. Expected frequencies are shown in parentheses.

| | | Some other labial and some other voiced obstruent and some other fricative? | | |
		Yes	No	Total
V?	Yes	136 (114)	11 (33)	147
	No	214 (236)	90 (68)	304
	Total	350	101	451

For example, according to this prediction, a voiced labial fricative V should be more frequent in systems having some other labial consonant such as B, F, or M, some other voiced obstruent such as B, D, or Z, and some other fricative such as F, X, or Z. This prediction can be tested by constructing a 2×2 contingency table as shown in table 2.2. (Uppercase letters here and below denote general feature-defined classes rather than specific phonetic values.) From left to right and top to bottom, the cells in this table present the number of languages that

• have V together with some other labial, some other voiced obstruent, and some other fricative (136);
• have V, but lack a labial, a voiced obstruent, or a fricative (11);
• lack V, but have another labial, another voiced obstruent, and another fricative (214);
• lack V, and also lack a labial, a voiced obstruent, or a fricative (90).

Parenthesized numbers show the values that would be statistically expected under the assumption that phonemes combine randomly, contrary to the predictions of Feature Economy.[11] For example, the number of languages that would be statistically expected to have V together with some other labial, some other voiced obstruent, and some other fricative on the assumption of random combination is 114, which is much lower than the 136 that we actually observe. The difference between observed and expected values in this case is highly significant under chi-square testing ($\chi^2 = 27.902$, $p < .0001$) and confirms prediction (8): V is indeed significantly more frequent in systems in which its distinctive features are independently present in other sounds. This trend reveals Feature Economy at work; the features [labial], [+voiced], and [+continuant], once present in a system, tend to recombine to form other sounds.

Table 2.3
Comparisons among pairs of stops sharing all manner features but differing in place of articulation. Symbols: P^- T^- K^- = plain voiceless stops, P^h T^h K^h = voiceless aspirated stops, P' T' K' = ejective stops, B D G = voiced unaspirated stops, B^h D^h G^h = voiced aspirated stops, and $B^<$ $D^<$ $G^<$ = implosive stops.

P^- vs. T^-	P^h vs. T^h	P' vs. T'
P^- vs. K^-	P^h vs. K^h	P' vs. K'
T^- vs. K^-	T^h vs. K^h	T' vs. K'
B vs. D	B^h vs. D^h	$B^<$ vs. $D^<$
B vs. G	B^h vs. G^h	$B^<$ vs. $G^<$
D vs. G	D^h vs. G^h	$D^<$ vs. $G^<$

Table 2.3 shows the result of testing 18 pairs of stop consonants for economy effects by this method. The consonants in each pair share all manner features, but differ in place. Feature Economy predicts that if a feature combination appears at one place of articulation, it should tend to appear at other places of articulation as well. For example, if a system contains a labial implosive, we expect it to contain a coronal implosive, and vice versa. (In this table, the symbols P, T, K stand for any voiceless labial, coronal, or dorsal stop, respectively, and B, D, G for any voiced labial, coronal, or dorsal stop. Diacritics indicate manner features as explained in the legend.) All these comparisons test positive at a high level of significance ($p < .0001$). That is, languages having one member of each pair are much more likely to have the other.

Let us return to the consonant inventory in (7). Under Feature Economy, though not under symmetry, we expect that a system containing the sounds /p, t, k/, /b, d, g/, and /f, s, x/ will also have the voiced fricatives /v, z, ɣ/, maximizing the use of [+voiced] and [+continuant]. This prediction is confirmed by chi-square testing. Voiced labial fricatives such as /v/ are considerably more frequent than expected in sample languages having all three of the sounds /p/, /b/, and /f/. Fully analogous results hold for /z/ and /ɣ/. These trends are significant at the .0001 level in all cases.

In Clements 2003b, I discuss other examples illustrating a variety of Feature Economy effects. These results show that sound systems are strongly structured by Feature Economy, a principle defined, as its name implies, in terms of features. Here again, phonetically based accounts do not appear to perform as well. One such alternative, Gestural Economy (Maddieson 1995), can be shown to be less adequate in predicting phoneme inventory structure, though it may correctly predict a tendency toward articulatory uniformity at the level of phonetic implementation.

To summarize, this section has reviewed evidence for a principle of Feature Economy according to which sound systems tend to maximize the use of their features.

The economy of a system can be quantified in terms of an economy index, E. Feature Economy places pressure on systems to increase this index, either by reducing the number of features or by increasing the number of sounds. This principle is confirmed by an examination of statistical trends in UPSID phoneme inventories.

2.6 Marked Feature Avoidance

Markedness, as it applies to inventories, can be understood as the tendency to avoid certain widely disfavored feature values—*marked* values (see Trubetzkoy 1969 [1939], Jakobson 1968 [1941], Greenberg 1966, Chomsky and Halle 1968, Kean 1975, Calabrese 1994, and others, as well as Rice 1999 and Gurevich 2001 for critical overviews). This section proposes a new approach to the study of inventory markedness based on a principle of Marked Feature Avoidance, which replaces the traditional notion of implicational universal.

2.6.1 Markedness and Feature Economy

Let us first consider how Markedness interacts with Feature Economy. In its strongest form, Feature Economy predicts that all languages make use of all possible combinations of all distinctive features in constructing their phoneme inventories. However, no language comes even close to achieving this goal. This is due to at least two factors. First, if some feature values are redundant—that is, predictable from other features—they are available to serve as secondary cues to the presence of other, distinctive features, especially in contexts where the primary cues to the distinctive feature are weak or absent. Second, some feature values—the marked values—appear less suited to speech communication than others for articulatory and perceptual reasons. If marked values are *under*used, not only is the redundancy of the system increased, aiding processing, but also the articulatory and perceptual complexity of the system is substantially reduced.

The English consonant system shown in (3) provides a good example of feature underutilization. If this system used all possible combinations of its 9 consonant features, it would have 2^9 or 512 consonants (including a number of highly unusual sounds) instead of the 24 relatively common sounds it actually contains. The English system is thus heavily constrained by markedness.

It is perhaps less obvious that Feature Economy also counteracts Markedness. However, this is also a strong effect. Once a feature value is present in a system, Feature Economy creates pressure for it to be used again, even if that value is marked. An example is provided by voiced fricatives, which bear the marked values [+voiced] and [+continuant]. These values are marked in fricatives presumably because they counteract the buildup of supraglottal air pressure required to produce the turbulence noise characteristic of obstruents (e.g., Stevens 1983). For this reason (and perhaps others), voiced fricatives are absent in roughly half the world's languages. However, because of Feature Economy, voiced fricatives are far more likely to occur in languages that have other voiced fricatives. This is demonstrated in (9), which shows the percentage of UPSID languages having voiced labial, coronal, and dorsal fricatives (1) overall, (2) in languages having one or more other voiced fricatives, and (3) in languages lacking other voiced fricatives. We see that languages are much more likely to have two or more voiced fricatives than to have just one. Again, English with its four voiced fricatives illustrates this trend.

(9) *Occurrence of voiced fricatives in UPSID languages*

		No. of languages	*Percentage*
[labial]	Overall:	147/451	32.6
	In languages having other voiced fricatives:	111/184	60.3
	In languages lacking other voiced fricatives:	36/267	13.5
[coronal]	Overall:	174/451	38.6
	In languages having other voiced fricatives:	129/175	73.7
	In languages lacking other voiced fricatives:	45/276	16.3
[dorsal]	Overall:	70/451	15.5
	In languages having other voiced fricatives:	62/212	29.2
	In languages lacking other voiced fricatives:	8/239	3.3

The tendency for Feature Economy to override Markedness can be shown in another way. Pericliev and Valdés-Pérez (2002) have documented the occurrence of what they call *idiosyncratic segments* in UPSID, that is, segments occurring in just one language. They find that if a language possesses several such segments, they strongly tend to share features that bind them together as a class. Thus, in 44 of the 53 languages having more than one idiosyncratic segment, all such segments share features, while in only 4 languages are all such segments unrelated. A study of Pericliev and Valdés-Pérez's data shows that in the great majority of cases, the shared features involve marked values, as in the case of Arrernte with its six unique nasally released stops or Shilha with its seven unique pharyngealized consonants. The likelihood of such configurations arising from random distribution is, of course, extremely small.

Thus, Feature Economy and Markedness operate antagonistically, Feature Economy tending to expand the size of an inventory and Markedness to contract it. Sound systems represent varying degrees of compromise between these two forces.

2.6.2   Which Value of a Feature Is Marked?

Markedness statements, like other types of phonological statements, usually refer to natural classes of sounds, taking the form of general statements such as "Nasal vowels are marked with respect to oral vowels" or "Fricatives are marked with respect to stops." Specific statements such as "/ã/ is marked with respect to /a/" or "/θ/ is marked with respect to /t/" are usually instances of broader generalizations such as these. Markedness is therefore a property of classes of sounds, as defined by marked feature values. Individual segments can be said to be marked just to the extent that they bear marked feature values.

Given this fact, markedness theory requires a criterion for determining the marked value of any feature, within and across languages. Linguists have generally taken one of two approaches here. One has sought to define markedness in terms of the substantive conditions that underlie the human capacity for speech production and speech processing. From this point of view, marked features are sometimes said to be those that are relatively difficult to implement, or that lack salient acoustic properties. A severe problem for this approach, however, is that the various fields embraced by phonetics—acoustics, physiology, neurology, aerodynamics, auditory perception, and so on—constitute a number of interacting complex systems, no one of which explains all aspects of speech, and which taken together often make conflicting predictions. There does not yet appear to be any general phonetic theory that predicts unambiguously, for any given feature, what its marked value must be.

A second approach to defining markedness is based on frequency, or likelihood of occurrence (e.g., Kean 1975). As pointed out by Greenberg (1966) and others, markedness tends to be reflected in frequency differences at many levels; thus, marked segments tend to be less frequent in the lexicon, in texts, in early stages of language acquisition, and in adult sound inventories, and tend to show fewer contextual variants. Moreover, it is well-established that humans are sensitive to frequency distributions in the data to which they are exposed from infancy onward (see, e.g., Jusczyk, Luce, and Charles-Luce 1994, Maye, Werker, and Gerken 2002, Anderson, Morgan, and White 2003). Though a frequency-based criterion cannot explain why some segments are more frequent than others, it has the advantage of relating markedness to quantitative trends that are observable by language learners and that plausibly form part of the input in the construction of the target grammar (Pierrehumbert 2003).[12]

For such reasons, it may be preferable to interpret markedness as an effect of frequency. The less frequent value of a feature is, by virtue of its relative unexpectedness in discourse, the more salient one, and for this reason it may exhibit the special properties often associated with marked values, such as their tendency to engage in assimilation, to trigger dissimilation, to "float" in the absence of segmental support, and so forth.

The markedness criterion that will be adopted here is based on a quantization of frequency in terms of nonuniversal vs. universal presence in inventories:

(10) A feature value is marked if it is absent in some languages; otherwise, it is unmarked.

A feature is counted as absent in a language if it does not occur in the primary allophone of any contrastive sound. For example, [+nasal] sounds are absent in this sense in some languages (including Quileute, Lushootseed, Pirahã, and Rotokas), while all known languages have [−nasal] sounds. It follows that [+nasal] is the marked value of the oral/nasal distinction. Features that are marked in terms of criterion (10) usually satisfy other markedness criteria as well. In the case of [+nasal], for example, we find that

• speech sound inventories tend to contain fewer [+nasal] sounds than [−nasal] sounds;
• most lexicons contain fewer [+nasal] sounds than [−nasal] sounds;
• in most languages, [+nasal] sounds tend to have lower text frequencies than [−nasal] sounds;
• in any inventory, [+nasal] stops usually imply corresponding [−nasal] stops;
• [+nasal] is more likely than [−nasal] to spread from one segment to another;
• [+nasal] sounds often neutralize to the nearest [−nasal] sound in nonassimilatory contexts, while the reverse is not true.

In evaluating a given feature by criterion (10), only classes of sounds in which the feature is potentially distinctive are considered. For example, since all vowels are redundantly [+sonorant] and [+continuant], vowels are not counted in evaluating these features. However, as these features are potentially distinctive in consonants, the marked value can be determined by examining consonants. Thus, we observe that some languages (e.g., Pirahã and Maxakalí) lack [+sonorant] consonants though all have obstruents, and that others (e.g., Auca, Dera, Angaatiha, and Ekari) lack [+continuant] consonants though all have stops. It follows from criterion (10) that [+sonorant] and [+continuant] are the marked values of these features.

Examples of marked feature values according to criterion (10) are shown in (11) (data source: UPSID).

(11)

Sounds that all languages have	*Sounds that some languages lack*	*Marked feature values*
Obstruents	Sonorant consonants	[+sonorant]
Stops	Continuants	[+continuant]
Oral sounds	Nasal sounds	[+nasal]
Nonstrident sounds	Strident sounds	[+strident]
Anterior coronal sounds	Posterior coronal sounds	[+posterior]
Nonlateral sounds	Lateral sounds	[+lateral]
Unaspirated sounds	Aspirated sounds	[spread glottis]

Nonglottalized sounds	Glottalized sounds	[constricted glottis]
Unrounded sounds	Rounded sounds	[+round]
Nonhigh vowels	High vowels	[+high]
Nonlow vowels	Low vowels	[+low]
Central and back vowels	Front vowels	[+front]

Not all features can be assigned marked values by criterion (10). For example, since all languages have both vowels and consonants, neither value of [±consonantal] can be considered marked by this criterion. UPSID does not give sufficient information to determine whether [±distributed] or [±ATR] ([advanced tongue root]) can be assigned marked values. (For further discussion of these features, see Clements 2001 and Casali 2003, respectively.)

Criterion (10) extends straightforwardly to one-valued features like [spread glottis]. As shown in (11), [spread glottis] is marked, since not all languages make use of it; the unmarked term is simply the absence of this feature. Similar considerations argue for the marked status of most articulator features. Thus, as consonant features, [labial] and [dorsal] are marked, since some languages (e.g., Wichita) have no primary labial consonants while others (e.g., Vanimo) have no primary dorsal consonants. In contrast, all known languages appear to have coronal consonants. (Hawaiian, often cited for its absence of /t/, has /n/ and /l/.) Criterion (10) therefore identifies [coronal] as unmarked.[13]

The feature [±voiced] requires special discussion. While most languages have voiceless obstruents, voiced obstruents are lacking in many languages. This suggests that [+voiced] is the marked value of this feature, as the earlier discussion has assumed.[14] However, UPSID includes four languages, all spoken in Australia, in which *all* obstruents are classified as voiced and are transcribed with the symbols *b*, *d*, *g*, and so on. It would follow from criterion (10) that neither value of this feature is marked.

A closer look at the facts, however, shows that the "voiced" obstruents in these languages are realized as voiceless in some circumstances. For example, in Mbabaram, according to a fairly recent description, "the allophony is as follows: (i) stops are normally voiceless in initial position, in final position, and in medial position after y; (ii) they are voiced after a nasal; (iii) they alternate between voiced and voiceless in medial position between vowels, or after l, r, or ɽ" (Dixon 1991:355). Most linguists would feel quite comfortable transcribing such sounds with the symbols *p*, *t*, *k*. However, the fact that they are often voiced between vowels shows that they are not quite the same as the voiceless stops of languages like French or Spanish. UPSID also records Dyirbal and Yidiny as having only voiced stops. Again, however, other sources show that they have regular voiceless variants. For Dyirbal /b/, Dixon observes, "The voiced allophone [b] is almost invariably heard between vowels (which are always voiced sounds); at the beginning of a word [p] is often heard, varying freely with [b] in this position. That is, [diban], [tiban] are the two commonest pronunciations of 'stone'. [dipan], [tipan] are heard much less often; but they are, unhesitatingly, taken as instances of the same word" (1980:127). For Yidiny, Dixon states, "Stops are almost always voiced. Partly voiced allophones are sometimes encountered word-initially" (1977:32). Generalizing over Australian languages, Yallop observes, "The plosives of aboriginal languages may be pronounced sometimes as voiced sounds (*b*, *d*, etc.) and sometimes as voiceless sounds (*p*, *t*, etc.)—but the voiced and voiceless counterparts are either freely interchangeable or in complementary distribution" (1982:56). The validity of this claim is confirmed by the study of some of the more detailed descriptions of individual Australian languages.[15]

Such realization patterns suggest that the "voiced" stops in question are produced with a laryngeal configuration in which the vocal cords are adducted as for modal voicing but neither tensed nor laxed. Phonetic studies show that whether the vocal cords vibrate in such a state is a function of the interacting articulatory and aerodynamic factors that regulate pressure drop across the glottis (see, e.g., Westbury 1983, Stevens 1998). Given this fact, the variably voiced stops of many Australian languages might be better analyzed as *lacking* any specification for voicing. The presence (or absence) of voicing would then be determined not by phonological features but by the phonetic context. Such an analysis can be easily expressed, for example, in the feature theory of Halle and Stevens (1971, 1991), which recognizes three categories of unaspirated, nonglottalized stops:

- voiced stops, bearing [+slack vocal cords],
- voiceless stops, bearing [+stiff vocal cords], and
- a third category of "intermediate" stops, bearing neither feature.

Stops that vary between voiced and voiceless, freely or according to the phonetic context, are quite naturally viewed as representing the third category of stops.[16] If voicing is reanalyzed in this way, the problem raised by Australian languages disappears. In these languages, stops lack specifications for both [stiff vocal cords] and [slack vocal cords]. In this analysis, [stiff vocal cords] and [slack vocal cords] are *both* marked features, since not all languages make use of them.

2.6.3   Marked Feature Avoidance

On the basis of these observations, we may state the principle of *Marked Feature Avoidance* as in (12).

(12) Within any class of sounds in which a given feature F is potentially distinctive, the number of sounds bearing marked values of F is less than ("<") the number bearing unmarked values of F.

This principle claims that languages tend to avoid marked feature values, regardless of the class of sounds they occur in. It predicts, for example, that [+nasal] sounds will be less numerous than [−nasal] sounds in the classes of vowels, liquids, sonorants, and so on. Like Feature Economy, this principle represents a force rather than a strict law, and it can be expected to have exceptions. We will examine several such exceptions in section 2.8, where we will see that they arise from interaction with a competing principle of Phonological Enhancement. The claim, then, is that (12) is one of a number of interacting principles that together govern the structure of sound inventories. Some specific claims that follow from (12) are shown in (13).

(13) a. Nasal vowels < oral vowels   Marked feature: [+nasal]
     b. Fricatives < stops   Marked feature: [+continuant]
     c. Sonorant consonants < obstruents   Marked feature: [+sonorant]

These statements bear a superficial resemblance to what are commonly called implicational universals. Such universals are usually given in the form "The presence of M implies the presence of U" (or more simply "M ⊃ U"), in which M is a marked term and U the corresponding unmarked term. Thus, we find statements such as those in (14).

(14) a. Nasal vowels ⊃ oral vowels
     b. Fricatives ⊃ stops
     c. Sonorant consonants ⊃ obstruents

We can observe that the truth of these statements follows strictly from the truth of those in (13). Thus, for example, if the number of nasal vowels in a language is always less than the number of oral vowels in accordance with (13a), it can never be the case that a language will have nasal vowels without oral vowels, violating (14a).

However, while the statements in (14) follow from those in (13), the reverse is not true. Languages can violate the statements in (13) without violating those in (14). Consequently, those in (13) make the stronger claim. To see this, let us compare the vowel systems in (15).

(15) *System A*   *System B*   *System C*
     i ĩ   u ũ   ĩ   ũ   ĩ   ũ
     e   o   ẽ   õ   ẽ   õ
          a ã   a ã   ã

Both (13a) and (14a) exclude system C, which has only nasal vowels. Both admit system A, in which nasal vowels form a proper subset of oral vowels. However, they differ in their predictions regarding system B. This system is admitted by the implicational universal (14a) since the presence of the single oral vowel satisfies the implied term U ("oral vowels"). However, it is excluded by Marked Feature Avoidance, since the number of nasal vowels exceeds the number of oral vowels.

Now it is a common observation that the number of nasal vowels in a vowel system is typically a proper subset of the number of oral vowels; systems like A are common, while those like B are apparently unattested (see, e.g., Williamson 1973, Maddieson 1984). It follows that even if we adopt the universal implication (14a), we *still* need principle (13a) to express this widespread trend. Once we admit (13a), however, (14a) becomes superfluous, as it is a logical consequence of (13). Thus, the implicational universal (14a) may be dispensed with. A similar line of reasoning applies to other implications such as (14b,c).

It may be objected that implicational universals such as those in (14) are still required because they are exceptionless by definition, while those in (13) state trends and are therefore not always true. For example, the existence of a single language with more nasal vowels than oral vowels would not weaken the statistical validity of (13a), but would disprove the implicational universal "nasal vowels ⊃ oral vowels." The claim, then, might be that "absolute" implications such as those in (14) are still required to state exceptionless patterns. This objection is ill-founded, however. "Absolute" implications of the type shown in (14) are exceptionless not because of any inherent link between the implying term and the implied term, but simply because the implied term occurs in all languages. Why is this? Recall that a material implication of the form P ⊃ Q is true if Q is true, no matter whether P is true or false. It follows that the statement "nasal vowels ⊃ oral vowels" is true by virtue of the fact that all languages have oral vowels—even those with no nasal vowels. Thus, the statements in (14) can be replaced by the simpler statements "All languages have oral vowels," and so on, from which they automatically follow.[17]

Marked Feature Avoidance is a more powerful tool than implicational universals in still another sense. Here are two more predictions made by Marked Feature Avoidance:

(16) a. In the class of uvular obstruents, fricatives < stops.
        marked feature: [+continuant]
    b. In the class of voiceless stops, ejectives < pulmonic stops.
        marked feature: [constricted glottis]

In these cases, there are no corresponding implicational universals.

• Uvular fricatives do not universally imply uvular stops: several languages, including Pashto, Armenian, Mandarin, Spanish, and Basque, have uvular fricatives without uvular stops.
• Voiceless ejective stops do not universally imply voiceless plain (unaspirated pulmonic) stops: at least one language, Berta, has a weakly ejective series without a voiceless plain stop series (Triulzi, Dafallah, and Bender 1976).

Nevertheless, these statements represent valid trends, as the data in (17) show.

	Sound type	No. of languages	No. of sounds	Average no. of sounds per language
a.	Uvular fricatives	49	100	2.0
	Uvular stops	69	169	2.4
b.	Ejective stops	68	248	3.6
	Plain stops	435	2,200	5.1

(with (17) labelling the set)

Overall, the marked member of each comparison is less frequent than the unmarked member, as predicted by Marked Feature Avoidance. Here, again, implicational universals have nothing to say.

There is an important class of exceptions to Marked Feature Avoidance that upon closer examination proves to be explained by its interaction with Feature Economy. Recall from the earlier discussion that Feature Economy tends to override Markedness. In its strongest form it predicts, contrary to Marked Feature Avoidance, that the marked members of a class should be equal in number to the unmarked members of a class. Now this is often true. For example, a fair number of languages have equal numbers of oral and nasal vowels. In a survey of 141 representative African vowel systems, I found that 45 had nasal vowels, and that of these, 7 or 15.6% had equal numbers of nasal and oral vowels. The system in (18), for example, is found in Ikwere, spoken in Nigeria (Clements and Osu 2005).

(18) i ĩ   u ũ
      ɪ ɪ̃   ʊ ʊ̃
      e ẽ   o õ
      ɛ ɛ̃   ɔ ɔ̃
          a ã

Similarly, many languages, including English (3), have equal numbers of voiced and voiceless fricatives, or voiced and voiceless stops, and so forth. In all such cases, Feature Economy overrides Marked Feature Avoidance. The combined prediction of these two principles is that the number of marked sounds may equal but will never *exceed* the number of corresponding unmarked sounds in a class.

While this prediction is very largely true across languages, there are nevertheless some cases in which marked sounds do outnumber the corresponding unmarked sounds. For example, Archi, a Lezghian language, has more uvular fricatives (12) than stops (10) (Colarusso 2004). It follows that a marked sound may have no unmarked counterpart at all. Thus, as noted in the discussion of (16), several languages have the uvular fricative /χ/ without a corresponding uvular stop /q/. It must be emphasized, however, that most such cases represent random minority patterns rather than general trends.[18]

2.6.4 Marked Segment Types Appear in Larger Inventories

A final prediction of Marked Feature Avoidance is stated in (19).

(19) The average number of sounds in languages containing a marked term M is greater than the average number of sounds in languages containing its unmarked counterpart U.

This is because, as we have just seen, languages having a marked class of sounds M generally contain an equal or larger number of sounds of the unmarked class U, while the reverse is not true. An example will make this clear. Consider typical systems containing an array of voiced and voiceless stops, with or without corresponding fricatives, as shown in (20). (It will be recalled that uppercase letters designate general feature-defined categories rather than specific sounds.)

(20) *System A*   *System B*   *System C*   *System D*

P T K	P T K	P T K	P T K
B D G	B D G	B D G	B D G
	F S	F S	
		V Z	V Z

Systems A, B, and C obey the predictions of Marked Feature Avoidance and Feature Economy. System D violates them, however, as it has more voiced fricatives (2) than voiceless ones (0). The prediction, then, is that systems of this type should tend not to occur. This proves to be strongly and significantly true; while many UPSID languages have both series of fricatives, as in system C, or just voiceless fricatives alone, as in system B, only seven have voiced fricatives alone ($\chi^2 = 22.377$, $p <$ .0001). The conclusion is that voiced fricatives will tend to be admissible in a system only if voiceless fricatives are already in place.

We expect, then, that systems with voiced fricatives will tend to have more consonants overall (since they must also have voiceless fricatives, as in system C) than will systems with voiceless fricatives (which need not have voiced fricatives, as in system B). This expectation is confirmed in UPSID, as shown in (21). Languages with voiced fricatives have, on average, about two consonants more than languages with voiceless fricatives.

(21)

Sound type	*No. of languages*	*Average no. of consonants*
Voiced fricatives	221	22.3
Voiceless fricatives	406	20.4

This prediction extends to more complex cases involving sounds with highly marked features. As an example, let us examine the distribution of plain dorsal stops K, labialized dorsal stops K^w, ejective dorsal stops K', and labialized-ejective dorsal stops $K^{w'}$. The three latter categories bear the marked features of glottal constriction and labialization. Marked Feature Avoidance predicts that the labialized ejective stops K^{w}' should tend to be present only in inventories that also have the plain labialized stops K^{w} and the simple ejective stops K', and that these in turn should tend to appear only in the still larger set of inventories that also have the plain nonejective stops K. As a consequence, K^{w}' should appear, on average, in languages with the largest consonant inventories, K^{w} and K' in languages with somewhat smaller inventories, and K in languages with the smallest inventories.

The numbers corresponding to each of these cases in UPSID are shown in (22).

(22)	Sound	Marked feature values	No. of languages	Average no. of consonants
a.	K^{w}'	2	23	35.8
b.	K'	1	68	29.0
	K^{w}	1	69	26.4
c.	K	0	450	19.7

Our expectation is confirmed. Languages containing K^{w}', bearing both marked features [constricted glottis] and [+round], have an average of 35.8 consonants; languages with K' and K^{w}, bearing just one of these features, have an average of 29.0 and 26.4 consonants, respectively; and languages containing K, bearing neither of these features, have an average of 19.7 consonants (equal to the average number of consonants in UPSID languages overall). In such examples, we find a positive correlation between the degree of markedness of a segment and the average size of the inventories containing it. This correlation is another consequence of Marked Feature Avoidance.

2.6.5 Summary

This section has made the following main points:

• Marked feature values can be defined as those that are not present in all languages.
• Inventories show a tendency to avoid segments bearing marked feature values.
• By Marked Feature Avoidance, this tendency holds in all classes of sounds.
• Marked Feature Avoidance interacts with other principles such as Feature Economy (see also the discussion of Phonological Enhancement in section 2.8).

However, the ultimate question of why some feature values are more frequent (and hence less marked) than others has not been addressed in this discussion, much less solved, and remains a question for further research.

2.7 Robustness

A further principle structuring sound inventories is one that will be called *Robustness*. This principle holds that there is a universal hierarchy of features such that, in constituting their inventories, languages draw upon higher-ranked features in the hierarchy before drawing upon lower-ranked features. (For this idea and related ones, see Jakobson 1968 [1941], Jakobson and Halle 1956, Chomsky and Halle 1968:409–410, Stevens and Keyser 1989, Dinnsen 1992, Calabrese 1994, 1995, Lang and Ohala 1996.)

The Robustness principle addresses a significant gap in the theory developed so far. Sound inventories do not typically consist of only vowels, or only fricatives, or only labial sounds. Instead, they typically draw their members from a wide variety of feature dimensions, including at least three major places of articulation and several manner categories (Maddieson 1984). Feature Economy does not predict this distribution. Markedness theory goes some way toward accounting for it, but does not explain why sound systems are not uniformly skewed toward unmarked categories. Why do we find no languages whose consonant inventories include only coronals, or only voiceless stops? Why are there no languages with only central vowels?

The answer seems to be that languages prefer to draw their sounds from a highly differentiated set of sounds that are distinguished along many acoustic/articulatory parameters. A language having only coronal consonants would fail to benefit from the rich auditory contrasts that become available once labial, dorsal, and laryngeal consonants are introduced. Similarly, a language with only voiceless stops would not fully exploit the resonance properties of the vocal tract, and a language with only central vowels would not make full use of the frequency spectrum. The point of drawing sounds from many well-differentiated phonetic dimensions is that the members of a system built up in this way are highly individualized and distinct from one another.[19]

Robustness theory, then, is based on the observation that some contrasts are highly favored in sound systems, others less favored, and still others disfavored. Contrasts can be arranged in terms of a probabilistic hierarchy according to the degree to which they are favored; contrasts high in the hierarchy tend to be present in most languages, while those lower in the hierarchy are present in fewer languages. It follows that contrasts lower on the list will tend to be present in an inventory only if contrasts higher on the list are also present.

The earlier literature often failed to distinguish Robustness from Markedness. The basic difference is that Markedness is a property of feature *values* while Robustness is a property of feature-based *contrasts*. Some examples of more and less robust contrasts are given in (23).

(23) *More robust*   *Less robust*

Sonorant vs. obstruent	Apical vs. nonapical
Labial vs. coronal vs. dorsal	Central vs. lateral
Nasal vs. oral	Aspirated vs. nonaspirated
Stop vs. continuant	Glottalized vs. nonglottalized
Voiced vs. voiceless	Implosive vs. explosive

Like Markedness, Robustness is ultimately rooted in phonetic and functional factors. The most robust features, as a class, have the property of ensuring a high degree of auditory dispersion of a "core" set of speech sounds. Robust features are, in general, those that maximize salience and economy at a low articulatory cost. They tend to permit one sound to be easily distinguished from another, even in rapid speech and under conditions of noise, and they are often mastered fairly early in the process of language acquisition, one criterion of articulatory ease. Another factor that supports Robustness is economy—the ability of a feature to combine freely with other features. Thus, for example, [±continuant] combines with all places of articulation, and [labial] with all manners of articulation. In contrast, many less robust features, such as [±strident], [±lateral], [±distributed], and [spread glottis], combine less easily, or not at all, with certain other features.[20]

However, as in the case of Markedness, the phonetic basis of Robustness is still poorly understood. Stevens and Keyser (1989) have suggested that "primary" features—in present terms, those that stand at the top of the robustness scale—provide a stronger auditory response than others. They state that "the three primary features are especially closely tied to fundamental capabilities of the auditory system for processing temporal and spectral aspects of sound" (p. 87). Thus, for example, [−continuant] obstruents (i.e., stops) are distinguished from [+continuant] obstruents (i.e., fricatives) by an abrupt decrease in amplitude over a wide range of frequencies with respect to neighboring vowels; contrasts of this type appear to trigger enhanced auditory responses in the peripheral auditory system (e.g., Delgutte and Kiang 1984). It is far from clear, however, that only primary features are characterized in this way. For example, clicks also involve rapid change in amplitude, yet these sounds are rare across languages. Stevens and Keyser themselves note, "We cannot, at this point, quantify the saliency of individual features in terms of auditory response mechanisms" (1989:85). Given these problems, a frequency-based diagnostic of Robustness will be adopted here, as in the case of Markedness.

(24) lists the commonest consonant contrasts in UPSID by order of frequency. These fall into four provisional groups, within which contrasts have roughly similar probabilities. Each contrast is illustrated by a typical pair, whose less probable member is shown first.[21] Percentages indicate how many languages have consonants representing each contrast (e.g., 91.6% of UPSID languages have contrasts between fricatives and stops). The features defining each contrast are given at the right.

(24) *Commonest consonant contrasts in UPSID*

	Example	Percentage (UPSID)	Feature(s)
a. Dorsal vs. coronal obstruent	K/T	99.6	[dorsal], [coronal]
Sonorant vs. obstruent	N/T	98.9	[±sonorant]
Labial vs. coronal obstruent	P/T	98.7	[labial], [coronal]

	Labial vs. dorsal obstruent	P/K	98.7	[labial], [dorsal]
	Labial vs. coronal sonorant	M/N	98.0	[labial], [coronal]
b.	Continuant vs. noncontinuant sonorant	J/N	93.8	[±continuant]
	Continuant vs. noncontinuant obstruent	S/T	91.6	[±continuant]
	Posterior vs. anterior sonorant	J/L	89.6	[±posterior]
c.	Voiced vs. voiceless obstruent	D/T	83.4	[±voiced]
	Oral vs. nasal noncontinuant sonorant	L/N	80.7	[±nasal]
d.	Posterior vs. anterior obstruent	Tʃ/T	77.6	[±posterior]
	Glottal vs. nonglottal consonant	H/T	74.5	[glottal]

Let us briefly consider contrasts based on [±strident], not included in this list. Two of the contrasts involving obstruents could also have been characterized in terms of [±strident]: the continuant versus stop contrast (e.g., S/T) and the anterior versus posterior contrast (e.g., T/Tʃ). In both cases, one member of the contrast is typically a strident sound. However, [±continuant] and [±posterior] have been chosen as the basis of the contrast, for two reasons. First, these features are used more frequently than [±strident] across languages to define minimal contrasts, even if we accept that [±strident] distinguishes simple stops and affricates (see Clements 1999, Kim 2001, Kehrein 2002). Specifically, 404 UPSID languages contrast coronal stops and fricatives (involving [±continuant]), 212 contrast anterior and posterior coronal stops (involving [±posterior]), and 187 contrast anterior and posterior fricatives ([±posterior] again). In contrast, only 178 contrast sibilant and nonsibilant coronal stops ([±strident]), and just 80 contrast sibilant and nonsibilant coronal fricatives ([±strident]). Of the three features, then, [±strident] is the least often used to define minimal contrasts. Second, [±strident] can be understood as a feature that enhances the acoustic properties of continuants (fricatives) and posterior sounds (such as palatoalveolars), in the sense of Stevens, Keyser, and Kawasaki (1986). It enhances fricatives by increasing the amplitude of the frication noise at higher frequencies, and posterior obstruents by making their characteristic lower-frequency noise component in the region of the third formant more audible (see further discussion in the next section). If one feature enhances another, the latter is considered more basic.

It seems appropriate, then, to regard [±continuant] and [±posterior] as the basis of these contrasts, even when [+strident] is also present in one member of the contrast. In the case of [±continuant], this choice is also supported by Feature Economy. While [±continuant] can be generalized to all oral places of articulation (labial, coronal, dorsal), [±strident] is restricted to coronal places (Sagey 1990) and thus tends to contribute less to the overall economy of a system. One would therefore expect [±continuant] to be the more basic feature even in segments in which both features are present.

A language having just the favored contrasts in (24) would typically include the consonants and glides shown in (25).

(25) P   T   Tʃ   K
         B   D   G
                S
         M   N
         W   L, R   J   H

Let us call this the *basic consonant inventory*. It contains the 15 commonest consonant types in UPSID, as defined by the feature contrasts in (24). Their frequencies
are shown in (26).

(26) *Sound*   *Typical phonetic*
      type   *Feature definition*   *Percentage*   *values*
      T   obs vl ant cor stop   98.2   t
      K   obs vl dor stop   97.8   k q
      N   son nas ant cor stop   95.6   n
      M   son nas lab stop   94.7   m
      P   obs vl lab stop   90.2   p
      S   obs vl cor cont   88.9   s ʃ
      J   son oral post cor cont   85.1   j
      L   son oral cor stop   81.4   l ʎ
      W   son oral lab cont   80.3   w
      H   glot   74.5   h ʔ
      B   obs vd lab stop   71.4   b
      R   son oral ant cor cont   71.0   r
      D   obs vd ant cor stop   70.3   d
      Tʃ   obs vl post cor stop   66.5   tʃ c
      G   obs vd dor stop   63.2   g

These consonant types are defined by the features [±sonorant], [labial], [dorsal],
[coronal], [±nasal], [±continuant], [±voiced], [±posterior], and [glottal], as shown in
the second column of (26). These features are presumably among the most robust for
consonants.[22]

   Based on these observations, a partial robustness scale is proposed in (27) for the
more important consonant features, with the most robust features placed at the top.
Features within each of the first three groups are unordered (ordering within group
(e) remains to be determined).

(27) *Robustness scale for consonant features*
         a. [±sonorant]
             [labial]
             [coronal]
             [dorsal]

    b. [±continuant]
       [±posterior]
    c. [±voiced]
       [±nasal]
    d. [glottal]
    e. others

(27) expands the two-point scale proposed by Stevens and Keyser (1989). According to (27), the most robust features are [±sonorant] and the three major place features, [labial], [coronal], and [dorsal] (group (a)). These features are used in the great majority of languages. The remaining groups are drawn upon with decreasing frequency as we descend the scale:

• [±continuant] and [±posterior] further expand the set of places and manners of articulation;
• [±voiced] and [±nasal] introduce the laryngeal and nasal dimensions, respectively;
• [glottal] is used here to designate sounds using a primary glottal articulator, namely, H-sounds and glottal stops.

Remaining features such as [±strident], [±distributed], [±lateral], [spread glottis], and [constricted glottis] are less widely drawn upon and tend to be used only if the higher-ranked ones are also exploited.

A language making full use of features (27a–d) in their most favored segmental contexts will have all members of the basic consonant inventory, as shown in (28).

(28)

	P	T	Tʃ	K	B	D	G	S	H	M	N	L	R	W	J
[sonorant]	−	−	−	−	−	−	−	−	−	+	+	+	+	+	+
[labial]	+				+					+				+	
[coronal]		+	+			+		+			+	+	+		+
[dorsal]				+			+							+	
[continuant]	−	−	−	−	−	−	−	+	+	−	−	−	+	+	+
[posterior]		−	+			−		−			−	−	−		+
[voiced]	−	−	−	−	+	+	+	−	−						
[nasal]	−	−	−	−	−	−	−	−	−	+	+	−	−	−	−
[glottal]									+						

On the basis of the robustness scale (27), we may formulate the *Robustness Principle* as in (29). It predicts, for example, that minimal contrasts involving [±strident] (group (27e)) will tend to be present only if minimal contrasts involving [±voiced] (group (27c)) are present, that those involving [±voiced] will be present only if those involving [±continuant] (group (27b)) are present, and so forth.

(29) *Robustness Principle*

   In any class of sounds in which two features are potentially distinctive, minimal contrasts involving the lower-ranked feature will tend to be present only if minimal contrasts involving the higher-ranked feature are also present.

As an illustration, let us consider the use of [±strident] and [±voiced] in the three stop systems in (30). All contain a plain coronal stop T and a coronal affricate, either anterior TS or posterior Tʃ.

(30) *System A*   *System B*   *System C*
   P   T   TS   K   P   T   Tʃ   K   P   T   TS   K
   B   D   DZ   G

Systems A and B are consistent with the Robustness Principle. System A has minimal contrasts involving [±strident] (TS/T, DZ/D) and [±voiced] (P/B, T/D, etc.); since higher-ranked [±voiced] is present, lower-ranked [±strident] is also allowed. System B contains no minimal contrast involving either feature. The contrast T/Tʃ is not minimal, as it involves two features, [±posterior] and [±strident]. Of these, the first is more robust, according to the robustness scale. Therefore, the fundamental contrast in this case involves [±posterior], with [±strident] serving as a redundant feature of enhancement (see the next section for further discussion). System C, however, violates the tendency expressed by the Robustness Principle, as it contains a minimal contrast involving lower-ranked [±strident]—namely, T/TS—while lacking a minimal contrast involving higher-ranked [±voiced].

The Robustness Principle would, of course, be too strong if it were taken to be an exceptionless law. As in the case of Feature Economy and Marked Feature Avoidance, it is proposed as one of several interacting forces and is intended to express significant trends rather than laws. As we would expect, then, some languages and language groups have exceptions to it. For example, Spanish with its /r/ versus /l/ contrast makes use of [±lateral] while abjuring the higher-ranked [glottal]. Similarly, as shown in (31), the Mexican language Zoque with its /t/ versus /ts/ contrast draws upon [±strident] in its native obstruent system while not exploiting the higher-ranked [±voiced] (Wonderly 1951–2).

(31) p   t   ts   tʃ   c   k
            s   ʃ

Interestingly enough, though the feature [±voiced] is not distinctive in the native lexicon of Zoque, it is distinctive in its substantial stock of Spanish-derived loanwords, and it also appears pervasively in the native phonology by virtue of a regular process that voices stops after nasals (Wonderly 1946, 1951–2). These redundantly voiced stops appear to be phonetically identical to the phonemically voiced stops of the Spanish-derived lexicon. Such observations suggest that feature contrasts that are passed over in phoneme inventories may have a high potential for subsequent incorporation as a result of contact or internal change.

Although we do, therefore, find a certain amount of crosslinguistic variation with respect to the robustness scale, such variation is within narrow limits. For example, no languages select all (or even most) of their features from the very bottom of the scale. Moreover, exceptions, when they exist, tend to be concentrated at the lower end of the scale, containing features that are easily dispensed with; while very few languages skip high-ranked features such as [±sonorant] or [labial], low-ranked features such as [±lateral] or [±distributed] can be passed over with relative ease.

Robustness interacts strongly with Feature Economy and Marked Feature Avoidance. First, as a result of Feature Economy, even though less robust features tend to be less frequent across languages, once they are present in a system they tend to generalize to other sounds, creating further contrasts. For example, though [spread glottis] is a lower-ranked feature, languages with distinctively aspirated stops tend to have many of them. Another interaction is that Feature Economy favors features that combine maximally with others, reinforcing Robustness. Thus, the robust feature [±sonorant], which cross-classifies all oral-cavity consonants, combines more readily with other sounds than the less robust feature [±strident], which cross-classifies only [coronal] sounds. The fact that [±strident], [±distributed], and [±lateral] are lower-ranked features is due, in part, to the fact that they combine poorly or not at all with noncoronal sounds.

Second, Marked Feature Avoidance limits the full generality with which even the most robust features are used. For example, labial and dorsal fricatives are absent in a majority of languages, even though [labial], [dorsal] and [±continuant] are highly robust, and Feature Economy favors their maximal use. The basic consonant inventory (25) reveals these gaps. The disfavored sounds are just those that combine the marked feature value [+continuant] with a marked articulator feature [dorsal] or [labial]. Other common gaps, also illustrated in the basic inventory, are the following:

• Dorsal nasals are missing: [+nasal] is disfavored with [dorsal] obstruents.
• Posterior fricatives are missing: [+continuant] is disfavored with [+posterior] obstruents.
• Posterior nasals are missing: [+nasal] is disfavored with [+posterior] sonorants.

In these cases, too, the missing combinations cumulate marked feature values. It is often the case that if an expected higher-ranked contrast is missing, it is missing in one or more marked categories. This follows directly from Marked Feature Avoidance. As a result, contextual conditions such as "[dorsal] only in [−continuant] obstruents" have an independent explanation and do not have to be built into the robustness scale itself.[23]

In summary, this section has outlined a Robustness Principle that states that languages tend to select their features from the more robust dimensions of contrast. Acting jointly, Feature Economy, Marked Feature Avoidance, and the Robustness Principle predict that languages tend to organize their sound systems by maximizing the use of a small number of highly valued features, favoring unmarked feature combinations.

2.8 Phonological Enhancement

Weak acoustic contrasts can be reinforced by increasing the acoustic difference between their members, a phenomenon termed *enhancement* (Stevens, Keyser, and Kawasaki 1986, Stevens and Keyser 1989). Enhancement is feature-based, as it typically affects natural classes of sounds rather than individual segments. Keyser and Stevens (2001) distinguish between Phonological Enhancement, in which reinforcement is achieved by introducing a redundant feature, and Phonetic Enhancement, in which reinforcement is achieved by introducing a supplementary articulation at the phonetic level. We will be concerned with Phonological Enhancement here.

Phonological Enhancement typically involves the introduction of a marked feature value to reinforce an existing contrast between two classes of sounds. A familiar example is the assignment of the feature [+round] to back vowels. The introduction of this feature has the effect of lowering the second formant (F2) of back vowels, increasing their auditory distance from front vowels, which are characterized by a high F2. Recall from (11) that [+round] is the marked value of the feature [±round]. In languages having this enhancement process, the marked value [+round] will be more frequent than the unmarked value [−round] in the class of back vowels, creating systematic violations of Marked Feature Avoidance.

The enhancement of posterior stops by the feature [+strident] is another example of this type. The addition of [+strident] to a posterior stop increases its auditory distance from a nonstrident anterior stop such as /t/. In this case, the increase is not along a uniform auditory dimension, but along a different one. This is because /tʃ/ differs from /t/ not only in terms of its lower burst and transition frequencies, which depend on the feature value [+posterior], but also in terms of the presence of high-pitched, high-amplitude turbulence noise following the burst, which depends on [+strident].[24]

It is not always clear whether a given enhancing property is due to a feature operating at the phonological level or to a gesture introduced at the phonetic level. In the case of English /tʃ/, /dʒ/, however, the enhancement is clearly due to the feature [+strident], for three reasons. First, the stridency following the release of /tʃ/, /dʒ/ is not variable or gradient, but appears to be similar in duration, prominence, and consistency to the distinctive stridency of affricates in languages in which they contrast minimally with nonstrident stops. Second, though this feature is redundant in the stops /tʃ/, /dʒ/ in English, it is distinctive in the fricatives /s/, /z/, which are minimally distinguished from /θ/, /ð/ by their stridency. The redundancy rule introducing [+strident] in the stops thus introduces a feature that is already distinctive in the system. Such "locally redundant features" (i.e., features redundant in some segments but distinctive in others) engage in Feature Economy effects just as fully distinctive features do (Clements 2003b), showing that they are phonologically present. Third, redundant values of [+strident] function in exactly the same way as distinctive values of [+strident] in English phonology. For example, both trigger an epenthetic vowel [ɨ] before the plural marker /-z/; compare nouns such as *matches* [. . . tʃɨz], with redundant [+strident], and *places* [. . . sɨz], with distinctive [+strident].

Examples of other common enhancement effects are shown in (32). All involve the introduction of a marked feature, in violation of Marked Feature Avoidance.[25]

(32) a. [+strident] enhances [+continuant] in coronal obstruents; thus, the strident /s/, with its high-energy noise component, is more distinct from nonstrident stops like /t/ than is a nonstrident fricative like /θ/.

   b. [+nasal] enhances [−continuant] in sonorant consonants; thus, the nasal stop /n/, with its pronounced nasal resonance, is more distinct from oral continuants like /ɾ/ or /ɹ/ than is an oral noncontinuant like /l/.

   c. [+posterior] enhances [coronal] in sonorant continuants; thus, the palatal glide /j/, with its extrahigh F2, is more distinct from noncoronals like /w/ than is a dental or alveolar continuant like /ɾ/ or the approximant /ð/.

   d. [+labiodental] enhances [+continuant] in labial sounds; thus, the labiodental fricative /f/, with its higher-amplitude fricative noise component, is more distinct from stops like /p/ than is a bilabial fricative like /ɸ/.

These examples are only illustrative, and others can be added.[26] All these enhancement effects can be expected to create reversals of the frequency patterns predicted by Marked Feature Avoidance.

That they do so is shown in (33), which illustrates several examples of Phonological Enhancement in consonants and vowels. The parenthesized number following a feature is the number of UPSID languages having that feature in the class of sounds described in the first column. For example, the first line shows that 450 languages have [−strident] anterior coronal stops. The final, boldfaced lines in each set represent enhancement contexts. They show that in these contexts, marked (plus) values are *more* frequent than unmarked values. (Phonetic symbols illustrate typical realizations.)

(33) *Frequency reversals resulting from Phonological Enhancement*

Segment class	More frequent	Less frequent
a. Anterior coronal stops	t [−strident] (450)	ts [+strident] (148)
Posterior coronal stops	**tʃ [+strident] (235)**	c [−strident] (138)
b. Coronal stops	t [−strident] (450)	tʃ [+strident] (291)
Coronal fricatives	**s [+strident] (397)**	θ [−strident] (105)
c. Vowels	a [−nasal] (451)	ã [+nasal] (102)
Obstruents	t [−nasal] (451)	ⁿt [+nasal] (57)
Sonorant continuants	r [−nasal] (433)	r̃ [+nasal] (5)
Sonorant noncontinuants	**n [+nasal] (435)**	l [−nasal] (368)
d. Obstruents	t [−posterior] (450)	c [+posterior] (355)
Sonorant noncontinuants	n [−posterior] (438)	ɲ [+posterior] (202)
Sonorant continuants	**j [+posterior] (384)**	r [−posterior] (320)
e. Labial stops	p [−labiodental] (446)	pf [+labiodental] (7)
Labial sonorants	β [−labiodental] (34)	ʋ [+labiodental] (7)
Labial fricatives	**f [+labiodental] (199)**	ɸ [−labiodental] (82)

The first two lines in (33) show that while [−strident] anterior coronal stops are present in more languages (450) than are [+strident] stops (148), the situation is reversed in the class of posterior stops, where [+strident] sounds hold the lead (235 vs. 138). The other boldfaced lines show similar frequency reversals.

The results for [±nasal] sounds in (33c) are of particular interest. As noted earlier, [+nasal] is the marked value of the nasal/oral dimension by most criteria, yet nasal sonorants are more frequent across languages than oral sonorants. Closer study shows that this effect is due mainly to the predominance of nasals in the subclass of sonorant noncontinuants, which contains nasal stops and laterals. Within this subclass, as shown in (33c), 435 languages have nasal or nasalized sounds while only 368 have [−nasal] sounds (laterals). Here it appears that [−continuant] is enhanced by [+nasal]. The explanation proposed in (32b) is that nasal stops like /m/ and /n/, with their pronounced nasal resonance, are more distinct from oral continuants like /ɾ/ or /ɹ/ than are oral noncontinuants like /l/.[27]

If this view is correct, it makes a strong prediction: nasal noncontinuants like /n/ should be much more frequent than oral noncontinuants like /l/ in languages having an oral continuant like /ɾ/. This prediction is borne out by an examination of the 320 UPSID languages that contain at least one R-sound (defined as any anterior coronal oral sonorant continuant) and one additional noncontinuant sonorant series, either nasal or lateral. In such "R-systems," as we might call them, the noncontinuant is almost invariably a nasal rather than a lateral:

• 54 R-systems have an anterior coronal nasal N but no anterior coronal lateral L, and
• just 2 R-systems have an anterior coronal lateral L but no anterior coronal nasal N.

This trend is highly significant ($\chi^2 = 20.446$, $p < .0001$). Let us consider the 2 non-conforming R-systems. Waris (a Papuan language) has no plain nasal stops but has prenasalized stops. In this system, replacement of the oral noncontinuant /l/ with the nasal /n/ would increase the auditory distance from the R-sound, but would risk confusion with the prenasalized stop /ⁿd/. Mixtec (a language of Mexico) has no coronal nasal, but has a velar nasal and a series of nasalized vowels; here, a coronal nasal would be competing with other nasal or nasalized sonorants.

While there is a similar preference for nasals in systems lacking R-sounds, this trend is much weaker. Of the 131 systems lacking R-sounds,

• 25 have an anterior coronal nasal N but no anterior coronal lateral L, and
• 5 have an anterior coronal lateral L but no anterior coronal nasal N.

This trend does not reach statistical significance ($p > .05$). Thus, the preference for nasal sonorants is largely due to their overwhelming preponderance in R-systems having just one additional noncontinuant sonorant series, as the enhancement-based account predicts.

We therefore find that a number of exceptions to the predictions of Marked Feature Avoidance can be explained in terms of Phonological Enhancement. This result has an important consequence. While most earlier work on inventory structure (including Clements 2001) has interpreted frequency reversals like those shown in (33) as "markedness reversals" in which the marked and unmarked values of a feature are reversed in certain contexts, enhancement theory allows us to maintain that the marked value of a feature is the same in all contexts, even those in which it is most frequent. In this view, for example, the value [+nasal] is marked even in the class of sonorant noncontinuants where it is more frequent than [−nasal]. Independent markedness criteria support this view; thus, [+nasal] is the typical (and perhaps unique) spreading value of [±nasal] regardless of the class of sounds in which it occurs. Had we maintained that [+nasal] is the unmarked value in sonorant continuants, we would have to maintain that the unmarked value spreads in just this special case.

To summarize this section, Phonological Enhancement is a principle by which weak acoustic contrasts are reinforced by redundant features. When the enhancing features are marked, the frequencies expected under Marked Feature Avoidance are typically reversed. In this way, enhancement theory accounts for a number of regular exceptions to the predictions of markedness theory.

2.9   Illustrations

We have discussed five feature-based principles that account for major trends in the structure of phonological inventories. One, Feature Bounding, is a principle that sets the limits within which the others act. The other four are forces that interact with each other to produce systems that exhibit their effects to varying degrees. Exceptions to one tend strongly to reflect the operation of another.

Let us now see how these forces operate to distinguish likely from unlikely consonant systems. We will consider small-inventory systems first. Under the principles discussed here, the same core set of relatively unmarked sounds should tend to be present in all systems, regardless of their size. This seems to be largely true.

(34) shows the 10 commonest consonant types across the UPSID phoneme inventories.

(34) P   T   K
         S
     M   N
     W   L ~ R   J   H ~ ?

Taken as a possible small-inventory system, (34) is not implausible. It reflects Feature Economy at labial and coronal places of articulation. It generally obeys Marked Feature Avoidance (except where Phonological Enhancement is involved, as in the case of the [+strident] S), and selects its features from groups (27a–d) of the robustness scale.

Small-inventory stems typically have most sounds of this set and sometimes add other members of the basic consonant inventory (25), such as voiced stops. However, they do not usually add highly marked sounds, in conformity with Marked Feature Avoidance. Six small-inventory languages are shown in (35).

(35) *Rotokas (Papuan)*   *Hawaiian (Austro-Tai)*   *Pirahã (Paezan)*
     p   t   k   p   k   ?   p   t   k   ?
     β   g   m   n   b   g
             r   w   l   h   s   h

     Roro (Austro-Tai)   *Gadsup (Papuan)*   *Maxakalí (Macro-Ge)*
     p   t   k   ?   p   t   k   p   t   tʃ   k   ?
     b   β   d   mb nd ndʒ ŋg
     m   n   m   n   h
         r   h   j   ?

Next, consider larger-inventory systems. Such systems tend to conform to the predictions of Feature Economy, Marked Feature Avoidance, Robustness, and Phonological Enhancement. Rather than examining representative examples of larger-inventory systems conforming to these principles, however, since these are commonplace, let us look at a number of hypothetical systems *violating* these principles. Several are shown in (36)–(39).

(36) *System A: Violates Feature Economy*

p t tʃ k
ɓ
   tʰ
      dʒ
         k'
m
  l
    j
      x
         h

This system contains the high-frequency consonants /p, t, tʃ, k/. However, it uses features uneconomically, as it has just one implosive, one aspirated stop, one voiced stop, one ejective, one nasal, one liquid, one glide, one fricative, and one glottal. Using 12 features to characterize 13 segments, it achieves an economy index of only 1.1.

(37) *System B: Violates Markedness*

p t k ʔ
b d g
bʰ dʰ gʰ
v z ɣ
m̥ n̥
  l
w j

This system contains a core set of high-frequency consonants and is relatively economical, but it violates Marked Feature Avoidance. This is because within UPSID languages,

• voiced fricatives usually imply the corresponding voiceless fricatives,
• voiceless nasals strictly imply voiced nasals,[28] and
• voiced aspirates strictly imply voiceless aspirates (within the database of Indian languages collected by Pandey (2003) as well as within UPSID).

The problem here, then, is that the missing series correspond to unmarked rather than marked feature values.

(38) *System C: Violates Robustness*

p t tʃ k ʔ
b d dʒ g
f s ʃ x h
v z

This system, like the others, contains a core set of high-frequency consonants. It is relatively economical and contains no highly marked segments. However, it violates the Robustness Principle ("Select higher-ranked features before lower-ranked features"), as it has no sonorant consonants. Only two UPSID languages lack sonorant consonants, and these are the small-inventory languages Pirahã and Maxakalí, shown in (35).

(39) *System D: Violates Phonological Enhancement*

p t t̠ k
b d d̠ ɡ
ɸ θ ç x
β ð
w ɾ l   h

This system satisfies previous criteria on most counts, but systematically fails to enhance weak contrasts. It chooses bilabial and nonsibilant fricatives instead of the preferred labiodentals and sibilants, incurring poor contrasts between, for example, /b/ and /β/, /β/ and /w/, /ɸ/ and /θ/. It selects nonsibilant posterior stops /t̠, d̠/ instead of the more distinctive sibilants /tʃ, dʒ/. It selects the oral sonorant /l/ instead of the nasal /n/, which provides a better contrast with /ɾ/.

To summarize, the principles discussed earlier operate together to correctly describe small-inventory consonant systems and to exclude many imaginable but unlikely larger-inventory systems. It appears that with nothing much more complicated than a ranked list of features indicating marked values, together with principles of economy and enhancement, we are in a good position to predict the preferred design features of phonological inventories to a reasonable first approximation.

2.10 Summary and Discussion

This chapter has offered evidence for a view that might be called economy theory, according to which phonological inventories are structured by a few feature-based principles. Feature Bounding, sets upper limits on the number of contrastive sounds that a language may have, while Feature Economy, Marked Feature Avoidance, Robustness, and Phonological Enhancement represent interacting forces that together define the set of preferred phonological systems within the limits set by Feature Bounding. The interaction of these principles accounts for the main design features of sound systems at the level where distinctive contrasts are taken into account. While these principles have been illustrated here primarily with consonants, they appear to hold for vowels as well; for example, the typical "symmetry" of vowel systems reflects Feature Economy. However, full discussion of vowels will require a separate study.

These results bear on the nature of the phonetics-phonology interface. Let us consider two theories of how phonology can be understood as constrained by phonetic factors: (1) a "direct access" theory, in which phonological generalizations make direct access to the potentially infinite number of articulatory and acoustic parameter values provided by phonetic theory; (2) a "feature-mediated" theory, in which phonetics constrains phonology through the mediation of the phonetic definitions associated with a small set of distinctive features. This chapter offers support for the second view: the major generalizations governing phonological inventories appear best captured in terms of principles stated over the features of which speech sounds are composed.

While this result confirms the central role of features in the organization of phonological inventories, it does not diminish the role of phonetics or of quantitative methods in understanding phonology. There are at least three reasons for this. First, the predictions of these general principles must be fine-tuned by quantitative modeling in order to determine the relative weight of each and the precise nature of their interaction. This cannot involve a simple ranking, as no single principle (setting aside Feature Bounding) ever outranks all others. Second, these principles must be complemented by principles operating purely at the level of phonetic realization. These include

• a theory of Gestural Economy, according to which sounds of a given class tend to have uniform articulatory realizations in a given language (Maddieson 1995, Keating 2003)—for example, anterior stops tend to be either dental or alveolar in UPSID (Clements 2003b);
• a theory of Phonetic Enhancement, according to which weak feature contrasts may be enhanced by appropriate, subfeatural articulatory gestures—for example, palatoalveolar fricatives tend to be somewhat rounded in many languages to increase their auditory difference from dental or alveolar fricatives (Keyser and Stevens 2001).

It is not clear at this point whether other proposed principles, such as a global measure of dispersion, will be needed in addition to these. It is of course sound scientific practice to reduce explanatory principles to the necessary minimum.

Third, sound systems are what they are because speakers and hearers prefer sounds that are easily distinguished and not too hard to produce, a central insight of phonetic theory over many decades. Phonological inventories would be much different if linguistic expressions were realized in another medium. Indeed, studies of sign languages such as ASL confirm that the inventories of sign languages conform to quite different constraints. For example, as Sandler and Lillo-Martin (2001) have noted:

Sign languages as well [as spoken languages] have constraints on the combination of elements. . . . For example, only one group of fingers may characterize the handshape within any sign. While either the finger group 5 (all fingers) or the group V (index plus middle finger) may occur in a sign, a sequence of the two shapes, *5-V is prohibited in the native signs of ASL and other sign languages.

This and many other constraints on sign language clearly are related to the specific nature of the medium and have no direct analogues in speech. However, it appears that sign languages, too, are characterized in terms of features (Brentari 1998), and one might ask whether the general principles discussed here generalize to basic design features of other linguistic media—a topic that must be left for future work.

Why, ultimately, should phonological inventories be structured in terms of features rather than directly in terms of the finer-grained phonetic primes that define them? I speculate that the answer may lie in quantal theory and the nature of early language acquisition, as reviewed in section 2.2. As was noted there, very young (including newborn) infants perceive speech sounds in terms of acoustic categories corresponding closely to feature categories of adult languages, and they are relatively insensitive to finer distinctions. These categories are typically determined by the natural boundaries that arise from the nonmonotonic relationships between articulatory parameters and their acoustic effects (as shown by many studies in quantal theory). It appears, then, that infants are biologically predisposed to perceive speech in terms of quantally defined features. This implies that the ability to distinguish sounds across the more robust feature categories does not emerge during the early months of language acquisition, but is in place at the outset, constituting a perceptual "grid" within which speech information is processed. In the process of early language acquisition, this grid becomes more finely tuned as categories that are not distinctive in the native language become merged. In short, speech is processed from the outset in a mode specifically adapted to feature categories that characterize the target language. If basic representational categories are fixed at a very early age, perhaps by the end of the first year (Jusczyk 1997, Peperkamp 2003), adult languages could be expected to preserve these categories, even though later phonetic training or prolonged exposure to another language may partly modify this effect.

What sort of consequences might we draw for the nature of phonological representations in adults? The principles reviewed here suggest that as a minimum, such representations must contain marked distinctive features. As marked values represent a cost, there will be a tendency to minimize them (Marked Feature Avoidance). However, this cost is lessened to the extent that such feature values are supported by other sounds that bear them (Feature Economy). Fully redundant features will tend to be absent (Feature Economy, acquisitional merger). Speech sounds that are identical in feature terms are treated as equivalent (Feature Bounding). All else being equal, more robust contrasts are preferred to less robust contrasts (Robustness), and weak contrasts tend to be reinforced both phonologically and phonetically (Enhancement). Representational systems must be designed in such a way as to favor such characteristics.[29]

Notes

This chapter has benefited from stimulating comments and suggestions received in the course of presentations in Paris, New York City, Ithaca, Copenhagen, and Odense. I would particularly like to thank Andrea Calabrese, Morris Halle, and Bert Vaux for their thoughtful comments on this chapter at the CUNY Phonology Forum Symposium on Architecture and Representation in Phonology, 20–21 February 2004.

1. The notion "inventory" is understood here as an abstraction over sets of distinctive segments (consonants and vowels) and subsegments (tones, autosegments) employed by a language in its phonological system, as defined by its active features.

2. As Halle (1983) and Halle and Stevens (1991) have pointed out, the mapping between the articulatory feature definitions and their acoustic consequences is not always one-to-one. This is because, first, the acoustic realization of a feature may depend on other features of the sound in which it occurs. Thus, for example, the proposed feature [stiff vocal cords] is realized as voicelessness in obstruents, but as high tone in vowels. Similarly, a given acoustic effect is not always associated with just one feature; for example, voicing implements [slack vocal cords] in obstruents but [+sonorant] in vowels, regardless of their tone.

3. Speech is not processed *only* in categorical terms. Speakers obviously also have knowledge of noncategorical aspects of speech sounds including intonation, voice quality, loudness, speech rate, and individual differences among speakers. Furthermore, fluent speakers of a language master fine details of phonetic realization that often differ considerably from one language to another. Categorical perception appears to be related to a phonological, as opposed to acoustic, mode of speech processing in which the listener parses the speech signal for discrete categories. Recent physiological studies give evidence that both modes of processing are used in listening to speech. For example, studies of adults by Näätänen et al. (1997) have shown that phonemic representations distinct from those used in acoustic processing are based on a neural network predominantly located in the left temporal lobe. Electrophysiological studies of infants described by Dehaene-Lambertz and Pena (2001) suggest that categorical representations are not computed after acoustic representations, but in parallel with them.

4. The actual number of sounds will be somewhat lower since in most feature systems, not all features combine freely. For example, in systems using [±high] and [±low], [+high] does not combine with [+low].

5. Here and below, binary features are named by their marked values, where these are known. For reasons that will become evident, "posterior" is the marked value of the anterior/posterior feature, and so this feature is renamed [±posterior] here.

6. Of course, caution must be exercised in taking articulatory labels found in the descriptive literature at face value. It is often hard to determine the exact value of sounds described as "dental," "alveolar," "palatal," and so forth, as such terms are often used impressionistically, or with different meanings from one writer to another.

7. Ladefoged and Bhaskakarao (1983:300) state that they are "unable to formulate phonetic criteria for deciding whether differences between sounds could be used phonologically within a language."

8. This analysis presupposes a feature hierarchy in which [±sonorant] and the place features [labial], [coronal], and [dorsal] outrank [±voiced], [±continuant], [±nasal], and [±lateral]. See further discussion in section 2.7.

9. It is assumed that the feature [coronal] is not usually required to distinguish coronal sounds from labial and dorsal sounds, for reasons given in Clements 2001. This feature is, however, phonologically active in English (Mohanan 1991, McCarthy and Taub 1992) and is assumed to be present as an active but nondistinctive feature in the phonological component.

10. This feature is probably [−obstruent] (Clements 2003b).

11. The expected frequency for any cell is given by the formula $(T_R * T_C)/T_S$, where T_R and T_C are the row and column totals corresponding to the cell in question and T_S is the total sample size.

12. A strong advantage of a frequency-based approach is that it is defined on broad tendencies across languages while still allowing for language-particular variation. In some languages, further factors may increase the frequency of a marked sound, as in the case of the fricative /ð/ in English, whose unexpectedly high frequency results from its occurrence in a small number of demonstratives (*the, this, then*, etc.) as well as from economy effects exerted by its voiceless counterpart /θ/. The high frequency of /ð/ need not necessarily be taken as evidence that voicing is unmarked in English fricatives. However, the high frequency of a sound may facilitate its acquisition by language learners, and some research has suggested that markedness and frequency factors interact to account for variation in phonological acquisition (Stites, Demuth, and Kirk 2004).

13. Other evidence supporting the view that [coronal] is unmarked is summarized in Paradis and Prunet 1991. See Hume and Tserdanelis 2002 and Hume 2003, however, for evidence that noncoronal places of articulation show unmarked behavior in some languages. Yoneyama, Beckman, and Edwards (2003) report that [dorsal] is a more frequent place feature than [coronal] in Japanese and that dorsal consonants tend to be acquired before coronal consonants, suggesting that [dorsal] may be less marked than [coronal] in that language.

14. Lombardi (1994) and I (Clements 2003b) argue that voiceless sonorants bear the feature [spread glottis]. If this analysis can be maintained in all languages, voicing need never be considered a distinctive feature of sonorants.

15. Some confusion has been created by the use of inconsistent transcription systems for variably voiced stops. As Dixon (1980:138) has observed, "A great deal of argument has gone on concerning whether *p, t, k* or *b, d, g* are most appropriate (at one time there was something in the nature of a feud, triggered by this issue, between the 'voiceless symbol' Adelaide school and the 'voiced symbol' Sydney school." Practical orthographies sometimes employ one series of symbols and sometimes the other. For such reasons, it is dangerous to rely on transcription symbols—as does UPSID in one case—in determining whether an Australian stop is voiced or voiceless.

16. Such an analysis could also be expressed by underspecifying [±voiced] in these stops on the assumption that nondistinctive values are phonetically underspecified in some languages (Keating 1988).

17. However, not all exceptionless implicational statements are of the type discussed here, in which the implied term occurs in all languages. For example, the statement "Dorsal fricatives imply dorsal stops" holds in all UPSID languages even though one UPSID language (Vanimo) lacks dorsal stops and fricatives. Here, the truth of the implication does not follow from the universal presence of the implied term. However, it does follow from the independent frequencies of dorsal stops (99.8%) and dorsal fricatives (33.6%) in UPSID, on the assumption that these sounds combine freely in languages. The expected frequency of systems having dorsal fricatives but lacking dorsal stops is a meager 0.07% (the product of .336 and 1-.998), which predicts that exactly .32 UPSID languages, or zero after rounding, should be of this type. Feature Economy further weighs against systems of this type, making them extremely improbable on statistical grounds. Implicational universals are not required to predict the quasi absence of such systems.

18. See section 2.8, however, for discussion of a significant class of principled exceptions.

19. This is perhaps the basic insight of dispersion theory, as developed in regard to vowel systems. In practice, however, dispersion theory has sought to define dispersion almost exclusively in terms of a two-dimensional (or sometimes three-dimensional) auditory space defined by formant values, and it has not so far been successfully extended to the study of nonmodal vowels, or to consonants. It is suggested here that the appropriate way of doing so is in terms of the principles of Robustness and Phonological Enhancement.

20. The robustness of a contrast also varies according to the context in which it occurs. For example, place-of-articulation contrasts tend to be most robust in prevocalic position, and may be neutralized in contexts where their auditory cues are weak (Steriade 2001), unless they are enhanced by secondary cues. The robustness scale reflects preferred contrasts in their most favored contexts.

21. As before, uppercase symbols stand for feature-defined classes of consonants rather than particular phonetic values: for example, T = any voiceless coronal stop (whether dental, palatal, labialized, ejective, geminate, etc.). *Sonorant* = sonorant consonant. The feature [±posterior] is restricted, of course, to coronal sounds.

22. UPSID does not provide information that would allow us to determine the frequency of contrasts based on the feature [±distributed], referring to the apical/nonapical distinction. This feature is often not recorded in primary descriptions, in part because relatively few languages make use of it for distinctive purposes. See Calabrese 1994 for a proposed preference scale for vowel features.

23. However, not all gaps involve segments that cumulate marked feature values. For example, most languages lack nasalized obstruents. In this case, though [+nasal] is a marked value, [−sonorant] is not. This and many other such gaps can be accounted for under enhancement theory, as discussed in section 2.8.

24. More exactly, in [+posterior] obstruents the lowest spectral prominence is associated with F3 of neighboring vowels, while in [−posterior] obstruents this prominence is associated with F4 or F5 of neighboring vowels (Stevens 1989). As for [±strident], the high-frequency spectral energy of [+strident] sounds exceeds that of neighboring vowels, while the spectral energy of [−strident] sounds is lower than that of neighboring vowels at all frequencies (Stevens 1983).

25. See further discussion and examples in Stevens, Keyser, and Kawasaki 1986 and Stevens and Keyser 1989. In (32c), the use of [+posterior] to enhance [+continuant] sonorants suggests that [±posterior] may be the lower-ranked of these two features, in spite of its nearly

equal frequency across languages. In (32d), [+labiodental] is used as an ad hoc feature to distinguish labiodental and bilabial sounds, on the view that [+strident] is restricted to coronal sounds. However, some linguists continue to use [+strident] for this purpose.

26. No data could be compiled for the features [±ATR] and [±distributed], which are not consistently recorded in UPSID. However, it is well-known that in African languages using [±ATR] as a distinctive feature, high vowels tend to be [+ATR] and low vowels tend to be [−ATR] (e.g., Archangeli and Pulleyblank 1994). These values reinforce acoustic distinctions, since [+ATR] and [+high] are realized with low F1 values and [−ATR] and [+low] with higher F1 values.

27. The preference for a nasal series over a lateral series is also explained by Feature Economy: while [+nasal] can be applied to all major places of articulation, [+lateral] is largely restricted to coronal places of articulation.

28. An isolated exception is Trumai, an Equatorial language of Brazil, which has two nasals, /m/ and /n/, of which the first is said to be typically voiceless (Monod-Becquelin 1975).

29. In Clements 2001, I have suggested a minimalist approach to phonological representation along these lines.

References

Anderson, Jennifer, James L. Morgan, and Katherine S. White. 2003. A statistical basis for speech sound discrimination. *Language and Speech* 46:155–182.

Archangeli, Diana, and Douglas Pulleyblank. 1994. *Grounded Phonology*. Cambridge, Mass.: MIT Press.

Basbøll, Hans. 1985. Review of *Patterns of sounds* by Ian Maddieson. *Phonology Yearbook* 2:343–353.

Best, Catherine T., Gerald W. McRoberts, and Elizabeth Goodell. 2001. Discrimination of non-native consonant contrasts varying in perceptual assimilation to the listener's native phonological system. *Journal of the Acoustical Society of America* 109:775–794.

Best, Catherine T., Gerald W. McRoberts, and Nomathemba M. Sithole. 1988. Examination of the perceptual reorganization for speech contrasts: Zulu click discrimination by English-speaking adults and infants. *Journal of Experimental Psychology: Human Perception and Performance* 14:345–360.

Boersma, Paul. 1997. Inventories in Functional Phonology. In *Proceedings of the Institute of Phonetic Sciences, Amsterdam 21*, 59–90. Amsterdam: University of Amsterdam, Institute of Phonetic Sciences. Reprinted as chapter 16 of *Functional Phonology*. The Hague: Holland Academic Graphics, 1998.

Bothorel, André. 1969–70. Contribution à l'étude descriptive des latérales de l'albanais. *Travaux de l'Institut de Phonétique de Strasbourg* 2:133–144.

Brentari, Diane. 1998. *A prosodic model of sign language phonology*. Cambridge, Mass.: MIT Press.

Browman, Catherine P., and Louis M. Goldstein. 1989. Articulatory gestures as phonological units. *Phonology* 6:201–251.

Browman, Catherine P., and Louis M. Goldstein. 1992. Articulatory Phonology: An overview. *Phonetica* 49:155–180.

Browman, Catherine P., and Louis M. Goldstein. 2000. Competing constraints on intergestural coordination and self-organization of phonological structures. *Les Cahiers de l'ICP, Bulletin de la Communication Parlée* 5:25–34.

Calabrese, Andrea. 1994. A constraint-based theory of phonological inventories. In *Phonologica 1992: Proceedings of the 7th International Phonology Meeting*, ed. by Wolfgang U. Dressler, Martin Prinzhorn, and John R. Rennison, 35–54. Turin: Rosenberg and Sellier.

Calabrese, Andrea. 1995. A constraint-based theory of phonological markedness and simplification procedures. *Linguistic Inquiry* 26:373–463.

Casali, Roderic F. 2003. [ATR] value asymmetries and underlying vowel inventory structures in Niger-Congo and Nilo-Saharan. *Linguistic Typology* 7:307–382.

Chomsky, Noam, and Morris Halle. 1968. *The sound pattern of English*. New York: Harper and Row.

Clements, G. N. 1999. Affricates as noncontoured stops. In *Proceedings of LP '98: Item order in language and speech*, ed. by Osamu Fujimura, Brian Joseph, and Bohumil Palek, 271–299. Prague: The Karolinum Press.

Clements, G. N. 2001. Representational economy in constraint-based phonology. In *Distinctive feature theory*, ed. by T. Alan Hall, 71–146. Berlin: Mouton de Gruyter.

Clements, G. N. 2003a. Feature economy as a phonological universal. In *Proceedings of the 15th International Congress of Phonetic Sciences, Barcelona, 3–9 August 2003*, ed. by María-Josep Solé, Daniel Recasens, and Joaquín Romero, 371–374. Rundle Mall, Australia: Causal Productions (CD-ROM); Barcelona: Futurgraphic (print).

Clements, G. N. 2003b. Feature economy in sound systems. *Phonology* 20:287–333.

Clements, G. N., and Elizabeth Hume. 1995. The internal organization of speech sounds. In *The handbook of phonological theory*, ed. by John Goldsmith, 245–306. Cambridge, Mass.: Blackwell.

Clements, G. N., and Sylvester Osu. 2005. Nasal harmony in Ikwere, a language with no phonemic nasal consonants. *Journal of African Languages and Linguistics* 26:165–200.

Colarusso, John. 2004. Georgian and other Caucasian languages. Ms., McMaster University.

Dehaene-Lambertz, Ghislaine, and Marcela Pena. 2001. Electrophysiological evidence for automatic phonetic processing in neonates. *Neuroreport* 12:3155–3158.

Delgutte, Bertrand, and Nelson Y.-S. Kiang. 1984. Speech coding in the auditory nerve, IV. Sounds with consonant-like dynamic characteristics. *Journal of the Acoustical Society of America* 75:897–907.

Dinnsen, Daniel A. 1992. Variation in developing and fully developed phonetic inventories. In *Phonological development: Models, research, implications*, ed. by Charles Ferguson, Lisa Menn, and Carol Stoel-Gammon, 191–210. Timonium, Md.: York Press.

Dixon, R. M. W. 1977. *A grammar of Yidiny*. Cambridge: Cambridge University Press.

Dixon, R. M. W. 1980. *The languages of Australia*. Cambridge: Cambridge University Press.

Dixon, R. M. W. 1991. Mbabaram. In *Handbook of Australian languages*, ed. by R. M. W. Dixon and Barry J. Blake, 4:349–402. Melbourne: Oxford University Press.

Flemming, Edward. 2002. *Auditory representations in phonology*. London: Routledge.

Greenberg, Joseph H. 1966. *Language universals.* The Hague: Mouton, 2nd ed., Berlin: Mouton de Gruyter, 2002.

Groot, A. W. de. 1931. Phonologie und Phonetik als Funktionswissenschaften. *Travaux du Cercle Linguistique de Prague* 4:116–147.

Gurevich, Naomi. 2001. A critique of markedness-based theories in phonology. *Studies in the Linguistic Sciences* 31 (2): 89–114.

Halle, Morris. 1983. On distinctive features and their articulatory implementation. *Natural Language and Linguistic Theory* 1:91–105. Reprinted in Halle 2002, 105–121.

Halle, Morris. 1992. Phonological features. In *Oxford international encyclopedia of linguistics*, ed. by William Bright, 207–212. New York: Oxford University Press.

Halle, Morris. 2002. *From memory to speech and back: Papers on phonetics and phonology 1954–2002*. Berlin: Mouton de Gruyter.

Halle, Morris, and G. N. Clements. 1983. *Problem book in phonology*. Cambridge, Mass.: MIT Press.

Halle, Morris, and Kenneth N. Stevens. 1971. A note on laryngeal features. In *Quarterly progress report 101*, 198–213. Cambridge, Mass.: MIT, Research Laboratory of Electronics. Reprinted in Halle 2002, 45–61.

Halle, Morris, and Kenneth N. Stevens. 1991. Knowledge of language and the sounds of speech. In *Music, language, speech, and brain*, ed. by Johan Sundberg, Lennart Nord, and Rolf Carlson, 1–19. London: Macmillan. Reprinted in Halle 2002, 176–195.

Harnad, Stevan, ed. 1987. *Categorical perception: The groundwork of cognition*. Cambridge: Cambridge University Press.

Hockett, Charles F. 1955. *A manual of phonology*. International Journal of American Linguistics 21 (4), Part 1, Memoir 1. Baltimore, Md.: Waverley Press. Reprinted, Chicago: University of Chicago Press, 1974.

Hume, Elizabeth. 2003. Language specific markedness: The case of place of articulation. *Studies in Phonetics, Phonology and Morphology* 9:295–310.

Hume, Elizabeth, and Georgios Tserdanelis. 2002. Labial unmarkedness in Sri Lankan Portuguese Creole. *Phonology* 19:441–458.

Jakobson, Roman. 1968. *Child language, aphasia and phonological universals*. The Hague: Mouton. Translation by Allan R. Keiler of *Kindersprache, Aphasie und allgemeine Lautgesetze*. Uppsala: Almqvist & Wiksell, 1941.

Jakobson, Roman, C. Gunnar M. Fant, and Morris Halle. 1952. Preliminaries to speech analysis: The distinctive features and their correlates. Technical Report 13. Cambridge, Mass.: MIT, Acoustics Laboratory. Expanded edition published, Cambridge, Mass.: MIT Press, 1961.

Jakobson, Roman, and Morris Halle. 1956. *Fundamentals of language*. The Hague: Mouton.

Jusczyk, Peter W. 1997. *The discovery of spoken language*. Cambridge, Mass.: MIT Press.

Jusczyk, Peter W., Paul A. Luce, and Jan Charles-Luce. 1994. Infants' sensitivity to phonotactic patterns in the native language. *Journal of Memory and Language* 33:630–645.

Kean, Mary-Louise. 1975. The theory of markedness in generative grammar. Doctoral dissertation, MIT.

Keating, Patricia. 1988. Underspecification in phonetics. *Phonology* 5:275–292.

Keating, Patricia. 2003. Phonetic and other influences on voicing contrasts. In *Proceedings of the 15th International Congress of Phonetic Sciences, Barcelona, 3–9 August 2003*, ed. by Maria-Josep Solé, Daniel Recasens, and Joaquín Romero, 375–378. Rundle Mall, Australia: Causal Productions (CD-ROM); Barcelona: Futurgraphic (print).

Kehrein, Wolfgang. 2002. *Phonological representation and phonetic phasing: Affricates and laryngeals.* Tübingen: Max Niemeyer Verlag.

Keyser, Samuel Jay, and Kenneth N. Stevens. 2001. Enhancement revisited. In *Ken Hale: A life in language*, ed. by Michael Kenstowicz, 271–291. Cambridge, Mass.: MIT Press.

Kim, Hyunsoon. 2001. A phonetically based account of phonological stop assibilation. *Phonology* 18:81–108.

Kirchner, Robert. 2001. Phonological contrast and articulatory effort. In *Segmental phonology in Optimality Theory*, ed. by Linda Lombardi, 79–117. Cambridge: Cambridge University Press.

Kuhl, Patricia K., Karen A. Williams, Francisco Lacerda, Kenneth N. Stevens, and Björn Lindblom. 1992. Linguistic experience alters phonetic perception in infants by 6 months of age. *Science* 55:606–608.

Ladefoged, Peter, and Peri Bhaskakarao. 1983. Non-quantal aspects of consonant production: A study of retroflex consonants. *Journal of Phonetics* 11:291–302.

Ladefoged, Peter, and Ian Maddieson. 1996. *The sounds of the world's languages.* Oxford: Blackwell.

Lang, Carrie E., and John J. Ohala. 1996. Temporal cues for vowels and universals of vowel inventories. In *Proceedings of the Fourth International Conference on Spoken Language Processing (ICSLP) 96.* http://www.asel.udel.edu/icslp.

Liberman, Alvin M., Franklin S. Cooper, Donald P. Shankweiler, and Michael Studdert-Kennedy. 1967. Perception of the speech code. *Psychological Review* 74:431–461.

Liberman, Alvin M., Katherine S. Harris, Howard S. Hoffman, and Belver C. Griffith. 1957. The discrimination of speech sounds within and across phoneme boundaries. *Journal of Experimental Psychology* 54:358–368.

Lieberman, Philip. 1970. Towards a unified linguistic theory. *Linguistic Inquiry* 1:307–322.

Lindblom, Björn. 1986. Phonetic universals in vowel systems. In *Experimental phonology*, ed. by John Ohala and Jeri J. Jaeger, 13–44. Orlando, Fla.: Academic Press.

Lindblom, Björn. 1992. Phonological units as adaptive emergents of lexical development. In *Phonological development: Models, research, implications*, ed. by Charles A. Ferguson, Lise Menn, and Carol Stoel-Gammon, 131–163. Timonium, Md.: York Press.

Lindblom, Björn, and Ian Maddieson. 1988. Phonetic universals in consonant systems. In *Language, speech, and mind*, ed. by Larry M. Hyman and Charles N. Li, 62–78. London: Routledge.

Lombardi, Linda. 1994. *Laryngeal features and laryngeal neutralization.* New York: Garland.

Maddieson, Ian. 1984. *Patterns of sounds.* Cambridge: Cambridge University Press.

Maddieson, Ian. 1991. Testing the universality of phonological generalizations with a phonetically specified segment database: Results and limitations. *Phonetica* 48 (2–4): 193–206.

Maddieson, Ian. 1995. Gestural economy. In *Proceedings of the 13th International Congress of Phonetic Sciences*, vol. 4, ed. by Kjell Elenius and Peter Branderud, 574–577. Stockholm: KTH and Stockholm University.

Maddieson, Ian, and Karen Precoda. 1989. Updating UPSID. In *UCLA working papers in phonetics 74*, 104–111. Los Angeles: UCLA, Department of Linguistics, Phonetics Lab.

Martinet, André. 1955. *Économie des changements phonétiques*. Bern: A. Francke.

Martinet, André. 1968. Phonetics and linguistic evolution. In *Manual of phonetics*, revised and extended edition, ed. by Bertil Malmberg, 464–487. Amsterdam: North-Holland. Reprinted from the first edition edited by Louise Kaiser, 1957, 252–273.

Maye, Jessica, Janet F. Werker, and LouAnn Gerken. 2002. Infant sensitivity to distributional information can affect phonetic discrimination. *Cognition* 82:B101–B111.

McCarthy, John, and Alison Taub. 1992. Review of *The special status of coronals: Internal and external evidence*, ed. by Carole Paradis and Jean-François Prunet. *Phonology* 9:363–370.

Mohanan, K. P. 1991. On the bases of radical underspecification. *Natural Language and Linguistic Theory* 9:285–326.

Monod-Becquelin, Aurore. 1975. *La pratique linguistique des indiens trumai (Haut-Xingu, Mato Grosso, Brésil)*. Vol. 1. Paris: SELAF and CNRS.

Näätänen, Risto, Anne Lehtokoski, Mietta Lennes, Marie Cheour, et al. 1997. Language-specific phoneme representations revealed by electric and magnetic brain responses. *Nature* 385:432–434.

Pallier, Christophe, Laura Bosch, and Núria Sebastián-Gallés. 1997. A limit on behavioral plasticity in speech perception. *Cognition* 64:B9–B17.

Pandey, Pramod. 2003. Sounds and their patterns in the languages of India. Part II: Phonological sketches. Ms., Jawaharlal Nehru University, New Delhi.

Paradis, Carole, and Jean-François Prunet, eds. 1991. *The special status of coronals: Internal and external evidence*. Phonetics and Phonology 2. San Diego, Calif.: Academic Press.

Peperkamp, Sharon. 2003. Phonological acquisition: Recent attainments and new challenges. *Language and Speech* 46:87–113.

Pericliev, Vladimir, and Raúl E. Valdés-Pérez. 2002. Differentiating 451 languages in terms of their segment inventories. *Studia Linguistica* 56:1–27.

Pierrehumbert, Janet. 2003. Probabilistic phonology: Discrimination and robustness. In *Probability theory in linguistics*, ed. by Rens Bod, Jennifer Hay, and Stefanie Jannedy, 177–228. Cambridge, Mass.: MIT Press.

Polka, Linda, and Janet F. Werker. 1994. Developmental changes in perception of non-native vowel contrasts. *Journal of Experimental Psychology: Human Perception and Performance* 20:421–435.

Repp, Bruno H. 1984. Categorical perception: Issues, methods, and findings. In *Speech and language: Advances in basic research and practice, vol. 10*, ed. by Norman J. Lass, 243–335. New York: Academic Press.

Rice, Keren. 1999. Featural markedness in phonology: Variation. Part 1. *Glot International* 4 (7): 3–6. Part 2. *Glot International* 4 (8): 3–7.

Sagey, Elizabeth. 1990. *The representation of features in nonlinear phonology: The articulator node hierarchy*. New York: Garland.

Sandler, Wendy, and Diane Lillo-Martin. 2001. Natural sign languages. In *Handbook of linguistics*, ed. by Mark Aronoff and Janie Rees-Miller, 533–562. Oxford: Blackwell.

Simpson, Adrian P. 1999. Fundamental problems in comparative phonetics and phonology: Does UPSID help to solve them? In *Proceedings of the 14th International Congress of Phonetic Sciences*, vol. 1, ed. by John J. Ohala, Yoko Hasegawa, Manjari Ohala, Daniel Granville, and Ashlee C. Bailey, 349–352. Berkeley: University of California.

Steriade, Donca. 2001. Directional asymmetries in place assimilation: A perceptual account. In *The role of speech perception in phonology*, ed. by Elizabeth Hume and Keith Johnson, 219–250. San Diego, Calif.: Academic Press.

Stevens, Kenneth N. 1972. The quantal nature of speech: Evidence from articulatory-acoustic data. In *Human communication: A unified view*, ed. by Edward E. David, Jr., and Peter B. Denes, 51–66. New York: McGraw-Hill.

Stevens, Kenneth N. 1983. Design features of speech sound systems. In *The production of speech*, ed. by Peter F. MacNeilage, 247–261. New York: Springer-Verlag.

Stevens, Kenneth N. 1989. On the quantal nature of speech. *Journal of Phonetics* 17:3–46.

Stevens, Kenneth N. 1998. *Acoustic phonetics*. Cambridge, Mass.: MIT Press.

Stevens, Kenneth N., and Samuel Jay Keyser. 1989. Primary features and their enhancement in consonants. *Language* 65:81–106.

Stevens, Kenneth N., Samuel Jay Keyser, and Haruko Kawasaki. 1986. Toward a phonetic and phonological theory of redundant features. In *Symposium on Invariance and Variability of Speech Processes*, ed. by Joseph Perkell and Dennis Klatt, 432–469. Hillsdale, N.J.: Lawrence Erlbaum.

Stites, Jessica, Katherine Demuth, and Cecilia Kirk. 2004. Markedness versus frequency effects in coda acquisition. In *Proceedings of the 28th Annual Boston University Conference on Language Development*, ed. by Alejna Brugos, Linnea Micciulla, and Christine E. Smith, 565–576. Somerville, Mass.: Cascadilla Press.

Trehub, Sandra E. 1976. The discrimination of foreign speech contrasts by infants and adults. *Child Development* 47:466–472.

Triulzi, A., A. A. Dafallah, and M. L. Bender. 1976. Berta. In *The non-Semitic languages of Ethiopia*, ed. by M. L. Bender, 513–532. East Lansing: Michigan State University, African Studies Center.

Trubetzkoy, Nikolai S. 1969. *Principles of phonology*. Berkeley and Los Angeles: University of California Press. English translation by Christiane A. M. Baltaxe of *Grundzüge der Phonologie*. Travaux du cercle linguistique de Prague VII, 1939. Reprinted, Göttingen: Vandenhoeck und Ruprecht, 1967.

Werker, Janet F., John H. V. Gilbert, Keith Humphrey, and Richard C. Tees. 1981. Developmental aspects of cross-language speech perception. *Child Development* 52:349–355.

Werker, Janet F., and Richard C. Tees. 1984. Cross-language speech perception: Evidence for perceptual reorganization during the first year of life. *Infant Behaviour and Development* 7:49–63.

Westbury, John R. 1983. Enlargement of the supraglottal cavity and its relation to stop consonant voicing. *Journal of the Acoustical Society of America* 73:1322–1336.

Williamson, Kay. 1973. More on nasals and nasalization in Kwa. *Studies in African Linguistics* 4:115–138.

Wonderly, William L. 1946. Phonemic acculturation in Zoque. *International Journal of American Linguistics* 12:92–95.

Wonderly, William L. 1951–2. Zoque (parts I–V). *International Journal of American Linguistics* 17 (1951): 1–9, 105–123, 137–162, 235–251; *International Journal of American Linguistics* 18 (1952): 35–48.

Yallop, Colin. 1982. *Australian aboriginal languages.* London: André Deutsch.

Yoneyama, Kiyomo, Mary E. Beckman, and Jan Edwards. 2003. Phoneme frequencies and acquisition of lingual stops in Japanese. Ms., Ohio State University.

3 Two Comments on "The Role of Features in Phonological Inventories"

Morris Halle

I am in complete agreement with Clements's thesis in chapter 2 of this volume that speech sounds are composite entities made up of features of the kind presented in *The Sound Pattern of English* (*SPE*; Chomsky and Halle 1968). The idea that speech sounds are composite entities (and not the atoms of language) was first advanced by Alexander Melville Bell in his 1867 book *Visible Speech*. This book presented Bell's phonetic alphabet, where each letter directly expressed the features that composed the sound represented (see figure 3.1). Thus, every consonant was represented by a crescent with the opening pointing in one of four directions: left, up, down, right. An opening to the left represented labial consonants; an opening upward, [+anterior] coronal consonants; an opening downward, [−anterior] coronal consonants; and an opening to the right, dorsal consonants. Other consonantal features were represented by diacritics: a bar across the opening represented stops, a dash opposite the opening [+voiced], and so on.

In commenting on his father's alphabet, Alexander Graham Bell, the inventor of the telephone, wrote in 1911:

The true element of articulation, I think, is a constriction or position of the vocal organs rather than a sound. Combinations of positions yield new sounds, just as combinations of chemical elements yield new substances. Water is a substance of very different character from either of the two gases of which it is formed; and the vowel *oo* is a sound of very different character from that of any of its elementary positions. (p. 38)

Prior to publication of *Visible Speech*, Alexander Melville Bell offered the alphabet to the British government for recording personal names and other non-English words in the colonies, among other things. His sole condition was that the government pay for casting the special typefaces needed to print texts in Visible Speech. Unfortunately, Bell's offer was rejected by the then prime minister, Lord Derby, on the grounds that there were no public funds for this purpose. Lord Derby was an accomplished classicist with a well-received translation of the *Iliad* to his credit, which perhaps made Bell hopeful of a more positive reaction.

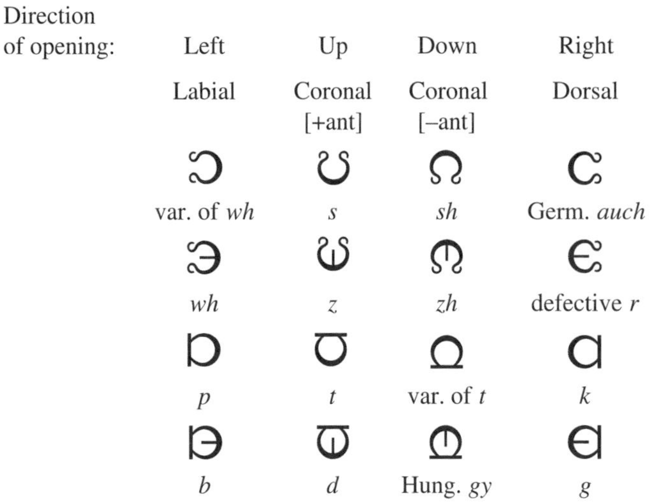

Direction
of opening: Left   Up   Down   Right

                   Labial   Coronal   Coronal   Dorsal
                                [+ant]   [−ant]

                     ɔ   ℧   ℧   Ɔ
                  var. of *wh*   *s*   *sh*   Germ. *auch*

                     ɘ   ℧   ℧   ℰ
                     wh   *z*   *zh*   defective *r*

                     ↼   ↽   ↽   ↺
                     p   *t*   var. of *t*   *k*

                     ↼   ↽   ↽   ↺
                     b   *d*   Hung. *gy*   *g*

Figure 3.1
Examples of Alexander Melville Bell's Visible Speech symbols. (After Bell 1911:56, 62. Visible
Speech symbols courtesy of Simon Ager, omniglot.com. Originally published in Morris Halle,
"Palatalization/Velar Softening: What It Is and What It Tells Us about the Nature of Lan-
guage," *Linguistic Inquiry* 36:27.)

As is well known, the prohibitive cost of casting the type was the reason why Bell's
alphabet was replaced with that of the International Phonetic Association (IPA),
where sounds are represented by letters of the Roman alphabet and diacritics available in most print shops. In fact, the IPA Principles expressly counsel writers against
use of diacritics, wherever possible. The replacement of Bell's alphabet by that of the
IPA had the unfortunate effect of obscuring and ultimately consigning to oblivion
Bell's important discovery that the atoms of language are not sounds, but features.

It is significant in this regard that Ladefoged and Maddieson's (1996) summa of
twentieth-century phonetic knowledge is titled *The Sounds of the World's Languages*,
taking sounds rather than features as the primitives of language. This important theoretical stance is taken without explicit argument, although the view of the speech
sound as a complex of features was reintroduced into linguistics in 1928 by Roman
Jakobson, Nikolai S. Trubetzkoy, and Serge Karcevsky and was fundamental to
some of the most important phonological studies of the twentieth century, including
Trubetzkoy's (1939) *Grundzüge der Phonologie* and Chomsky and Halle's (1968) *The
Sound Pattern of English (SPE)*.

In view of Clements's important contributions to feature theory, beginning with
his 1985 paper on feature geometry, I was disappointed that in his remarks here

about various phonetic problems, Clements adopts very traditional views and has little to say about alternatives to them. I focus here on two such "blemishes."

First, like Ladefoged and Maddieson, Clements refers to the phonetic feature [±palatalized]. This feature, which figured in Jakobson, Fant, and Halle 1952 under the label [sharp], was eliminated in *SPE* for reasons that are worth recalling. In the IPA system, vowels and consonants are characterized with different sets of features, as they were also in Bell's Visible Speech. One of Jakobson's important innovations was to eliminate that bifurcation as artificial, because, as Jakobson often remarked, humans have only one vocal tract and its actions produce both vowels and consonants; both types of sounds should therefore share features.

This insight lay behind Jakobson's introduction of the acoustic features compact-diffuse and grave-acute. (See Jakobson 1938 and Jakobson, Fant, and Halle 1952.) From an articulatory point of view, these two features were not especially intuitive, because they equated distinctions in tongue body positions in the vowels with distinctions of the main active articulator (the designated articulator) in the consonants.

These Jakobsonian features had another undesirable consequence: they required that the feature system include the feature [±palatalized] (or [±sharp]) in order to characterize the so-called soft consonants of Russian and other Slavic languages. In particular, the process palatalizing consonants before front vowels, which is central to Slavic phonology, had to be formulated as in (1).

(1) [−pal] → [+pal] in env ＿＿＿ [−grave]

(1) fails utterly to capture the fact that from an articulatory point of view palatalization is a natural process, whereby the front tongue position of the vowel spreads to the preceding consonant. The process can be expressed as one of feature spreading once the two acoustic features [±grave] and [±palatalized] are replaced by the single articulatory feature [±back], as was done in *SPE*.

My second comment about Clements's chapter is this. In various places, Clements refers to the feature [±voiced], overlooking, as it were, the conclusion reached in Halle and Stevens 1971 that the universal feature set does not include such a feature. In that paper, Stevens and I argued that the voicelessness of obstruents and the high pitches of vowels both manifest the single articulatory gesture (feature) vocal cord stiffness. We noted that voicing and pitch are in complementary distribution: voicing contrasts are found in obstruents, whereas pitch contrasts are never found in obstruents, but only in sonorants. Both voicing and pitch are, of course, produced by actions of the vocal cords, but the two classes of sound differ fundamentally with respect to the pressure drop across the cords: the pressure drop is relatively large in sonorants, but significantly smaller in obstruents, and this difference has important consequences for the behavior of the cords. When slack, the cords vibrate in both obstruents and sonorants. On the other hand, when the cords are stiffened, vocal cord vibration depends on the pressure drop across them. In sonorants, with their large pressure drop, the cords vibrate as before; in fact, the increase in stiffness causes the rate of vibration to increase. By contrast, in obstruents, where the pressure drop across the cords is small, increased stiffness prevents the cords from being set into motion, and as a result the sound is voiceless.

In sum, voiceless obstruents and high-pitch vowels (sonorants) are produced with stiff vocal cords, whereas voiced obstruents and low-pitch vowels are produced with slack vocal cords. This fact accounts also for the well-documented phenomenon that in an obstruent-vowel sequence, the pitch of the initial portion of the vowel is higher when the obstruent is voiceless and lower when the obstruent is voiced (House and Fairbanks 1953). These are simple examples of inertia in the speech production process, rather than parts of the speech-planning process, as suggested by Kingston and Diehl (1994).

Replacing the two acoustic features [±low pitch] and [±voiced] with the single articulatory feature [±slack vocal cords] has further desirable consequences. Simple feature spreading can now account for the tonogenesis facts in the East Asian languages where the tones of vowels are raised after voiceless obstruents and lowered after voiced obstruents (see, e.g., Bao 1990). There are also cases where the slackness feature spreads from a vowel to the adjacent obstruent, the most famous being the Indo-European case described by Verner's Law. Verner (1876) explained the unexpected appearance of voiced obstruents in Germanic by noting that it occurred always and exclusively after unstressed syllables. In light of the preceding discussion, we can characterize the fact that unstressed syllables have lower pitch than their stressed cognates by assigning to unstressed syllables the feature [+slack vocal cords]. Verner's Law is then the result of a rule that spreads this feature to the following vowel. Verner's Law differs from East Asian tonogenesis in that in Verner's Law the feature spreads from vowel to obstruent, whereas in tonogenesis the feature spreads in the opposite direction, from obstruent to vowel.

References

Bao, Zhiming. 1990. On the nature of tone. Doctoral dissertation, MIT.

Bell, Alexander Graham. 1911. *The mechanics of speech.* New York: Funk and Wagnalls.

Bell, Alexander Melville. 1867. *Visible Speech: The science of universal alphabetics.* London: Simkin, Marshall.

Chomsky, Noam, and Morris Halle. 1968. *The sound pattern of English.* New York: Harper and Row.

Clements, G. N. 1985. The geometry of phonological features. *Phonology Yearbook* 2:223–252.

Halle, Morris. 2002. *From memory to speech and back: Papers on phonetics and phonology 1954–2002.* Berlin: Mouton de Gruyter.

Halle, Morris, and Kenneth N. Stevens. 1971. A note on laryngeal features. In *Quarterly progress report 101*, 198–213. Cambridge, Mass.: MIT, Research Laboratory of Electronics. Reprinted in Halle 2002, 45–61.

House, Arthur S., and Gordon Fairbanks. 1953. The influence of consonant environment upon the secondary acoustical characteristics of vowels. *Journal of the Acoustical Society of America* 25:105–113.

Jakobson, Roman. 1938. Observations sur le classement phonologique des consonnes. Reprinted in Jakobson 1971, 272–279.

Jakobson, Roman. 1971. *Selected writings II: Word and language.* The Hague: Mouton.

Jakobson, Roman, C. Gunnar, M. Fant, and Morris Halle. 1952. Preliminaries to speech analysis: The distinctive features and their correlates. Technical Report 13. Cambridge, Mass.: MIT, Acoustics Laboratory. Expanded edition published, Cambridge, Mass.: MIT Press, 1961.

Jakobson, Roman, Serge Karcevsky, and Nikolai S. Trubetzkoy. 1928. Quelles sont les méthodes les mieux appropriés à un exposé complet et pratique d'une langue quelconque? Reprinted in Jakobson 1971, 3–6.

Kingston, John, and Randy Diehl. 1994. Phonetic knowledge. *Language* 70:419–454.

Ladefoged, Peter, and Ian Maddieson. 1996. *The sounds of the world's languages.* Oxford: Blackwell.

Trubetzkoy, Nikolai S. 1939. *Grundzüge der Phonologie.* Travaux du cercle linguistique de Prague VII. Reprinted, Göttingen: Vandenhoeck und Ruprecht, 1967.

Verner, Karl. 1876. Eine Ausnahme der ersten Lautverschiebung. *Zeitschrift für vergleichende Sprachwissenschaft* 23:97–130.

4 The Role of Features in a Symbolic Theory of Phonology

Bert Vaux

4.1 Introduction

The importance of Clements's novel arguments in chapter 2 for the centrality of features in phonology should not be underestimated, coming as they do on the heels of increasingly common attempts by phoneticians and connectionists to deny the existence of features, rules, abstract underlying representations, and other higher-order symbolic categories and operations in human linguistic cognition. The most recent such attempt is Flemming's (2005) retreat to a system of phonetic primitives that abandons more than 50 years' worth of evidence for the existence of distinctive features (see, e.g., Jakobson, Fant, and Halle 1952, Miller and Nicely 1955, Chomsky and Halle 1968, McCawley 1972, Fromkin 1973, Kiparsky 1974, Singh 1976, Baltaxe 1978, Brakel 1983, Hall 2001, Ruszkiewicz 2001). Clements rightly notes that this effort (to which one could add Shattuck-Hufnagel and Klatt 1979, Soli and Arabie 1979, Lisker 1985, and much work in Articulatory Phonology[1]) reveals "a bias toward phonetic reductionism."[2]

Clements then presents a number of compelling arguments in support of feature-based phonology, such as the fact that "the features [±posterior] and [±distributed] successfully characterize the set of primary coronal contrasts that are actually attested across languages" (p. 27), and asserts that phonetic theories that eschew features are unable to account for the same facts. Clements's work is an impressive complement to the above-mentioned classical arguments for features, to which one can add more recent arguments for distinctive feature theory from experimental linguistics:

- *Psycholinguistics* Wickelgren 1965, 1966, Anisfeld, Barlow, and Frail 1968, Anisfeld and Gordon 1968, Martin 1975, Derwing and Nearey 1986, Bedoin 2003, Krifi, Bedoin, and Mérigot 2003, Pycha et al. 2003
- *Neurolinguistics* Lawson and Gaillard 1981, Phillips, Pellathy, and Marantz 2000, Obleser, Eulitz, and Lahiri 2004

- *Aphasia*   Martin 1972, Testut 1980, Milberg, Blumstein, and Dworetzky 1988
- *Perception*   Tannahill 1971, Hayden 1976, Eimas et al. 1978, Hillenbrand 1983, Blumstein and Stevens 1985, Lahiri and Jongman 1990, Green and Kuhl 1991, Espy-Wilson 1994, Marslen-Wilson and Warren 1994, Bitar and Espy-Wilson 1995, Stevens 1995, 2003, Wode 1997, Jusczyk, Goodman, and Baumann 1999, Lukatela and Turvey 2001
- *Production*   Anisfeld, Barlow, and Frail 1968, McReynolds and Engmann 1975, Jaeger 1992, Rogers and Storkel 1998, Goldrick 2004
- *Production and perception*   Singh 1976, Goldstein 1980
- *Acquisition*   Humphrey 1977 (first language acquisition), Wall 1976 (second language acquisition)
- *Orthography*   Sawyer, Wade, and Kim 1999
- *Rhyme*   Zwicky 1976, Berg 1990

Clements's focus on articulatory rather than auditory features (following Chomsky and Halle 1968 and other works in the *SPE* tradition, and pace Brakel 1983, Flemming 1995) draws support from studies finding that features are grounded in activities of articulators rather than acoustic targets. Tatham (1979), for instance, cites evidence from an electromyographic study by Tom Shipp of the VA Hospital in San Francisco showing that in English word-final underlyingly voiced obstruents that surface as voiceless (i.e., do not undergo periodic abduction of the vocal cords), the larynx is actually in the configuration for voicing ([−stiff vocal cords] in present terms). The key here is that the phonological feature that characterizes the class of "voiced" segments in English is clearly indexed to an articulatory activity—setting the vocal cords to a particular range of stiffness—rather than to a particular auditory event such as voice onset time. Further evidence for the articulatory underpinnings of the phonological feature [stiff vocal cords] can be found in its multiplicity of acoustic manifestations, including formant cutback (Liberman, Delattre, and Cooper 1958, Lisker 1975), spectral characteristics of the release burst (Winitz, LaRiviere, and Herriman 1975, Williams 1977, Hutters 1985:17), differences in the degree and temporal extent of formant transitions (Cooper et al. 1952, Stevens and Klatt 1974, Summerfield and Haggard 1974), and differences in F0 change following release (Haggard, Ambler, and Callow 1970, Fujimura 1971). It is relatively straightforward to correlate the suite of phonological voicing behaviors with a single articulatory activity, stiffening of the vocal cords, whereas it does not satisfyingly correlate with any single acoustic event.

Kim (1970) and Iverson and Salmons (1995) make similar observations for [spread glottis] in English, where the phonological instruction to spread the vocal cords may or may not result in greater airflow through the vocal tract, thus producing either a voiceless unaspirated stop or a voiceless aspirated stop. Kim (1970) found for instance that the /t/'s in both *tar* and *star* involve significant spreading of the glottis (i.e., they are [+spread glottis]), but owing to the presence of a preceding [s] the latter /t/ surfaces with significantly less acoustic aspiration, because the burst of air produced by the lungs has been consumed by the [s]. This mismatch between the surface acoustics on the one hand and the phonological representation and the articulatory facts on the other again suggests that phonological features are based in articulations rather than acoustics.

The articulatory basis of features makes sense in light of increasingly robust evidence that animals (including humans) cognitively model relevant actions and events in terms of the physical activities necessary to execute them (Motor Theory; Ribot 1890, Taylor 1962, Tettamanti et al. 2005, etc., and for language (pace Ohala 1996) Liberman et al. 1963, Williams and McReynolds 1975, Borden, Harris, and Raphael 1980, Liberman and Mattingly 1985, Fadiga et al. 1995, Calvert et al. 1997, Fadiga et al. 2002, Tremblay, Shiller, and Ostry 2003). The claims of Motor Theory have recently been bolstered by imaging studies of the activity of mirror neurons in the premotor area of the monkey brain, which are activated by both execution and observation of manual and oral actions by both first and third person agents (Gallese et al. 1996, Ferrari et al. 2003, Fogassi and Ferrari 2004).

With these important appeals of Clements's feature theory in mind, I would like to address some relatively minor questions raised by its empirical and formal components.

4.2 Faulty Database

The main problem lies in the use of the UCLA Phonological Segment Inventory Database (UPSID; http://www.langmaker.com/upsidlanguages.htm) as the empirical base upon which Clements builds his theory. UPSID has serious phonetic and phonological flaws, as I detail below, and therefore should not be used as the empirical basis for crosslinguistic phonetic or phonological theories.[3] Both the current electronic form of the database and the well-known summary of its contents in book form (Maddieson 1984) appear to be the product of a grant obtained at UCLA by Ian Maddieson and Peter Ladefoged to synthesize what is known about the phonetic content of phonological inventories in a representative sampling of the world's languages. Maddieson is an ideal linguist to carry out such a project, as he is known for the high quality of his groundbreaking phonetic studies of diverse and lesser-known languages. Unfortunately, UPSID appears to have been built not on phonetically reliable work such as his, or phonologically reliable work such as François Dell's treatments of French and Berber, but on relatively arbitrary old grammars and articles. The database contains not only coding errors (such as the omission of

Russian *ы* [ɨj]; see Basbøll 1986), but also unwittingly imported phonetic and phonological errors from the source materials, examples of which are given in (1).

(1) *Some imported errors in Maddieson 1984*
   a. Russian /tʃʲ/ is described as nonpalatalized (p. 266).
   b. Eastern Armenian is reported as having only one rhotic (it has two, a tap and a trill).
   c. Eastern Armenian is characterized as opposing unaspirated, aspirated, and ejective voiceless stops, when in fact these three series are voiced, voiceless aspirated, and voiceless unaspirated, respectively.
   d. Both phonemic and allophonic vowel length are omitted in Tuvan, Yakut, and Khalaj.
   e. Bashkir /ð/ is rendered as */z/ (it is written as a form of ⟨z⟩ in the Bashkir script), while /θ/ is correctly rendered as /θ/, not */s/.
   f. Kirghiz velars are not represented, even though its separate uvular series is.

4.2.1 Phonetics

Maddieson's UCLA database contains several significant phonetic mischaracterizations as well.

For instance, older Mongolian grammars (Street 1963, Luvšanvandan 1964, Hangin 1968) and by extension Maddieson 1984 erroneously claim that the Khalkha (Halh) dialect contains only one high front unrounded vowel and organizes its vowel system in terms of backness and roundness. In reality, as shown in phonetic studies by Rialland and Djamouri (1984) and Svantesson (1985), Khalkha also features an [ɪ], which does not appear in traditional descriptions because it is not represented in the writing system, and organizes its vowel system in terms of [ATR]. (Traditional descriptions forced these [ATR] contrasts into the more familiar [back] contrasts of other Altaic languages, especially of the Turkic family.) According to Maddieson (1984:281), Khalkha Mongolian has the vowel inventory in (2), whereas the phonetic study by Rialland and Djamouri shows that it actually has the inventory in (3).

(2) *Khalkha Mongolian vowel inventory according to Maddieson (1984:281)*

	Short			Long	
High	iᵢ ʉ	ɷ		ʉː	
Higher mid	e			e[ː]	
Mid		"e"	"o"	"eː"	"oː"
Lower mid		ɔ		ɔː	
Low		ɑ		ɑː	

(3) *Khalkha (short) vowel inventory according to Rialland and Djamouri (1984)*
([ɪ] is a harmonic allophone of /i/, and is not included here)

Traditional label	i	e	a	ü	u	ö	o
IPA value	i	ε	ɑ	u	ʊ	o	ɔ
F2	2525	2350	1500	630	825	925	1060
F1	250	420	900	275	400	400	630
F2 – F1	2275	1930	600	355	425	525	430

UPSID in fact generally fails to capture the actual phonetics of vowel systems, which unfortunately facilitates claims about dispersion patterns in vowel systems by, for example, Liljencrants and Lindblom (1972) and Flemming (2004), though careful phonetic study of a representative range of vowel systems has shown these claims to be unjustified (Disner 1983).

The database (as presented in Maddieson 1984) also incorrectly presents many languages with aspirated stops as not aspirating these stops, including Aleut (Taff et al. 2001:239), Amharic (UCLA Phonetics Lab Archive), Evenki (Li 1996), German (Wagner 2002), Goldi (Li 1996), Manchu (Li 1996), Tuvan (Li 1996), and Yakut (Krueger 1962). This flaw, which results from the fact that most writers of grammars do not indicate aspiration in their transcriptions even if they are aware of its existence, has the unfortunate consequence of leading both Maddieson (1984) and Clements (p. 36, (11)) to conclude that nonaspiration is the unmarked state for voiceless stops, even though closer examination of the actual phonetic and phonological facts casts this popular generalization into doubt (for further details, see Vaux and Samuels 2005). Excessively literal and uncritical renditions of simplified transcriptions like this abound in the consonantal domain: for example, the well-documented Sinhalese implosive stops are nowhere to be found in the inventory on page 272 of Maddieson 1984, presumably because they are not written as such in the orthographic system. However, these errors are perhaps even more rampant in the vocalic component of UPSID: for example, the famously rounded Farsi [ɒ] is rendered as ⟨ɑ⟩ (1984:268), and the Turkish [æ] allophone of /e/ that occurs before {r, l, m, n} is omitted from the Osmanli inventory on page 277, presumably because it is not conveyed in the orthography.

UPSID also fails to reflect idiolectal and dialectal variation that is essential in formulating accurate typological generalizations, such as the variation found in the English-speaking world between individuals who oppose unaspirated fully voiced and voiceless series (e.g., Lisker and Abramson (1964) observe that one of their four English speakers systematically has large voicing lead for the "voiced" stop series; also see Scobbie 2002) and those who oppose plain and aspirated series, with the plain series varying in voicing depending on segmental and prosodic context.

Other phonetic generalizations extracted from UPSID need to be used with caution because they may reflect artifacts of perception and transcription, rather than actual phonological patterns in the languages being described. For example, Clements's generalization from UPSID that having one voiced fricative makes it more likely that another will occur in the same inventory can follow directly from whether or not the individuals who did the original transcriptions were able to hear voicing in obstruents successfully. This is no trivial matter, as shown by the fact that only the most observant phoneticians and phonologists are aware that speakers of English generally devoice word-initial and word-final obstruents (e.g., Haggard 1978, Pierrehumbert and Talkin 1992:109).

4.2.2 Phonology

At the phonological level, matters become even more complicated. For example, UPSID is inconsistent in the level of phonological representation it describes.[4] On the one hand, UPSID seems to be describing surface (i.e., allophonic) representations, since for example it renders Eastern Armenian as having a retroflex voiced nonsibilant fricative (Maddieson 1984:273) that is a surface allophone of the language's two rhotic phonemes /ɾ/ and /r/ but not a phoneme in its own right, and it includes the diphthong [ie] (actually [jɛ]), a word-initial allophone of /e/ and again not an independent phoneme. On the other hand, UPSID's representations sometimes appear phonemic: for instance, they do not include Eastern Armenian [vo], a surface allophone of underlying /o/ whose distribution is exactly parallel to that of [jɛ]; nor do they include [ɛ], an allophone of /e/ in certain prosodic positions. Similarly, Maddieson (1984:267) renders French ⟨r⟩ as a voiced uvular trill /r/, without mentioning its allophones [ʁ] and [χ], again implying that the inventories are based on underlying rather than surface representations. The list of confusions between underlying and surface representations in UPSID can be extended at length; illustrative examples are provided in (4).[5]

(4) *Conflicting levels of representation in UPSID*
    a. *Allophonic*
        i. French is listed as having /j/ and /w/, which are only surface allophones (of /i/ and /u/, respectively).
        ii. The Spanish chart includes the allophonic (but not phonemic) voiced fricative series.
        iii. Turkish is described as having a glottal stop (p. 277), which to the best of my knowledge appears only allophonically in word-initial position.
    b. *Phonemic*
        i. The [ə] allophone of Russian /a/ and /o/ is not included.
        ii. Turkish /cʰ/ and /ɟʰ/ are labeled as occurring only in loanwords, which is true of the phonemes (which appear primarily in Arabic and Persian

      loans) but not the allophones (which are regular allophones of /k/ and /g/ in [−back] spans).

  iii. Turkish is listed as not having /ŋ/, which is true phonemically but not allophonically.

  iv. The uvular allophones of dorsal obstruents in Yakut and Evenki are not included.

   v. Kabardian is stated to have only two short vowels, which is true underlyingly but not on the surface (see Colarusso 1992).

Clements is aware of this problem, and discusses several manifestations of it in section 2.3; he also discusses the problem of Southern Nambiquara in the 2003 version of his theory (Clements 2003:316). In the present volume, however, he does not indicate which level of representation (if either) he desires his theory to be built upon, beyond mentioning in his introduction (p. 20) that he is interested in inventories of contrastive speech sounds. One is left wondering whether it makes sense to conflate surface contrasts and underlying segments in this way.

Moreover, Clements's examples vacillate between using phonemic and allophonic representations. For instance, he states that "dorsal nasals are missing: [+nasal] is disfavored with [dorsal] obstruents" (p. 49), a generalization that holds only for underlying inventories, given that most languages fitting this description actually possess a dorsal nasal allophone. In many other instances, though, Clements seems to be operating with surface inventories.

Clements again indicates awareness of the phoneme/allophone issue when he states that "the sounds selected as the basic allophone or variant of a consonant phoneme in UPSID are typically those that appear [in the surface representation] in strong positions such as the onset. The rationale for this choice is that consonants that appear elsewhere can often be regarded as reduced or lenited realizations of this basic variant" (p. 24). This again implies an interest in focusing on phonemes rather than phones, which of course is problematic given UPSID's abundant use of surface rather than underlying representations. The decision criterion that Clements imports from Maddieson[6] raises a deeper problem as well, in that the allophones of segments that appear in onsets are not always the basic or underlying form, as in the many languages with onset fortition (e.g., Spanish dialects with onset fortition (Harris and Kaisse 1999), and languages that aspirate stops in onset position, such as English). Thanks primarily to the crosslinguistic frequency of enhancement in strong positions, of which /y/ fortition and stop aspiration are two examples, we must look elsewhere (no pun intended) for an algorithm that can identify underlying representations. The logical choice is what we learn in introductory phonology class: the basic/underlying variant should be the form that appears in the elsewhere case, not the one that appears most frequently, in strong positions, and so on.

4.2.3 Summary of Database Flaws

The basic problem facing us is keeping our levels of phonological representation distinct. As described above, this is particularly problematic in UPSID, which therefore should not be used as a basis for typological phonological analyses. Some have argued that the sheer number of inventories included in UPSID should compensate for the empirical and conceptual flaws just discussed, but this is incorrect: adding more flawed data to an already flawed base makes it worse, not better. Conducting statistical analysis of this flawed database will not rectify matters either; p values and percentages may look comfortingly solid and objective, but they are no better than the data from which they are derived. (As Best (2001) states, "Some statistics are born bad"; or put in computer science terms, "Garbage in, garbage out.")

This is not to say that Clements's project is ill-conceived or on the wrong track; quite the contrary. In order to pursue his research program safely, though, we must first construct a new database from reliable phonetic and phonological studies. Fortunately, we already have the phonetic and phonological sophistication to build such a database; suitable starting points would include Ladefoged's and Maddieson's phonetic studies, as well as explicit, clear, and detailed phonological studies such as Dell 1980, 1995 for French, and Kiparsky 2003 for Arabic.

4.3 Problems with the Feature Set

Another issue that needs to be resolved in Clements's theory of feature economy involves the nature of the features the theory is to be based on. Currently, many (and perhaps most) practitioners of Optimality Theory (OT) employ privative features (see Steriade 1995), but there is good reason to believe (see Kim 2002) that features are generally either binary (+/−) or equipollent (+/−/Ø). Clements actually uses all three options at different points in chapter 2: binary (e.g., binary [posterior] and [distributed] in figure (1)), privative [spread glottis] on page 36, and equipollent [slack vocal cords] and [stiff vocal cords] on page 37. (The idea that surface segments unspecified for laryngeal features can vary widely in acoustic properties associated with laryngeal activities such as voice onset time is developed in greater detail in Vaux and Samuels 2005.) It is conceivable that all three types are in fact needed (and nothing rules this out in a theory like OT), but such a powerful claim needs to be explicitly motivated with relevant arguments and data.

Any theory that manipulates features must also take a stand on underspecification. Clements appears to use full specification, even though he otherwise seems to be operating at the level of the phoneme, which is generally agreed to be underspecified to some extent (see especially the Toronto school of contrastive underspecification; Keating 1988, Choi 1992, Harrison and Kaun 2000, Eulitz et al. 2003). Until we know what features are employed, how they are specified, and at what level of representation their specifications are being assessed, it is not possible to make coherent feature-based computations of the sort Clements's theory of feature economy relies on.

4.4 Markedness

Clements's theory also relies heavily on the notion of phonological markedness in order to explain why some feature values appear more than others. This raises larger questions concerning the ontogeny and ontology of markedness, and the role of markedness in the grammar. For instance, Clements states that "if [the English] system used all possible combinations of its 9 consonant features, it would have 2^9 or 512 consonants... instead of the 24 relatively common sounds it actually contains. The English system is thus heavily constrained by markedness" (p. 32). But how much evidence for markedness activity does the English system actually provide? Probably none, in cases where speakers acquire the exact system to which they are exposed. Generally speaking, markedness effects only appear clearly in historical changes, acquisition errors, and the like that cannot be more plausibly explained by competing factors such as misanalysis, conflicting dialectal input, and so on.

Clements continues by saying that "some feature values—the marked values— appear less suited to speech communication than others for articulatory and perceptual reasons" (p. 32), and he discusses these reasons persuasively and at great length. It should be noted, though, that Clements's single-feature-based theory of markedness stands in opposition to the contrast-based theory of markedness employed in much recent OT work (Padgett 2003, Flemming 2004), which is closer to Clements's principle of Robustness ("Robustness is a property of feature-based contrasts," p. 43). Which of these two approaches to markedness is on the right track remains to be determined conclusively, though a point in favor of Clements's view is the fatal empirical and theoretical problems encountered by the contrast-based markedness model's dispersion-driven analyses (see Nevins and Vaux 2004, Vaux and Samuels 2004).

Clements next argues that idiosyncratic segments provide evidence that Feature Economy trumps Markedness, to the extent that "if a language possesses several such segments, they strongly tend to share features that bind them together as a class" (p. 33). But group behavior of this sort also results from the well-known fact that sound changes operate on features rather than phonemes and hence generally affect, create, and/or eliminate entire classes of segments. The robustly attested fact that historical sound changes involve entire natural classes of sounds rather than individual sounds or arbitrary groupings thereof thus strongly supports a distinctive feature theory of the sort Clements proposes, but does not actually support (or disconfirm, for that matter) his scenario wherein Feature Economy overrides Markedness.

Clements's discussion of markedness also suffers from at least one factual problem (which may again be the fault of UPSID). He states (p. 39) that voiceless ejective stops do not universally imply voiceless unaspirated stops, and he cites the case of Berta. Such systems are in fact quite common, occurring for example in the Ethiopic group of Semitic languages and in Caucasian languages such as Abkhaz and Georgian (see Žgent'i 1965). The frequency of such systems can be plausibly attributed to the unmarkedness of aspiration in stops, which in part involves Enhancement (Vaux and Samuels 2005).

One final comment on Clements's treatment of markedness. In his search to determine the unmarked value of individual features, Clements focuses primarily on static distributional patterns. Recent work by Andrea Calabrese and his associates suggests that there may be another way of identifying marked and unmarked values of individual features, namely, rules that are sensitive only to marked feature specifications. Rules of this type include Japanese Rendaku (Calabrese 1995:413–418) and Sibe uvularization (Nevins and Vaux 2004).

4.5   What and Where Is Economy?

My final concern with Clements's theory of Economy is the notion of Economy itself. It is not clear from Clements's proposals whether his Economy system is part of the grammar, a general cognitive phenomenon, or just an emergent property of systems from evolution or mathematics.[7] Is there something in the head that makes phonological inventories tend to change in certain ways, or can the attested patterns be derived as Ohala suggests, via perception, acquisition, misanalysis, and diffusion?

The same question can be raised about the role of the acquisition process versus Economy in producing historical sound changes. Clements states that "increasing the number of sounds while holding the number of features constant [one of Clements's two types of Feature Economy] is reflected in historical changes that create new phonemes by recombining existing features (Martinet 1955)" (p. 28). But is it actually Feature Economy driving such changes, and if so, how can we prove this? Clements gives as an example "the historical creation of a new series of [+nasal] vowels in French through the historical deletion of syllable-final [+nasal] consonants" (p. 28). However, since this case (arguably) involves surface allophones rather than phonemes (a problem for Clements's implied focus on underlying rather than surface representations) and can be accounted for at least as plausibly in terms of misanalysis by the language learner as it can by Feature Economy, it does not constitute a compelling argument for the activity of Economy in historical sound change.

4.6 Conclusions

Notwithstanding the issues with Economy just discussed, the overall thrust and empirical content of Clements's arguments for a feature-based system of Economy remains convincing. Clements's focus on discrete phonological features governed by abstract combinatorial principles (as opposed to phonetic categories emerging from lower-level gradient processes) not only makes sense considering the phonological and psycholinguistic evidence discussed in this chapter, but also dovetails well with the ample evidence for feature-based processing in other domains of human cognition[8] such as

- sign language phonologies (e.g., Stokoe 1960, Sandler 1996),
- morphology (Jakobson 1962, Katz and Fodor 1963, Greenberg 1967:218, Janda 1987, Neidle 1988, Gvozdanović 1991, McCreight and Chvany 1991, Janda and Joseph 1992, Halle and Marantz 1993, Franks 1995, McGinnis 1995, Halle 1997, Miozzo and Caramazza 1997, Noyer 1997, Calabrese 1998, 2002, Halle and Vaux 1998, Fitzpatrick, Nevins, and Vaux 2004, Wunderlich 2004),
- semantics (Hjelmslev 1953:44, Katz and Fodor 1963, Collins and Quillian 1969, Schank 1972, Rips, Shoben, and Smith 1973, Rosch 1973, Collins and Loftus 1975, Warrington 1975, Rosch et al. 1976, Wilks 1976, Carey 1978, Barsalou 1982, Warrington and McCarthy 1983, 1987, Warrington and Shallice 1984, Rumelhart 1990, Rapp and Caramazza 1991, De Renzi and Lucchelli 1994, McCarthy and Warrington 1994, Masson 1995, Plaut 1995, Gonnerman et al. 1997, McRae, de Sa, and Seidenberg 1997, Frenck-Mestre and Bueno 1999),
- alphabet processing (Gibson 1969, Steinheiser 1970, Campbell 1974, Cleghorn 1978, Keren and Baggen 1981, Rapp and Caramazza 1997),
- object perception (Biederman 1987, Schyns, Goldstone, and Thibaut 1998, Carneiro and Jepson 2003, Lowe 2004, Lu, Hager, and Younes 2004),
- cuisine (Lévi-Strauss 1963:86–87), and
- ethnosemantics, including componential analysis of kinship systems (Kroeber 1909, Greenberg 1966, 1967, Fox 1979).

In this last connection, Clements's Economy theory is reminiscent of Jones's generalization about kinship systems: "The discussion of distinctive features and markedness above implies that kin terminologies are built around two contradictory commandments: 'Thou shalt preserve information about distinctive features,' and 'Thou shalt avoid marked terms.' These commandments reflect two opposing tendencies in language, toward exactness and economy of communication" (2003:308). Clements wisely points out, though, that his Economy principles "cannot involve a simple ranking, as no single principle . . . ever outranks all others" (p. 57), leaving one wondering whether strict domination, one of the cornerstones of orthodox OT, has any place in the grammar at all.

Notes

Thanks to Nick Clements, Andrew Nevins, Morris Halle, Colin Phillips, and Chuck Cairns for comments on drafts of this chapter.

1. As Ladefoged 2004:7 notes, "Most practitioners of articulatory phonology are not adherents to the principles of universal grammar and see no need for a universal set of features."

2. For parallel philosophical arguments against reductionism in philosophy, psychology, and biology, see Mill 1843, Putnam 1967, 1973, Mayr 1970, 1982, Fodor 1974, 1981, Hull 1974, Wimsatt 1976, Pylyshyn 1984, Fodor and Pylyshyn 1988, van Gulick 1993, Hardcastle 1998.

3. Clements (2003:298–299) notes this problem, but adds that the data can in his opinion be used as long as they are interpreted with care and cross-checked against original sources when questions arise about their reliability. He also gives an extended case study of such error-detection and correction (2003:316–318).

4. Maddieson (1984:6) states that "in the database each segment which is considered phonemic is represented by its most characteristic allophone . . . UPSID, unlike the S[tanford] P[honological] A[rchive], makes no attempt to include information on allophonic variation," but this principle is inherently misleading and, as detailed below, is not followed consistently.

5. Clements (pers. comm.) comments that

Dell considers /j/, but not [w] as a phoneme in French (see e.g., the phoneme chart in *Les règles et les sons, 2nd edition*, p. 101 [Dell 1973], or his article on the palatal glide in French, Dell 1972 as cited in his book). I have discussed this issue with him at length in the past and agree with him that in the framework of classical generative analysis, /j/ probably would have phonemic status, while /w/ is phonemic at best only in loanwords like *whisky* where it behaves like a consonant in not triggering vowel deletion (*le whisky*, **l' whisky*). Phonemic palatal glides /j/ in native French words are largely those that descend from earlier palatal l, as in *fille*, *abeille*.

6. Maddieson also employs the less "relaxed" of two variants as the basic form in some cases (1991:196), but also states that the criterion used "in most cases" is frequency; that is, the allophone that occurs in the most contexts is selected. He adds two further criteria in his lengthier discussion in *Patterns of Sounds* (1984:162–163).

7. As George Miller stated concerning Zipf's-Mandelbrot's Law in his introduction to Zipf 1965,

Faced with this massive statistical regularity, you have two alternatives. Either you can assume that it reflects some universal property of human mind, or you can assume that it reflects some necessary consequence of the laws of probabilities. Zipf chose the synthetic hypothesis and searched for a principle of least effort that would explain the apparent equilibrium between uniformity and diversity in our use of words. Most others who were subsequently attracted to the problems chose the analytic hypothesis and searched for a probabilistic explanation. Now, thirty years later, it seems clear that the others were right. Zipf's curves are merely one way to express a necessary consequence of regarding a message source as a stochastic process.

8. As well as other domains such as Aristotelian physics; see Greenberg 1967.

References

Anisfeld, Moshe, Judith Barlow, and Catherine Frail. 1968. Distinctive features in the pluralization rules of English speakers. *Language and Speech* 11:31–37.

Anisfeld, Moshe, and Malcolm Gordon. 1968. On the psychophonological structure of English inflectional rules. *Journal of Verbal Learning and Verbal Behavior* 7:973–979.

Baltaxe, Christiane. 1978. *Foundations of distinctive feature theory.* Baltimore, Md.: University Park Press.

Barsalou, Lawrence W. 1982. Context-independent and context-dependent information in concepts. *Memory and Cognition* 10:82–93.

Basbøll, Hans. 1986. Review of *Patterns of sounds* by Ian Maddieson. *Phonology Yearbook* 2:343–353.

Bedoin, Nathalie. 2003. Sensitivity to voicing similarity in printed stimuli: Effect of a training programme in dyslexic children. *Journal of Phonetics* 31 (3–4): 541–546.

Berg, Thomas. 1990. Unreine Reime als Evidenz für die Organisation phonologischer Merkmale. *Zeitschrift für Sprachwissenschaft* 9:3–27.

Best, Joel. 2001. *Damned lies and statistics: Untangling numbers from the media, politicians and activists.* Berkeley and Los Angeles: University of California Press.

Biederman, Irving. 1987. Recognition-by-components: A theory of human image understanding. *Psychological Review* 94:115–147.

Bitar, Nabil, and Carol Espy-Wilson. 1995. A signal representation of speech based on phonetic features. In *Proceedings of the 1995 IEEE Dual-Use Technologies and Applications Conference, May 22–25, SUNY Inst. of Tech.,* 310–315. Utica/Rome.

Blumstein, Sheila, and Kenneth N. Stevens. 1985. On some issues in the pursuit of acoustical invariance in speech: A reply to Lisker. *Journal of the Acoustical Society of America* 77:1203–1204.

Borden, Gloria, Katherine Harris, and Lawrence Raphael. 1980. *Speech science primer: Physiology, acoustics and perception of speech.* Baltimore, Md.: Williams and Wilkins.

Brakel, Arthur. 1983. *Phonological markedness and distinctive features.* Bloomington: Indiana University Press.

Calabrese, Andrea. 1995. A constraint-based theory of phonological markedness and simplification procedures. *Linguistic Inquiry* 26:373–463.

Calabrese, Andrea. 1998. Some remarks on the Latin case system and its development in Romance. In *Theoretical analyses on Romance languages,* ed. by José Lema and Esthela Treviño, 71–126. Amsterdam: John Benjamins.

Calabrese, Andrea. 2002. On impoverishment and fission in the verbal morphology of the dialect of Livinallongo. In *Studies on Italian dialects*, ed. by Christina Tortora, 3–33. Oxford: Oxford University Press.

Calvert, Gemma, Edward Bullmore, Michael Brammer, Ruth Campbell, Steven Williams, Philip McGuire, Peter Woodruff, Susan Iversen, and Anthony David. 1997. Activation of auditory cortex during silent lipreading. *Science* 276.5312:593–596.

Campbell, Hugo. 1974. Phoneme recognition by ear and by eye: A distinctive feature analysis. Doctoral dissertation, Katholieke Universiteit te Nijmegen.

Carey, Sue. 1978. The child as word learner. In *Linguistic theory and psychological reality*, ed. by Morris Halle, Joan Bresnan, and George Miller, 264–293. Cambridge, Mass.: MIT Press.

Carneiro, Gustavo, and Allan Jepson. 2003. Multi-scale phase-based local features. Computer Vision and Pattern Recognition. In *Proceedings of IEEE Conference on Computer Vision and Pattern Recognition (CVPR03), Madison, June 2003*.

Choi, John. 1992. Phonetic underspecification and target interpolation: An acoustic study of Marshallese vowel allophony. Doctoral dissertation, UCLA.

Chomsky, Noam, and Morris Halle. 1968. *The sound pattern of English.* New York: Harper and Row.

Cleghorn, G. Dean. 1978. Analysis of simultaneous, successive and distinctive feature visual-discrimination training and paired-associate learning of confusable letters. Doctoral dissertation, University of Tennessee, Knoxville.

Clements, G. N. 2003. Feature economy in sound systems. *Phonology* 20:287–333.

Colarusso, John. 1992. *A grammar of the Kabardian language.* Calgary: University of Calgary Press.

Collins, Allan, and Elizabeth Loftus. 1975. A spreading-activation theory of semantic processing. *Psychological Review* 82:407–428.

Collins, Allan, and M. Ross Quillian. 1969. Retrieval time from semantic memory. *Journal of Verbal Learning and Verbal Behavior* 8:240–248.

Cooper, Franklin, Pierre Delattre, Alvin Liberman, John Borst, and Louis Gerstman. 1952. Some experiments on the perception of synthetic speech sounds. *Journal of the Acoustical Society of America* 24:597–606.

Dell, François. 1972. Une règle d'effacement de *i* en français. *Recherches Linguistiques* 1:63–87. University of Paris VIII-Vincennes.

Dell, François. 1973. *Les règles et les sons: Introduction à la phonologie générative.* Paris: Collection Savoir Hermann.

Dell, François. 1980. *Generative phonology and French phonology.* Cambridge: Cambridge University Press.

Dell, François. 1995. Consonant clusters and phonological syllables in French. *Lingua* 95:5–26.

De Renzi, Ennio, and Federica Lucchelli. 1994. Are semantic systems separately represented in the brain? The case of living category impairment. *Cortex* 30:3–25.

Derwing, Bruce, and Terrance Nearey. 1986. Experimental phonology at the University of Alberta. In *Experimental phonology*, ed. by John Ohala and Jeri Jaeger, 187–209. Orlando, Fla.: Academic Press.

Disner, Sandra. 1983. Vowel quality: The relation between universal and language-specific factors. Doctoral dissertation, UCLA.

Eimas, Peter, Vivien Tartter, Joanne Miller, and Nancy Keuthen. 1978. Asymmetric dependencies in processing phonetic features. *Perception and Psychophysics* 23:12–20.

Espy-Wilson, Carol. 1994. A feature-based semivowel recognition system. *Journal of the Acoustical Society of America* 96:65–72.

Eulitz, Carsten, Aditi Lahiri, Jonas Obleser, and Henning Reetz. 2003. Brain electric activity reflects the underspecification of phonological features in the mental lexicon. In *Proceedings of the 15th International Congress of Phonetic Sciences, Barcelona, 3–9 August 2003*, ed. by Maria-Josep Solé, Daniel Recasens, and Joaquín Romero, 1631–1634. Rundle Mall, Australia: Causal Productions (CD-ROM); Barcelona: Futurgraphic (print).

Fadiga, Luciano, Laila Craighero, Giovanni Buccino, and Giacomo Rizzolatti. 2002. Speech listening specifically modulates the excitability of tongue muscles: A TMS study. *European Journal of Neuroscience* 15:399–402.

Fadiga, Luciano, Leonardo Fogassi, Giovanni Pavesi, and Giacomo Rizzolatti. 1995. Motor facilitation during action observation: A magnetic stimulation study. *Journal of Neurophysiology* 73:2608–2611.

Ferrari, Pier Francesco, Vittorio Gallese, Giacomo Rizzolatti, and Leonardo Fogassi. 2003. Mirror neurons responding to the observation of ingestive and communicative mouth actions in the monkey ventral premotor cortex. *European Journal of Neuroscience* 17:1703–1714.

Fitzpatrick, Justin, Andrew Nevins, and Bert Vaux. 2004. Exchange rules and feature-value variables. Paper presented at the 3rd North American Phonology Conference, Concordia University, Montréal, Québec.

Flemming, Edward. 1995. Auditory representations in phonology. Doctoral dissertation, UCLA.

Flemming, Edward. 2004. Contrast and perceptual distinctiveness. In *Phonetically based phonology*, ed. by Bruce Hayes, Robert Kirchner, and Donca Steriade, 232–276. Cambridge: Cambridge University Press.

Flemming, Edward. 2005. Deriving natural classes in phonology. *Lingua* 115:287–309.

Fodor, Jerry. 1974. Special sciences, or The disunity of science as a working hypothesis. *Synthese* 28:97–115.

Fodor, Jerry. 1981. *Representations.* Cambridge, Mass.: MIT Press.

Fodor, Jerry, and Zenon Pylyshyn. 1988. Connectionism and cognitive architecture: A critical analysis. *Cognition* 28:3–71.

Fogassi, Leonardo, and Pier Francesco Ferrari. 2004. Mirror neurons, gestures and language evolution. *Interaction Studies* 5:345–363.

Fox, Robin. 1979. Kinship categories as natural categories. In *Evolutionary biology and human social behavior: An anthropological perspective*, ed. by Napoleon A. Chagnon and William Irons, 132–144. North Scituate, Mass.: Duxbury.

Franks, Steven. 1995. *Parameters of Slavic morphosyntax.* Oxford: Oxford University Press.

Frenck-Mestre, Cheryl, and Steve Bueno. 1999. Semantic features and semantic categories: Differences in rapid activation of the lexicon. *Brain and Language* 68:199–204.

Fromkin, Victoria. 1973. *Speech errors as linguistic evidence.* The Hague: Mouton.

Fujimura, Osamu. 1971. Remarks on stop consonants: Synthesis experiments and acoustic cues. In *Form and substance: Phonetic and linguistic papers presented to Eli Fischer-Jørgensen,* ed. by L. L. Hammerich, Roman Jakobson, and Eberhard Zwirner, 221–232. Odense: Akademisk Forlag.

Gallese, Vittorio, Luciano Fadiga, Leonardo Fogassi, and Giacomo Rizzolatti. 1996. Action recognition in the premotor cortex. *Brain* 119:593–609.

Gibson, Eleanor. 1969. *Principles of perceptual learning and development.* New York: Appleton-Century-Crofts.

Goldrick, Matthew. 2004. Phonological features and phonotactic constraints in speech production. *Journal of Memory and Language* 51:586–603.

Goldstein, Louis. 1980. Categorical features in speech perception and production. *Journal of the Acoustical Society of America* 67:1336–1348.

Gonnerman, Laura M., Elaine S. Andersen, Joseph T. Devlin, Daniel Kempler, and Mark Seidenberg. 1997. Double dissociation of semantic categories in Alzheimer's disease. *Brain and Language* 57:254–279.

Green, Kerry, and Patricia Kuhl. 1991. Integral processing of visual place and auditory voicing information during phonetic perception. *Journal of Experimental Psychology: Human Perception and Performance* 17:278–288.

Greenberg, Joseph. 1966. *Language universals, with special reference to feature hierarchies.* The Hague: Mouton.

Greenberg, Joseph. 1967. The first (and perhaps only) non-linguistic distinctive feature analysis. *Word* 23:214–220.

Gulick, Robert van. 1993. Who's in charge here? And who's doing all the work? In *Mental causation,* ed. by John Heil and Alfred Mele, 233–256. Oxford: Clarendon Press.

Gvozdanović, Jadranka. 1991. Syncretism and paradigmatic patterning of grammatical meaning. In *Paradigms,* ed. by Frans Plank, 133–160. Berlin: Mouton de Gruyter.

Haggard, Mark. 1978. The devoicing of voiced fricatives. *Journal of Phonetics* 6:95–102.

Haggard, Mark, Stephen Ambler, and Mo Callow. 1970. Pitch as a voicing cue. *Journal of the Acoustical Society of America* 47:613–617.

Hall, T. Alan, ed. 2001. *Distinctive feature theory.* Berlin: Mouton de Gruyter.

Halle, Morris. 1997. Distributed Morphology: Impoverishment and fission. In *Papers at the interface,* ed. by Benjamin Bruening, Yoonjung Kang, and Martha McGinnis, 425–449. MIT Working Papers in Linguistics 30. Cambridge, Mass.: MIT, MIT Working Papers in Linguistics.

Halle, Morris, and Alec Marantz. 1993. Distributed Morphology and the pieces of inflection. In *The view from Building 20,* ed. by Kenneth Hale and Samuel Jay Keyser, 111–176. Cambridge, Mass.: MIT Press.

Halle, Morris, and Bert Vaux. 1998. Theoretical aspects of Indo-European nominal morphology: The nominal declensions of Latin and Armenian. In *Mír curad: Studies in honor of Calvert Watkins,* ed. by Jay Jasanoff, H. Craig Melchert, and Lisi Oliver, 223–240. Innsbrucker Beiträge zur Sprachwissenschaft. Innsbruck: Universität Innsbruck, Institut für Sprachen und Literaturen.

Hangin, John. 1968. *Basic course in Mongolian*. Bloomington: Indiana University Press.

Hardcastle, Valerie. 1998. On the matter of minds and mental causation. *Philosophy and Phenomenological Research* 58:1–25.

Harris, James, and Ellen Kaisse. 1999. Palatal vowels, glides and obstruents in Argentinean Spanish. *Phonology* 16:117–190.

Harrison, David, and Abigail Kaun. 2000. Pattern-responsive underspecification. In *Proceedings of North East Linguistic Society (NELS) 30*, ed. by Masako Hirotani, Andries Coetzee, Nancy Hall, and Ji-yung Kim, 327–340. Amherst: University of Massachusetts, Graduate Linguistic Student Association.

Hayden, Mary. 1976. Distinctive feature use in the perception of speech under binaural and dichotic conditions. Doctoral dissertation, University of Houston.

Hillenbrand, James. 1983. Perceptual organization of speech sounds by infants. *Journal of Speech and Hearing Research* 26:268–282.

Hjelmslev, Louis. 1953. *Prolegomena to a theory of language*. Trans. by Francis J. Whitfield. Supplement to *International Journal of American Linguistics* 19 (1).

Hull, David L. 1974. *The philosophy of biological science*. Englewood Cliffs, N.J.: Prentice-Hall.

Humphrey, Jean. 1977. Distinctive feature generalization in children's speech: A clinical study. Master's thesis, Southern Illinois University.

Hutters, Birgit. 1985. Vocal fold adjustments in aspirated and unaspirated stops in Danish. *Phonetica* 42:1–24.

Iverson, Gregory, and Joseph Salmons. 1995. Aspiration and laryngeal representation in Germanic. *Phonology* 12:369–396.

Jaeger, Jeri. 1992. Phonetic features in young children's slips of the tongue. *Language and Speech* 35:189–205.

Jakobson, Roman. 1962. Beitrag zur allgemeinen Kasuslehre: Gesamtbedeutungen der russischen Kasus. In *Selected writings*, 2:23–71. The Hague: Mouton.

Jakobson, Roman, C. Gunnar M. Fant, and Morris Halle. 1952. Preliminaries to speech analysis: The distinctive features and their correlates. Technical Report 13. Cambridge, Mass.: MIT, Acoustics Laboratory. Expanded edition published, Cambridge, Mass.: MIT Press, 1961.

Janda, Richard. 1987. On the motivation for an evolutionary typology of sound-structural rules. Doctoral dissertation, UCLA.

Janda, Richard, and Brian Joseph. 1992. Pseudo-agglutinativity in Modern Greek verb inflection and "elsewhere." In *Proceedings of Chicago Linguistic Society (CLS) 28*, ed. by Costas P. Canakis, Grace P. Chan, and Jeannette Marshall Denton, 1:251–266. Chicago: University of Chicago, Chicago Linguistic Society.

Jones, Doug. 2003. The generative psychology of kinship. Part 1, Cognitive universals and evolutionary psychology. *Evolution and Human Behavior* 24:303–319.

Jusczyk, Peter, Mara Goodman, and Angela Baumann. 1999. Nine-month-olds' attention to sound similarities in syllables. *Journal of Memory and Language* 40:62–82.

Katz, Jerrold, and Jerry Fodor. 1963. The structure of a semantic theory. *Language* 39:170–210.

Keating, Patricia. 1988. Underspecification in phonetics. *Phonology* 5:275–292.

Keren, Gideon, and Stan Baggen. 1981. Recognition models of alpha-numeric characters. *Perception and Psychophysics* 29:234–246.

Kim, Chin-Wu. 1970. A theory of aspiration. *Phonetica* 21:107–116.

Kim, Yuni. 2002. Phonological features: Privative or equipollent? Bachelor's thesis, Harvard University.

Kiparsky, Paul. 1974. A note on the vowel features. In *Proceedings of North East Linguistic Society (NELS) 5*, ed. by Ellen Kaisse and Jorge Hankamer, 162–171. Cambridge, Mass.: Harvard University, Department of Linguistics.

Kiparsky, Paul. 2003. Syllables and moras in Arabic. In *The syllable in Optimality Theory*, ed. by Caroline Féry and Ruben van de Vijver, 147–182. Cambridge: Cambridge University Press.

Krifi, Sonia, Nathalie Bedoin, and Anne Mérigot. 2003. Effects of voicing similarity between consonants in printed stimuli in normal and dyslexic readers. *Current Psychology Letters: Behaviour, Brain and Cognition* 10.1. http://cpl.revues.org.

Kroeber, Alfred. 1909. Classificatory systems of relationship. *The Journal of the Royal Anthropological Institute of Great Britain and Ireland* 39:77–84.

Krueger, John. 1962. *Yakut manual.* Bloomington: Indiana University Press.

Ladefoged, Peter. 2004. Phonetics and phonology in the last 50 years. In *UCLA working papers in phonetics 103*, 1–11. Los Angeles: UCLA, Department of Linguistics, Phonetics Lab.

Lahiri, Aditi, and Allard Jongman. 1990. Intermediate level of analysis: Feature or segments? *Journal of Phonetics* 18:435–443.

Lawson, Everdina, and Anthony Gaillard. 1981. Mismatch negativity in a phonetic discrimination task. *Biological Psychology* 13:281–288.

Lévi-Strauss, Claude. 1963. *Structural anthropology.* Trans. by Claire Jacobson and Brooke Grundfest Schoepf. New York: Basic Books.

Li, Bing. 1996. *Tungusic vowel harmony: Description and analysis.* Amsterdam: Universiteit van Amsterdam.

Liberman, Alvin M., Franklin S. Cooper, Katherine Harris, and Peter MacNeilage. 1963. A motor theory of speech perception. In *Proceedings of the Symposium on Speech Communication Seminar, Royal Institute of Technology, Stockholm.* Vol. 2, Paper D3.

Liberman, Alvin M., Pierre C. Delattre, and Franklin S. Cooper. 1958. Some cues for the distinction between voiced and voiceless stops in initial position. *Language and Speech* 1:153–167.

Liberman, Alvin M., and Ignatius Mattingly. 1985. The motor theory of speech perception revised. *Cognition* 21:1–36.

Liljencrants, Johan, and Björn Lindblom. 1972. Numerical simulation of vowel quality systems: The role of perceptual contrast. *Language* 48:839–862.

Lisker, Leigh. 1975. Is it VOT or a first-formant transition detector? *Journal of the Acoustical Society of America* 57:1547–1551.

Lisker, Leigh. 1985. The pursuit of invariance in speech signals. *Journal of the Acoustical Society of America* 77:1199–1202.

Lisker, Leigh, and Arthur S. Abramson. 1964. A cross-language study of voicing in initial stops: Acoustical measurements. *Word* 20:384–422.

Lowe, David G. 2004. Distinctive image features from scale-invariant keypoints. *International Journal of Computer Vision* 60 (2): 91–110.

Lu, Le, Gregory Hager, and Laurent Younes. 2004. A three tiered approach for articulated object action modeling and recognition. http://books.nips.cc/papers/files/nips17/NIPS2004_0497.pdf.

Lukatela, Georgije, and Michael Turvey. 2001. Does visual word identification involve a sub-phonemic level? *Cognition* 78:B41–B52.

Luv Šanvandan, S. 1964. The Khalkha-Mongolian phonemic system. *Acta Orientalia* 17:175–185.

Maddieson, Ian. 1984. *Patterns of sounds.* Cambridge: Cambridge University Press.

Maddieson, Ian. 1991. Testing the universality of phonological generalizations with a phonetically specified segment database. *Phonetica* 48:193–206.

Marslen-Wilson, William, and Paul Warren. 1994. Levels of perceptual representation and process in lexical access: Words, phonemes and features. *Psychological Review* 101:653–675.

Martin, Albert. 1972. Phonological impairment in aphasia: A distinctive feature analysis of a repetition task. Doctoral dissertation, Columbia University.

Martin, Charles. 1975. The prediction of similarity judgments with a distinctive feature system and the relative frequency of occurrence of distinctive features in the English language. Doctoral dissertation, Southern Illinois University.

Martinet, André. 1955. *Économie des changements phonétiques.* Bern: A. Francke.

Masson, Michael E. J. 1995. A distributed memory model of semantic priming. *Journal of Experimental Psychology: Learning, Memory, and Cognition* 21:3–23.

Mayr, Ernst. 1970. *Populations, species, and evolution.* Cambridge, Mass.: Belknap Press of Harvard University Press.

Mayr, Ernst. 1982. *The growth of biological thought: Diversity, evolution, and inheritance.* Cambridge, Mass.: Belknap Press of Harvard University Press.

McCarthy, Rosaleen, and Elizabeth Warrington. 1994. Disorders of semantic memory. *Philosophical Transactions of the Royal Society, London* B346:89–96.

McCawley, James. 1972. The role of a system of phonological features in a theory of language. In *Phonological theory*, ed. by Valerie Makkai, 322–328. New York: Holt, Rinehart and Winston.

McCreight, Katherine, and Catherine Chvany. 1991. Geometric representation of paradigms in a modular theory of grammar. In *Paradigms*, ed. by Frans Plank, 91–111. Berlin: Mouton de Gruyter.

McGinnis, Martha. 1995. Fission as feature-movement. In *Papers on minimalist syntax*, ed. by Robert Pensalfini and Hiroyuki Ura, 165–187. MIT Working Papers in Linguistics 27. Cambridge, Mass.: MIT, MIT Working Papers in Linguistics.

McRae, Ken, Virginia de Sa, and Mark Seidenberg. 1997. On the nature and scope of featural representations of word meaning. *Journal of Experimental Psychology: General* 126:99–130.

McReynolds, Leija, and Deedra Engmann. 1975. *Distinctive feature analysis of misarticulations.* Baltimore, Md.: University Park Press.

Milberg, William, Sheila Blumstein, and Barbara Dworetzky. 1988. Phonological processing and lexical access in aphasia. *Brain and Language* 34:279–293.

Mill, John Stuart. 1843. *A system of logic, ratiocinative and inductive: Being a connected view of the principles of evidence and the methods of scientific investigation.* London: J. W. Parker.

Miller, George, and Patricia Nicely. 1955. An analysis of perceptual confusions among some English consonants. *Journal of the Acoustical Society of America* 27:338–352.

Miozzo, Michele, and Alfonso Caramazza. 1997. Retrieval of lexical-syntactic features in tip-of-the-tongue states. *Journal of Experimental Psychology: Learning, Memory, and Cognition* 23:1410–1423.

Neidle, Carol. 1988. *The role of case in Russian syntax.* Dordrecht: Kluwer.

Nevins, Andrew, and Bert Vaux. 2004. The transparency of contrastive segments in Sibe: Evidence for relativized locality. Paper presented at GLOW (Generative Linguistics in the Old World) 27, Thessaloniki.

Noyer, Rolf. 1997. Features, positions and affixes in autonomous morphological structure. New York: Garland. Revised version of Doctoral dissertation, MIT, 1992.

Obleser, Jonas, Carsten Eulitz, and Aditi Lahiri. 2004. Magnetic brain response mirrors extraction of phonological features from spoken vowels. *Journal of Cognitive Neuroscience* 16:31–39.

Ohala, John. 1996. Speech perception is hearing sounds, not tongues. *Journal of the Acoustical Society of America* 99:1718–1725.

Padgett, Jaye. 2003. The emergence of contrastive palatalization in Russian. In *Optimality Theory and language change*, ed. by Eric Holt, 307–335. Dordrecht: Kluwer.

Phillips, Colin, Tom Pellathy, and Alec Marantz. 2000. Phonological feature representations in auditory cortex. http://www.ling.udel.edu/colin/research/papers/feature_mmf.pdf.

Pierrehumbert, Janet, and David Talkin. 1992. Lenition of /h/ and glottal stop. In *Gesture, segment, prosody: Papers in laboratory phonology II*, ed. by Gerard J. Docherty and D. Robert Ladd, 90–117. Cambridge: Cambridge University Press.

Plaut, David C. 1995. Semantic and associative priming in a distributed attractor network. In *Proceedings of the 17th Annual Conference of the Cognitive Science Society*, ed. by Johanna D. Moore and Jill Fain Lehman, 37–42. Hillsdale, N.J.: Lawrence Erlbaum.

Putnam, Hilary. 1967. Psychological predicates. In *Art, mind and religion*, ed. by William Captain and Daniel Merrill, 37–48. Pittsburgh, Pa.: Pittsburgh University Press.

Putnam, Hilary. 1973. Reductionism and the nature of psychology. *Cognition* 2:131–146.

Pycha, Anne, Pawel Novak, Eurie Shin, and Ryan Shosted. 2003. Phonological rule-learning and its implications for a theory of vowel harmony. In *WCCFL 22: Proceedings of the 22nd West Coast Conference on Formal Linguistics*, ed. by Gina Garding and Mimu Tsujimura, 423–435. Somerville, Mass.: Cascadilla Press.

Pylyshyn, Zenon. 1984. *Computation and cognition.* Cambridge, Mass.: MIT Press.

Rapp, Brenda, and Alfonso Caramazza. 1991. Lexical deficits. In *Acquired aphasias*, ed. by Martha Taylor Sarno, 181–222. 2nd ed. San Diego, Calif.: Academic Press.

Rapp, Brenda, and Alfonso Caramazza. 1997. From graphemes to abstract letter shapes: Levels of representation in written spelling. *Journal of Experimental Psychology: Human Perception and Performance* 23:1130–1152.

Rialland, Annie, and Redouane Djamouri. 1984. Harmonie vocalique, consonantique et structures de dépendance dans le mot en mongol khalkha. *Bulletin de la Société de Linguistique de Paris* 79:333–383.

Ribot, Théodule. 1890. *Psychologie de l'attention.* Paris: Alcan.

Rips, Lance, Edward Shoben, and Edward Smith. 1973. Semantic distance and the verification of semantic relations. *Journal of Verbal Learning and Verbal Behavior* 12:1–20.

Rogers, Margaret, and Holly Storkel. 1998. Reprogramming phonologically similar utterances: The role of phonetic features in pre-motor encoding. *Journal of Speech, Language, and Hearing Research* 41:258–274.

Rosch, Eleanor. 1973. On the internal structure of perceptual and semantic categories. In *Cognitive development and the acquisition of language*, ed. by Timothy E. Moore, 111–144. New York: Academic Press.

Rosch, Eleanor, Carolyn Mervis, Wayne Gray, David Johnson, and Penny Boyes-Braem. 1976. Basic objects in natural categories. *Cognitive Psychology* 8:382–439.

Rumelhart, David. 1990. Brain style computation: Learning and generalization. In *An introduction to neural and electronic networks*, ed. by Steven F. Zornetzer, Joel L. Davis, and Clifford Lau, 405–420. San Diego, Calif.: Academic Press.

Ruszkiewicz, Piotr. 2001. *Distinctive feature theory: Origins, development and current practice.* Gdansk: Wydawnictwo Uniwerstytetu Gdanskiego.

Sandler, Wendy. 1996. Phonological features and feature classes: The case of movements in sign language. *Lingua* 98:197–220.

Sawyer, Diane, Sally Wade, and Jwa Kim. 1999. Spelling errors as a window on variations in phonological deficits among students with dyslexia. *Annals of Dyslexia* 49:135–159.

Schank, Roger. 1972. Conceptual dependency: A theory of natural language understanding. *Cognitive Psychology* 3:552–631.

Schyns, Philippe, Robert Goldstone and Jean-Pierre Thibaut. 1998. The development of features in object concepts. *Behavioral and Brain Sciences* 21:1–54.

Scobbie, James. 2002. Flexibility in the face of incompatible English VOT systems. Paper presented at Eighth Conference on Laboratory Phonology (LABPHON 8).

Shattuck-Hufnagel, Stefanie, and Dennis Klatt. 1979. The limited use of distinctive features and markedness in speech production: Evidence from speech error data. *Journal of Verbal Learning and Verbal Behavior* 18:41–55.

Singh, Sadanand. 1976. *Distinctive features: Theory and validation.* Baltimore, Md.: University Park Press.

Soli, Sigfrid, and Phipps Arabie. 1979. Auditory versus phonetic accounts of observed confusions between consonant phonemes. *Journal of the Acoustical Society of America* 66:46–59.

Steinheiser, Frederick. 1970. Phonemic distinctive feature encoding from visual information storage. Doctoral dissertation, University of Cincinnati.

Steriade, Donca. 1995. Underspecification and markedness. In *The handbook of phonological theory*, ed. by John Goldsmith, 114–174. Cambridge, Mass.: Blackwell.

Stevens, Kenneth N. 1995. Applying phonetic knowledge to lexical access. In *Proceedings of Eurospeech '95*, ed. by José Pardo, 1:3–10. Madrid: European Speech Communication Association.

Stevens, Kenneth N. 2003. Acoustic and perceptual evidence for universal phonological features. In *Proceedings of the 15th International Congress of Phonetic Sciences, Barcelona, 3–9 August 2003*, ed. by Maria-Josep Solé, Daniel Recasens, and Joaquín Romero, 33–38. Rundle Mall, Australia: Causal Productions (CD-ROM); Barcelona: Futurgraphic (print).

Stevens, Kenneth N., and Dennis Klatt. 1974. Role for formant transitions in the voiced-voiceless distinction for stops. *Journal of the Acoustical Society of America* 55:643–659.

Stokoe, William. 1960. *Sign language structure*. Buffalo, N.Y.: University of Buffalo Press.

Street, John. 1963. *Khalkha structure*. Bloomington: Indiana University Press.

Summerfield, A. Quentin, and Mark Haggard. 1974. Perceptual processing of multiple cues and contexts: Effects of following vowel upon stop consonant voicing. *Journal of Phonetics* 2:279–295.

Svantesson, Jan-Olof. 1985. Vowel harmony shift in Mongolian. *Lingua* 67:283–327.

Taff, Alice, Lorna Rozelle, Taehong Cho, Peter Ladefoged, Moses Dirks, and Jacob Wegelin. 2001. Phonetic structures of Aleut. *Journal of Phonetics* 29:231–271.

Tannahill, Curtis. 1971. An experimental study of consonant discrimination as a function of distinctive feature differences. Doctoral dissertation, University of Kansas.

Tatham, Mark. 1979. Some problems in phonetic theory. In *Current issues in the phonetic sciences*, ed. by Harry Hollien and Patricia Hollien, 93–106. Amsterdam: John Benjamins.

Taylor, James. 1962. *The behavioral basis of perception*. New Haven, Conn.: Yale University Press.

Testut, Eldred. 1980. Distinctive feature analyses of the speech of profoundly hearing impaired children. Doctoral dissertation, University of Oklahoma.

Tettamanti, Marco, Giovanni Buccino, Maria Cristina Saccuman, Vittorio Gallese, Massimo Danna, Paola Scifo, Ferruccio Fazio, Giacomo Rizzolatti, Stefano F. Cappa, and Daniela Perani. 2005. Listening to action-related sentences activates fronto-parietal motor circuits. *Journal of Cognitive Neuroscience* 17:273–281.

Tremblay, Stéphanie, Douglas Shiller, and David Ostry. 2003. Somatosensory basis of speech production. *Nature* 423:866–869.

UCLA Phonetics Lab Archive. http://archive.phonetics.ucla.edu/Language/AMH/amh_word-list_1966_01.html#1, http://archive.phonetics.ucla.edu/Language/AMH/amh_word-list_1966_01.mp3.

Vaux, Bert, and Bridget Samuels. 2004. Explaining vowel systems: Dispersion theory vs. evolution. Paper presented at the annual meeting of the Linguistic Society of America, Boston.

Vaux, Bert, and Bridget Samuels. 2005. Aspiration and laryngeal markedness. *Phonology* 23:395–436.

Wagner, Michael. 2002. The role of prosody in laryngeal neutralization. In *Phonological answers (and their corresponding questions)*, ed. by Anikó Csirmaz, Zhiqiang Li, Andrew Nevins, Olga Vaysman, and Michael Wagner, 357–376. MIT Working Papers in Linguistics 42. Cambridge, Mass.: MIT, MIT Working Papers in Linguistics.

Wall, Nancy. 1976. Foreign accent: A distinctive feature analysis of adult misarticulations. Master's thesis, Utah State University.

Warrington, Elizabeth. 1975. The selective impairment of semantic memory. *Quarterly Journal of Experimental Psychology* 27:635–657.

Warrington, Elizabeth, and Rosaleen McCarthy. 1983. Category specific access dysphasia. *Brain* 106:859–878.

Warrington, Elizabeth, and Rosaleen McCarthy. 1987. Categories of knowledge: Further fractionations and an attempted integration. *Brain* 110:1273–1296.

Warrington, Elizabeth, and Tim Shallice. 1984. Category specific semantic impairments. *Brain* 107:829–853.

Wickelgren, Wayne. 1965. Distinctive features and errors in short term memory for English vowels. *Journal of the Acoustical Society of America* 38:583–588.

Wickelgren, Wayne. 1966. Distinctive features and errors in short term memory for English consonants. *Journal of the Acoustical Society of America* 39:388–398.

Wilks, Yorick. 1976. Parsing English II. In *Computational semantics*, ed. by Eugene Charniak and Yorick Wilks, 155–184. Amsterdam: North Holland.

Williams, Gail, and Leija McReynolds. 1975. The relationship between discrimination and articulation training in children with misarticulations. *Journal of Speech and Hearing Research* 18:401–412.

Williams, Lee. 1977. The voicing contrast in Spanish. *Journal of Phonetics* 5:169–184.

Wimsatt, William. 1976. Reductionism, levels of organization and the mind-body problem. In *Consciousness and the brain*, ed. by Gordon Globus, Grover Maxwell, and Irvine Savodnik, 199–267. New York: Plenum Press.

Winitz, Harris, Conrad LaRiviere, and Eve Herriman. 1975. Variations in VOT for English initial stops. *Journal of Phonetics* 3:41–52.

Wode, H. 1997. Where do features come from? A perception-based approach. In *New Sounds 97: Proceedings of the Third International Symposium on the Acquisition of Second-Language Speech*, ed. by Jonathan Leather and Allan James, 343–350. Klagenfurt, Austria: University of Klagenfurt.

Wunderlich, Dieter. 2004. Is there any need for the concept of directional syncretism? In *Explorations in nominal inflection*, ed. by Lutz Gunkel, Gereon Müller, and Gisela Zifonun, 373–396. Berlin: Mouton de Gruyter.

Žgent'i, S. 1965. Harmonische Komplexe der Konsonanten in der Khartvelischen Sprachen. *Zeitschrift für Phonetik, Sprachwissenschaft und Kommunikationsforschung* 18:143–148.

Zipf, George. 1965. *The psycho-biology of language: An introduction to dynamic philology.* Cambridge, Mass.: MIT Press.

Zwicky, Arnold. 1976. Well, this rock and roll has got to stop. Junior's head is hard as a rock. In *Papers from the Twelfth Regional Meeting, Chicago Linguistic Society, April 23–25, 1976*, ed. by Salikoko Mufwene et al., 676–697. Chicago: University of Chicago, Chicago Linguistic Society.

II The Syllable

5   The Appendix

Bert Vaux and Andrew Wolfe

5.1   Introduction

Work on phonology since the time of the structuralists, and especially since *The Sound Pattern of English* (*SPE*; Chomsky and Halle 1968), has been characterized by tension between on the one hand formalists, who favor abstraction, formal elegance, and explanatory adequacy, and on the other hand functionalists, broadly defined, who favor concreteness and descriptive adequacy. Over the 25 years following *SPE*, formalist theories of rules and representations attained a high level of intricacy, sophistication, and breadth of empirical coverage, but also a degree of abstraction that did not sit well with some of the more phonetically and functionally inclined. The rise in 1993 of Optimality Theory (OT), with its emphasis on naturalness and the avoidance of abstract representational stages, opened the door for the return of phoneticians, functionalists, and other supporters of surface-oriented approaches. This tension shows up clearly in syllable theory, which by 1993 had for many phonologists become highly articulated and abstract, with numerous elements that were not readily apparent in the acoustic signal such as syllables themselves, rimes and nuclear heads, sonority, and unsyllabified segments, as well as principles that were often not surface-true, such as Final Consonant Extraprosodicity (Borowsky 1986, Ito 1986, Iverson 1990, Vaux 2003, etc.) and the Sonority Sequencing Principle (Sievers 1881, Jespersen 1904, Clements 1990, etc.). Since 1993, most phonologists have favored a simple moraic conception of the syllable that ignores the phenomena that gave rise to its more intricate predecessors, and some (see, notably, Ohala 1990, Ohala and Kawasaki-Fukumori 1997, Samuels 2008) have gone so far as to advocate eliminating the syllable and its attendant baggage altogether, citing the absence of clear phonetic correlates for syllable breaks and subconstituents (Nolan 1994), inconsistency of native-speaker intuitions regarding syllabification, unclear motivation for syllabic versus segmental or phonetic conditioning (Steriade 1998, 1999), and so on. On this matter we side with Anderson (1982:546), who states that if we ask for a justification of the notion of phonetic segments, we see quickly that the facts of acoustics and of articulatory co-articulation make it quite impossible to segment and identify the speech stream directly in terms of such units. Their justification comes not from our ability to find them clearly in the physical facts of speech, but rather (like any other theoretical entity) from the degree of coherence and order they bring to our understanding of those facts.... The justification for including syllable structure in our representation cannot possibly be expected to come directly from the observable facts of speech, but rather must derive from the augmentation in our understanding of those facts that results from the assumption of its presence.

In this chapter, we will show how careful examination of a wide range of complex internal and external linguistic facts reveals interesting abstract properties of the phonology. More specifically, we will be dealing with the behavior and representational status of consonants that do not fit neatly into canonical syllable templates, such as the *s* in *stop*, the final [ʁ] in French *mordre*, or the *ktkt* in Klamath [gankənktkt-damna]. Many phonologists have suggested that such consonants do not in fact attach to syllables in the normal way (at least at some point in the derivation), but such stipulations are usually formulated on an ad hoc, language-specific basis, and without regard for the behavior of other phenomena that in different ways also suggest the existence of extrasyllabicity. Our purpose here is to bring together a wide range of linguistic evidence and arguments that have been adduced in support of extrasyllabicity and to synthesize a representational theory that accounts for the subset of these that should be accounted for. We will show that some of the more famous phenomena cited as evidence for the appendix[1] are not actually probative; instead, on the basis of ample other evidence we will suggest that phonological segments can attach to prosodic nodes higher than the syllable, as in (1), and that the specific locus of attachment can vary both between and within languages.

(1) *A word-final appendix*

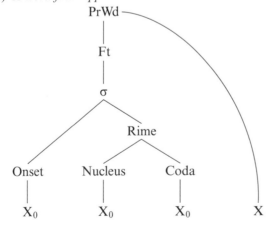

The facts to be explained range from the phonetic, to the phonological (including sonority sequencing, aspiration, glide formation, epenthesis, implicational universals, and prosodic phenomena such as stress assignment, metrical scansion, lengthening, and shortening), to the morphological (reduplication, infixation, syllable-counting rules), to external linguistic phenomena involving child language acquisition, aphasia, and psycholinguistic experiments.

The most prevalent rationale for positing extrasyllabicity comes from an examination of sonority sequencing. From as early as Whitney 1865, linguists have ranked speech sounds by relative sonority or stricture (for a brief historical review, see Clements 1990:284). The Sonority Sequencing Generalization, or Sonority Sequencing Principle (henceforth SSP), as it is often named in the recent literature, captures the basic crosslinguistic fact that syllables rise in sonority through the onset to the syllable peak, then fall in sonority through the coda. Stating the SSP as a linguistic universal rather than a tendency makes definite predictions about the nature of the syllable, but it leaves numerous counterexamples to be accounted for parsimoniously. We will examine data providing evidence of the nontautosyllabicity of clusters that violate the SSP.

Linguists have long allowed for other forms of extrasyllabicity, as well, that are not motivated by violation of the SSP. As surveyed by Iverson (1990), cases of extraprosodicity, in which final segments do not count toward weight, often prompt the use of extrasyllabic measures—for instance, in Cairene Arabic, where CVC syllables are heavy in medial but not final position (Kiparsky 2003). Other phonological and morphological rules such as English's closed-syllable shortening have been formulated to refer to extrasyllabic segments at some derivational stage (Kenstowicz 1994:261). Treiman, Gross, and Cwikiel-Glavin (1992) argue on the basis of their psycholinguistic experiments that English s + sonorant clusters, though of rising sonority, are nontautosyllabic. The same holds for Nxaʔamxcín OR clusters (Czaykowska-Higgins and Willett 1997).[2] Segments that cannot be incorporated into a syllable given a language's inventory of possible core syllables, as well as segments affected by Final Consonant Extraprosodicity, may be formalized as appendices even when their inclusion in neighboring syllables does not violate the SSP. We take note of these approaches below, but our focus remains primarily on those deriving from SSP violations, the complementary set to those reviewed by Iverson (1990).

Conversely, some apparent phenomena bundled into this inquiry are illusory and should not be explained. Marlo (2004) suggests that speakers allow particular extrasyllabic segments that are required by the morphology; for instance, English allows extrasyllabic [t] in *apt* because of the past tense marker [t].[3] While this hypothesis may or may not obtain in the English, Spokane Salish, or Sipakapense Maya data adduced by Marlo, it does not, for instance, apply in French *s*C- clusters, as French has no [s] morpheme.[4] Scheer (2004) claims that only one extrasyllabic segment may appear per extrasyllabic sequence, but one need look no further than Polish (*krtań* 'larynx', etc.) to counter this contention, not to mention Spokane Salish [sčkʷλ'kʷλ'] 'little eyes'.[5] Most work on extrasyllabicity assumes that extrasyllabic segments are limited to the word periphery (e.g., Clements 1990, Rubach and Booij 1990a, Scheer 2004, McCarthy 2005), since word-internal sequences such as VLOV will be syllabified VL.OV rather than V.LOV. While extrasyllabicity may be more common at word or morpheme edges, this premise does not hold universally. Numerous examples defy this hypothesis, such as English *extra* and *abstract*, or Klamath [gankənktktdamna]. Likewise, many scholars have proposed restricting extrasyllabic segments to coronals, or to some other specific subset of the phonemic inventory (Hall 2002, Kiparsky 2003, and many others). While one may justifiably limit extrasyllabic sequences to the class of coronal segments in a language-particular setting (e.g., in English[6]), it is not our aim here to explicate the constraints of any one language but to propose that the formal device of the appendix best covers the breadth of what is attested, which includes Nxaʔamxcín [pʰtiχʷ] 'spit', Armenian [kurtskʰ] 'breast', French [mɛtχ] 'meter', and so on. Even in a language-particular setting, arguments for a theory of extrasyllabicity that are based on static phonotactic distribution (e.g., "Only coronal segments may be extrasyllabic") rather than phonological processes may be misleading, as distributional gaps may arise from historical accident (Cho and King 2003:186).

Many theories have been proposed to account for the range of extrasyllabic phenomena, as summarized in (2)[7,8], but to the best of our knowledge they have yet to be systematically compared, and the phenomena on which they are based have yet to be considered as a unified set.

(2) *Possible treatments of these consonant sequences and representative diagrams*

  a. Complex margins: More complex onset/coda clusters are allowed at edges of certain prosodic constituents.

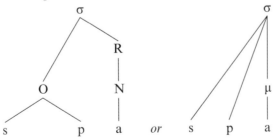

  b. Degenerate syllables: Odd segments belong to syllables lacking nuclei and/or moras.

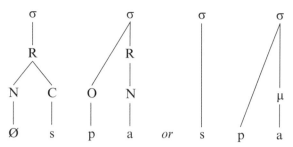

c. Appendices: Segments attach directly to a higher-level prosodic node (normally PrWd).

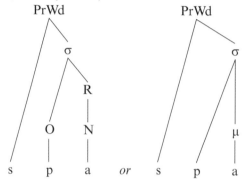

d. Stray segments: Stray segments do not attach to any higher-level prosodic structure.

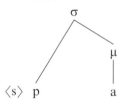

Since theory (2a) is the most concrete of these options, in the sense that it requires no new formal elements, we critique it first in section 5.2. In section 5.3, we lay out our analysis making use of the appendix (2c) and explore how it is represented, including a brief discussion of analyses with permanently stray segments (2d). In section 5.4, we contrast the appendix with degenerate syllable theory (2b). In section 5.5, we offer concluding remarks.

5.2 Complex Onsets and Codas

Appendices, degenerate syllables, and stray segments would not be needed if the consonant sequences in question could be simply included in the onset or coda.

Such a theory can be made to follow naturally from a modified form of Clements's (1992) Dispersion Principle, a sonority-driven algorithm for computing the relative complexity of syllable margins represented in (3) and (4). According to the Dispersion Principle, onsets crosslinguistically prefer to rise sharply and steadily in sonority whereas codas prefer to decline gradually along the sonority scale, which for Clements distinguishes five classes: obstruent, nasal, liquid, glide, and vowel. Thus, evenly distributed initial demisyllables[9] like OLV [bra] and [pla] appear less complex than ONV [bna] and [tma] (obstruent and nasal occupy adjacent spots on the sonority scale) or OGV [bja] and [kwa] (obstruent and glide are separated by two intervening classes). Similarly, glide-vowel demisyllables imply the presence of stop-vowel demisyllables but not vice versa. As for final position, a CVG syllable is simpler, for example, than a CVL syllable, CVL than CVO, and so on. Codas permit less dispersed clusters as in [arm], the reverse of which, [mra], constitutes a relatively more marked onset.

(3) *The Dispersion Principle (Clements 1992)*
    a. The preferred initial demisyllable maximizes sonority dispersion.
    b. The preferred final demisyllable minimizes sonority dispersion.
    c. $D = \Sigma_{i=1 \text{ to } m} 1/d_i^2$ (where D is the measure of a demisyllable's dispersion; m is the number of segments in the demisyllable, including nonadjacent pairs; and d is the distance in sonority rank between members of each pair).

The formula in (3c)[10] forms the basis of a complexity ranking for demisyllables, as in (4).[11]

(4) *Complexity rankings for initial and final demisyllables*

Initial	D	Final	D	
OV	.06	V	—	Least complex
		VGL	2.25	
		VLN, VGN	1.36	
		VNO, VGO	1.17	
NV	.11	VG	1.00	
LV	.25	VL	.25	
OLV	.56	VLO	.56	
GV	1.00	VN	.11	
ONV, OGV	1.17			
NLV, NGV	1.36			
LGV	2.25			
V	—	VO	.06	Most complex

By refining the formula in (3c) to distinguish in sonority between obstruents and fricatives—as we need to already for languages like Imdlawn Tashlhiyt Berber—

and to distinguish positive values for rising sonority and negative values for falling sonority, we can generate values for clusters that violate the SSP, not just well-behaved clusters of the type in (4). The extended complexity hierarchy resulting from these modifications would look something like (5) for initial demisyllables.[12]

(5) *Revised complexity hierarchy for initial demisyllables*

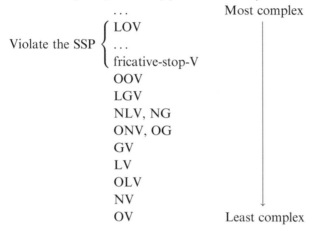

In this scheme, the words *star* and *tsar* would have the representations in (6), wherein both clusters are assigned to complex onsets; the former is simply more complex than the latter.

(6) a.

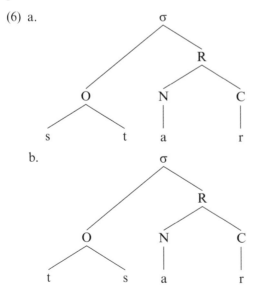

b.

This neo-Clementsian tautosyllabic approach encounters a number of problems on top of the infinity issue mentioned in note 12. Basically, it runs afoul of the fact that *s*T- clusters appear to be less complex than canonical onset clusters. Calabrese and Romani (1998), for instance, find that Italian-speaking aphasics tend to simplify complex onsets but not *s*T clusters. In the realm of first language acquisition, Gierut (1999) observes that children learn *s*T clusters faster than complex onsets.[13] In Pima, infixing reduplication creates less marked syllables (Riggle 2003), but this includes forms like [kosvuɹ] → [koksvuɹ] 'cocoons' and [kuʃva] → [kukʃva] 'lower skulls'. Perceptual studies by Engstrand and Ericsdotter (1999) have shown that *s*T- and -*s*T sequences in fact have a perceptual advantage over onset and coda clusters that obey the SSP. Perhaps most damaging to a theory in which clusters violating the SSP belong to complex onsets is the existence of languages like Acoma that allow supposedly highly complex *s*C- clusters but disallow OC- clusters (Miller 1965, Goad and Rose 2004).[14]

Given the number and severity of these problems, it is reasonable to propose that the quirky segments under consideration do not in fact form tautosyllabic clusters with their more well-behaved neighbors.[15] The same arguments can be leveled against the hypothesis that our quirky consonants form complex monosegments with their neighbors, as has been proposed by Fudge (1969), Selkirk (1982), Iverson and Salmons (1999), Duanmu (2002), and Broselow (e.g., Broselow 1991).

The notion that such clusters are nontautosyllabic is buttressed by ample phonetic and phonological evidence, as we will show for French and several other languages below.

5.3 The Appendix

To deal with this phenomenon of extrasyllabic segments, many linguists have proposed that they instead attach to a higher node in the prosodic hierarchy, as what we will henceforth call an *appendix*. Until recently, this was the favored strategy of phonologists (cf., e.g., Haugen 1956, Fujimura 1979, Kiparsky 1979, Halle and Vergnaud 1980, Fujimura and Lovins 1982, Steriade 1982, Vennemann 1982, 1988, Clements and Keyser 1983, Trommelen 1984, van der Hulst 1984, Charette 1985, Levin 1985, de Haas 1986, Kager and Zonneveld 1986, Wiese 1988, Trommelen and Zonneveld 1989, Davis 1990, Goldsmith 1990, Rubach and Booij 1990a, Giegerich 1992, Hall 1992, Fikkert 1994, Harris 1994, Kenstowicz 1994, Sherer 1994, Spaelti 1994, Vaux 1994, 1998b, 2003, Berens 1996, Spencer 1996:99, Grijzenhout and Joppen 1998, Siptar and Törkenczy 2000, Duanmu 2002, Törkenczy 2003, McCarthy 2005). Supporters of the appendix generally maintain that the SSP holds only over the syllable; appendices, since they do not belong to syllables, are immune to its requirements (see Vennemann 1988). Appendices moreover are constructed by the syllabification algorithm only as a last resort (Törkenczy 2003); many derivational phonologists combine this postulate with rule ordering to get certain rules to ignore appendices, as with English Shortening, and to get certain other rules to treat the appendix as part of the coda, as in German final devoicing (see Kiparsky 1981, Hayes 1985, Bagemihl 1991, Clements 1992:64). While we leave open the possibility of late adjunction, the lines of reasoning pursued below do not require it.

5.3.1 Evidence for the Appendix

Some researchers have been reluctant to accept the appendix hypothesis, because it violates the Strict Layering Hypothesis (Selkirk 1984), requires a formal addition to the set of representational primitives provided by the core syllabification algorithm, and sometimes seems to contradict native-speaker intuitions about syllable affiliations. Why then do we need such a formal device? Many different sorts of evidence, both internal and external, have been adduced in its defense; in the next part of this chapter, we survey the range of phenomena most commonly invoked.

5.3.1.1 External Evidence In addition to the internal phonological and morphological evidence, which we find the most compelling and will therefore focus on at the end of this chapter, there is a host of external evidence for the appendix in the domains of child and aphasic speech production, psycholinguistic experiments and adult speech errors, language typology, and metrical scansion.

5.3.1.1.1 Child Language Errors Numerous studies have found that a significant subset of children acquiring English, Dutch, and German go through a stage where their treatment of initial clusters displays what Goad and Rose (2004) call the Head Pattern, wherein s + stop and stop + sonorant clusters retain the stop but s + sonorant clusters retain the sonorant, as depicted in (7).

(7) *The Head Pattern (Goad and Rose 2004)*
   a. OR → O, sO → O, sR → R
   b. Dutch (Fikkert 1994, Gilbers and den Ouden 1994), English (Velten 1943, Smith 1973), German (Elsen 1991)
      i. English blow → bo, spun → pun, slug → lug (Smith 1973)
      ii. German klein → [kain], Spiegel → [pigəl], snell → [nel] (Elsen 1991)

Spencer (1986) and Goad and Rose (2004) interpret this phenomenon in terms of a preference for structural heads to survive, which relies on a theory of syllable structure in which the /s/ in sC clusters is an appendix whereas all initial OR clusters are onsets.[16]

5.3.1.1.2 Aphasic Speech Calabrese and Romani (1998) find similar patterns in the speech of the Italian aphasic DB, who tends to simplify complex onsets (8) but makes only one error with sT clusters out of 391 initial clusters of this type.

(8) *Percentages of deletion errors according to cluster type, ranked from least to most*
    complex according to Clements's hierarchy (from Calabrese and Romani 1998)

Cluster type	Percentage errors	Number of errors/chances	
a. OL	2.1	24/1161	Least complex
b. OG	7.0	61/865	
c. NG	16.3	17/104	
d. LG	34.4	136/396	Most complex
e. OO	0.26	1/391	(Appendix)

The data from child and aphasic speech production thus suggest that $s +$ stop clusters are qualitatively different from initial clusters of rising sonority, which we can straightforwardly capture by assuming that the former are nontautosyllabic whereas the latter are tautosyllabic.

5.3.1.1.3 Psycholinguistic Evidence A wide range of psycholinguistic experiments manipulating word chunks support the same division. For instance, Treiman, Gross, and Cwikiel-Glavin (1992) found in a battery of three syllable-manipulation tasks that English speakers treat *s*T and *s*R clusters but not TR clusters as nontautosyllabic, and suggested on this basis that initial *s*-clusters are syllabified with an appendix. Prior examination of English speakers' hyphenation of polysyllabic words by Treiman and Zukowski (1990) had shown that speakers intuitively group medial TR clusters together, as in *Madrid* (85% of subjects hyphenated it *Ma-drid*), but break up medial *s*T clusters, as in *estate* (69% divided it *es-tate*). Treiman, Gross, and Cwikiel-Glavin (1992) expanded this in their first experiment to nonwords *nuspeem* and *nu-fleem*, finding 68% and 62% preferences, respectively, for an analogous syllable division. Oral syllabification tasks reported in both Treiman and Zukowski 1990 and Treiman, Gross, and Cwikiel-Glavin 1992 produced similar results (55% for *nus-peem* and 46% for *nu-fleem*).[17] A third experiment specifically tested vowel reduction in the production of nonwords *wospeem* and *wofleem*, with the expectation that a strong initial syllable would be protected from reduction (Fudge 1984, Hayes 1985). Comparing only those cases where the subject stressed the second syllable, more than five times as many subjects left the first vowel of *wospeem* full ([wɑspˈim] 22%) than reduced it to schwa ([wəspˈim] 4%), suggesting a syllable break of *wospeem*. Reduction was more common for *wofleem* than for *wospeem* ([wəflˈim] 11%), although more of the subjects chose not to reduce the vowel ([wɑflˈim] 15%).

Similarly, Treiman and Fowler (1991) used a speeded task in which subjects had to move just the first consonant of a consonant cluster. They found that *s* clusters were easier to break up than clusters of rising sonority. Finally, Stemberger and Treiman (1986) found that *s* is more likely to be lost in speech errors than are the first consonants of initial clusters of rising sonority.

Most recently, Pierrehumbert and Nair (1995) taught test subjects a language game that infixes [ət] at beginning of word, as in *log* → *l*[ət]*og*. Training stimuli contained only monoconsonantal onsets. Interestingly, they found that when asked to apply the game to forms beginning in complex onsets, their subjects tended to insert the [ət] sequence inside obstruent + liquid clusters, but after *s* + stop clusters, suggesting that the *s* in such clusters is not tautosyllabic with the stop.

All of these psycholinguistic results support the hypothesis that *s* + stop clusters are nontautosyllabic in English.

5.3.1.1.4 Typology As mentioned briefly above, the existence of languages that allow appendices but do not allow complex onsets suggests that the two have distinct prosodic structures. The presence of one does not imply the presence of the other. In the native vocabulary of Acoma (Miller 1965),[18] the syllable inventory comprises CV and CVV syllables but no CVC or CCV(V). The only systematic exception to this is *s*O clusters, as shown in (9).[19]

(9) *Acoma nontautosyllabic clusters*

    a. <u>sb</u>úuná   'pottery'
       <u>sp</u>aat'i   'mockingbird'
       <u>sd</u>ák'aci   'tangled hair'
       <u>sk</u>'aašu   'fish'
    b. w'ii<u>sp</u>'i   'cigarette'
       ʔúča<u>st</u>áan'i 'walking cane'
       su<u>st</u>'á   'I took water'
       ʔúu<u>sd</u>yúuci   'drum'
       gui<u>st</u>yasa   'knot'
       <u>sk</u>úuy'u   'giant'
       ʔé<u>sg</u>á   'rawhide'

The full array of 12 stop phonemes, with the possible exception of the glottalized palatal, appears with a preceding *s*. It is interesting to note that none of Acoma's 10 sonorants ([m, n, w, r, y] and their glottalized counterparts) are found directly following *s*, the combination of which would form a complex onset according to the SSP.

A similar example is found in Ladakhi (Koshal 1979, Bell and Saka 1983), which allows initial liquid-obstruent clusters (/lg-/, /lz-/, /rb-/, /rg-/, etc.) but not the reverse.

5.3.1.1.5 Metrical Scansion In the domain of metrical scansion, it is well-known at least since Steriade 1982 that Classical Greek treats noncanonical clusters such as *gn*, *sm*, and *kt* as nontautosyllabic, even in word-initial position; at the phrase level, light CV syllables preceding such clusters are resyllabified as heavy CVC syllables (see Green 2003 for a summary of the facts). These metrical facts of course cannot reveal anything about the syllabification of such clusters in absolute initial position, but their behavior in other positions is consistent with their initial members' being appendices, especially when considered in tandem with the arguments in section 5.2 against their being tautosyllabic.

5.3.1.2 Internal Evidence
Even more persuasive than this suite of external evidence is the wide range of internal phonetic, phonological, and morphophonological evidence supporting the existence of appendices. This evidence ranges from coarticulation to weight-based phenomena such as shortening, lengthening, and stress assignment to phonological rules sensitive to syllable affiliation or position to prosodic morphological processes such as reduplication, infixation, and truncation.

5.3.1.2.1 Phonetics
Two sorts of phonetic arguments have been adduced in support of extrasyllabicity, both involving the degree of cohesion between neighboring segments. Huffman (1972) and Lovins (1977) found that falling-sonority initial clusters in Cambodian have a "weak intruded vocalism" between their segments, suggesting a looser connection of the outer segments of these clusters to the rest of the syllable.[20] More persuasive is Rialland's finding that French extrasyllabic consonants do not show the same degree of coarticulation with following segments as complex onsets do (1994:136). In French, onset but not coda consonants coarticulate with a tautosyllabic vowel, whether or not other consonants intervene, so for example in forms like *oucri* [ukʁi], *k* shows significant effects from the *i*, despite the intervening liquid (Zerling 1981, Vaissière 1988, Rialland 1994:144). Crucially, comparable coarticulation does not appear with appendices, as with the *k* in *knout* [k.nut] 'short whip'. These facts make good sense if we assume that coarticulation effects of the relevant sort are syllable-bound, and segments like the *k* in [knut] are extrasyllabic.[21]

5.3.1.2.2 Phonotactics and Sonority
Moving to phonological lines of reasoning, one of the favorite arguments for appendices in the literature involves phonotactics. Such arguments are closely linked to the theory of the sonority hierarchy and the Sonority Sequencing Principle. As Blevins (1995:240) observes for Klamath, "Attested word-initial clusters do not appear to be constrained by any version of the SSG, as they include sonorant-obstruent clusters.... Rather than weaken the theory of syllable structure to allow blatant sonority violations, word-initial segments which cannot be syllabified are extraprosodic."

Many languages allow more complex clusters (in terms of sonority sequencing) at word edges; Blevins (1995:219) cites Totonac, English, Nisqually, Gilyak, Tamazight Berber, Cairene Arabic, Spanish, Dakota, Italian, and Mokilese as allowing more complex final clusters, and Klamath, Sedang, Italian, and Piro as allowing more complex initial clusters; this list can be expanded ad infinitum. Arguments for the existence of appendices based on phonotactic distribution include those adduced by Chierchia (1986) for Italian, Pierrehumbert (1994) for English, Green (2003) for Irish, and many more.

5.3.1.2.3 Phonological Rules   In our opinion, though, static sonority-related phonotactics are not entirely convincing; evidence of active phonological processes sensitive to corresponding differences in prosodic structure is more persuasive. Rialland (1994) provides a convincing array of such cases for French, summarized in (10)–(14).

First, she shows that glide formation optionally applies to the first of two vowels if the onset contains only one consonant. Since French allows only CL and CG complex onsets, the resultant CG onset of C + glide formation is permitted (10a), whereas with CL onsets, glide formation cannot occur, as it would produce an ungrammatical CLG onset (10b). The fact that forms like *skier* and *ptyaline* allow glide formation (10c) shows that their initial consonant is not part of the same syllable as the glide.

(10) *French glide formation (Rialland 1994:137)*
   a. C onset   lier 'to bind' [lje] ∼ [lije], nouer 'to tie' [nwe] ∼ [nue]
   b. CL onset   plier 'to fold' [plije] not *[plje]
   c. Appendix   skier 'to ski' [skje] ∼ [skije], ptyaline 'ptyalin' [ptjalin] ∼ [ptijalin]

(11) *Rialland's representation of extrasyllabicity in* skier *(1994:138)*

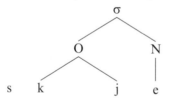

Second, laxing changes /ə/ and /e/ to [ɛ] in closed syllables, as in (12) (Selkirk 1972, Dell 1995). Cases like the initial [e] in *étriqué* [e.tʁi.ke] 'tight' (12b) show that OL clusters form licensed onsets (i.e., it is not *[ɛt.ʁi.ke]); the fact that *s*C clusters by contrast normally trigger laxing as in *espérer* [ɛs.pe.ʁe] 'to hope' (12c) suggests that they are not tautosyllabic, and is consistent with the extrasyllabic analysis in (11).[22]

(12) *French closed-syllable laxing (Rialland 1994:139–140)*
   a. [ə] and [e] only in open syllables; → [ɛ] in closed syllables
   b. CL: étriqué [e.tʁi.ke] *[ɛt.ʁi.ke] 'tight'
   c. *s*C: espérer [ɛs.pe.ʁe] 'to hope'

Rialland (1994:140) notes that medial C in CCC and CCCL clusters is extrasyllabic, as in *expert* [ɛk.s.pɛʁ] and *expier* [ɛk.s.pje] 'to expiate'. Dell (1995) disagrees, claiming that in such cases, *s* belongs in the following onset, but this does not square with a case such as *expier* in which glide formation can apply as well.

Third, word-final liquids can optionally delete before a consonant or pause, but only when syllabified as appendices, as in *arbre* 'tree' (Rialland 1994:149, Dell 1995). Fourth, the optional rule of schwa deletion between identical segments followed by a liquid or glide, as in (13a), is not allowed before extrasyllabic consonants, as in (13b).

(13) *French schwa deletion with geminates (Rialland 1994:153)*
    a. Optional schwa deletion allowed / C_1__C_1(L,G)
        il viendra c(e) soir [. . . sswaʁ]
        il n'y a pas d(e) drap [. . . paddʁa]
    b. Not allowed before extrasyllabic consonant
        *il n'a jamais pratiqué c(e) sport *[. . . sspɔʁ]

Fifth, French contrasts single consonants with their false geminate counterparts at word boundaries, as shown in (14), but does not allow this contrast when the second member is extrasyllabic.

(14) *French false geminates at word boundary (Rialland 1994:154)*
    a. / __ V   *laisse s'établir* [lɛsse . . .] 'allows to become established'
    b. / __ CL, CG   *un bac crevé* [. . . bakkʁə . . .] 'a ruptured tank'
    c. Disallowed before extrasyllabic C   *laisse strier* 'allows to striate' does not contrast with *laisse trier* 'allows to select'

Finally, the phoneme /r/ is realized as a glide in coda position (Simon 1967). When the schwa is deleted in cases such as *On r(e)commence?* [ɔ̃ʁkɔmãs] 'Shall we start again?', one would expect the initial *r* to syllabify as a coda. The fact that it surfaces as a uvular trill, not a glide, suggests that it is not a coda; since French phonotactics prevent it from resyllabifying into the onset of the following syllable as well, it must be extrasyllabic.

5.3.1.2.4 Syllable Weight Many prosodic phenomena in various languages support Rialland's arguments for the appendix, such as Italian and Icelandic vowel lengthening in stressed open syllables (Chierchia 1986, Harris and Gussmann 1998, Green 2003). In Icelandic (Green 2003, from earlier sources), metrical lengthening requires stressed (i.e., initial) open syllables to contain a long vowel. Only steep-rising clusters of *s* or stop + *r* or glide are tautosyllabic internally; these clusters syllabify as onsets for the second syllable, triggering lengthening in the open first syllable (15a). The first consonant of medial heterosyllabic clusters, however, closes the first syllable so that the environment for lengthening does not obtain (15b). All other clusters that are permitted initially (e.g., *s* or stop + *l/n*, nasal or liquid + *j*) are heterosyllabic internally (15c). Most interestingly, in one-syllable words, single word-final consonants and most word-final consonant clusters do not count toward determining vowel length (15d) (Harris and Gussmann 1998, Green 2003). As Thráinsson (1994:150) concludes, "Either we need a more sophisticated theory of syllables, namely one that does not consider final consonants and certain final consonant clusters part of the preceding syllable in some sense, or the length of stressed vowels in Icelandic does not depend on syllable boundaries." Under the strong hypothesis, the length of stressed vowels in Icelandic is, in fact, predictable from the syllable boundaries, given final consonant (or perhaps final coda) extrasyllabicity. Cases such as [knai.va] in (15c) show that Icelandic at least appears to allow extrasyllabic segments in those initial clusters that are heterosyllabic medially (i.e., [k.nai.va]).

(15) *Icelandic*
   a. tʰr: [bɛː.tʰrɪ] 'better'
   b. nt: [pan.ta] 'order' (not *[paː.nta])
   c. [knai.va] 'to project', but [ɛk.na] 'to bait' (not *[ɛː.kna])
   d. [tʰaːl] 'number', [snyːpr] 'scolding', etc.

Conversely, English and Wolof closed-syllable shortening does not apply in final syllables (e.g., *dream* /drɛːm/ → [driːm], *dreamt* /drɛːm-t/ → [drɛmt]), suggesting that a word-final consonant is extrasyllabic in these languages, at least at the stage in the derivation where shortening applies (Charette 1985, Kenstowicz 1994:261).

In another similar case, Hayes (1985) and Blevins (1995:240–241) note that Cairene Arabic stress rules treat CVC as light word-finally, but heavy word-internally. This is best explained by assuming a rule of word-final consonant extrametricality, $C \rightarrow \langle C \rangle \, / \, \_\#\#$.

(16) *Cairene Arabic stress assignment*

	Nonfinal	*Final*
CV	light	light
CVC	heavy	light
CV:	heavy	heavy
CVCC	heavy	heavy

In the cases of Icelandic, English, Wolof, and Cairene Arabic examined in this section, the primary argument for extrasyllabicity has centered on segments that do not violate the SSP, such as the [l] of Icelandic [tʰaːl] and the [m] of *dream*. While scholars have adduced these sorts of arguments in favor of extrasyllabicity and of the formalism of the appendix, our primary lines of support are drawn from evidence involving SSP violations.

5.3.1.2.5 Rules That Refer to Syllable Affiliation or Position Rules that refer to syllable affiliation or position can also sometimes be used to identify appendices. The most famous case of this type is Italian *raddoppiamento sintattico*, but this turns out to be problematic for various reasons and hence will not be considered here (see McCrary 2002 for further details). A better example is aspiration in Nxaʔamxcín, which applies to voiceless stops everywhere but in syllable onsets (17b). The fact that the initial *p* in 'spit' and the initial *kt* in 'I covered it' in (17a) all aspirate suggests that they are not in the onset with the following unaspirated stops, from which we can conclude that they must be extrasyllabic. The facts in (17) fall out nicely if one assumes maximal CVC syllables + extrasyllabicity, as suggested by Czaykowska-Higgins and Willett (1997), following Bagemihl (1991).

(17) *Nxaʔamxcín aspiration (Czaykowska-Higgins and Willett 1997:405)*

    a. pʰtiχʷ   'spit'
        kʰtʰpanaʔəʔan   'I covered it'
    b. ʔarasikʷʰ   'turtle'
        t'ʌkʷʰpʰ   'burst'
        qʷupʰsaʔ   'great-great-grandparent/child'

Davidsen-Nielsen (1974) has suggested that the English aspiration rule can also be used as a diagnostic for syllabification, under the assumption that it targets syllable-initial voiceless stops (see Kahn 1976). If, for example, the /s/ of *fastidious* belongs to the first syllable, then the *t* should aspirate since it begins the second syllable. Davidsen-Nielsen concludes that since such *t*'s are normally unaspirated, these words are divided before the *s*.[23] There are a few problems with this analysis, though. First, if Fudge (1984) and others are right that English unstressed vowel reduction happens in open but not closed syllables, then the *s* in *fastidious*, *gastronomy*, and so on, should attach to the preceding syllable. Second, as the cases in (18) illustrate, aspiration appears to be the elsewhere case in English, failing to surface on voiceless stops only when overridden by more specific rules like flapping and glottalization. Were it not the elsewhere case, we would have trouble deriving cases of non-syllable-initial aspiration like the one in (18b).

(18) *English aspiration*

    a. [pʰətʰero] 'potato'
    b. [hætʰ] ~ [hæʔt̚] 'hat'
    c. [dɪ.stɛnd] vs. [dɪs.tʰest] 'distend', 'distaste'
    d. [wɪs.kʰɑn.sn̩] vs. [wə.skɑn.sn̩] 'Wisconsin'

Third, Kim (1970) has demonstrated that the voiceless stop in *s*T clusters is actually produced with [spread glottis], even though this articulatory specification does not produce its normal acoustic correlate, aspiration. If the voiceless stops in words like *ski* actually undergo the aspiration rule, then we cannot use its effects as evidence for syllabic affiliation.

The picture is further complicated by the data in (18c,d), which indicate that (contrary to popular belief) stops sometimes do show up with acoustic aspiration after *s*, as in *distaste* and exophonic *Wisconsin*. It appears that there is a nontrivial mismatch between the phonological feature [spread glottis] and its primary acoustic correlate, aspiration. We suggest a resolution along the lines proposed in *SPE* and Iverson and Salmons 1995, wherein all of the stops are specified as [spread glottis] when not superseded by competing phonological rules, and this feature specification surfaces in different guises according to the prosodic context. Specifically, let us assume the syllabifications in (18c,d) and the representations in (19)—in which with bound morphemes *s* adjoins to the foot and shares its [spread glottis] specification with the following stop—and let us postulate that one of the phonetic realization rules for [spread glottis] in English is that it surfaces as degree-zero aspiration (i.e., no aspiration) when preceded by tautopodic *s*. With these assumptions, one should find appendix *s* only at the beginnings of words or of stressed syllables. It is not clear how one could derive this intricate set of facts without assuming that *s* can be an appendix.

(19) *Relevant representations*
   a. distend

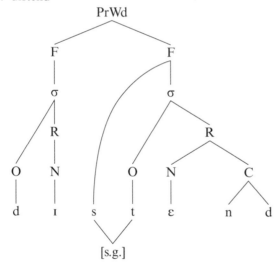

b. distaste

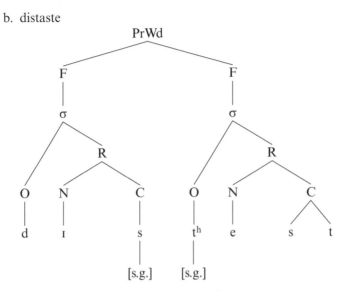

5.3.1.2.6 Prosodic Morphological Processes Let us turn next to prosodic morphological processes that provide evidence for extrasyllabicity.

5.3.1.2.6.1 Reduplication The most famous cases involve partial reduplication in Greek, Sanskrit, and Bella Coola, as outlined in (20)–(23).

The Greek perfect aspect (Steriade 1982:197) copies the initial consonant of the verbal base if it is syllabified, employing it as the onset of the fixed vowel -e- (20a); if the initial consonant is extrasyllabic, no copying takes place, and the -e- is prefixed to the base (20b).[24]

(20) *Greek*

	Verb	*Gloss*	*Perfect aspect*
a.	graphō	'to write'	ge-graph-
	thlibō	'to oppress'	te-thlib-
	krinō	'to judge'	ke-krin-
	plēroō	'to fill'	pe-plēro-
	traumatizō	'to wound'	te-traumatis-
	phrissō	'to shudder'	pe-phris-
	chrusō (chrusoō)	'to gild'	ke-chruso-
b.	skandalizō	'to cause to be caught'	e-skandalis-
	speirō	'to sow'	e-spar-
	stephanō (stephanoō)	'to crown'	e-stephano-
	sphragizō	'to seal'	e-sphragis-
	strateuō	'to do military service'	e-strateu-
	schizō	'to split'	e-schis-

mnēsteuō	'to betroth'	e-mnēsteu-
bdelussō	'to abhor'	e-bdelus-
ktizō	'to create'	e-ktis-
ksērainō	'to dry'	e-ksēra-
phtheirō	'to destroy'	e-phthar-
psōriō (psōriaō)	'to have a rough surface'	e-psōria-

Compare Spokane Salish, which makes use of a similar form of reduplication with fixed segmentism: its repetitive infix /-e-/ (realized as [a] if followed by a uvular anywhere in the word) is preceded by a copy of the root-initial consonant as in (21a), but if the initial consonant is unsyllabified, the copy attaches to its right as in (21b).

(21) *Spokane Salish repetitive formation (Bates and Carlson 1992:654)*
    a. √šil 'chop' → š-e-šil 'chopped repeatedly'
                REP-chop
    b. √ptaχ^w 'spit' → s-n-p-e-taχ^w-mn → (sn')pataχ^wm'n' 'spittoon'
              NOM-in-REP-spit-INSTR

These data suggest that the initial consonants in (20b) and (21b) are extrasyllabic. Similar reasoning holds for the Sanskrit and Bella Coola cases in (22)–(23), where extrasyllabic material evades duplication.

(22) *Sanskrit (e.g., Steriade 1982, Frampton 2007)*
    a. du-droh-   'be hostile'
    b. si-ṣṇeh-   'be sticky'
    c. ti-ṣṭha-   'stand'

(23) *Bella Coola (Nater 1984, 1990, Bagemihl 1991)*
    a. OO   pɬa

b. (C)OR	stn	s-tn-tni	'tree-diminutive'
	pɬtkn-ɬp	pɬt-kn-kn-ɬp	'bitter cherry tree'
	sma	sm-sma	'tell a story'

According to Bagemihl's (1991) analysis, Bella Coola reduplication involves prefixing a reduplicative template (e.g., CV) to the initial (core) syllable, a maximally CRVC syllable built around the word's first sonorant or vowel. Consonants preceding that first core syllable remain unsyllabified.

    Though the extrasyllabic approach to the reduplication facts is appealing, it encounters at least one problem, namely, that it is also possible to analyze the same facts in terms of ignoring the prosodic structure of the base and fitting as much segmental material into the reduplicant syllable as possible, subject to reduplicant-specific markedness constraints. If one is justified in having such morpheme-specific constraints, as practitioners of OT assume, then these reduplicative processes say nothing about the syllable structure of the base, as Carlson (1997) and Cho and King (2003) point out.

5.3.1.2.6.2 Infixation We believe that Nxaʔamxcín infixation may circumvent the domain-specific markedness arguments that practitioners of OT could employ against the extrasyllabic analysis of reduplication and truncation. As can be seen in (24), various reduplicative processes in Nxaʔamxcín are infixational in character, and Czaykowska-Higgins and Willett (1997) demonstrate that the locus of infixation can be characterized insightfully if one assumes extrasyllabicity and core syllabification almost identical to that proposed for Bella Coola by Bagemihl. An allomorph of the inchoative morpheme, shown in (24a), appears as a glottal stop after the first vowel in CVC roots (24ai) and as an epenthetic [a] + glottal stop after the first consonant in CCVC roots (24aii). Czaykowska-Higgins and Willett generalize the process as infixing the glottal stop after the first mora of the foot, whether that is the first vowel (as in CVC roots) or the first moraic extrasyllabic consonant (as in CCVC roots). The same generalization applies in the out of control reduplication shown in (24b),[25] which copies the second consonant into the same position—after the first mora—in CVC (24bi) and in CCVC (24bii). The C_1C_2 of a CCVC root in Nxaʔamxcín cannot, it is argued, form a complex onset, because infixation never breaks up complex onsets. Another reduplicative process, characteristic, shown in (24c), suffixes the reduplicant syllable to the first maximal syllable of the root.[26] In CVC syllables and CVCC alike, it surfaces after C_2. Thus, where the reduplicative processes of inchoative and out of control delimit the onset of the root's core syllable, characteristic reduplication demarcates its coda.

(24) *Nxaʔamxcín infixation (Czaykowska-Higgins and Willett 1997)*
       a. *Inchoative infixation (pp. 394–395)*
            i. p'iq →   p'iʔq   'gets warm'
            ii. c'q'ʷunm →   c'aʔq'ʷunm'   'read'
       b. *Out of control reduplication (p. 395)*
            i. cək →   cəkək   'get hit'
               q'al'xʷ →   q'al'l'xʷ   'something hanging'
            ii. tkay →   tkkayi   'urinate out of control'
               ptiχʷ-mix →   pttiχʷəxʷ   'spitting a lot'
       c. *Characteristic reduplication (p. 402)*
            q'il →   q'il-q'il-t   'it hurts'
            picχʷ →   pic-pic-χʷ-t   'disgusting'

Much recent work on reduplication has centered on the principle of the emergence of the unmarked (TETU; McCarthy and Prince 1995), according to which reduplicants tend to feature less marked structures than in the language in general. Lines of reasoning that argued for a language's syllable structure from the structure of its reduplicants (see Bagemihl 1991 for Bella Coola) were rendered obsolete (see Carlson 1997). In the Nxaʔamxcín data examined above, however, we base our maximal CVC syllable analysis on the locus for infixation. Picking a locus for infixation does not involve identifying a set of reduplicant-specific markedness constraints. One can come up with another, unrelated set of constraints to select the infixational locus, but this loses the connection between the various infixational and reduplicative processes that was captured in the extrasyllabic analysis.

5.3.1.2.6.3 Morpheme Selection   Another phenomenon at the morphology-phonology nexus that is relevant to extrasyllabicity involves rules of vocabulary insertion that are sensitive to the phonological content of the bases to which they are added. One can find rules of this type that distinguish between appendices and syllabified clusters, such as those forming the Spanish diminutive (Harris 1983:5), the Polish comparative (Booij and Lieber 1993), the Homshetsma tree suffix (Berens 1996), and the Armenian plural. As Vaux (2003) argues, Armenian generally selects one plural allomorph for monosyllabic stems and another for all other stems, but in Western Armenian the selection process ignores appendices whereas in Eastern Armenian it does not. Some representative forms and representations are provided in (25)–(29).

(25) *Western Armenian plurals (Istanbul dialect)*

	Singular	*Plural*	*Gloss*
a.	tsʰi	tsʰi-eɾ	'horse'
	kʰaɾ	kʰaɾ-eɾ	'rock'
	kʰiɾ-kʰ	kʰiɾ-kʰ-eɾ	'book'
	asdʁ	asdʁ-eɾ	'star'
	ɾazm	ɾazm-eɾ	'battle'
	dakʰɾ	dakʰɾ-eɾ	'brother-in-law'
b.	moɾukʰ	moɾukʰ-neɾ	'beard'
	jeɾeχa	jeɾeχa-neɾ	'child'

Several of the forms in (25) include SSP violations, but for Istanbul Armenian, the decision of which plural morpheme to select comes down to the number of syllables (or, formally, syllable nodes) in the word. Words with a single syllable node take [eɾ] as a plural marker; words with multiple syllables use [neɾ].

(26) *Vocabulary insertion rules governing the plural in Istanbul Armenian*
     In the context [+plural, __]:

     σ   ⇔   -eɾ
     elsewhere   ⇔   -neɾ

The same rules in Eastern Armenian, by contrast, are sensitive to the presence of appendices, as shown in (27).

(27) *Eastern Armenian plural selection with appendices (Atʃarjan 1957, 1971)*

Singular	Plural	Gloss
skizb	skizb-neɾ	'beginning'
spɑ	spɑ-neɾ	'officer'
stɑk	stɑk-neɾ	'money, coin'
stoɾ	stoɾ-neɾ	'window shade'
pɑɾt-kʰ	pɑɾt-kʰ-neɾ	'debt'
kuɾts-kʰ	kuɾts-kʰ-neɾ	'breast'
vɑgɾ	vɑgəɾ-neɾ	'tiger'
astʁ	astʁ-neɾ	'star'

Here, even the nontautosyllabicity of *s*C-clusters triggers the choice of the [neɾ] allomorph, as does that of final obstruent clusters. Only a word in which a single syllable node exhaustively dominates all of the word's segments uses the [eɾ] plural (compare the two-morpheme, one-syllable [giɾ-kʰ] 'book' → [gəɾkʰeɾ] 'books'). For all others, [neɾ] is selected (28).

(28) *Standard Eastern Armenian plural selection*
In the context [+plural, __]:
minimal σ   ⇔   -eɾ
elsewhere ⇔   -neɾ

The prosodic structures of some relevant forms at the time of plural selection—valid for both dialects—appear in (29).[27]

(29) *Prosodic structure in Armenian*
  a. *Initial appendix*

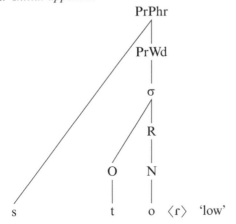

b. *Final appendix*

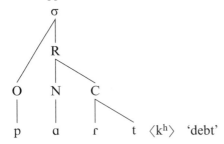

p   ɑ   ɾ   t ⟨kʰ⟩   'debt'

5.3.2 Formal Representation of the Appendix

It should be clear from the phenomena just surveyed that certain segments are clearly not tautosyllabic with their neighbors. How exactly should we capture this fact? Numerous theories have been proposed, which can be lumped into three categories: appendices, degenerate syllables, and stray consonants + lack of Stray Erasure. After briefly addressing the stray consonants option, we focus, in this section and the next, on the two most popular strategies, involving appendices and degenerate syllables.

Although an examination of the logical permutations leads us to the option of leaving extrasyllabic consonants stray without a mechanism of stray erasure, we know of no studied and delineated defense of this approach as such. For example, diagrams in Clements and Keyser 1983, Pierrehumbert 1994, and Grijzenhout and Joppen 1998 include unparsed appendices or extrasyllabic segments, but then again they give no indication of suprasyllabic structure, and the text does not make immediate reference to the question of Stray Erasure. In his remarks on Bagemihl 1991, Cook (1994) argues for limitations on the application of Stray Erasure in Bella Coola, while restricting the environments in which it is needed; in his conclusion he suggests, without further discussion, that the stray extrasyllabic segments that do exist in the language (because of the SSP) may be spared Stray Erasure so as to be pronounced.[28]

Under scrutiny, it becomes clear that leaving segments completely stray is not a viable option. For one, while the present study has largely abstracted away from language-particular constraints on appendices, some languages (Armenian, for example) do restrict which segments can appear in their appendices. What would be the domain over which such restrictions would apply, or the edge to which the markedness constraints would align? Such formulations necessarily make reference to the prosodic hierarchy. If, as it is sometimes presented, it is an appendix node dominating multiple extrasyllabic segments that specifies the features of those segments, then the constituency of such a node must be justified. If such a grouping exists, one would expect to see evidence of its acting in phonological processes as a unit distinct from the coda, the syllable, and the word. Since we do not know of any such evidence, we cannot defend the addition of an appendix node to the prosodic structure, and the problem remains. In addition, the proponent of such a theory would be burdened with proving that no language with SSP violations actually utilized Stray Erasure. Finally, Stemberger and MacWhinney (1984) object that unsyllabified stray consonants do not encode sufficient information for linear order and motor programming (though see Raimy 2000 for a theory of linear precedence that avoids this problem).

Let us then assume that the appendix does attach to the prosodic structure. Where in the prosodic structure should it attach? Almost every conceivable locus has been proposed in the literature, as summarized in (30).[29]

(30) *Loci of appendix attachment*
    a. *Onset* (See Cairns and Feinstein 1982 (for *asparagus*), Steriade 1982, Harris 1983, Calabrese and Romani 1998:92.)
    b. *Coda* (See Hall 1992:122—attached to coda (late in derivation) in German *Jagd* 'hunt', etc., to get devoicing.)
    c. *Mora* (See McCarthy and Prince 1990, Bye 1997. Also used in much OT work as intermediary between extrasyllabic segment and PrWd (moraic licensing); see Hyman 1985 for Gokana, Zec 1988 for Bulgarian, Bagemihl 1991 for Bella Coola, Buckley 1994 for Kashaya, Lin 1995, 1997 for Piro, Czaykowska-Higgins and Willett 1997, Kiparsky 2003.)
    d. *Rime* (See Lapointe and Feinstein 1982, Dell 1995.)
    e. *Syllable* (See Fujimura 1979, Halle and Vergnaud 1980, Cairns and Feinstein 1982, Charette 1985, Giegerich 1992, Sherer 1994, Spencer 1996:98–99, Gierut 1999:709, Törkenczy 2003. Also attached to the syllable in English words like *constable* by van der Hulst (1984), Levin (1985), Zonneveld (1993), Booij (1995), and Goad and Rose (2004), even though some or all of these authors say the default pattern is to attach the appendix to the Prosodic Word; McCarthy (1979) and Harris (1999) use something like Chomsky-adjunction of the appendix to the syllable.)
    f. *Foot* (May be needed for English aspiration and internal appendices. Also see Hagstrom 1997 on Mohawk and Passamaquoddy, Kiparsky 2003:168 on Piro initial geminates, Green 2003 on Irish consonant clusters. NB: Foot attachment does not work for Arabic (unless appendices are nonmoraic), because appendices do not count for prosodic minimality and stress (Kiparsky 2003:160).)
    g. *Prosodic Word* (See Steriade 1982 for Greek, Borowsky 1986, Goldsmith 1990, Rubach and Booij 1990a, Harris 1994:62, Rialland 1994:148, Rubach 1997, Dyck 1999 on Cayuga, Kiparsky 2003:151 on Arabic, Goad and Rose 2004, McCarthy 2005.)
    h. *Prosodic Phrase* (See Vaux 1998b for word-initial appendices in Armenian.)

i. *Variable* (See Rialland 1994:156, Vaux 1994, 1998b, 2003, Green 2003, Kiparsky 2003:153.)

Attaching quirky segments to the syllable or any of its dependents fails to account for the evidence of nontautosyllabicity discussed earlier, so we can immediately eliminate theories (30a–e). Theories in which quirky segments attach to moras (30c) create additional problems. First, appendices do not count for stress, as in Georgian and Polish (Cho and King 2003:206). Second, appendices do not count for weight, as in Der ez-Zor Arabic (Jastrow 1978, Kiparsky 2003:157). Finally, such a theory does not work well for nonmoraic languages.

This leaves us with the Foot, the Prosodic Word, and the Prosodic Phrase. Kiparsky (2003:153) points out that OT, because of violability and free ranking, predicts appendices at any and every level of the prosodic hierarchy, adding (2003:154) that one expects the attachment to be as low in the hierarchy as possible, to avoid greater violations of strict layering. Variability in appendix attachment was already proposed by Rialland (1994) and Vaux (1994), in order to account for schwa deletion + voicing assimilation in French and phrasal syllabification in Armenian, respectively. Green (2003) adduces similar arguments for Irish. Though there is good evidence for appendices at the Foot, Prosodic Word, and Prosodic Phrase levels, it appears that they most often adjoin to the Prosodic Word.

To bring variable appendix attachment to the Prosodic Word and Prosodic Phrase nodes into contrast in French, we now look at voicing assimilation after schwa deletion (Rialland 1994:156). When a consonant left by schwa deletion belongs to the same word as the following consonant, voicing assimilation may apply to it (*s(e)cond* [zgõ] 'second'), but when the two are in separate words, the stranded consonant does not undergo voicing assimilation (*il va t(e) gronder* 'he's going to scold you' [...tg...], not *[...dg...]). These facts follow from an analysis in which word-internal appendices attach to the PrWd node, whereas clitic appendices attach to the PrPhr node. A characteristic representation is shown in (31).

(31) t(e) renverser *(Rialland 1994:156)*

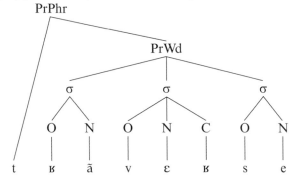

5.4 Degenerate Syllables

The variable appendix theory is not out of the woods yet, though. Several scholars
have objected that it overgenerates, predicting the existence of more cluster types
than actually occur. Broselow (1995) takes issue in particular with the type of moraic
licensing account of extrasyllabicity that Bagemihl (1991) uses for Bella Coola, pointing out that it allows "virtually any sequence of segments" (p. 203) to be a word.
Cho and King (2003:200) specify that Rubach and Booij's (1990a) appendix-based
analysis for Polish makes room for "unlimited obstruent sequences, or multiple
obstruents with stray adjoined segments, such as initial *mpt*, *kpt*, medial *kmnpt*,
kmsnpt," and so on. In a strong and general statement of the argument, Scheer
(2004) cites the lack of cooccurrence restrictions on appendices and proposes that
"as a matter of fact, such monster clusters (as [fdgltprkot]) do not occur at edges of
any natural language."

To address this (apparent) problem, many scholars have suggested that the consonants under consideration here actually belong to degenerate syllables or semisyllables,[30] that is, syllables with a null nucleus (e.g., Fudge 1976, Aoun 1979, Selkirk
1981, Anderson 1982, Svantesson 1983, Kaye and Lowenstamm 1984, McCarthy
and Prince 1990, Burzio 1994, Nepveu 1994, Dell 1995; also used in Government
Phonology, as in Kaye, Lowenstamm, and Vergnaud 1990, Charette 1991, Gussmann and Kaye 1993, Harris 1994, Scheer 2004) or lacking a nuclear position altogether (e.g., Shaw 1993, 1996, Cho 1997, Cho and King 2003, Féry 2003). For many
researchers, the basic idea here is to piggyback on the phonotactic constraints already required for core syllables in order to limit the inventory of possible quirky
segments and sequences. Most practitioners of OT treat semisyllables as onsets,
though they disagree about whether they are attached to moras or not: for Kiparsky
(2003) they are moraic, whereas for Cho and King (2003) and Féry (2003) they are
moraless and attach instead to degenerate syllable nodes.

Degenerate syllable theories encounter several problems. First, their importation
of core syllable phonotactics works well for some languages like French and Polish,
where historical vowel deletion processes have left behind onset clusters, but since
vowel deletion is not the only source of quirky consonant sequences (borrowing,
affixation, and others have also been at work), it constrains some appendices too
much (as in Bella Coola, which basically allows any imaginable appendix sequence)
and some too little (as in Armenian, which has a highly articulated core syllable but
allows only single-segment appendices consisting of *s* or aspirated *k*[h]).

Bella Coola deserves further comment, since it stands out as one of the most striking examples of a language with long strings of unsyllabified consonants (see Bagemihl 1991). Vowelless and nearly vowelless words such as those in (32) have been
attested.

(32) *Bella Coola words*
    a. c'ktskwc'   'he arrived'
    b. q'pssttχ   'taste it'
    c. st'qʷlus   'black bear snare'
    d. ɬχʷtɬcχʷ   'you spat on me'

To address the overgeneration issues brought up above, Cho and King introduce a peripherality condition stating that "there is at most one semisyllable per morpheme edge" (2003:194). Attempting to make Bella Coola syllable structure line up with this peripherality condition, they propose that fricatives in Bella Coola are nuclear; hence, words like [q'pssttχ] syllabify as [q'.psst.tχ]. Bella Coola reduplication processes, however, regularly bypass initial obstruent sequences to construct a reduplicant with the first sonorant or vowel of the word as its peak + a simple onset (and sometimes a simple coda), as in (33).

(33) *Bella Coola reduplication*
    a. qpsta   →   qpstata   'taste'/'taste' (iterative)
        pɬtkn   →   pɬtknkn-ɬp   'bark of bitter cherry tree'/'bitter cherry tree'
        stan   →   stantan-mc   'mother'/'all one's female relatives on the
                                       mother's side'
        p'ɬa   →   p'ɬaɬa   'wink'/'wink' (continuative)
        sma   →   smsma   'story'/'tell a story'
        milixʷ   →   milmilixʷ-ɬp   'bear berry'/'bear berry plant'
    b. *qpspsta
        *pɬpɬtkn
        *p'ɬp'ɬa

To avoid the ungrammatical forms in (33b), Cho and King posit a constraint against fricatives in syllabic peaks that holds only in the reduplicant, in accordance with TETU.

Cho and King's (2003) positive evidence for fricative nuclei proves weak, however. They cite a "preference for fricatives to be syllabified in codas and stops in onsets, as evidenced by alternation among dorsal obstruents," concluding that "in this respect as well, fricatives behave like the syllable peak" (2003:203). The dorsal alternation to which they presumably refer involves the neutralization of dorsal and uvular contrasts among the segments [k, kʷ, q, qʷ, k', kʷ', q', qʷ', x, xʷ, χ, χʷ] to [x] in the coda of the reduplicant. By way of TETU, this only serves to demonstrate the cross-linguistic fact that singly articulated fricatives are less marked in coda position than other obstruents. It has no bearing on syllable peaks or moraic nuclei. Cho and King also point, without supporting evidence, to a disproportionate number of fricatives in vowelless words.

Finally, Cho and King claim that stops fail to aspirate before vowels, sonorants, and fricatives, as in [pɬtʰ] 'thick'. Vaux (1998a) has shown that voiceless fricatives (the class to which all of Bella Coola's fricatives belong) are, in fact, [+spread glottis]. Consequently, teasing apart the aspiration of voiceless stops from the aspiration of voiceless fricatives that follow immediately after without an intervening schwa is exceedingly difficult, as shown by transcriptional variation in the literature—Newman (1947) indicates aspiration in forms such as [pɬtʰ] 'thick' whereas Hoard (1978) and Nater (1984) do not—and by Bagemihl's own admission (1991:624);[31] careful phonetic testing would be needed to determine with confidence (if possible) the glottal specifications of Bella Coola stops in this context.

Without coupling with some form of peripherality condition or length limitation, degenerate syllable theory loses much of its explanatory appeal, since a string of degenerate syllables could easily overgenerate to the same degree that it is claimed variable appendix theory does. Yet many words even in English do not conform to such peripherality, displaying stop-fricative-stop sequences morpheme-internally: *midst*, *betwixt*, *abstract*, *extra*, *Baxter* (the proper name), *expand*, *experiment*, *expect*, *extreme*, *rapscallion*, *substance*, and—ironically—*obstruent*, to name a few. Although a number of these may have polymorphemic historical roots, from a synchronic standpoint there is no reason to believe that an unschooled native speaker would parse them into more than one morpheme. Unlike some other bound morphemes like *-ceive*, which behaves as one morpheme in *perceive/perception*, *receive/reception*, *conceive/conception*, *deceive/deception*, and so on, or like the *ex-* of *export* with its distinct semantics (opposing the /in-/ of *import*, for instance), these examples have few obviously living relatives. English is not alone in this matter, either; Nxaʔamxcín has a small number of single-morpheme roots with internal unsyllabified segments (Czaykowska-Higgins and Willett 1997): [ʔal'sqaʔ] 'outside' and [samckiyaʔ] 'sticks at end of spear pole'.

Second, it is unclear what part of the syllable the segments pattern with, and how. This is especially true for theories defining the semisyllable as a nonmoraic syllable (e.g., Cho and King 2003), in those problem languages (such as Georgian and Polish) in which consonants are not counted toward weight. Since in a simple moraic framework onset effects and coda effects have to be derived via ALIGN-L and ALIGN-R constraints, respectively, a single special segment (i.e., both the left and the right edge of the semisyllable) would fall under the purview of both sets of constraints. It should be subject to phonotactic restrictions not only on onsets but also on coda inventory, so one cannot say (contra Féry (2003) and others) that degenerate syllables are onsets without nuclei. To prevent coda (i.e., ALIGN-R) constraints from applying to semisyllables, one would have to refer to the distinction between full syllable and semisyllable in the domain of the ALIGN constraint. In so doing, one would in effect subvert the very motivation for positing a syllable-like structure for extrasyllabic sequences.[32] The situation is further complicated by the lack of consensus in the literature about whether degenerate syllables are moraic or not. For those who prefer a moraic degenerate syllable, it should pattern with "nuclei" or "rimes," because the latter are distinguished from "onsets" and (sometimes) "codas" by being moraic, but here again significant complication is needed to obviate the application of both left- and right-syllable-edge constraints.

This edge-effect confusion reaches its peak in Government Phonology's (e.g., Harris 1994) casting of degenerate syllable theory, which forces all CVC syllables to syllabify as CV.C[V] (where [V] is an empty nucleus). Many languages allow, or require, stops in coda position to be unreleased, yet in Government Phonology these stops are not codas at all but onsets of headless syllables. The neutralization of laryngeal contrasts in coda position, as in Sanskrit, fits into this category of objection as well. Government Phonology does not appear to generate weight-controlled stress systems well either: a regularity as simple as "Stress the leftmost heavy syllable" becomes "Stress the leftmost syllable followed by a syllable containing an empty nucleus."

Third, because it postulates many extra syllables, degenerate syllable theory runs afoul of facts regarding syllable count. Rialland (1994) points out that her appendix-based account of French not only captures the sequencing facts, but also explains why words like *stricte* are perceived and scanned as monosyllables; degenerate syllable theory is unable to do so. Nor can it explain why Russian words with quirky consonants like *mgla* 'mist' count as monosyllabic with respect to stress and versification (Kiparsky 2003:155). We expect degenerate syllable theories to also fail to account for syllable-counting processes similar to the Armenian plural selection rule in (26), especially if some were to be found in languages of the Salish family where variable appendix theory and degenerate syllable theory diverge so widely in the number of syllables they predict (see (34)).[33]

(34) *Relevant representations with reference to syllable-counting phenomena: Bella Coola [q'psttχ] 'taste it'*
   a. *Bagemihl 1991*

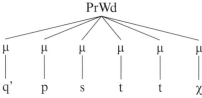

b. *Cho and King 2003:205*

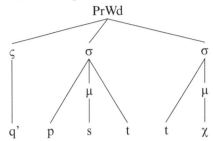

We would like to add that what Scheer (2004) claims to be an important advantage of Government Phonology's version of degenerate syllable theory is actually a liability for the theory. He states that "my best argument is the fact that languages produce only one extrasyllabic consonant at a time. In all extrasyllabic scenarios that I know, nothing withstands the existence of five or twenty extrasyllabic consonants. Since empty Nuclei are subject to the ECP [Empty Category Principle] and every extra consonant implies the existence of an additional empty Nucleus, there can be one extrasyllabic consonant at most." This prediction is rampantly falsified by the data, as we demonstrate briefly in (35); many languages allow long strings of quirky consonants, both peripherally and medially.

(35) *Virtually limitless extrasyllabic sequences*
   a. "[In languages like Bella Coola and Sipakapense Maya] there is essentially no limit to the number of unsyllabified initial segments" (Marlo 2004:94).
   b. Spokane Salish sčkwλ'kwλ' 'little eyes' (Bates and Carlson 1992)
   c. Sipakapense Maya ʃtqsb'χaχ 'they are going to whack him/her/it' (Barrett 1999)
   d. Pima totpk 'purr' (Riggle 2003)

We attribute the common limitation of appendices to one segment to historical reasons, not formal or computational ones.

When it is stripped of a viable peripherality or length condition and divorced from the phonotactics of full syllables, the only justification for degenerate syllable theory lies in its satisfaction of the Strict Layering Hypothesis (Selkirk 1984), according to which every prosodic node is immediately dominated by a prosodic node of the next highest layer, without skipping layers. Appendices violate the hypothesis by attaching directly to the PrWd node without belonging to a mora, syllable, or foot.

Recent literature on prosodic structure since Ito and Mester's landmark 1992 paper (updated as Ito and Mester 2003) on weak layering has suggested that strict layering may, in fact, not be so strict. In OT, as noted above, Kiparsky (2003) has pointed out that with violability and free ranking of constraints, violations of the

Strict Layering Hypothesis are expected. In other words, satisfying the hypothesis does not by itself give degenerate syllable theory any significant advantage over variable appendix theory.

5.5 Conclusions

To summarize, we have argued that there is ample evidence of many different sorts—phonetic, phonological, morphological, and psycholinguistic, internal and external—for the existence of extrasyllabicity. We have suggested that these facts are best modeled by a variable appendix theory, which attaches quirky segments directly to prosodic nodes above the syllable, the choice of node varying both within and across languages.

This investigation has several larger implications. First, it argues against superficial statistically driven phonological models that attempt to derive syllabic generalizations solely from the distribution of initial and final clusters (e.g., Pulgram 1970, Hooper 1972, Selkirk 1982, Steriade 1998). Second, it argues against those who are unwilling to look inside the linguistic black box and prefer to imagine that reality consists of nothing more than what the box emits, in this case phonetics. Pace Ohala (1990:324), syllable appendices are not "purely ad hoc strategies designed like the Ptolemaic epicycles 'to save the appearances' of the data." Instead, in the spirit of *SPE* and of Anderson 1982, appendices are justified by the insight and coherence that they bring to the facts. By postulating highly abstract formal entities such as syllables and appendices, we begin to bring order to a vast array of seemingly disparate facts that would otherwise remain unconnected and unhelpful.

Notes

Many thanks to Chuck Cairns, Morris Halle, and Donca Steriade for comments on earlier versions of this chapter.

1. Also sometimes referred to as an affix (Fujimura and Lovins 1982, Treiman, Gross, and Cwikiel-Glavin 1992), termination (Fudge 1969), premargin (Cairns and Feinstein 1982), adjunct (Gierut 1999), or semisyllable (Kiparsky 2003).

2. Unless otherwise noted, O refers to obstruent, T to stop, R to resonant, L to liquid, G to glide, N to nasal, C to consonant, and V to vowel.

3. Marlo suggests that even tautomorphemic initial extrasyllabic sequences such as in *sport* are licensed because since "the morphology requires that these final fricatives be realized, the English speaker is forced to accept that this class of sounds is tolerated outside the syllable" (p. 94).

4. French *ce*, as mentioned below, sometimes surfaces as extrasyllabic—for example, *ce drap* [sdra]. This results, however, from an optional schwa deletion rule, hardly sufficient to "force" the French speaker into accepting *s*C-clusters.

5. While the native vocabulary of English does not allow noncoronal segments in appendices, English speakers have at times borrowed words violating this popular generalization; witness for example the Siberian place names *Irkutsk* and *Yakutsk* in the popular Parker Brothers board game Risk™.

6. Gussmann (1992), developing an observation by Kuryłowicz (1952), notes that Polish allows initial clusters consisting of what appear to be two consecutive onsets. In our analysis, as we show below, the first of these two apparent onset sequences is best analyzed as a string of appendix segments governed by the same internal sequencing constraints as regular onsets are.

7. Another alternative advanced in Cairns and Feinstein 1982 makes use of a highly articulated theory of the syllable in the style of Fudge 1969 with a branching, multitiered onset that adheres to the phrase structure rules in (i).

(i) *Cairns and Feinstein's (1982:200) onset structure*
    Onset → Margin (Adjunct)
    Margin → (Premargin) Margin Core

Under this view, appendices fall into the Premargin, whereas complex onsets such as OR-make use only of the Margin and Adjunct positions. While this model captures both the distinct nature of appendices vis-à-vis complex onsets and the markedness facts covered in (8a) below, it explicitly rejects the SSP as a basis of syllable structure and is founded instead solely upon markedness facts. This loses the explanatory power of the SSP, and moreover fails to account for the nontautosyllabic behavior of *s*T clusters documented extensively in this chapter. Research is also needed to explore how this formalism would treat long strings of appendices, as well as *final* extrasyllabic and extraprosodic segments.

8. For simplicity's sake, foot structure and other prosodic structure not essential to the discussion is not shown. Diagrams are inspired by Hall 2002 (for (2a)), Harris 1994 and Cho and King 2003 (for (2b)), Rialland 1994 and Kiparsky 2003 (for (2c)), Clements and Keyser 1983 (for (2d)).

9. Clements uses the term *demisyllable* to refer to onset + vowel or vowel + coda sequences. By his definition, the word /tal/ 'tall' has two demisyllables, /ta/ and /al/.

10. A similar equation is used in physics in the computation of forces in potential fields; Liljencrants and Lindblom (1972) propose its use for the dispersion of vowels in the vowel space. As Clements explains, "we need not attribute such computation to the explicit knowledge of native speakers in any sense.... We can detect whether billiard balls are evenly dispersed on a billiard table without doing computations on a pocket calculator" (1990:311).

11. Although this chart does not show it, being organized by the demisyllables' values for D, two-segment demisyllables are ranked separately from three-segment demisyllables. Final VGL sequences are certainly not less complex than final VG sequences, but VG sequences *are* less marked than VO sequences, and VGL is the least complex of three-segment demisyllables.

12. We have not included numerical calculations for OOV, fricative-stop-V, and LOV because it is not immediately clear how to alter Clements's algorithm to rank these in a coherent manner. Our intuition is that sonority plateaus like OOV are more complex initial demisyllables than ONV and less complex than NOV, for example, but Clements's algorithm generates a problematic dispersion value of ∞ (infinity) for OOV (and all other sonority plateaus).

13. Given that studies on the order of acquisition of onset clusters have not produced entirely uniform results (see McLeod, van Doorn, and Reed 2001), we hesitate to adopt this sort of

acquisition data as a fine-tuned metric for determining ranks of cluster complexity. Even so, the data generally support the view that *s*T-onsets are *less* complex, not more complex, than complex onset clusters.

14. See Morelli 2003 for further discussion of *s*T as the least-marked cluster, and see section 5.3.1.1.4 for further data from Acoma.

15. Before proceeding to arguments in favor of the appendix, we feel it is important to address Hall's (2002) optimality-based reanalysis of German and English extrasyllabicity. Hall argues that it is unnecessary to treat English and German SSP-violating segments as extrasyllabic, proposing instead a set of crosslinguistically motivated markedness constraints from which follows a fully syllabified account of all German and English clusters.

In our view, Hall's analysis is inadequate in several respects. First, he shows that an analysis of the German and English facts that does not employ extrasyllabicity is *sufficient*, but he does not show that it is *necessary*, as demonstrated by his section 4 in which he proposes that Irish does in fact make use of extrasyllabicity. He never proves that an extrasyllabic analysis does not, or cannot, work. Second, while he takes care to establish crosslinguistic perceptual bases for constraints such as **pk* and **tk*, he specifically formulates SON to apply to English and German but not Polish, to avoid its nasal sequences. The question of how such constraints would have to be recast and supplemented for other languages is left unsatisfyingly open. Third, dividing the SSP into a number of subsidiary constraints—a measure Hall takes to fine-tune his analysis to the distributional facts of German and English—loses the sense of a "conspiracy of constraints" in which those microconstraints all work together to achieve, even approximately, the goal of sonority sequencing. In other words, it loses the crosslinguistic explanatory elegance of the SSP. Fourth, Hall fails to consider the crosslinguistic evidence for the appendix.

16. Initial *s*R-clusters do not violate the SSP. Goad and Rose (2004) argue, in fact, that it is this case that distinguishes their Head Pattern from the Sonority Pattern proposed by many previous researchers, because *s*R-patterns with other *s*-initial onsets and not with other SSP-compatible complex onsets. In either case, whether acquisition cluster-simplification data on the whole favor the Head Pattern proposed by Spencer (1986) and Goad and Rose (2004) or the Sonority Pattern proffered by other researchers, a clear distinction is drawn between complex onsets and extrasyllabic /s/.

17. The lower percentages are due to the wider range of possibilities in oral syllabification: not only *nu-speem* and *nus-peem* but ambisyllabic *nus-speem* and *nusp-peem* as well.

18. Medial nasal + stop clusters (as well as one medial nasal + affricate cluster and one medial nasal + fricative cluster) are found in some loanwords and probable loanwords. Other initial clusters (listed exhaustively from Miller 1965:10) include the /ny-/ of *nyáanyaa* 'to nurse' (baby talk), the /hy-/ of *hyêesta* 'fiesta, feast day', the /sw-/ of *swêera* 'sweater', the /gr-/ of *hisugrístu* 'Jesus Christ', and the /sč-/ allomorph of the distributive dubitative prefix, which falls into the appendix pattern.

19. In Miller's orthography, *dy* and *ty* represent voiced and voiceless palatal stops, respectively.

20. Bell and Saka (1983) show evidence that in Pashto, unlike in Huffman's and Lovins's Cambodian data, the reversed-sonority initial clusters *lm-*, *wl-*, and *wr-* are true clusters, in terms of their coarticulation, duration, intensity, and voicing, and that sonority does not provide an insightful explanation into the differences that do exist between Pashto initial clusters

of rising and falling sonority. Further investigation is needed to determine the significance of these findings in the context of Pashto phonology in general and of phonetic arguments more broadly. In any case, Bell and Saka's observations do not detract from the Cambodian findings.

21. Sequences of stop + nasal do not violate the SSP per se, but are often considered extrasyllabic on the basis of their violating minimal sonority distance requirements. Such requirements are linked to the discussion in section 5.2 of the sonority scale and dispersion in sonority, with the idea that licensed complex onsets do not contain sequences of consonants from adjacent sonority ranks.

22. Laxing does not always occur across morpheme boundaries, so r[ə]stériliser (Dell 1995:10).

23. Treiman, Gross, and Cwikiel-Glavin (1992:398) respond that aspiration may not be a good test, because according to Kahn (1976), voiceless stops may only aspirate when unambiguously syllable-initial. The s may be ambisyllabic, which would block aspiration.

24. Two possible exceptions are ktōmai (ktaomai) 'procure for oneself, acquire', whose perfect is attested both as ke-ktēmai (Arndt 1957) and as e-ktēmai (Liddell and Scott 1940), and ptussō 'fold up', whose perfect appears in the forms e-ptugmai and pe-ptuktai. Others include obstruent-nasal sequences: thnēskō 'die', pft. te-thnēka; knaō 'scrape', pft. kata-ke-knēsmai; pneō 'blow', pft. pe-pneumai; pnigō 'choke', pft. pe-pnigmai; but compare gnōrizō 'make known', pft. e-gnōrika. Nevertheless, most roots with initial extrasyllabic consonants (especially in OO sequences) do not copy the initial consonant, and no complex onsets that we have found fail to reduplicate the initial consonant. Sequences of s + nasal may pattern with s + stop clusters: smurnizō 'treat with myrrh', pft. part. e-smurnismenos. Exceptions may be due to dialectal or diachronic variation.

25. Czaykowska-Higgins and Willett (1997:402) support their suffixal analysis vis-à-vis a possible prefixal analysis on the basis that whereas prefixes are always unstressed in Nxaʔamxcín, the first of the two identical syllables here is stressed. See Czaykowska-Higgins 1993 and van Eijk 1997 for further discussion of this reduplicative pattern.

26. Sometimes an epenthetic schwa breaks up the two copies of C_2.

27. PrPhr = Prosodic Phrase; PrWd = Prosodic Word. The [ɾ] in (29a) is extraprosodic on this cycle, owing to Final Consonant Extraprosodicity. See Vaux 2003 for further discussion. This detail does not affect the representation of the initial appendix.

28. For other presentations including permanently stray elements, see Newman 1947 and Bye 1997.

29. That the French appendix attaches to the PrWd (30g) is shown by the fact that it undergoes regressive voicing assimilation, which is a word-level phonological rule, not syllable-level (as shown by the fact that liaison consonants do not participate).

30. Some researchers prefer the term semisyllable to degenerate syllable and/or make a formal distinction between the two; we will use both terms interchangeably here. Note that Kiparsky (2003) defines semisyllables as unsyllabified moras that attach higher in the prosodic hierarchy (licensed moras).

31. He footnotes, "it is...not entirely clear that aspirated and unaspirated stops would be acoustically distinct before fricatives, and I was not in fact able to detect any such difference in the speech of my consultants" (p. 624).

32. One can imagine a taxonomy of ALIGN constraints wherein some apply only to full syllables (coda constraints), some to both full and degenerate syllables (onset constraints), and
some only to degenerate syllables (to further constrain certain languages' semisyllables, such
as Armenian's). We believe this lacks explanatory elegance—for instance, why would only
ALIGN-R constraints refer to full syllables?—not to mention that it destroys the essential unity
semisyllable theorists have attempted to establish. Alternatively, proponents of degenerate syllable theories could readopt Onset and Coda nodes into their analyses.

33. If one were to abstract away from Bagemihl's (1991) and Cho and King's (2003) interpretation of what constitutes a syllabic nucleus in Bella Coola, an appendix theorist might posit as
many as one syllable (compared with Bagemihl's zero syllables) and a degenerate syllable theorist as many as six (compared with Cho and King's three).

References

Anderson, Stephen. 1982. The analysis of French shwa, or How to get something for nothing.
Language 58:534–573.

Aoun, Youssef [Joseph]. 1979. Is the syllable or the supersyllable a constituent? In *Papers
on syllable structure, metrical structure, and harmony processes*, ed. by Ken Safir, 140–148.
MIT Working Papers in Linguistics 1. Cambridge, Mass.: MIT, MIT Working Papers in
Linguistics.

Arndt, William F. 1957. *A Greek-English lexicon of the New Testament and other early Chris-
tian literature; a translation and adaptation of Walter Bauer's* Griechischdeutsches Wörterbuch
zu den Schriften des Neuen Testaments und der übrigen urchristlichen Literatur. 4th rev. and
augm. ed., 1952, by William F. Arndt and F. Wilbur Gingrich. Chicago: University of Chicago Press.

Atʃarjan, Hratʃʰja. 1957. *Liakatar kʰerakanutʰjun hajotsʰ lezvi* [Complete grammar of the
Armenian language]. Vol. 3, *Morphology*. Erevan: Hajkakan SSH GA Hrataraktʃʰutʰjun.

Atʃarjan, Hratʃʰja. 1971. *Liakatar kʰerakanutʰjun hajotsʰ lezvi* [Complete grammar of the
Armenian language]. Vol. 6, *Phonology*. Erevan: Hajkakan SSH GA Hrataraktʃʰutʰjun.

Bagemihl, Bruce. 1991. Syllable structure in Bella Coola. *Linguistic Inquiry* 22:589–646.

Barrett, Edward. 1999. A grammar of Sipakapense Maya. Doctoral dissertation, University of
Texas, Austin.

Bates, Dawn, and Barry Carlson. 1992. Simple syllables in Spokane Salish. *Linguistic Inquiry*
23:653–659.

Bell, Alan, and Mohamad Saka. 1983. Reversed sonority in Pashto initial clusters. *Journal of
Phonetics* 11:259–275.

Berens, Sally. 1996. The phonetics and phonology of Homshetsma. Bachelor's thesis, Harvard
University.

Blevins, Juliette. 1995. The syllable in phonological theory. In *The handbook of phonological
theory*, ed. by John Goldsmith, 206–244. Cambridge, Mass.: Blackwell.

Booij, Geert. 1995. *The phonology of Dutch*. Oxford: Clarendon Press.

Booij, Geert, and Rochelle Lieber. 1993. On the simultaneity of morphological and prosodic
structure. In *Studies in Lexical Phonology*, ed. by Sharon Hargus and Ellen Kaisse, 23–44.
Phonetics and Phonology 4. San Diego, Calif.: Academic Press.

Borowsky, Toni. 1986. Topics in the Lexical Phonology of English. Doctoral dissertation, University of Massachusetts, Amherst.

Broselow, Ellen. 1991. The structure of fricative-stop onsets. Paper presented at the Conference for the Organization of Phonological Features. Santa Cruz, July 1991.

Broselow, Ellen. 1995. Skeletal positions and moras. In *The handbook of phonological theory*, ed. by John Goldsmith, 175–205. Cambridge, Mass.: Blackwell.

Buckley, Eugene. 1994. *Theoretical aspects of Kashaya phonology and morphology*. Stanford, Calif.: CSLI Publications.

Burzio, Luigi. 1994. *Principles of English stress*. Cambridge: Cambridge University Press.

Bye, Patrik. 1997. Representing 'overlength': Against trimoraic syllables. In *Phonology in progress—Progress in phonology*, ed. by Geert Booij and Jeroen van de Weijer, 61–101. The Hague: Holland Academic Graphics.

Cairns, Charles, and Mark Feinstein. 1982. Markedness and the theory of syllable structure. *Linguistic Inquiry* 13:193–226.

Calabrese, Andrea, and Cristina Romani. 1998. Syllabic constraints in the phonological errors of an aphasic patient. *Brain and Language* 64:83–121.

Carlson, Katy. 1997. Sonority and reduplication in Nakanai and Nuxalk (Bella Coola). Ms., University of Massachusetts, Amherst.

Charette, Monik. 1985. The appendix in parametric phonology. *Studies in African Linguistics*. Suppl. 9:49–53.

Charette, Monik. 1991. *Conditions on phonological government*. Cambridge: Cambridge University Press.

Chierchia, Guglielmo. 1986. Lunghezza, sillabificazione ed il ciclo fonologico in italiano (Length, syllabification, and the phonological cycle in Italian). *Journal of Italian Linguistics* 8:5–34.

Cho, Young-mee Y. 1997. Semisyllables and Georgian consonant clusters. Paper presented at the 10th Biennial Non-Slavic Languages Conference, Chicago.

Cho, Young-mee Y., and Tracy Holloway King. 2003. Semisyllables and universal syllabification. In *The syllable in Optimality Theory*, ed. by Caroline Féry and Ruben van de Vijver, 183–212. Cambridge: Cambridge University Press.

Chomsky, Noam, and Morris Halle. 1968. *The sound pattern of English*. New York: Harper and Row.

Clements, G. N. 1990. The role of the sonority cycle in core syllabification. In *Papers in laboratory phonology I*, ed. by John Kingston and Mary Beckman, 283–333. Cambridge: Cambridge University Press.

Clements, G. N. 1992. The sonority cycle and syllable organization. In *Phonologica 1988*, ed. by Wolfgang U. Dressler, Hans C. Luschützky, Oskar E. Pfeiffer, and John R. Rennison, 63–76. Cambridge: Cambridge University Press.

Clements, G. N., and Samuel Jay Keyser. 1983. *CV phonology*. Cambridge, Mass.: MIT Press.

Cook, Eung-Do. 1994. Against moraic licensing in Bella Coola. *Linguistic Inquiry* 25:309–326.

Czaykowska-Higgins, Ewa. 1993. The phonology and semantics of CVC reduplication in Moses-Columbian Salish (Nxaʔamxcín). In *American Indian linguistics and ethnography in honor of Laurence C. Thompson*, ed. by Anthony Mattina and Timothy Montler, 47–72. Occasional Papers in Linguistics 10. Missoula: University of Montana.

Czaykowska-Higgins, Ewa, and Marie Louise Willett. 1997. Simple syllables in Nxaʔamxcín. *International Journal of American Linguistics* 63:385–411.

Davidsen-Nielsen, Niels. 1974. Syllabification in English words with medial *sp, st, sk*. *Journal of Phonetics* 2:15–45.

Davis, Stuart. 1990. Italian onset structure and the distribution of *il* and *lo*. *Linguistics* 28:43–55.

Dell, François. 1995. Consonant clusters and phonological syllables in French. *Lingua* 95:5–26.

Duanmu, San. 2002. Two theories of onset clusters. *Journal of Chinese Phonology* 11:97–120.

Dyck, Carrie. 1999. Cayuga syllable structure. *Linguistica Atlantica* 21:69–105.

Eijk, Jan van. 1997. CVC reduplication in Salish. In *Salish languages and linguistics: Theoretical and descriptive perspectives*, ed. by Ewa Czaykowska-Higgins and M. Dale Kinkade, 453–476. Berlin: Mouton de Gruyter.

Elsen, Hilke. 1991. *Erstspracherwerb: Der Erwerb des deutschen Lautsystems*. Wiesbaden: Deutscher Universitäts-Verlag.

Engstrand, Olle, and Christine Ericsdotter. 1999. Explaining a violation of the sonority hierarchy: Stop place perception in adjacent [s]. In *Proceedings from the XIIth Swedish Phonetics Conference*, 49–52. Göteborg, Sweden: Göteborg University, Department of Linguistics.

Féry, Caroline. 2003. Onsets and nonmoraic syllables in German. In *The syllable in Optimality Theory*, ed. by Caroline Féry and Ruben van de Vijver, 213–237. Cambridge: Cambridge University Press.

Fikkert, Paula. 1994. On the acquisition of prosodic structure. Doctoral dissertation, Leiden University/HIL. Published, The Hague: Holland Academic Graphics, 1994.

Frampton, John. 2007. Root vowel syncope and reduplication in Sanskrit. In *CLS 39*. Vol. 1, *The Main Session*, ed. by Jon Cihlar, Amy Franklin, David Kaiser, and Irene Kimbara, 75–91. Chicago: University of Chicago, Chicago Linguistic Society.

Fudge, Erik. 1969. Syllables. *Journal of Linguistics* 5:253–286.

Fudge, Erik. 1976. Phonotactics and the syllable. In *Linguistic studies offered to Joseph Greenberg*, ed. by Alphonse Juilland, 381–398. Saratoga, Calif.: Anma Libri.

Fudge, Erik. 1984. *English word-stress*. London: Allen and Unwin.

Fujimura, Osamu. 1979. An analysis of English syllables as cores and affixes. *Zeitschrift für Phonetik, Sprachwissenschaft und Kommunikationsforschung* 32:471–476.

Fujimura, Osamu, and Julie Lovins. 1982. Syllables as concatenative phonetic units. Bloomington: Indiana University Linguistics Club.

Giegerich, Heinz J. 1992. *English phonology: An introduction*. Cambridge: Cambridge University Press.

Gierut, Judith. 1999. Syllable onsets: Clusters and adjuncts in acquisition. *Journal of Speech, Language, and Hearing Research* 42:708–726.

Gilbers, Dicky, and Dirk-Bart den Ouden. 1994. Compensatory lengthening and cluster reduction in first language acquisition: A comparison of analyses. In *Language and Cognition 4,*

Yearbook 1994 of the Research Group for Linguistic Theory and Knowledge Representation of the University of Groningen, ed. by Ale de Boer, Helen de Hoop, and Henriëtte de Swart, 69–82. Groningen: University of Groningen.

Goad, Heather, and Yvan Rose. 2004. Input elaboration, head faithfulness and evidence for representation in the acquisition of left-edge clusters in West Germanic. In *Fixing priorities: Constraints in phonological acquisition*, ed. by René Kager, Joe Pater, and Wim Zonneveld, 109–157. Cambridge: Cambridge University Press.

Goldsmith, John. 1990. *Autosegmental and metrical phonology.* Oxford: Blackwell.

Green, Antony. 2003. Extrasyllabic consonants and onset well-formedness. In *The syllable in Optimality Theory*, ed. by Caroline Féry and Ruben van de Vijver, 238–253. Cambridge: Cambridge University Press.

Grijzenhout, Janet, and Sandra Joppen. 1998. First steps in the acquisition of German phonology: A case study. SFB 282 Working Paper Nr. 110. Utrecht: Utrecht University, Department of English. Updated as Janet Grijzenhout and Sandra Joppen, 2002, http://www.ling.uni-potsdam.de/kurse/SpracherwerbPhonologie-SS04/german.pdf.

Gussmann, Edmund. 1992. Resyllabification and delinking: The case of Polish voicing. *Linguistic Inquiry* 23:29–56.

Gussmann, Edmund, and Jonathan Kaye. 1993. Polish notes from a Dubrovnik café I: The yers. In *SOAS working papers in linguistics and phonetics 3*, 427–462. London: University of London, School of Oriental and African Studies.

Haas, Wim de. 1986. Partial syllabification and schwa epenthesis in Dutch. *Gramma* 10:143–162.

Hagstrom, Paul. 1997. Contextual metrical invisibility. In *PF: Papers at the interface*, ed. by Benjamin Bruening, Yoonjung Kang, and Martha McGinnis, 113–181. MIT Working Papers in Linguistics 30. Cambridge, Mass.: MIT, MIT Working Papers in Linguistics.

Hall, T. Alan. 1992. *Syllable structure and syllable-related processes in German.* Tübingen: Max Niemeyer Verlag.

Hall, T. Alan. 2002. Against extrasyllabic consonants in German and English. *Phonology* 19:33–75.

Halle, Morris, and Jean-Roger Vergnaud. 1980. Three-dimensional phonology. *Journal of Linguistic Research* 1:83–105.

Harris, James. 1983. *Syllable structure and stress in Spanish.* Cambridge, Mass.: MIT Press.

Harris, James. 1999. High vocoids in Spanish syllables. Ms., MIT.

Harris, John. 1994. *English sound structure.* Oxford: Blackwell.

Harris, John, and Edmund Gussmann. 1998. Final codas: Why the West was wrong. In *Structure and interpretation in phonology: Studies in phonology*, ed. by Eugeniusz Cyran, 139–162. Lublin: Folia.

Haugen, Einar. 1956. The syllable in linguistic description. In *For Roman Jakobson*, ed. by Morris Halle, Horace G. Lunt, Hugh McLean, and Cornelius van Schooneveld, 213–221. The Hague: Mouton.

Hayes, Bruce. 1985. *A metrical theory of stress rules.* New York: Garland.

Hoard, James E. 1978. Syllabication in Northwest Indian languages, with remarks on the nature of syllabic stops and affricates. In *Syllables and segments*, ed. by Alan Bell and Joan B. Hooper, 59–72. Amsterdam: North Holland.

Hooper, Joan Bybee. 1972. The syllable in phonological theory. *Language* 48:525–540.

Huffman, Franklin. 1972. The boundary between the monosyllable and the disyllable in Cambodian. *Lingua* 29:54–66.

Hulst, Harry van der. 1984. The diminutive suffix and the structure of Dutch syllables. In *Linguistics in the Netherlands 1984*, ed. by Hans Bennis and W. U. S. van Lessen Kloeke, 73–83. Dordrecht: Foris.

Hyman, Larry. 1985. *A theory of phonological weight*. Dordrecht: Foris.

Ito, Junko. 1986. Syllable theory in prosodic phonology. Doctoral dissertation, University of Massachusetts, Amherst.

Ito, Junko, and Armin Mester. 1992. Weak layering and word binarity. Ms., Linguistic Research Center, LRC-92–09, University of California, Santa Cruz. Revised version in *A new century of phonology and phonological theory: A festschrift for Professor Shosuke Haraguchi on the occasion of his sixtieth birthday*, ed. by Takeru Honma, Masao Okazaki, Toshiyuki Tabata, and Shinichi Tanaka, 26–65. Tokyo: Kaitakusha, 2003.

Iverson, Gregory. 1990. The stipulation of extraprosodicity in syllabic phonology. *Language Research* 26:515–552.

Iverson, Gregory, and Joseph Salmons. 1995. Aspiration and laryngeal representation in Germanic. *Phonology* 12:369–396.

Iverson, Gregory, and Joseph Salmons. 1999. Glottal spreading bias in Germanic. *Linguistische Berichte* 178:135–151.

Jastrow, Otto. 1978. *Die mesopotamisch-arabischen qəltu-Dialekte*. Wiesbaden: Steiner.

Jespersen, Otto. 1904. *Lehrbuch der Phonetik*. Leipzig and Berlin.

Kager, René, and Wim Zonneveld. 1986. Schwa, syllables, and extrametricality. *The Linguistic Review* 5:197–221.

Kahn, Daniel. 1976. Syllable-based generalizations in English phonology. Doctoral dissertation, MIT.

Kaye, Jonathan, and Jean Lowenstamm. 1984. De la syllabicité. In *Forme sonore du langage*, ed. by François Dell, Daniel Hirst, and Jean-Roger Vergnaud, 123–159. Paris: Hermann.

Kaye, Jonathan, Jean Lowenstamm, and Jean-Roger Vergnaud. 1990. Constituent structure and government in phonology. *Phonology* 7:193–231.

Kenstowicz, Michael. 1994. *Phonology in generative grammar*. Oxford: Blackwell.

Kim, Chin-Wu. 1970. A theory of aspiration. *Phonetica* 21:107–116.

Kiparsky, Paul. 1979. Metrical structure assignment is cyclic. *Linguistic Inquiry* 10:421–441.

Kiparsky, Paul. 1981. Remarks on the metrical structure of the syllable. In *Phonologica 1980*, ed. by Wolfgang U. Dressler, Oskar E. Pfeiffer, and John R. Rennison, 245–256. Innsbruck: Institut für Sprachwissenschaft Innsbruck.

Kiparsky, Paul. 2003. Syllables and moras in Arabic. In *The syllable in Optimality Theory*, ed. by Caroline Féry and Ruben van de Vijver, 147–182. Cambridge: Cambridge University Press.

Koshal, Sanyukta. 1979. *Ladakhi grammar*. Delhi: Motilal Banarsidass.

Kuryłowicz, Jerzy. 1952. Uwagi o polskich grupach spółgłoskowych [Remarks on Polish consonantal groups]. *Biuletyn Polskiego Towarzystwa Jezykoznawczego* 11:54–69.

Lapointe, Steven, and Mark Feinstein. 1982. The role of vowel deletion and epenthesis in the assignment of syllable structure. In *The structure of phonological representations II*, ed. by Harry van der Hulst and Norval Smith, 69–120. Dordrecht: Foris.

Levin, Juliette. 1985. A metrical theory of syllabicity. Doctoral dissertation, MIT.

Liddell, Henry George, and Robert Scott. 1940. *A Greek-English lexicon*, revised and augmented throughout by Sir Henry Stuart Jones, with the assistance of Roderick McKenzie. Oxford: Clarendon Press.

Liljencrants, Johan, and Björn Lindblom. 1972. Numerical simulation of vowel quality systems: The role of perceptual contrast. *Language* 48:839–862.

Lin, Yen-Hwei. 1995. Extrasyllabic consonants and compensatory lengthening. In *Proceedings of the Thirteenth West Coast Conference on Formal Linguistics*, ed. by Raul Aranovich, William Byrne, Susanne Preuss, and Martha Senturia, 93–105. Stanford, Calif.: CSLI Publications.

Lin, Yen-Hwei. 1997. Syllabic and moraic structures in Piro. *Phonology* 14:403–436.

Lovins, Julie. 1977. A phonetic reanalysis of some common and uncommon constraints on syllables structure. Paper presented at the annual meeting of the Linguistic Society of America, 28–30 December.

Marlo, Michael. 2004. CVX theory in CCCCCVX languages. *Journal of Universal Language* 5:75–99.

McCarthy, John. 1979. Formal problems in Semitic phonology and morphology. Doctoral dissertation, MIT.

McCarthy, John. 2005. Optimal paradigms. In *Paradigms in phonological theory*, ed. by Laura Downing, T. Alan Hall, and Renate Raffelsiefen, 170–210. Oxford: Oxford University Press.

McCarthy, John, and Alan Prince. 1990. Prosodic morphology and templatic morphology. In *Perspectives on Arabic linguistics II*, ed. by Mushira Eid and John McCarthy, 1–54. Amsterdam: John Benjamins.

McCarthy, John, and Alan Prince. 1995. Faithfulness and reduplicative identity. In *Papers in Optimality Theory*, ed. by Jill Beckman, Suzanne Urbanczyk, and Laura Walsh Dickey, 249–384. University of Massachusetts Occasional Papers in Linguistics 18. Amherst: University of Massachusetts, Graduate Linguistic Student Association.

McCrary, Kristie. 2002. Vowel length, consonant length and raddoppiamento-sintattico: Segment duration in Italian revisited. Paper presented at the 10th Manchester Phonology Meeting, Manchester.

McLeod, Sharynne, Jan van Doorn, and Vicki A. Reed. 2001. Normal acquisition of consonant clusters. *American Journal of Speech-Language Pathology* 10:99–110.

Miller, Wick R. 1965. *Acoma grammar and texts*. Berkeley and Los Angeles: University of California Press.

Morelli, Frida. 2003. The relative harmony of /s + stop/ onsets: Obstruent clusters and the Sonority Sequencing Principle. In *The syllable in Optimality Theory*, ed. by Caroline Féry and Ruben van de Vijver, 356–371. Cambridge: Cambridge University Press.

Nater, Hank F. 1984. *The Bella Coola language*. National Museum of Man Mercury Series, Canadian Ethnology Service Paper No. 92. Ottawa: National Museums of Canada.

Nater, Hank. 1990. *A concise Nuxalk-English dictionary*. National Museum of Man Mercury Series, Canadian Ethnology Service Paper No. 115. Hull, Quebec: Canadian Museum of Civilization.

Nepveu, Denis. 1994. Georgian and Bella Coola: Headless syllables and syllabic obstruents. Master's thesis, University of California, Santa Cruz.

Newman, Stanley. 1947. Bella Coola I: Phonology. *International Journal of American Linguistics* 13:129–134.

Nolan, Francis. 1994. Phonetic correlates of syllable affiliation. In *Phonological structure and phonetic form: Papers in laboratory phonology III*, ed. by Patricia A. Keating, 107–135. Cambridge: Cambridge University Press.

Ohala, John. 1990. Alternatives to the sonority hierarchy for explaining segmental sequential constraints. In *Papers from the 26th Regional Meeting of the Chicago Linguistic Society*. Vol. 2, *The Parasession on the Syllable in Phonetics and Phonology*, ed. by Michael Ziolkowski, Manuela Noske, and Karen Deaton, 319–338. Chicago: University of Chicago, Chicago Linguistic Society.

Ohala, John, and Haruko Kawasaki-Fukumori. 1997. Alternatives to the sonority hierarchy for explaining segmental sequential constraints: The shape of morphemes. In *Studies for Einar Haugen*, ed. by Stig Eliasson and Ernst Håkon Jahr, 343–365. Berlin: Mouton de Gruyter.

Pierrehumbert, Janet. 1994. Syllable structure and word structure: A study of triconsonantal clusters in English. In *Phonological structure and phonetic form: Papers in laboratory phonology III*, ed. by Patricia A. Keating, 168–188. Cambridge: Cambridge University Press.

Pierrehumbert, Janet, and Rami Nair. 1995. Word games and syllable structure. *Language and Speech* 38:78–114.

Pulgram, Ernst. 1970. *Syllable, word, nexus, cursus*. The Hague: Mouton.

Raimy, Eric. 2000. *The phonology and morphology of reduplication*. Berlin: Mouton de Gruyter.

Rialland, Annie. 1994. The phonology and phonetics of extrasyllabicity in French. In *Phonological structure and phonetic form: Papers in laboratory phonology III*, ed. by Patricia A. Keating, 136–159. Cambridge: Cambridge University Press.

Riggle, Jason. 2003. Infixing reduplication in Pima and its theoretical consequences. Ms., UCLA. Paper presented at the annual meeting of the Linguistic Society of America.

Rubach, Jerzy. 1997. Extrasyllabic consonants in Polish: Derivational Optimality Theory. In *Derivations and constraints in phonology*, ed. by Iggy Roca, 551–581. New York: Oxford University Press.

Rubach, Jerzy, and Geert Booij. 1990a. Edge of constituent effects in Polish. *Natural Language and Linguistic Theory* 8:427–463.

Rubach, Jerzy, and Geert Booij. 1990b. Syllable structure assignment in Polish. *Phonology* 7:121–158.

Samuels, Bridget. 2008. The syllable mirage. Handout from a talk presented at Penn Linguistics Colloquium 32. http://www.people.fas.harvard.edu/~bdsamuel/pdfs/syllablemirage.pdf.

Scheer, Tobias. 2004. There is no extrasyllabicity. http://www.unice.fr/dsl/tobweb/papers/posterManch.pdf.

Selkirk, Elisabeth. 1972. The phrase phonology of English and French. Doctoral dissertation, MIT.

Selkirk, Elisabeth. 1981. Epenthesis and degenerate syllables in Cairene Arabic. In *Theoretical issues in the grammar of Semitic languages*, ed. by Hagit Borer and Youssef [Joseph] Aoun, 209–232. MIT Working Papers in Linguistics 3. Cambridge, Mass.: MIT, MIT Working Papers in Linguistics.

Selkirk, Elisabeth. 1982. The syllable. In *The structure of phonological representations*, ed. by Harry van der Hulst and Norval Smith, 2:337–383. Dordrecht: Foris.

Selkirk, Elisabeth. 1984. *Phonology and syntax: The relation between sound and structure.* Cambridge, Mass.: MIT Press.

Shaw, Patricia. 1993. The prosodic constituency of minor syllables. In *Proceedings of the 12th West Coast Conference on Formal Linguistics*, ed. by Eric Duncan, Donka Farkas, and Philip Spaelti, 117–132. Stanford, Calif.: CSLI Publications.

Shaw, Patricia. 1996. Degenerate syllables. Paper presented at the 8th International Phonology Conference, Vienna, November 1996.

Sherer, Tim. 1994. Prosodic phonotactics. Doctoral dissertation, University of Massachusetts, Amherst.

Sievers, Eduard. 1881. *Grundzüge der Phonetik*. Leipzig: Breitkopf und Hartel.

Simon, Péla. 1967. *Les consonnes du français: Mouvements et positions articulatoires à la lumière de la radiocinématographie*. Paris: Klincksieck.

Siptar, Peter, and Miklos Törkenczy. 2000. *The phonology of Hungarian*. Oxford: Oxford University Press.

Smith, Norval. 1973. *The acquisition of phonology: A case study*. Cambridge: Cambridge University Press.

Spaelti, Philip. 1994. Weak edges and final consonants in Swiss German. Rutgers Optimality Archive ROA-18. http://roa.rutgers.edu.

Spencer, Andrew. 1986. Toward a theory of phonological development. *Lingua* 68:3–38.

Spencer, Andrew. 1996. *Phonology*. Oxford: Blackwell.

Stemberger, Joseph, and Brian MacWhinney. 1984. Extrasyllabic consonants in CV phonology: An experimental test. *Journal of Phonetics* 12:355–366.

Stemberger, Joseph, and Rebecca Treiman. 1986. The internal structure of word-initial consonant clusters. *Journal of Memory and Language* 25:163–180.

Steriade, Donca. 1982. Greek prosodies and the nature of syllabification. Doctoral dissertation, MIT.

Steriade, Donca. 1998. The grammatical bases of speakers' judgments of syllable division. Ms., UCLA.

Steriade, Donca. 1999. Alternatives to the syllabic interpretation of consonantal phonotactics. In *Proceedings of LP '98: Item order in language and speech*, ed. by Osamu Fujimura, Brian Joseph, and Bohumil Palek, 205–242. Prague: The Karolinum Press.

Svantesson, Jan-Olof. 1983. *Kammu phonology and morphology*. Travaux de l'Institut de Linguistique de Lund 18. Lund, Sweden: CWK Gleerup.

Thráinsson, Höskuldur. 1994. Icelandic. In *The Germanic languages*, ed. by Ekkehard König and Johan van der Auwera, 142–189. London: Routledge.

Törkenczy, Miklos. 2003. English phonetics and phonology. Class handout in AN/ANN/AFN-241 (Spring 2003), Hungarian Academy of Sciences, Research Institute for Linguistics. http://ny01.nytud.hu/~tork/engphon2003/EngPhonLec2003s_09.pdf.

Treiman, Rebecca, and Carol A. Fowler. 1991. Differences in cohesiveness among different types of word-initial consonant clusters. Paper presented at the meeting of the Psychonomic Society, San Francisco.

Treiman, Rebecca, Jennifer Gross, and Annemarie Cwikiel-Glavin. 1992. The syllabification of /s/ clusters in English. *Journal of Phonetics* 20:383–402.

Treiman, Rebecca, and Andrea Zukowski. 1990. Toward an understanding of English syllabification. *Journal of Memory and Language* 29:66–85.

Trommelen, Mieke. 1984. *The syllable in Dutch*. Dordrecht: Foris.

Trommelen, Mieke, and Wim Zonneveld. 1989. *Klemtoon en metrische fonologie*. Muiderberg: Coutinho.

Vaissière, Jacqueline. 1988. Prediction of velum movement from phonological specifications. *Phonetica* 45 (2–4): 122–139.

Vaux, Bert. 1994. Armenian phonology. Doctoral dissertation, Harvard University.

Vaux, Bert. 1998a. The laryngeal specifications of fricatives. *Linguistic Inquiry* 29:497–512.

Vaux, Bert. 1998b. *The phonology of Armenian*. Oxford: Clarendon Press.

Vaux, Bert. 2003. Syllabification in Armenian, Universal Grammar, and the lexicon. *Linguistic Inquiry* 34:91–125.

Velten, Harry V. 1943. The growth of phonemic and lexical patterns in infant language. *Language* 19:281–292.

Vennemann, Theo. 1982. Zur Silbenstruktur der deutschen Standardsprache. In *Silben, Segmente, Akzente*, ed. by Theo Vennemann, 261–305. Tübingen: Max Niemeyer Verlag.

Vennemann, Theo. 1988. *Preference laws for syllable structure and the explanation of sound change: With special reference to German, Germanic, Italian, and Latin*. Berlin: Mouton de Gruyter.

Whitney, William Dwight. 1865. The relation of vowel and consonant. *Journal of the American Oriental Society* 8. Reprinted in William Dwight Whitney, *Oriental and linguistic studies, second series*. New York: Charles Scribner's Sons, 1874.

Wiese, Richard. 1988. *Silbische und lexikalische Phonologie: Studien zum Chinesischen und Deutschen*. Tübingen: Max Niemeyer Verlag.

Zec, Draga. 1988. Sonority constraints on prosodic structure. Doctoral dissertation, Stanford University.

6 Phonological Representations and the Vaux-Wolfe Proposal

Charles E. Cairns

6.1 Introduction

Vaux and Wolfe (VW) show that syllabification is not exhaustive; in particular, many consonants are left unsyllabified. In diagram (2) of their chapter, they present an array of models for representing the sequence /spa/. VW's basic theory is that unsyllabified consonants are appendices, which they define as segments dominated directly by prosodic nodes higher than the syllable. Clearly, the success of their analysis of most unsyllabified consonants as "appendices" depends on the validity of the overall framework in which their analysis is couched. This response argues for a theory of representation different from any in VW's figure (2); further, although the model described here still countenances unsyllabified consonants (hereafter notated as C′), they are arguably not dominated by any prosodic constituents, and there are many fewer than VW postulate.

In this response, I pursue two distinct yet inextricably intertwined issues. One is how to analyze consonants that VW claim are "appendices," and the second is to develop a theory of syllable structure that is different from VW's. This is accomplished in six parts. In section 6.2, I discuss the notion of prosodic licensing, because it is one of VW's justifications for their theory of the appendix. In section 6.3, I present four alternative models of phonological representation, I demonstrate the implications of Raimy's (2000) theory for indicating precedence relationships, and I question the role of the prosodic hierarchy; this discussion suggests that it is certainly undesirable, and probably unnecessary, to analyze unsyllabified consonants as dominated by suprasyllabic constituents. Obviously, any theory of unsyllabified consonants rests upon a theory of syllable structure; accordingly, in section 6.4 I describe Cairns and Feinstein's (1982) theory of syllable structure, which contains substantially more internal structure than VW's account and therefore tolerates more tautosyllabic consonant sequences. Because Cairns and Feinstein's (CF's) theory allows tautosyllabic sequences of consonants that violate the Sonority Sequencing Principle (SSP),[1] I take up this principle in section 6.5. VW cast Rialland's (1994) observations about certain

French phenomena into their framework in their section 5.3.1.2.3; in section 6.6, I reanalyze these phenomena in the framework sketched here. I present overall conclusions in section 6.7. I emphasize that for reasons of space I do not present and defend a complete alternative to VW's theory; I can only outline an approach here.

6.2 Prosodic Licensing

VW assume that the SSP is a necessary condition for syllabification. What happens to a consonant that cannot be syllabified with a neighbor in accordance with the SSP? There are two possibilities. One is that the consonant is analyzed as an orphan and not as a terminal member of any prosodic category at all; VW reject this option, but I advocate it below. Alternatively, the consonant may be considered to be an "appendix," which means, according to VW, that it is dominated by some prosodic category higher than the syllable. This option is not available within the theory sketched here, because, as I will argue, phonological theory does not contain any prosodic categories higher than the syllable. Other authors (see, e.g., Kenstowicz 1994:260, Tranel 1995:82) have postulated that the offending consonant is part of the syllable after all, but dependent from the syllable node in some fashion. VW do not discuss these possibilities, and we can dispense with this approach because it is ad hoc and without empirical foundation.

One reason why VW choose the appendix as a way to handle disobedient consonants is to provide a formal means of constraining what segments may appear as C' (section 5.3.2). This is essentially similar to prosodic licensing (PL), the notion that if a segment is not dominated by some prosodic category, it is not interpretable, hence not pronounceable. Ito (1986), who introduced this concept into the literature, points out that some languages insert a vowel to "save" such consonants, whereas others delete them. Therefore, it is necessary to stipulate for each C' whether or not it is subject to stray erasure or is to be saved by epenthesis. However, the appendix approach does not allow us to escape stipulation. Ito says, "Our hypothesis is that both stray operations [erasure and epenthesis] bring the representations into conformity with Prosodic Licensing at the end of each phonological cycle. Stray Erasure is universal and always available as a last resort. Stray Epenthesis, on the other hand, is subject to parametric variation (the unmarked option is [off]...)" (1986:116). It follows, then, that PL is superfluous because we must still stipulate for each language whether an unsyllabified consonant is deleted, whether it is saved by epenthesis, or whether nothing happens and it is pronounced anyway. If PL is not part of linguistic theory, then it cannot be used to support VW's appendix analysis.

Below, I adumbrate Raimy's (2000) theory of precedence relations, which makes explicit the notions "follow" and "precede." These relations are sufficient to replace PL as the principle guiding what gets interpreted. Precedence relations ensure that segments are pronounceable or interpretable, and (nonexhaustive) syllabification provides a scaffold for the organization of the word, accounting for (most of) phonotactics. And, of course, we will expect deletion and epenthesis rules to "clean up" the representations at some points in derivations.

6.3 The Prosodic Hierarchy and 3-D Phonology

Prosodic hierarchy theory, which has appeared in various incarnations since Nespor and Vogel 1986, is the first of four models of phonological representation I will discuss here. Although prosodic hierarchy (PH) theories differ in details, the basic idea is that segments are dominated by syllables, syllables by feet, feet by prosodic words, and so on; moras intervene between segments and syllables in some versions of PH theory. Crucially, levels can occasionally be (nonoptimally) skipped, so a segment might be connected directly to a node higher than the syllable. An optimistic view holds that the constituents defined by PH theory not only account for stress patterns, but are supported by other phonological evidence as well. Phonological operations, be they constraints or rules, all work on the constituents or terminal nodes defined by PH theory. Although the name is a great oversimplification, I call this the *two-dimensional (2-D) model* because the information relevant to stress and other phonological operations can be encoded in one plane (= tier), the prosodic plane (PP).[2] (A graphic display of this model appears in figure 6.1.)

As an alternative to PH theory, Halle and his associates (e.g., Halle and Vergnaud 1980) propose the *3-D model*. Here, syllable and stress information belong on orthogonal planes, the metrical and syllabic tiers, where segments are arrayed along the line defined by their intersection (see figure 6.1). This is a 3-D model in the sense that the two relevant planes must exist in a three-dimensional space. 3-D theorists claim their model can account for all the phenomena used to justify PH theory without recourse to prosodic categories that hierarchically dominate the syllable.

The metrical tier of the 3-D model and rules for its construction are the subject of Idsardi's contribution to this volume. The syllabic tier contains no constituents higher than the syllable node; syllables (which must have some internal structure; see below) are simply concatenated and are not embedded in any hierarchical structure. If a consonant fails to be syllabified, there is no higher prosodic constituent to which it is attached—it must remain an orphan either at the edge of a word or between two syllables.

The notion "foot" is entirely different in PH theory and the 3-D model. The prosodic foot, an element of PH theory, is defined in terms of the hierarchical nodes with which it coexists in that theory. The metrical foot, as defined in 3-D theory, is a group of marks defined by brackets on lines of the metrical tier. There is no sense in which metrical feet gather up or dominate syllables or segments, directly or

2-D model

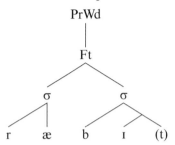

Stress is derived directly from the geometry of the prosodic hierarchy. Terminal segments are optimally dominated by the syllable node, but may also be dominated by higher nodes. This model is empirically inadequate because it falsely predicts the nonoccurrence of violations of Syllable Integrity.

3-D model

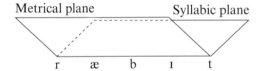

One of these two planes is defined by the metrical grid. The other contains syllables and unsyllabified (and extrametrical) consonants.

Hybrid 3-D model

Vaux adopts 3-D representation, but substitutes the prosodic plane for the syllabic plane of the classical 3-D model.

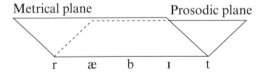

Figure 6.1
Three models of phonological representation. Each model assumes other planes, or tiers, for representing information about features, morphology, and so on. These diagrams depict only the representations relevant to relating stress to prosodic information.

indirectly, because feet and syllables are not on the same plane. The metrical and syllabic planes are related in two ways. First, they intersect along the segmental line. Second, rules (see Idsardi, this volume) relate elements on the metrical plane to elements on the syllabic plane (as well as to segmental and morphological information); in fact, information can flow both ways between planes.

At first glance, it is not obvious which of the models discussed above is the more restrictive or complex; there is a rough trade-off between the elaborate structure of PH theory and the extra dimension and attendant rules of 3-D theory. As it turns out, however, this question is immediately rendered moot by evidence that 2-D theory is empirically inadequate. As I argue in Cairns 2002, 2-D theory cannot account for violations of Syllable Integrity (SI), which are cases where a foot boundary bisects a syllable.

The third model is created by substituting the prosodic plane for the syllabic plane in 3-D phonology. This *hybrid 3-D model* is clearly more complex than the two sketched above, because it posits more structure. The trade-off mentioned in the previous paragraph is eliminated. Thus, there must be compelling evidence to accept the hybrid model. VW's approach clearly implies this model. Vaux (1998, 2003) proposes representations involving the PH, as he and Wolfe do in this volume. Furthermore, Vaux accepts the metrical plane as the way to account for stress; this is clear from his analysis of Armenian stress (Vaux 1998) as well as from personal communications. Because appendix theory is embedded in PH theory and its authors accept 3-D phonology, any critique of the hybrid model applies to appendix theory.

Before we turn to arguments evaluating the hybrid model, it behooves us to examine recent advances in understanding how precedence relationships are represented. Raimy (2000) proposes a formal procedure for representing and manipulating sequential relationships between segments, which could in principle be combined with any of the three models discussed so far. As Raimy notes, precedence is traditionally represented simply as left-to-right ordering of elements across the page. He shows that an explicit theory of precedence relationships opens the way to deepening insight into phonological phenomena. Precedence relationships are formally represented as illustrated in (1) for the English word *rabbit*.

(1) $\# \to X \to X \to X \to X \to X \to \%$

r æ b ɪ t

The symbol $\to$ represents the relationship "precede," and # and % are arbitrary symbols representing "beginning" and "end," respectively. Celebrated facts of reduplication were at the heart of the initial motivation for this theory; the interested reader may pursue this by reading Raimy 2000.

Raimy's theory seems a likely contender as part of a general theory of phonological representation, so I adopt it here and will embed it within the models discussed above. The fourth model to be discussed here, then, is simply the *3-D model with Raimy's precedence relationships* explicitly indicated.

I make the working assumptions that precedence relationships are primary and syllable structure is derived, that syllabification is the first process that applies to lexical items, and that syllabification applies cyclically. The syllabified representation of *rabbit* would be (2); I explain the angle brackets around the final /t/ below. For the purposes of this chapter, we can remain agnostic about the formal devices for deriving syllable structure. I propose that syllable structure is built on structures like those in (1), yielding structures like those in (2). Under Raimy's proposal, phonological theory must contain a process of linearization to "ensure that sequences of elements are interpretable at the motor/perceptual interface" (Raimy 2000:6).

(2)

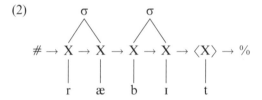

Raimy's theory provides an attractive alternative to the notion of prosodic licensing discussed above. A segment can be interpreted by peripheral mechanisms (i.e., is "pronounced") if it is in a linearized string as defined by graphs like that in (1); prosodic structure is irrelevant to any concept of licensing.

I have argued that two-dimensional PH theory must be rejected on empirical grounds (Cairns 2002), so we are left with choosing between the simple 3-D model and the hybrid model; either must at this point be supplemented with an explicit theory of precedence. It now seems clear that this move renders the PH otiose, so we must also reject the hybrid model. Accordingly, we are left with the classical Hallean 3-D model, amended with precedence relationships.

Recall that the burden of proof must fall upon proponents of the hybrid model, as it is more complex than the simple 3-D model. VW give two principal arguments for including the PH in a theory of phonological representation. Arguing that suprasyllabic prosodic structures are required to account for restrictions that some languages place on what may occur as unsyllabified segments, they ask, "What would be the domain over which such restrictions would apply, or the edge to which the markedness constraints would align?" (p. 123). They go on to claim that "such formulations necessarily make reference to the prosodic hierarchy" (p. 123). It is legitimate to question the "necessity" of this conclusion. I see no compelling reason to reject, a priori, statements that constrain the class and/or sequencing of stray segments.

VW also suggest that suprasyllabic prosodic structure is needed to account for the phenomena that motivated the notion of prosodic licensing, which I have argued against above. Furthermore, Raimy (2000:105, 109, 114) proposes rules for effectively deleting segments by inserting a "jump-link" arrow around the segment to be deleted, as illustrated in (3); we will look at a relevant example later in this chapter.[3]

(3) $\cdots \rightarrow X_1 \rightarrow X_2 \rightarrow X_3 \rightarrow \cdots$

6.4   The Internal Structure of the Syllable

There is an inverse relationship between the amount of infrasyllabic structure and the number of extrasyllabic consonants posited by any particular theory.[4] Each particular theory of syllable structure determines what must be C′. I will argue that CF's theory of syllable structure allows far fewer instances of C′ than VW's theory allows. Some reduplication facts constitute the primary evidence here; phonotactic evidence is sketched later. The main point of this section is to show that an empirically adequate theory of syllable structure must have a richly articulated infrasyllabic hierarchical organization.

To see the interplay between infrasyllabic structure and the number of consonants rendered extrasyllabic, note that Idsardi (this volume) proposes a flat syllable structure with no internal structure, in the spirit of Kahn 1976, Clements and Keyser 1983, and other work. He goes further and suggests that consonants do not close syllables, yielding a great many extrasyllabic consonants. By contrast, Fudge (1969), CF (1982), Selkirk (1982), and Goldsmith (1990) propose theories of syllable structure with elaborated internal structure containing branching rhymes and codas that can accommodate many consonants that sparser theories render extrasyllabic.

Idsardi's proposal cannot be valid as stated because syllables must contain codas at virtually every level of the grammar. For example, Vaux (1998) demonstrates that the selection of the plural allomorph in Standard Eastern Armenian must distinguish between coda and extrametrical consonants, indicating that any syllabification algorithm must admit codas at even the highest level of the phonology. Furthermore, Borowsky (1986, 1989) argues that at the lexical level, English syllables can be no longer than C_0VX, where X is either a consonant or the extension of the vocalic nucleus. She also shows that not only does this level tolerate at most one word-final extrametrical consonant, it in fact analyzes any word-final consonant as C′; the angle brackets around the final /t/ in *rabbit* in (2) indicate word-final extrametricality. Borowsky's observation explains alternations such as *mean* ∼ *meant*, *keep* ∼ *kept*, *wide* ∼ *width*. In the lexicon, the stems *mean*, *keep*, *wide* have a long vowel as the nucleus of the syllable, and the stem-final consonants are extrametrical. The addition of a single-consonant suffix at the lexical level pushes the stem-final consonant into the coda of the syllable, forcing the vowel to shorten to adhere to the C_0VX canonical structure. This analysis relies crucially on the presence of a coda. We may conclude, then, that the representation of syllables must allow codas and that Idsardi's proposal is too austere for syllabification at every level of phonology.

This conclusion does not settle the question whether a CVC syllable is flat or has an internal onset/rhyme distinction, as most phonologists assume. Although space limits prevent a thorough defense of the internal structure view, the literature contains many convincing arguments that syllables must have an internal constituent break between an onset and a rhyme and that the latter splits into a nucleus and a coda. There is by no means a consensus on whether the onset and/or coda have internal structure; below I present a model with onset-internal structure that was first proposed by CF (1982) and more recently explored by Idsardi and Raimy (2005) in connection with language-play phenomena.

CF's model of the syllable posits the onset structure in (4), where each position within a syllable is given a specific label by Universal Grammar (UG). All simple onsets occupy the MC position. P and A positions occur only if the onset is a cluster. Some languages allow either a P position (but not A), some allow A (but not P), and some (e.g., English) allow both. Universal laws that define phoneme inventories, like those described by Clements (this volume), determine what segments may appear in each position. For many languages, these laws allow only /s/ in the P position and sonorants in the A slot.[5] Any consonant in a language's inventory may appear in the MC position. However, there are cooccurrence restrictions on adjacent segments within the onset, discussed below.

(4) *The Cairns-Feinstein (1982) model of the syllable*
    Parentheses indicate optionality; O = onset; R = rhyme (rhyme structure is simplified here for expository reasons); M = margin; P = premargin; MC = margin core; A = adjunct; N = nucleus; C = coda.
    a. *General template*

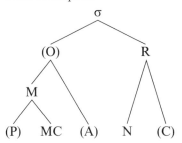

b. *The word* strap

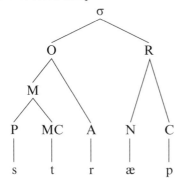

CF's theory of syllable structure and Raimy's theory of precedence relations fit together nicely to explain some otherwise recalcitrant facts of reduplication. Raimy's theory of reduplication sometimes refers to syllabic constituents to define anchor points for the arrows defining precedence relations. Fleischhacker (2005), extending proposals by Steriade (1988), presents a taxonomy (cast within Optimality Theory) of reduplication patterns where only a portion of the onset is copied. The following examples show the utility of constituent structure within the onset, particularly of the MC position.

Gothic, for instance, appears to copy the entire M constituent, as in (5a) (Braun 1883, Kiparsky 1979, CF 1982, Steriade 1988).[6] The analysis in (5b,c) is adapted from Raimy 2002. The diagram in (5c) means that a morphological rule inserts the curved arrow and the vowel /e/; the linearization algorithm spells out new material before underlying material. Therefore, linearization will first spell out the entire initial consonant sequence, followed by the vowel /e/; then it will repeat the consonant sequence, followed by the rest of the base.[7]

(5) *Cluster simplification in Gothic reduplication*
    a. *Data from Braun 1883, via Fleischhacker 2005*
       ste-stald   'possessed'
       ske-sked   'separated'
       ge-grot   'wept'
       se-slept   'slept'

b. *Syllable structure for Gothic*

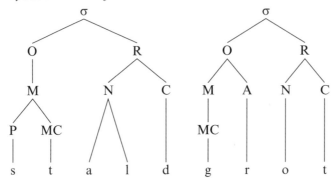

c. *Gothic rule*
   The reduplicant morpheme is the entire M + /e/.

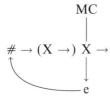

   In Sanskrit, on the other hand, the reduplicant consists of the bare MC node followed by the stem vowel, as depicted in (6b). As the reduplication rule is formulated in Raimy's framework (see (6c)), the first element in the spelled-out reduplicated form begins with the MC, followed by the N, followed by the entire base. (The parentheses around P constituents mean, as usual, optionality and disjunctive ordering; see below.) The syllabification clearly rests on the syllabic analysis whereby /s/ followed by a sonorant is an MC-A sequence, unlike in Gothic (or English; see below); the onset /mn/ must also be an MC-A sequence. Kessler (1994), who applies CF's model of syllable structure to these and other Sanskrit facts, provides justification for these conclusions.[8]

(6) *Cluster simplification in Sanskrit reduplication*
   a. *Data from Steriade 1982, via Fleischhacker 2005*
      tu-tud   'pushed'
      pa-prac   'asked'
      si-smi   'smiled'
      tu-stu   'praised'
      ma-mna:-u   'noted'

b. *Syllable structure for Sanskrit*

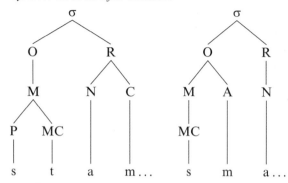

c. *Sanskrit rule*
RED = MC + N copy

$$\# \to (P \to) \, MC \to (A \to) \, N \to \cdots$$

The Greek examples provided by VW (see their (20)) are also readily explained in this theory. Observe that reduplication simply fails if there is a segment before the MC; therefore, the rule for this case is as in (7). (7a) says that an MC that begins a root is reduplicated and /e/ is inserted between the two occurrences of MC. The example *graphō*, *ge-graph-* 'write' (from VW (20)) illustrates this; the root begins with MC, /g/, so this segment is reduplicated and /e/ inserted. In examples from VW's (20) like *speirō*, *e-spar-* 'sow' and *ktizō*, *e-ktis-* 'create', the root does not begin with MC, so (7a) cannot apply. In conformity with the Elsewhere Condition, the more general rule (7b) applies; this rule simply inserts an /e/ before the first segment of the root.

(7) *Greek perfect reduplication rule*
a.   MC
       |
   \# → X → ⋯
       e

b. \# → X → ⋯
       e

Idsardi and Raimy (2005) invoke CF's model of the onset to account for some facts of Germanic alliteration. These facts also make use of the initial consonant sequence minus the A. In Idsardi and Raimy's examples, as well as in the reduplication examples discussed above, the analysis of /s/ as a P constituent is not crucial; it could just as well be unsyllabified, as in VW's analysis. Similarly, all the accounts of reduplication in VW's chapter can be recast in CF's framework,[9] so the reduplication examples discussed here and in VW's chapter are not critical to proving the existence of the P node. However, these reduplication examples and the alliteration facts discussed by Idsardi and Raimy (2005) do show the utility of the MC node. This suffices to make the point that the onset has internal hierarchical structure. I make the case for the P node in the next section, where I argue that the SSP is not part of UG.

6.5 The Sonority Sequencing Principle

VW propose that the SSP is a necessary condition for determining syllable constituency. It is clear that the SSP is not a sufficient condition; as Vaux agrees (pers. comm.), English and many other languages systematically exclude /tl-/ and /dl-/ as syllable-initial sequences, despite adhering to the SSP. I propose in this section that the SSP is also not a necessary condition for deciding whether two adjacent consonants are tautosyllabic. CF's model posits that /s/ is tautosyllabic with a following obstruent in English and many (but not all) other languages, so it eschews the SSP as a necessary condition for defining syllables. As this is clearly a minority position in the field, it is incumbent on me to justify it. I sketch such an argument in the next few paragraphs, followed by a few general comments about the SSP.

Sequences like /sn-/ and /sm-/ obey the SSP, so these sequences are arguably tautosyllabic in any theory. Yet nasals occur in second position in an English syllable only after /s/. CF propose that these sequences are allowed because /s/ occupies the P position within a complex onset, and nasals may occupy the MC position. Similarly, /sl-/ obeys the SSP and is also presumably a tautosyllabic sequence. The sequence /sl-/ is the only example of a coronal followed by /l/ in English; /tl-/, /dl-/, and /θl-/ are excluded because if MC is occupied by a coronal, /l/ may not appear in the A position. The admissibility of the /sl-/ onset follows straightforwardly in CF's theory because /s/ is the only segment allowed in P position in English. A theory that did not accept such a notion of onset structure would require a more complicated set of statements to allow /sl-/ and disallow other coronal-/l/ sequences.

English also allows /ʃ/ in initial position preceding /l, m, n/ in many recent loanwords, mostly from Yiddish, such as *schlep*, *schnook*, *schmuck*. There are two possibilities here: either the /ʃ/ irregularly occupies the P slot in these words or it is unsyllabified. In loanwords like *Irkutsk* and *Yakutsk*, I propose that the final /k/ is indeed unsyllabified.

The arguments in the preceding paragraph involve only sequences that obey the SSP. CF claim that the presence of the P position allows for a broad array of consonants in the MC position, including voiceless stops, a situation that clearly violates the SSP. It has been noted that words like those in (8) are absent from the English lexicon (Fudge 1969, 1987, Clements and Keyser 1983, Cairns 1988, Davis 1991). Coetzee (2004) has shown that experimental subjects tend to reject forms like the last three in (8b).

(8) a. *stask, *spast, *skusp
   b. *smum, *snun, *slul, *shrear, *klull, *krear, *plall, *trear, *spap, *skuck, ?stit

Given the frequency of each of the sounds involved in these nonwords, linguistic theory arguably must account for the words' nonoccurrence. The forms in (8a) seem to suggest that if an /s/ occupies the P position of the onset, then /s/ may not occur in the coda; those in (8b) are perhaps accounted for by the constraint in (9).

(9) $*(C_1C_2VC_3)$, where $C_2 = C_3$ and V is short

The final example in (8b) is marginally acceptable; the similar form *stet* is an editorial term, and *stat* is a frequent abbreviation for *statistics* and is used in medicine to mean 'right now'. However, all these forms are unquestionably odd; note that words like *strut* and *skunk*, which do not meet the structural description of (9), are actual words and do not sound odd at all. The constraint in (9) is quite unusual; Menn (1978) reports that children frequently impose pansyllabic constraints against repeated occurrence of the same or similar phonemes within a given syllable. The /s/ must belong to the syllable for this formulation of the constraint.

The kind of constraint in (9) is qualitatively dissimilar from the kind that governs cooccurrence within subsyllabic constituents. Intraconstituent constraints can be expressed as suppressing the occurrence of marked feature values. For example, the presence of /s/ in the P position eliminates from the MC position all segments defined as marked for any features other than place; and the presence of a segment in the A position eliminates all segments marked for both continuance and voicing from the MC position. This is further justification for CF's structure of the onset; constraints within a constituent defined by UG can be formulated using categories naturally available within phonological theory. Constraints that span the onset-rhyme boundary, on the other hand, are usually constraints against the recurrence of identical or similar segments in specific syllabic positions (see Fudge 1987).

An even stronger case can be made for the tautosyllabicity of word-internal /s/ and an immediately following consonant.[10] Let us first consider a clear example of C′ within a word. The /t/ in a word like *antler* must be C′, owing to the inadmissibility of syllable rhymes longer than VX and of /tl-/ onsets. Borowsky (1986, 1989) observes that in all English words where a rhyme appears to be longer than VX, the offending consonant (which I analyze as C′) is homorganic with the following onset; *mountain* and *council* are other examples. Pierrehumbert (1994) makes a similar observation. An internal C′ apparently cannot license its own point of articulation; it must borrow it from the following onset.

We now turn to the word *abscond*. If the /s/ in this word were C′, it would have to get its point of articulation from the following onset; however, the /k/ is not coronal, so /s/ cannot be C′. In fact, /s/ is the only segment that can occur in this position. *Abfcond is distinctly odd; if it is at all acceptable, perhaps it is because the /f/ borrows its point of articulation from the preceding /b/. Certainly the word *agfcond is completely impossible in English. The most parsimonious explanation for these distributional facts is that the /s/ in *abscond* is the P constituent of the onset of the second syllable, and only /s/ may occur in this slot.[11]

If we accept these arguments that /s/ may be tautosyllabic with a following obstruent, then the SSP is not a necessary condition for syllables. Another fact about English onsets makes the SSP dubious as a linguistic principle. Basing their argument on Clements's Dispersion Principle, VW claim that the SSP suggests a hierarchy of admissible tautosyllabic sequences; languages will move down the scale of SSP violations. That is, if a language allows TN- onsets, it should also allow TL- onsets, but not vice versa, because TN- violates the SSP more than does TL-. (Recall that *T* is any stop, *N* any nasal, and *L* any liquid.) Furthermore, if a language allows N in the second position in a syllable, it should allow a stop in the first position before it allows a fricative there; the TN- cluster violates the SSP less than does an SN- sequence. English does have tautosyllabic SN- sequences, yet it does not have TN-onsets.[12] Therefore, the SSP fails to make a valid prediction here. The crucial point is that the relevant UG principles do not govern sequences; rather, they govern the definitions of positions within the syllable.

I propose that the relationship between the SSP and the distributional facts within syllables is like the relationship between vowel lengthening and iambic footing. Giving perception-based arguments, many phonologists (e.g., Hayes 1995, Kager 1999) propose as a principle of UG that long vowels are favored over short vowels in the head of an iambic foot. However, Halle and Idsardi (2000:206) disagree, writing that "instead of importing nonlinguistic auditory perceptual biases into UG, we suggest instead that these biases provide preferred perceptions to the learners, which they try to maintain if they can." The moral here is that UG is not the only source of explanation; the perceptual system and its interaction with the language acquisition device can also explain crosslinguistic tendencies. In a similar vein, I propose that the SSP is not part of UG, but instead belongs to one or more of the phonetic sciences. The role of UG is to define the positions and constituency within a syllable, and not necessarily to delimit which segments may occur in each position.

One of VW's arguments against the tautosyllabicity of *s*T clusters is that they appear "less complex than canonical onset clusters" (p. 108), and VW go on to refer to perceptual and language acquisition observations, as well as purely linguistic facts. For example, Engstrand and Ericsdotter (1999) indicate that *s*T clusters are rich in cues for identifying the phonemes. These authors found that the stop in *s*T- onsets was readily perceptible on the basis of acoustic information in the /s/, and they conclude "that the commonly encountered initial [s] + stop and final stop + [s] clusters, in which the onset and coda sequences are mirror images of each other, may have a perceptual basis." Their basic idea is that "stop place of articulation will be signaled more efficiently in these onsets and codas than in those in which consonants appear in the reversed order, the reason being that place information is then present both before and after the stop, i.e., both in [s] and in the vowel" (p. 49).

Morelli (1999), reporting her study of universal patterns of phonotactics, indicates the presence of implicational universals favoring *s*T- onsets over sequences of two stops, two fricatives, or a stop followed by a fricative. Studies such as Engstrand and Ericsdotter's, as well as the plausible assumption that an *s*T- onset provides rich cues for segmentation as well as segment identification, provide a phonetic basis for these observations. There is no need to encode them in UG if we employ reasoning like Halle and Idsardi's cited above.

6.6 Reanalysis of Facts from Rialland 1994

VW (section 5.3.1.2.3) discuss a number of interesting facts due to Rialland (1994). In this section, I show how CF's model of the syllable, coupled with Raimy's (2000) theory of precedence, can handle these facts.

VW argue that French words like *skier*, optionally [skje], show that the /s/ must be extrasyllabic; if it were not, the /j/ would not be allowed, because only two segments are allowed in the French onset. However, in CF's model it is straightforward to assign the /s/ to the P position, the /k/ to the MC position, and the /j/ to the A position. Words like **plje* are impossible because only one segment at a time is allowed in the A position, and /p/ is not allowed in the P position. French does indeed have C′ word-initially, as shown by Rialland's discussion of *knout* 'short whip'. However, there is no reason to believe that /s/ is C′ in the forms VW list in their (10).

VW remind us that the vowels /ə/ and /e/ relax to [ɛ] in closed syllables in French. The data in VW's (12) show that intervocalic *s*T sequences are syllabified with the /s/ as the coda of the left syllable and the stop as the onset of the right one—this is no surprise, and does not, in fact, speak at all to their extrasyllabic analysis. The facts related to postlexical dropping of /ə/ are of particular interest and show the utility of CF's model of syllable structure, especially in conjunction with Raimy-type rules.

The French deletion phenomena take place at the postlexical level, after words and clitics have been concatenated. Furthermore, deletion is quite variable, depending apparently on speech rate and social factors. There is, therefore, some question whether the facts need to be accounted for fully within phonological theory; phonetic theories should also play a role. It is unclear just how to partition the analysis of this phenomenon between phonetic and phonological theories.

Referring to the facts depicted in VW's (13), it appears that [ə] may delete in a sequence of . . . $V \rightarrow C_1 \rightarrow ə \rightarrow C_1 \rightarrow R$ . . ., where R is a sonorant and $C_1 \rightarrow ə$ constitutes a grammatical formative. However, deletion does not take place if the second C_1 is a member of the P constituent. In other words, the deletion rule starts with an MC position and ends with an MC position. It cannot end in a P position. See the formulation of the rule in (10).

(10)

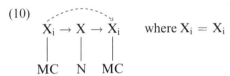

$$X_i \rightarrow X \rightarrow X_i \qquad \text{where } X_i = X_i$$

| | | |
| MC | N | MC |

This rule operates under conditions not relevant here.

Rule (10) says that the N position may be skipped just in case it is flanked by two identical segments, each of which occupies the MC position of an onset. It succeeds in accounting for all of the examples in VW's (13). The facts in (13a) are accounted for by assuming that /sw/ may be analyzed as an MC-A sequence. And the rule does not apply in cases like (13b), because the structural description is not met; the /s/ in *sport* occupies the P position, not the MC position.

6.7   Conclusion

I have argued that it is undesirable to incorporate the PH in a theory of phonological representation because it adds unnecessary components to our theoretical repertoire. Raimy (2000) uses facts about reduplication to justify a general theory of precedence that, in conjunction with a more richly articulated theory of syllable structure, can handle many, if not all, of the facts that VW adduce in support of the PH. I conclude, then, that the Hallean 3-D theory of phonological representations, enriched by Raimy-style rules, is the most parsimonious available.

Phonologists (except for mora theorists) commonly accept that syllables must have an onset-rhyme constituent structure, with the rhyme in turn divided into a nucleus and a coda.

Reduplication phenomena that involve partial copy of the onset suggest that the onset in turn has a constituent structure. Because I reject the SSP as part of UG on the grounds that it properly belongs to one or more of the phonetic sciences, there is no reason to disallow fricative-stop sequences in an onset. In fact, I have adduced phonotactic evidence from English in favor of just such an analysis.

There is arguably no net gain from substituting the richly articulated syllable structure of CF's theory for the complexity of the PH embedded in the hybrid model. However, there are no compelling empirical or theoretical arguments in favor of positing any structure above the level of the syllable, whereas there is evidence in favor of positing infrasyllabic structure. Furthermore, I have argued against both of VW's motivations for the PH, namely, the notions of prosodic licensing and the idea that suprasyllabic structure is required to account for constraints on what may appear in unsyllabified positions within the string.

There is no empirical or theoretical reason to reject the occurrence of unsyllabified segments; in fact, I have suggested (in connection with words like *Irkutsk*) that consonants in loanwords that clearly disobey a language's phonotactic constraints may be best analyzed as prosodic orphans. However, the theory described here posits far fewer occurrences of C' than does VW's.

This chapter cannot be taken as a "refutation" of VW's appendix theory because space does not permit a thorough exploration of anywhere near all their observations. The goal here was to sketch and briefly motivate an alternative approach to phenomena similar to those they focus on; this alternative would need considerably more investigation to be taken as definitive.

Notes

I am indebted to Bert Vaux, who commented at length on an earlier version of this chapter and whose comments prompted extensive revisions. I also thank Eric Raimy, who provided detailed and very helpful comments. Of course, all responsibility still lies directly with me. I also thank my wife and colleague Helen Cairns for detailed commentary and moral encouragement. My puppies Leander and Pazuzu kept me focused and provided contentment throughout the writing of this chapter.

1. The SSP is the principle "that syllables rise in sonority through the onset to the syllable peak, then fall in sonority through the coda" (VW, p. 103). The SSP has sometimes been referred to as the "sonority hierarchy" (see, e.g., Engstrand and Ericsdotter 1999). The term "sonority hierarchy" is used here (as in most of the phonology literature) to refer to the theory that segments are dominated by syllables, syllables by feet, and so on, as discussed extensively in this chapter.

2. Strictly speaking, there is not really a 2-D model, because other linguistically relevant information must exist on other planes. For example, feature information, with its distinct geometry, must lie on a separate plane. These other planes may intersect with the models discussed here in complex ways beyond the scope of this chapter. *2-D* refers only to the fact that no more than two dimensions need be posited to represent phonological structures that trigger and/or undergo phonological processes.

3. Bear in mind that the foregoing criticism of VW's theory rests upon its having been recast in an explicit theory of precedence relationships that VW themselves did not consider.

4. Some terminological notes are in order. An *extrasyllabic* segment is simply one that is not included in a syllable. If such a segment is also attached to a higher prosodic node (in VW's theory), then it is an *appendix*. An *extrametrical* segment is an extrasyllabic segment that is invisible to the syllabification algorithm, usually because it is at a word edge. Thus, a segment may be extrasyllabic because it cannot fit into the canonical syllable structure of a language (like the /t/ in *antler*, discussed later), or because it is word-final, like the /t/ in *rabbit*. *C′* notates extrasyllabic segments; I indicate in the text wherever it is relevant to specify that it means 'extrametrical', not just 'extrasyllabic' (I reject appendices, because I reject suprasyllabic structure).

5. Many languages allow various segments in the P position, which is frequently the locus of violations of the SSP (see Kessler 1994).

6. Klamath has a pattern similar to that of Gothic, except with more lexical variability (Barker 1964:84, Fleischhacker 2005).

7. Note that the behavior of the reduplicant in *se-slept* 'slept' shows that the /s/ is analyzed here as the MC and the /l/ as the A; further research is required to justify this analyis.

8. Note that the final example, [ma-mna:-u], shows that it is not feasible to formulate this Sanskrit reduplication in terms of sonority, whereby the least sonorant segment is copied; /m/ and /n/ are of equal sonority.

9. VW do not in fact provide formal analyses of any of the reduplication phenomena they adduce in favor of appendix theory.

10. The syllabification of medial /s/ is subject to some lexical variation. For example, VW note two possible syllabifications of *Wisconsin*, either between the /s/ and the /k/, or to the left of the /s/. Also, *plas.tic* is usually syllabified as indicated in New York City Dialect and the [æ] is pronounced as a tense and diphthongized vowel typical of a closed syllable; contrast this word with *a.stronaut*, which has lax [æ] and is analyzed as indicated.

11. VW specifically reject the use of phonotactics as a basis for formulating linguistic generalizations, because it is not always possible to distinguish a historical from a true linguistic generalization; therefore, they do not accept the arguments made here. They also disagree with Borowsky's generalizations, and Vaux says (pers. comm.) that *abfcond* sounds fine to him (I have not asked him about *agfcond*). Although the rejection of *abfcond* may not be as robust as, say, the rejection of *ftprk*, there are no words in the English lexicon that violate Borowsky's generalizations about the licensing of word-internal C′. I submit that it is unlikely that this gap is due to historical accident, because of the size of the English vocabulary and the lexical frequency of the sounds involved.

12. Words beginning with /sn-/ are straightforwardly analyzed in CF's theory.

References

Barker, Muhammad Abd-al-Rahman. 1964. *Klamath grammar*. Berkeley and Los Angeles: University of California Press.

Borowsky, Toni. 1986. Topics in the Lexical Phonology of English. Doctoral dissertation, University of Massachusetts, Amherst.

Borowsky, Toni. 1989. Structure preservation and the syllable coda in English. *Natural Language and Linguistic Theory* 7:145–166.

Braun, Wilhelm. 1883. *Gothic grammar, with selections for reading and a glossary*. London: Sampson Low, Marston, Searle, and Rivington.

Cairns, Charles. 1988. Phonotactics, markedness and lexical representation. *Phonology* 5:209–236.

Cairns, Charles. 2002. Foot and syllable in Southern Paiute. Ms., City University of New York. http://www.cunyphonologyforum.net/papers/20Sopai.pdf.

Cairns, Charles, and Mark Feinstein. 1982. Markedness and the theory of syllable structure. *Linguistic Inquiry* 13:193–226.

Clements, G. N., and Samuel Jay Keyser. 1983. *CV phonology*. Cambridge, Mass.: MIT Press.

Coetzee, Andries. 2004. What it means to be a loser: Non-optimal candidates in Optimality Theory. Doctoral dissertation, University of Massachusetts, Amherst. Rutgers Optimality Archive ROA 687-0904. http://roa.rutgers.edu.

Davis, Stuart. 1991. Coronals and the phonotactics of nonadjacent consonants in English. In *The special status of coronals: Internal and external evidence*, ed. by Carole Paradis and Jean-François Prunet, 49–60. San Diego, Calif.: Academic Press.

Engstrand, Olle, and Christine Ericsdotter. 1999. Explaining a violation of the sonority hierarchy: Stop place perception in adjacent [s]. In *Proceedings from the XIIth Swedish Phonetics Conference*, 49–52. Göteborg, Sweden: Göteborg University, Department of Linguistics.

Fleischhacker, Heidi. 2005. Similarity in phonology: Evidence from reduplication and loan word adaptation. Doctoral dissertation, UCLA.

Fudge, Erik. 1969. Syllables. *Journal of Linguistics* 5:253–286.

Fudge, Erik. 1987. Branching structure within the syllable. *Journal of Linguistics* 23:359–377.

Goldsmith, John A. 1990. *Autosegmental and metrical phonology*. Oxford: Blackwell.

Halle, Morris, and William Idsardi. 2000. Stress and length in Hixkaryana. In *A review of Optimality Theory*, ed. by Nancy Ritter, special issue, *The Linguistic Review* 17 (2–4): 199–218.

Halle, Morris, and Jean-Roger Vergnaud. 1980. Three-dimensional phonology. *Journal of Linguistic Research* 1:83–105.

Hayes, Bruce. 1995. *Metrical stress theory: Principles and case studies*. Chicago: University of Chicago Press.

Idsardi, William, and Eric Raimy. 2005. Remarks on language play. http://www.ling.umd.edu/~idsardi/work/2005lgplay.pdf.

Ito, Junko. 1986. Syllable theory in prosodic phonology. Doctoral dissertation, University of Massachusetts, Amherst.

Kager, René. 1999. *Optimality Theory*. Cambridge: Cambridge University Press.

Kahn, Daniel. 1976. Syllable-based generalizations in English phonology. Doctoral dissertation, MIT.

Kenstowicz, Michael. 1994. *Phonology in generative grammar*. Oxford: Blackwell.

Kessler, Brett. 1994. Sandhi and syllables in Classical Sanskrit. In *Proceedings of the 12th West Coast Conference on Formal Linguistics*, ed. by Eric Duncan, Donca Farkas, and Philip Spaelti, 35–50. Stanford, Calif.: CSLI Publications.

Kiparsky, Paul. 1979. Metrical structure assignment is cyclic. *Linguistic Inquiry* 10:421–441.

Menn, Lisa. 1978. Phonological units in beginning speech. In *Syllables and segments*, ed. by Alan Bell and Joan B. Hooper, 157–171. Amsterdam: North Holland.

Morelli, Frida. 1999. The phonotactics and phonology of obstruent clusters in Optimality Theory. Doctoral dissertation, University of Maryland, College Park.

Nespor, Marina, and Irene Vogel. 1986. *Prosodic phonology*. Dordrecht: Foris.

Pierrehumbert, Janet. 1994. Syllable structure and word structure: A study of triconsonantal clusters in English. In *Phonological structure and phonetic form: Papers in laboratory phonology III*, ed. by Patricia A. Keating, 168–188. Cambridge: Cambridge University Press.

Raimy, Eric. 2000. *The phonology and morphology of reduplication*. Berlin: Mouton de Gruyter.

Raimy, Eric. 2002. Minimalist reduplication. Talk given at the CUNY Linguistics Colloquium, City University of New York, 28 February.

Rialland, Annie. 1994. The phonology and phonetics of extrasyllabicity in French. In *Phonological structure and phonetic form: Papers in laboratory phonology III*, ed. by Patricia A. Keating, 136–159. Cambridge: Cambridge University Press.

Selkirk, Elisabeth. 1982. The syllable. In *The structure of phonological representations*, ed. by Harry van der Hulst and Norval Smith, 2:337–383. Dordrecht: Foris.

Steriade, Donca. 1988. Reduplication and syllable transfer in Sanskrit and elsewhere. *Phonology* 5:73–155.

Tranel, Bernard. 1995. Current issues in French phonology: Liaison and position. In *The handbook of phonological theory*, ed. by John Goldsmith, 798–816. Cambridge, Mass.: Blackwell.

Vaux, Bert. 1998. *The phonology of Armenian*. Oxford: Clarendon Press.

Vaux, Bert. 2003. Syllabification in Armenian, Universal Grammar, and the lexicon. *Linguistic Inquiry* 34:91–125.

7 Does Sonority Have a Phonetic Basis?

G. N. Clements

In their chapter, Vaux and Wolfe argue that syllabification conforms universally to the Sonority Sequencing Principle (SSP), according to which the segments in a syllable rise in sonority from the margin to the peak. Segments that cannot be gathered into syllables in this way remain extrasyllabic, linking to higher levels of prosodic structure such as the foot, the prosodic word, or the prosodic phrase.

The driving concept behind this view is *sonority*. Though this concept has a venerable history in phonology and phonetic studies, dating well back into the nineteenth century (Whitney 1865, Sievers 1881), precise phonetic correlates for it have proven elusive, and several scholars have maintained that it has no phonetic basis. This issue, which Vaux and Wolfe do not discuss, is an important one, and I would like to comment on it briefly in this chapter.

As Vaux and Wolfe point out, not all phonological concepts have phonetic correlates. For example, though the syllable is an essential unit in phonology (and underlies many aspects of phonetic and prosodic patterning as well), it has no universally valid phonetic definition. This fact is not surprising once we recognize that the syllable is primarily a phonological construct, defined over sequences of discrete phonological segments rather than over phonetic primes as such. At this level of abstraction (which includes most of phonology), few constructs have direct phonetic definitions. Vaux and Wolfe rightly emphasize that the ultimate justification for such concepts depends on their success in bringing order to a vast array of seemingly disparate facts. The syllable does just that.

Although sonority can also be justified on these grounds, it does not appear to be an abstract category in the same sense. It does not seem very likely that the ranking of various types of speech sounds in a sonority scale is entirely unrelated to their physical and perceptual properties. If sonority were completely abstract, as some linguists have maintained, a scale such as Vowel > Semivowel > Liquid > Nasal > Obstruent would be inherently arbitrary. We might just as well have expected syllables to conform to any random permutation of this scale, such as the (unattested) reverse order in which obstruents are the most favored syllable nucleus and vocoids the preferred margin. As I have pointed out elsewhere, the absence of a consistent, physical basis for characterizing sonority in language-independent terms would make it impossible to explain the nearly identical nature of sonority constraints across languages (Clements 1990:291).

Not all phoneticians maintain that sonority has no phonetic content, however. Many, from Sievers (1881) onward, have suggested that sonority is correlated in some way with audibility, in the sense that more audible sounds occupy a higher position on the sonority scale. This view was adopted in much subsequent work, for example by Heffner, who stated that "sonority is a quality attributed to a sound on the basis of its seeming fullness or largeness, and when attributed to speech sounds, sonority is correlated very largely with the degree to which the voice is audible. There is very little discernable difference between the sonority of any two speech sounds produced without voice. For this reason sonority may be equated more or less correctly with acoustic energy and its quantities determined accurately by electronic methods" (1950:74). A similar view was proposed by Ladefoged (1993), who suggested that sonority can be defined in terms of the loudness of a sound, which is related to its acoustic energy relative to other sounds having the same length, stress, and pitch.[1]

Several methods of ranking speech sounds in terms of power and relative audibility have been described by Fletcher (1972:82–86). Of the various measures proposed, the one that yields a result closest to the sonority scale is a composite measure of relative phonetic power, taking the power of the weakest sound as the basis of comparison. The ratio of powers between the weakest sound, $/\theta/$, and the most powerful sound, $/ɔ/$, is 680, amounting to a difference of 28 dB. The full ranking of English speech sounds is given in (1).

(1)	ɔ	680	u	310	tʃ	42	k	13
	a	600	ɪ	260	n	36	v	12
	ʌ	510	i	220	dʒ	23	ð	11
	æ	490	r	210	ʒ	20	b	7
	o	470	l	100	z	16	d	7
	ʊ	460	ʃ	80	s	16	p	6
	e	370	ŋ	73	t	15	f	5
	ɛ	350	m	52	g	12	θ	1

It can be seen that by this measure, the relative ranking of English sounds is low vowels > mid vowels > high vowels > r > l > nasals > obstruents, with few discrepancies. This ranking fits commonly proposed sonority scales quite well. The major anomaly is the high rank of voiceless sibilants, one of which, $/ʃ/$, outranks all nasals. Sibilants, though rather noisy sounds, do not pattern as high-sonority sounds in most languages. In English, for example, they precede rather than follow nasals in syllable onsets (*small*, *snail*, but **msall*, **nsail*).

I would like to suggest that sonority is related not to loudness or audibility as such, but to the relative *resonance* of speech sounds. While the words *sonority* and *resonance* overlap in their everyday meaning, *resonance* adds a suggestion of repetition to the base meaning of *sonority* (resonance = re + sonance). A resonant sound can be understood as one whose inherent sonority is repeated, prolonged, or augmented in some way.[2]

Resonance is, of course, a familiar notion in both physics and acoustics. In acoustic theory, resonance is measured in terms of the amplitude at which an object vibrates at its natural frequency. In speech, resonance is a property of a vibrating body of air contained within one or more vocal tract cavities. In an acoustic system like the vocal tract, the natural frequencies (or resonances) of the vibrating air are determined by its size, shape, and elasticity. Sounds perceived as sonorant tend to be characterized by high acoustic energy and a relatively low degree of resistance or acoustic loss, leading to a slow decay of formant oscillation, manifested in the spectrum as a reduction in formant bandwidth (i.e., as more sharply peaked formants). In contrast, sounds perceived as having low sonority have lower energy and/or a relatively high degree of resistance or loss, leading to a faster decay of formant oscillation and a consequent increase in formant bandwidth (in the limit case, a flat spectrum).

The most resonant speech sounds are therefore those with an auditorily prominent, relatively undamped formant structure. Resonance is enhanced by voicing, which provides a strong and efficient excitation source: "the resonators respond to both . . . hiss and voice, but generally with more sharply-tuned resonances—a greater concentration of acoustic energy into particular frequency bands—in voiced sounds, particularly vowels" (Catford 1977:57). Sounds having this property include not only vowels, the resonants par excellence, but also semivowels, liquids, and nasals—the traditional class of resonant consonants. Speech sounds not perceived as resonant do not have these properties, either because their resonances are not enhanced by voicing (as in voiceless vowels) or because they have a relatively flat spectrum (as in the case of many voiced fricatives). Resonance, in this sense, is not quite the same thing as loudness or audibility. Loud noises are audible by definition, but they are not necessarily resonant. For example, the chiming of a bell is resonant, but the hiss of a teakettle or the burst of a firecracker is not.

If we understand sonority in this sense, we may be in a better position to understand why the sonority scale has the form it has. Vowels stand at the top of the scale because they are characterized by a prominent, well-defined formant pattern. Other sonorants on the scale have this property to a decreasing degree (Kent and Read 1992, Fujimura and Erickson 1997, Stevens 1997):

• *Approximant consonants* (including liquids and semivowels) differ from vowels in generally having a reduced low-frequency spectrum amplitude, an additional decrease in amplitude at higher frequencies, and reduced prominence of the second or third formant peak.

• Within the class of approximants, *liquids* differ from semivowels in having a brief, intermittent, or partial constriction in the oral tract, which further reduces their spectral energy and formant prominence.

• *Nasals* differ from approximants in having a complete closure in the oral tract and an open passage to the nasal cavity, a configuration that creates a heavily damped nasal murmur of which only one component, the so-called nasal formant, has an amplitude comparable to that of vowel formants.

A further acoustic difference between laterals and nasals is that the nasals have a more abrupt transition to a neighboring vowel in the middle- and high-frequency range, aligning them more closely with obstruents (Stevens and Keyser 1989). Obstruents, including sibilants, generally involve considerable noise (burst and/or frication), but little if any sustained resonance, though voiced obstruents, especially fricatives, often show some lower-frequency formants.

These differences among major sound types are reflected in the ranking of major sonority classes shown in (2), where all sonorants are understood as voiced, and all sounds but vowels are understood as nonsyllabic. Highest-sonority sounds occur at the top and lowest-sonority sounds at the bottom.

(2)

	[syllabic]	[vocoid]	[approximant]	[sonorant]	Total *"yes"*
V (vowel)	yes	yes	yes	yes	4
S (semivowel)	no	yes	yes	yes	3
L (liquid)	no	no	yes	yes	2
N (nasal)	no	no	no	yes	1
O (obstruent)	no	no	no	no	0

As this chart shows, these classes are fully distinguished from each other by phonological features, except for vowels, which are distinguished from semivowels by their function as syllable peaks. The positive value of each feature is generally more resonant than the negative value, all else being equal. A basic sonority hierarchy is created by this scale, quantifiable by the number of "yes" responses in each row as shown in the column at the right (Clements 1990). More elaborate hierarchies recognizing subdivisions within these categories, which depend on the specific characteristics of subclasses of these sounds, can be (and have been) proposed. The sonority scale may thus be grounded in the perceived resonance of major classes of speech sounds, as defined in terms of the features shown at the head of each column in (2).

The main properties just attributed to resonance—notably, the presence of prominent formant peaks—can also be considered defining properties of the feature [+sonorant].[3] The sonority scale then corresponds to the degree to which a given segment possesses the characteristic properties of [+sonorant] sounds. Vowels possess these properties to the highest degree and stand at the top of the scale, while (oral) stops and fricatives possess them to the lowest degree (or not at all) and stand at the bottom of the scale. Note that (2) does not include a column for voicing. Though sonorant sounds are typically voiced, we do not want to incorporate the feature [+voiced] into the definition of [+sonorant], as this would involve defining one feature in terms of another. Instead, we may consider voicing (like some minimum of duration) as a precondition for the perception of resonance in speech sounds. If this is correct, only voiced sounds count as [+sonorant], an analysis that seems generally consistent with crosslinguistic patterning.[4]

The view that sonority corresponds to perceived resonance provides a basis for understanding the way the sonority scale functions to organize segments into syllables. Some familiar principles of sonority-based syllabification are summarized in (3):

(3) a. *Sonority Sequencing*
       Segments are syllabified in such a way that sonority increases from the margin to the peak.
   b. *Sonority-Syllabicity Alignment*
       Sonority peaks correspond to syllable peaks and vice versa.
   c. *Sonority Dispersion*
       Sonority is maximally dispersed in the initial demisyllable and minimally dispersed in the final demisyllable.
   d. *Syllable Contact*
       Sonority drops maximally across syllable boundaries.

These principles express preferences rather than absolute laws: a syllable is highly valued to the extent that it conforms to these properties. Though violations of these principles do occur, the presence of a syllable violating one of them in a language usually implies the presence of otherwise similar syllables that do not, while the reverse is not true.

All these principles make sense if sonority is related to perceived resonance. For example, if sonority is based on perceived resonance, we can better understand why sonority peaks should constitute preferred syllable peaks, as required by Sonority-Syllabicity Alignment (3b). Resonant sounds are optimal bearers of the prosodic properties that are typically associated with syllables. Vowels, as the highest-sonority sounds, are ideally suited to the function of anchoring the distinctive F0 variations found in tone, pitch-accent, and intonation systems. Liquids and nasals may or may not constitute syllable peaks, depending on the language. While some languages, such as Tashlhiyt Berber as described by Dell and Elmedlaoui (2002), also allow obstruents to function as syllable peaks, such syllables poorly convey F0-based prosodic information, and this fact may have consequences for the prosodic system as a whole. In the case of Berber, for instance, Dell and Elmedlaoui point out that significant pitch events are confined to sonorant peaks:

If Imdlawn Tashlhiyt has a phenomenon that could be called stress or accent, it is likely that it is a property of units larger than words. Our preliminary observations suggest that in general, the main pitch event in an intonational phrase occurs near its end, viz on the last or next-but-last syllable nucleus *which is a sonorant*. (Dell and Elmedlaoui 2002:14; emphasis added)

One would have trouble imagining the opposite situation, in which the main pitch event in a language is aligned with the last *non*sonorant syllable nucleus. In contrast, a fully abstract view of sonority would treat both situations as equally likely.

The view that sonority is based in perceived resonance may also help explain the preference for high-sonority final demisyllables (rhymes), as stated by Sonority Dispersion (3c), after Clements (1990). Time-varying prosodic differences such as falling and rising tones are often sequenced across two segments of the syllable rhyme and can be most easily perceived if both members of the rhyme are high in sonority, that is, if both are vowels or sonorants (Gordon 2004). Though stress-accent languages (in which contour tones do not occur) often allow obstruent-final syllables (English is an example), tone languages typically avoid them, and when they do have them, tonal distinctions are often neutralized on obstruent-final syllables. An example is present-day Hanoi Vietnamese, in which six tones contrast on sonorant-final syllables, but only two on syllables ending in one of the voiceless stops /p, t, k/ (Michaud 2004). Words illustrating each tone (with its traditional tone label and a brief description) are shown in (4).

(4) a. *Sonorant-final syllables*

ma	'ghost'	A1 (ngang)	High-level modal
mà	'which, whom'	A2 (huyền)	Low-falling modal
má	'cheek'	B1 (sắc)	High-rising modal
mạ	'young rice plant'	B2 (nặng)	High-falling glottalized
mả	'tomb'	C1 (hỏi)	High-falling rising modal; (other speakers: falling with final laryngealization)
mã	'plumage; code'	C2 (ngã)	Falling-rising with medial glottal constriction

b. *Stop-final syllables*

mát	'fresh; refreshing'	D1 (sắc)	High-rising modal
mạt	'sawdust'	D2 (nặng)	High-falling modal

It will be noted that not only the pitch of the tones but also their laryngeal quality is neutralized in stop-final syllables, whose tones are produced with modal voice.

A further sonority-related principle of syllables is Syllable Contact (3d), which favors a maximal drop in sonority across a syllable boundary (e.g., Murray and Vennemann 1983, Vennemann 1988). This principle prefers a word like *metro* to be syllabified as *me.tro* rather than *met.ro*, since sonority drops from *e* to *t* in the first syllabification but rises from *t* to *r* in the second. It predicts that syllable sequences with large drops in sonority across syllable boundaries should be favored across languages, except where language-particular constraints on syllable structure override it (for example, *met.ro* would be preferred to *me.tro* in languages that systematically disallow complex onsets). Syllable Contact, like Sonority Sequencing (3a), may facilitate parsing of the syllable, as a sharp drop in sonority will typically coincide with the point at which a new syllable begins.

Not all these principles are independent, of course. In particular, Syllable Contact is closely related to Sonority Dispersion and may derive from it, at least in part. This is because the syllable sequences preferred by Syllable Contact are generally those whose individual syllables, taken in isolation, are preferred by Sonority Dispersion. (To see this point, consider again the preferred syllabification *me.tro*; both syllables conform to Sonority Dispersion in having low-sonority initials and high-sonority finals, and it is just because of this that their combination satisfies the requirements of Syllable Contact.) The main argument for treating these two principles as independent has been that many languages, including English, French, and Vietnamese, allow word-final stops and fricatives quite freely, creating syllables that violate Sonority Dispersion while not infringing Syllable Contact. However, few languages favor obstruent-final syllables over sonorant-final syllables, and those that allow them usually place heavy restrictions on them, as does English. Furthermore, as Vaux and Wolfe point out, in a number of languages, such as Icelandic, word-final consonants behave as extrasyllabic, in which case they do not count as syllable codas at all. Thus, there is good reason to believe that Sonority Dispersion operates on codas in many languages that at first sight seem to show the opposite.

To summarize, it appears that sonority plays a fundamental role in accounting for preferred phonotactic patterns across languages and that this role may reflect its phonetic basis in relative power or perceived resonance. At the same time, however, it is necessary to point out that sonority does not explain everything (an alleged shortcoming of sonority theory according to some critics), and to mention a few things that it does not do.

First, sonority theory does not explain all phonotactic patterns—nor was it ever intended to. Many common constraints have little or nothing to do with syllable structure and lie entirely outside the domain of sonority theory. One example is the common constraint that requires obstruent clusters to agree in voicing. This constraint operates not only within syllable constituents but also across syllable boundaries in many languages (e.g., French, Russian, Catalan), showing that it can be entirely independent of syllabification. Furthermore, even some syllable-based constraints have nothing to do with sonority. An example here is the common rule of obstruent devoicing in syllable codas; this phenomenon is unrelated to sonority, since devoicing makes the coda less rather than more sonorant, contrary to Sonority Dispersion. Sonority-based syllabification is just one among several interacting principles that together account for trends in phonotactic patterning.

Second, the constraints in (3) are not exceptionless "laws" but count among a number of constraints that interact, and occasionally compete, to favor some syllabifications over others. Thus, as mentioned above, one constraint that often overrides Syllable Contact is the prohibition of complex syllable onsets. Turkish provides an example. In this language, sonority sequencing plays a role in determining the set of possible word-final clusters. If a cluster consists of a sonorant + obstruent (or ends in one of a small set of obstruent clusters), it is well-formed and requires no epenthetic vowel (5a). In all other cases, an epenthetic vowel, showing the expected vowel harmony, appears between its two members (Nominative column of (5b)). The accusative forms listed in the Accusative column show that no epenthetic vowel appears when the cluster is intervocalic. The forms in (5c) are included to show that underlying vowels are not deleted in the accusative.

(5)

		Nominative	Accusative	Underlying
a.	'Turk'	türk	türk-ü	/türk/
	'steep'	sarp	sarp-ɨ	/sarp/
	'color'	renk	reng-i	/reng/
b.	'text'	metin	metn-i	/metn/
	'belly'	koyun	koyn-u	/koyn/
	'idea'	fikir	fikr-i	/fikr/
c.	'copper'	bakɨr	bakɨr-ɨ	/bakɨr/
	'poor'	fakir	fakir-i	/fakir/
	'sheep'	koyun	koyun-u	/koyun/

Sonority Sequencing thus requires epenthesis in word-final clusters with poor sonority profiles, even when such epenthesis merges underlying minimal pairs ('belly' vs. 'sheep').

Since sonority requirements apply word-finally in Turkish, we might expect them to control word-internal clusters as well. However, this is not the case. All intervocalic clusters are separated by a syllable boundary (C.C), regardless of their segmental composition, because of a more basic constraint that rules out complex onsets. As a result, intervocalic clusters systematically disobey Syllable Contact, as is shown by examples like *an.la* 'understand' or *mis.ra:* 'poem line'. The Complex Onset constraint operates with full generality in Turkish, ruling out word-initial clusters in the native vocabulary and explaining the fact that initial clusters in loanwords are ordinarily separated by an epenthetic vowel (e.g., *pirens* 'prince'). It also explains the fact that obstruents undergo devoicing both word-finally and before other consonants,

since in both cases they occupy coda position (e.g., *kap/kaplar* 'container' (sg./pl.);
cf. *kaba* (dative), *kabɨ* (possessed)). In addition, it accounts for a more subtle observation regarding compensatory lengthening. As Sezer (1985) points out, the consonants /v, h, y/ optionally delete under certain conditions. When they do, the
preceding vowel may undergo compensatory lengthening, but only if the deleted consonant occupies the syllable coda in the corresponding full form that is its source
(6a). If the deleted consonant is in the onset, the preceding vowel does not lengthen
(6b).

(6) a. savmak ∼ sa:mak   'to get rid of'
        övmek ∼ ö:mek   'praise'
        kahya ∼ ka:ya   'steward'
    b. davul ∼ daul   'drum'
        tohum ∼ toum   'seed'
        ishal ∼ isal   'diarrhea'

The fact that the vowel lengthens in a word like [sa:mak], derived from /savmak/,
confirms that the syllabification prior to *v*-deletion is *sav.mak*, with *v* in the coda as
required by the Complex Onset constraint. To summarize, we see that this constraint
systematically takes precedence over Syllable Contact in Turkish.

A third necessary qualification is that the principles in (3) need not apply as uniform, all-or-nothing constraints. Although earlier analyses have occasionally treated
them as such, attempts to apply these principles to complex data have shown that
they may have to be parceled into families of more specific constraints applying to
specific subparts of the syllable (onset, coda, initial demisyllable, final demisyllable,
etc.) or to specific types of violations (sonority reversals vs. sonority plateaus, etc.).
Exactly what this family of constraints might consist of is a subject of ongoing research (for suggestions, see Zec 1995, Clements 1997, Davis and Shin 1999, Dell
and Elmedlaoui 2002, and Green 2003, among others).

In conclusion, Vaux and Wolfe have provided a very useful overview of evidence
for the appendix, emphasizing the wide variety of phenomena that it helps to explain.
While I agree with their analysis in most respects, I have suggested that the notion of
sonority that underlies their syllabification algorithm is not phonetically arbitrary,
but may be rooted in the property of perceived resonance. This suggestion is admit-
tedly tentative, and I hope that future experimental studies will be able to test it and
to make corrections if necessary.

Notes

1. Other phoneticians, from Jespersen (1932) to Beckman, Edwards, and Fletcher (1992), have
related sonority to the degree of opening of the vocal tract.

2. In a related suggestion, Nathan (1989) has proposed that sonority is a function of relative loudness, voicing, *svara* (formant structure), and prolongability.

3. For reasons discussed in Clements and Osu 2002, [sonorant] and [obstruent] may constitute distinct features.

4. This analysis can be stated formally as a constraint against the feature combination *[+sonorant, −voiced]. It appears that many so-called voiceless sonorants, if not all, can be better analyzed as bearing the feature [spread glottis] (e.g., Lombardi 1994, Clements 2003); whether these sounds ever pattern as true sonorants remains an open question.

References

Beckman, Mary, Jan Edwards, and Janet Fletcher. 1992. Prosodic structure and tempo in a sonority model of articulatory dynamics. In *Gesture, segment, prosody: Papers in laboratory phonology II*, ed. by Gerard J. Docherty and D. Robert Ladd, 68–86. Cambridge: Cambridge University Press.

Catford, John C. 1977. *Fundamental problems in phonetics*. Bloomington: Indiana University Press.

Clements, G. N. 1990. The role of the sonority cycle in core syllabification. In *Papers in laboratory phonology I*, ed. by John Kingston and Mary Beckman, 283–333. Cambridge: Cambridge University Press.

Clements, G. N. 1997. Berber syllabification: Derivations or constraints? In *Derivations and constraints in phonology*, ed. by Iggy M. Roca, 289–330. Oxford: Oxford University Press.

Clements, G. N. 2003. Feature economy in sound systems. *Phonology* 20:287–333.

Clements, G. N., and Sylvester Osu. 2002. Explosives, implosives, and nonexplosives: The linguistic function of air pressure differences in stops. In *Laboratory phonology 7*, ed. by Carlos Gussenhoven and Natasha Warner, 299–350. Berlin: Mouton de Gruyter.

Davis, Stuart, and Seung-Hoon Shin. 1999. The syllable contact constraint in Korean: An optimality-theoretic analysis. *Journal of East Asian Linguistics* 8:285–312.

Dell, François, and Mohamed Elmedlaoui. 2002. *Syllables in Tashlhiyt Berber and in Moroccan Arabic*. Dordrecht: Kluwer.

Fletcher, Harvey. 1972. *Speech and hearing in communication*. Huntington, N.Y.: Robert E. Krieger.

Fujimura, Osamu, and Donna Erickson. 1997. Acoustic phonetics. In *The handbook of phonetic sciences*, ed. by William J. Hardcastle and John Laver, 65–115. Oxford: Blackwell.

Gordon, Matthew. 2004. Syllable weight. In *Phonetic bases for phonological markedness*, ed. by Bruce Hayes, Robert Kirchner, and Donca Steriade, 277–312. Cambridge: Cambridge University Press.

Green, Anthony Dubach. 2003. Extrasyllabic consonants and onset well-formedness. In *The syllable in Optimality Theory*, ed. by Caroline Féry and Ruben van de Vijver, 238–253. Cambridge: Cambridge University Press.

Heffner, Roe-Merrill S. 1950. *General phonetics*. Madison: The University of Wisconsin Press.

Jespersen, Otto. 1932. *Lehrbuch der Phonetik*. 5th ed. Leipzig: B. G. Teubner.

Kent, Ray D., and Charles Read. 1992. *The acoustic analysis of speech*. San Diego, Calif.: Singular Publishing.

Ladefoged, Peter. 1993. *A course in phonetics*. 3rd ed. (International edition.) Orlando, Fla.: Harcourt Brace.

Lombardi, Linda. 1994. *Laryngeal features and laryngeal neutralization*. New York: Garland.

Michaud, Alexis. 2004. Final consonants and glottalization: New perspectives from Hanoi Vietnamese. *Phonetica* 61:119–146.

Murray, Robert W., and Theo Vennemann. 1983. Sound change and syllable structure in Germanic phonology. *Language* 59:514–528.

Nathan, Geoffrey S. 1989. Preliminaries to a theory of phonological substance: The substance of sonority. In *Linguistic categorization*, ed. by Roberta Corrigan, Fred Eckman, and Michael Noonan, 56–67. Amsterdam: John Benjamins.

Sezer, Engin. 1985. An autosegmental analysis of compensatory lengthening in Turkish. In *Studies in compensatory lengthening*, ed. by Leo Wetzels and Engin Sezer, 227–250. Dordrecht: Foris.

Sievers, Eduard. 1881. *Grundzüge der Phonetik*. Leipzig: Breitkopf und Hartel.

Stevens, Kenneth N. 1997. Articulatory-acoustic-auditory relationships. In *The handbook of phonetic sciences*, ed. by William J. Hardcastle and John Laver, 462–506. Oxford: Blackwell.

Stevens, Kenneth N., and Samuel Jay Keyser. 1989. Primary features and their enchancement in consonants. *Language* 65:81–106.

Vennemann, Theo. 1988. *Preference laws for syllable structure and the explanation of sound change*. Berlin: Mouton de Gruyter.

Whitney, William Dwight. 1865. The relation of vowel and consonant. *Journal of the American Oriental Society* 8. Reprinted in William Dwight Whitney, *Oriental and linguistic studies: Second series*. New York: Charles Scribner's Sons, 1874.

Zec, Draga. 1995. Sonority constraints on syllable structure. *Phonology* 12:85–129.

8   A Case of Appendicitis

Eric Raimy

8.1   Introduction

Vaux and Wolfe (this volume) propose a very strict view of syllabification and the prosodic status of unsyllabified segments. Put simply, a phoneme must either be syllabified directly or be associated to a higher prosodic level via an appendix structure. The purpose of this commentary is two-fold. First, as I will show, analyses of one pattern of infixation and one pattern of reduplication in Nxaʔamxcín (Czaykowska-Higgins and Willett 1997, henceforth CHW) demonstrate that these processes may in fact be completely agnostic about prosodic structure. Consequently, the behaviors of these processes do not provide evidence relevant to determining the prosodic structure present in the language. Second, the analysis of a reduplication pattern in Thao (Chang 1998) demonstrates that a syllabification scheme utilizing degenerate syllables is necessary to account for the pattern. VW's explicit rejection of degenerate syllables raises the question of whether their strict claims about the nature of the syllable are tenable. Thus, the spirit of this commentary is to suggest that we must be careful before ruling out classes of analyses on the basis of VW's arguments. Instead, we should further investigate VW's examples in order to fully determine what import they have for constructing a theory of syllabification for phonology.

8.2   Reduplication and Infixation in Nxaʔamxcín

To begin evaluating whether an appendix-based analysis of syllable structure is helpful in understanding nonconcatenative morphological processes in Nxaʔamxcín, let us look at the out of control (OOC) reduplication forms in (1). The reduplicated consonants are underlined.

(1) *Out of control reduplication in Nxaʔamxcín (CHW 1997:395)*

	Out of control	Gloss	Root
a.	k'íp'əp'	'get pinched'	(k'ip')
	cə́kək	'get hit'	(cək)
	q'ál'l'xʷ	'something hanging'	(q'al'xʷ)
b.	c'q'ʷq'ʷúnl'əxʷ	'land gets named'	(c'q'ʷu-n-ul'əxʷ)
	pt̲t̲íx̲ʷəxʷ	'spitting a lot'	(ptix̲ʷ-mix)
	tk̲kayi	'urinate (out of control)'	(tkay)

CHW convincingly demonstrate that Nxaʔamxcín has a simple syllable canon consisting of a maximal syllable of CVC for roots. Following Bagemihl (1991), CHW suggest that the initial consonant in CCVC roots is not syllabified (and that, more generally, consonants that cannot be parsed into a CVC syllable are not syllabified).[1] Thus, the forms in (1) are split into two groups on the basis of whether they begin with a syllabified consonant (1a) or an unsyllabified consonant (1b). Since VW explicitly reject the position that unsyllabified segments are not associated with any prosodic structure, the initial consonant in the forms in (1b) would be an appendix. (2) presents the data from (1) again, but focuses on the prosodic structure of the roots under an appendix-based analysis and the resulting reduplication pattern. For present purposes, I indicate syllables with curly brackets, { }, and I enclose segments in appendices in square brackets, [ ].

(2) *Appendix analysis of out of control reduplication*

a. *No initial appendix: #{CV . . .*

Root	Gloss	Out of control
{k'ip'}	'get pinched'	k'íp'əp'
{cək}	'get hit'	cə́kək
{q'al'}[xʷ]	'something hanging'	q'ál'l'xʷ

b. *Initial appendix: #[C]{CV . . .*

Root	Gloss	Out of control
[c']{q'ʷu}	'land gets named'	c'q'ʷq'ʷúnl'əxʷ
[p]{tix̲ʷ}	'spitting a lot'	pt̲t̲íx̲ʷəxʷ
[t]{kay}	'urinate (out of control)'	tk̲kayi

Displaying the OOC reduplication data as grouped in (2) highlights the difference with respect to which consonant is repeated as part of reduplication.[2] In (2a) the consonant in a coda position is copied, whereas in (2b) the onset consonant is copied. Syllabification provides no useful generalization because sometimes the onset reduplicates, and sometimes the coda. Therefore, whether the unsyllabified consonants are in appendices or not becomes moot.

The best generalization about the OOC reduplication pattern in Nxaʔamxcín does not use syllabic information at all. Informally stated, it says that the second consonant is reduplicated.[3] To formalize this insight, I will review the core proposals in Raimy 2000 about the nature of precedence in phonology.

In Raimy 2000, I argue that classical phonological representations such as the one for *cat* in (3a) do not formalize phonological precedence sufficiently for scientific investigation. Instead, representations such as (3b) that contain explicit marking of precedence relations (via $\rightarrow$) are necessary.

(3) *Precedence in phonological representations*
    a. cat   kæt
    b. cat $\# \rightarrow k \rightarrow æ \rightarrow t \rightarrow \%$

(3b) explicitly notates the precedence relations between the segments in the word *cat*. The symbols $\#$ and $\%$ indicate the beginning and end of the representation, respectively; they are necessary to determine well-formedness. Explicit representations of precedence in phonology enable us to better form questions about the nature of precedence. An immediate question that can be asked is whether a segment can be associated with more than one precedence relation. The answer is yes, and the bulk of Raimy 2000 demonstrates the utility of this answer in explicating the nature of reduplication.

One way to associate a segment with more than one precedence relation is to have a phonological representation contain a "loop" in its precedence structure.[4] Consider characteristic morphology reduplication in NxaɁamxcín.

(4) *Characteristic morphology in NxaɁamxcín (CHW 1997:403)*

	Characteristic	*Base*	*Gloss*
a.	Ɂac-pəkpək	pək	'spotted'
b.	qilqil-t	qil	'it hurts'
c.	picpicxʷ	picxʷ	'disgusting'
d.	ɁitɁitxʷ-ul	Ɂitxʷ	'he overslept'

Characteristic morphology in NxaɁamxcín is expressed by CVC suffixing reduplication. As proposed in Raimy 2000, we can account for reduplication by saying that the morphology component creates a representation with a "loop" in the precedence structure. The resulting representations for characteristic morphology reduplication in NxaɁamxcín are shown in (5).

(5) *Application of characteristic morphology reduplication in NxaɁamxcín (affixes suppressed)*

    Root (base)   *Characteristic morphology*
    a. $\# \rightarrow q \rightarrow i \rightarrow l \rightarrow \%$ $\# \rightarrow q \rightarrow i \rightarrow l \rightarrow \%$

    b. $\# \rightarrow p \rightarrow i \rightarrow c \rightarrow xʷ \rightarrow \%$ $\# \rightarrow p \rightarrow i \rightarrow c \rightarrow xʷ \rightarrow \%$

On the left in (5) are the roots that undergo characteristic morphology reduplication. The phonological change caused by the spell-out of characteristic morphology is the addition of a precedence relation that states, "The segment after the first vowel precedes the first segment." The resulting phonological structures are on the right in (5). A bare output condition (Chomsky 1995) on the phonological component requires that phonological representations be legible at the phonetic interface.[5] Clearly, the interface cannot interpret segments with multiple precedence relations like those in (5). Linearization is the operation within the phonological component that ensures that any precedence structure created by the morphology ends up being interpretable; therefore, the reduplicated structures in (5) must be linearized. For present purposes, we only need to know that linearization will cause segmental material that is within a loop to be repeated. (6) presents the input-output mappings for the pre- and post-linearized structures in (5).

(6) *Linearization*

       Prelinearization structure   *Postlinearization structure*

    a. $\# \to q \to i \to l \to \%$ $\# \to q \to i \to l \to q \to i \to l \to \%$

    b. $\# \to p \to i \to c \to x^w \to \%$ $\# \to p \to i \to c \to p \to i \to c \to x^w \to \%$

In (6a), the entire root is contained "within the loop," so linearization creates the surface effect of total reduplication (which in this case is ambiguously CVC reduplication also). In (6b), only the segments /p/, /i/, and /c/ of the root are in the loop. Consequently, only these segments are repeated during linearization, giving the surface effect of CVC reduplication.

Surface reduplication patterns are the result of the description of the precedence relation added by the morphology that creates the loop. Precedence relations added by the morphology are described by the *anchor points* (Raimy 2000, 2005, this volume) that specify the segment at the beginning and the segment at the end of the added precedence link. For a phonological representation to be well-formed from a segmental point of view, each segment must have two precedence relations, one that specifies what it follows and one that specifies what it precedes. From a precedence relation point of view, each precedence relation must have segments (or the terminal symbols, # and %) associated with both its beginning and its end.

In Raimy 2005, I present a constrained theory of the set of possible anchor points, based in part on proposals about infixation made by Yu (2003). Yu argues that crosslinguistic variation with respect to the positioning of infixes is limited to a small set of pivot points. In Raimy 2005, I suggest that Yu's pivot points are identical to anchor points. For example, we can understand the CVC-prefixing pattern of reduplication found in Nxaʔamxcín as the result of the pairing of the anchor points "after the first vowel" and "first segment." Both of these anchor points are identical to pivot points suggested by Yu (2003:54–55).

With this background, we can return to the OOC reduplication pattern in Nxaʔamxcín. This pattern can be captured by adding a precedence link that begins and ends at the "second consonant," as shown in (7).

(7) *Out of control reduplication*
  Root   *Out of control (reduplicated)*
  a. # → k' → i → p' → %   # → k' → i → p' → %
                                        ⤸

  b. # → c' → q'ʷ → u → %   # → c' → q'ʷ → u → %
                                        ⤸

Although Yu does not include "second consonant" as a pivot point attested in infixation patterns, McCarthy (1985, 1986) suggests that this way of describing a phonological environment is central to understanding Obligatory Contour Principle (OCP) effects in Semitic. McCarthy (1985) argues for an autosegmental view of phonological representations with separate consonant and vowel tiers. The ability to separate consonants and vowels onto distinct tiers allows operations to be calculated over consonants and/or vowels only. Calculating only over consonants or vowels is a core component in explaining OCP effects in many languages. As McCarthy (1986) discusses, gemination and antigemination are also best accounted for by positing a separate consonant tier. Thus, the phonological environment "second consonant" is simply "the segment that follows the initial segment on the consonant tier." The essence of OCP effects in Semitic roots is that the first and second (or last and next to last) consonants may not be identical. The fact that OCP effects are seen across vowels indicates that "second consonant" must be a viable structural description for phonology.

The analysis using "second consonant" is the most parsimonious analysis for the OOC reduplication pattern in Nxaʔamxcín because it explains the choice of consonant for reduplication. Since the calculation is conducted only on the consonant tier, the resulting syllable structure, which requires vowels to appear in certain locations, is irrelevant to which consonant is being repeated. (8) presents the linearization of the forms in (7) with OOC morphology and schwa inserted in the appropriate place.[6]

(8) *Postlinearization out of control forms*
  Prelinearization structure   *Postlinearization structure with epenthesis*
  a. # → k' → i → p' → %   # → k' → i → p' → ə → p' → %
          ⤸

  b. # → c' → q'ʷ → u → %   # → c' → q'ʷ → q'ʷ → u → %
          ⤸

To summarize: proposals in Raimy 2000 about the nature of precedence relations in phonological environments, combined with proposals in Yu 2003 about pivot points, allow a novel analysis of the NxaɁamxcín OOC reduplication pattern. This proposed analysis simply states that the OOC morphology adds a precedence link, which creates a reflexive precedence relation on the second consonant. When the representation containing this loop is linearized, the surface result is reduplication of the second consonant. The final, correct surface forms for this pattern are created by epenthesis of a schwa in appropriate places via NxaɁamxcín phonology that is not discussed here. Since this analysis does not refer to syllable structure, this pattern of reduplication provides no evidence for or against any model of syllabification. Consequently, the NxaɁamxcín facts do not support VW's proposals about the appendix; an appendix analysis would simply be superfluous.

Analysis of the inchoative morphology in NxaɁamxcín further supports the utility of the "second consonant" anchor point. Examples of inchoative morphology on strong roots in NxaɁamxcín are presented in (9). The allomorph of the inchoative morpheme for strong roots is an infixed glottal stop; the other allomorph is a suffixed /p/ (CHW 1997:394). Only the infixed glottal stop is of interest here.

(9) *Inchoative infixation in NxaɁamxcín (CHW 1997:395)*

	Root		Inchoative root	
a.	cíx	'lukewarm'	na-cí-Ɂ-x	'water gets warm'
	p'íq	'ripe, bake'	p'í-Ɂ-q	'it's ripe, gets warm'
b.	təmtəmút-n	'clothes'	ta-Ɂ-mút	'round hemp bag'
	t'uwáy't	'cry hard'	s-t'a-Ɂ-wáy't-s	'cry continuously'
	łuwám	'go, pl.'	ła-Ɂ-wám	'walk around'
c.	c'q'ʷú-n-m	'say, name'	c'-aɁ-q'ʷú-n-m	'read'

With respect to segmental makeup of the root, the pattern in (9) is similar to the OOC reduplication pattern. The roots in (9a) are CVC in composition and are completely parsed into a single syllable. The roots in (9b) have a predictable schwa that breaks up the root-initial obstruent-resonant sequence (CHW 1997:390); note that [ł] is classified as an obstruent. The predictable schwa alternates with /u/ before /w/ and with /a/ before a pharyngeal segment. Finally, (9c) presents a CCVC root where the first and second Cs are heterosyllabic (CHW 1997:393). The resulting inchoative form does have a predictable schwa, here triggered by the glottal stop; glottal stop patterns with resonants in NxaɁamxcín in that it triggers schwa epenthesis (which alternates with /a/, as described above).

Considering the analysis of OOC reduplication developed above, we can see that an appendix-based analysis of NxaɁamxcín syllabification is not helpful in understanding infixation of the glottal stop. (10) presents the different types of syllable structure that VW's proposals would assign to the forms in (9).

(10) *Appendix-based analysis of Nxaʔamxcín roots*
   Root syllabification *Infixation*
  a. {cíx}   {cí-ʔ-x}
  b. {t'u}{wáy't}   {t'a-ʔ}{wáy't}
  c. [c']{q'ʷú}   {c'-aʔ}{q'ʷú}

When prosodic structures are built for the data in (10) according to VW's appendix theory, there is no clear generalization for infixing the glottal stop. For the forms that do not have an appendix, (10a,b), we could posit that the infix occurs after the first vowel (in line with Yu's (2003) proposals on the nature of infixation). However, this generalization does not hold for the form in (10c) that does have an appendix. It appears that an appendix-based analysis of Nxaʔamxcín is not beneficial because positing an appendix structure prevents a uniform description of the locus of infixation.

The above analysis of the OOC pattern, relying on the anchor point "second consonant," suggests a generalization for identifying where to infix the inchoative-marking glottal stop: it precedes the second consonant and follows what precedes the second consonant. This generalization creates the following derivation of the inchoative form for strong roots:

(11) *Inchoative morphology on strong roots*
   Root   *Inchoative*

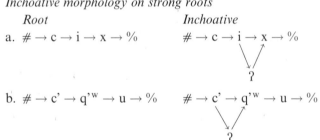

The same principles of linearization that hold for patterns that create a loop in the precedence structure also hold for infixation patterns that create a "detour." However, since there is no loop, no reduplication occurs; linearization instead creates the surface effect of infixation. (12) presents the linearization of (11a,b) with the resulting epenthesis triggered by the glottal stop.

(12) *Linearization and epenthesis in inchoative forms*
   Prelinearization structure *Postlinearization structure with epenthesis*

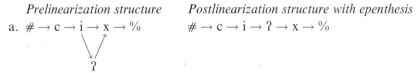

b. $\# \to c' \to q'^w \to u \to \%$ $\# \to c' \to a \to ? \to q'^w \to u \to \%$

$?$

The most important thing to note about the present analysis of the Nxaʔamxcín infixation pattern is that it is agnostic about the actual syllable structure of the root. Because the calculation of where the infix goes only considers a linear sequence of consonants, it is moot whether root-initial members of consonant clusters are in an appendix or not.

These two phenomena from Nxaʔamxcín, then, do not provide evidence in favor of (or against) VW's proposals. The most parsimonious analyses for these phenomena are completely agnostic about any kind of prosodic structure. Note also that in both cases, adding the relevant morphology to the root creates marked unsyllabified segments that are sometimes but not always repaired by epenthesis of a schwa. The clearest examples of this aspect of these patterns are repeated in (13), with syllable structure indicated.

(13) *The creation of unsyllabified segments*

a. *Root*	*Out of control*	*Gloss*
{q'al'}xʷ	{q'ál'}l'xʷ	'something hanging'
c'{q'ʷu}	c'q'ʷ{q'ʷún}{l'əxʷ}	'land gets named'
p{tix̣ʷ}	pt{tí}{x̣ʷəxʷ}	'spitting a lot'
t{kay}	tk{ka}{yi}	'urinate (out of control)'
b. *Root*	*Inchoative*	
{cíx}	{na}{cíʔ}x	'lukewarm'/'water gets warm'
{p'íq}	{p'íʔ}q	'ripe, bake'/'it's ripe, gets warm'

All of the forms in (13a) with OOC morphology end up with two unsyllabified segments even though the root began with just one. The forms in (13b) with inchoative morphology end up desyllabifying the coda of the root since Nxaʔamxcín does not allow complex codas (CHW 1997:398–402). The production of phonological forms containing marked structure that may or may not be repaired by general processes in the language is a predicted result of analyses that are agnostic about syllabification. This result would be an anomaly for any approach based on the goal of producing well-formed prosodic structures.

8.3 Reduplication in Thao

While the previous sections' analyses of OOC reduplication and inchoative morphology on strong forms in Nxaʔamxcín are orthogonal to syllabification, the analysis of reduplication in Thao to be developed here crucially relies on syllable structure.

Chang (1998) provides a description of Thao and in particular the reduplication pattern in (14).

(14) *Thao rightward reduplication (Chang 1998:284)*

Base	Reduplicated form	Gloss
šnara	pa-šnara-nara	'ignite'/'burn s.t. repeatedly'
kikaɬi	kikaɬi-kaɬi	'ask'/'ask around'
qriuʔ	q-un-riu-riuʔ	'steal'/'steal habitually'
patihaul	matihau-haul	'spell'/'cast a spell'
ag.qtu	agqtu-qtu	'contemplate'/'think about'
ar.faz	m-arfa-rfaz	'fly'/'fly continuously'
m-ig.kmir	igkmi-kmir-in	'grasp'/'roll into a ball'
bu.qnur	mia-buqnu-qnur	'anger'/'be irritable'

Fitzpatrick (to appear) points out the theoretical importance of this pattern, stemming from the fact that the reduplicated region of the word (underlined in (14)) varies among CVCV, CCV, and CVV sequences. This set of consonant-vowel sequences defies any sort of prosodic characterization and often cuts across syllable boundaries. The most interesting aspect of the data, though, is that as Fitzpatrick points out, they follow directly from a classical Marantzian CV template analysis (Marantz 1982). If a CVCV template is infixed after the final vowel, right-to-left association will produce the correct reduplication pattern. However, this classical Marantzian template is not available to contemporary models of reduplication.

Fitzpatrick points out that like other contemporary analyses of reduplication, the precedence model is unable to make a clean generalization for rightward reduplication in Thao. This conclusion is correct if a surface syllabification of the data with complex onsets and codas is assumed. If a more abstract syllabification is posited instead, a clean generalization is possible.

The abstract syllabification required to account for Thao posits strict CV syllables with both empty nuclei and empty onsets to break up consonant-vowel clusters; final consonants are analyzed as extraprosodic. Consider the abstract syllabification for relevant Thao forms in (15). Empty nuclei are represented as Ø, empty onsets are represented as O, and angle brackets indicate extraprosodic consonants.

(15) *Abstract syllabification in Thao*

Stem	Syllabification	"Reduplicant"
kikaɬi	{ki}{ka}{ɬi}	{ka}{ɬi}
qriuʔ	{qØ}{ri}{Ou}⟨ʔ⟩	{ri}{Ou}
patihaul	{pa}{ti}{ha}{Ou}⟨l⟩	{ha}{Ou}
ag.qtu	{Oa}{gØ}{qØ}{tu}	{qØ}{tu}
ar.faz	{Oa}{rØ}{fa}⟨z⟩	{rØ}{fa}

Once this abstract syllabification is posited, the classical Marantzian template effect can be captured in the precedence model of reduplication. The reduplication pattern is that the "last vowel" precedes the "next to last onset." Again, the concept "second" proves useful, but instead of being calculated on the consonant tier, it is being calculated on the syllable tier, specifically on onsets.

The relevance of this Thao reduplication pattern is that in order to produce an elegant analysis, one must posit an abstract syllabification. Because VW (section 5.4) reject the idea of degenerate syllables, it is hard to see how their theory can insightfully account for these phenomena. The important question at hand about the Thao data is whether syllabification changes during the derivation. It may be that the proposed abstract syllabification for Thao exists only early in the derivation. As the derivation progresses, processes could occur that convert the empty onsets and nuclei into complex syllables. Only further research on Thao will answer this question. The surface syllabification of Thao clearly allows complex onsets, but this level of syllabification does not appear to be relevant to the reduplication pattern. Thus, I find VW's rejection of some possible analyses of syllabification to be unjustified.

8.4 Conclusion

These brief comments are meant to be taken as complementary to the main proposals made by VW in this volume. My goal here has been to provide some insight into further issues in determining the most appropriate theory of syllabification. I wholeheartedly agree with VW's position that the types of evidence required to investigate syllable structure should be based in morphological and phonological processes. One complication that VW only hint at is that syllabification is likely not uniform through an entire derivation. CHW (1997) strongly suggest that this is the case for Nxaʔamxcín in that consonant clusters in roots are repaired differently than nonroot consonant clusters. This observation has a very natural account in any model of phonology that is stratal or derivational in nature. The complexity that arises, though, is that early syllabification (e.g., cyclic syllabification) may be distinct from later syllabification (e.g., noncyclic syllabification), and this could produce either false or conflicting data about the nature of syllabification in a particular language.

In conclusion, VW argue persuasively that the idea of an appendix in syllable structure is a useful theoretical construct and that it explains a variety of linguistic phenomena. What I do not accept, though, is the conclusion that only an appendix-based account of unsyllabified consonants should be utilized. The brief examples discussed here suggest that there are classes of linguistic phenomena that are best accounted for without reference to syllable structure or can only be accounted for with a non-appendix-based syllabification system. Because of these types of linguistic phenomena, of which many more exist beyond the few examples presented here, an exclusively appendix-based approach to unsyllabified segments cannot be accepted.

Notes

I would like to thank the participants and audience at the CUNY Phonology Forum Symposium on Architecture and Representation in Phonology for discussion of these issues. Further discussion occurred with Bill Idsardi, and Chuck Cairns has spent a large amount of time helping sift these ideas. All errors of fact and interpretation that remain are mine.

1. CHW also follow Bagemihl (1991) in claiming that unsyllabified consonants are moraically licensed. I follow Cook (1994) in rejecting the position of moraic licensing because "extending the notion of Prosodic Licensing to such syllabically unaffiliated obstruents entails serious erosion of the explanatory power of the overriding principle" (p. 326). Instead, Cook suggests that languages that tolerate unsyllabified segments simply lack the operation of Stray Erasure, a proposal I follow here.

2. The $/x^w/$ in the last form of (2a) has been designated as an appendix under assumptions based on VW's proposals and CHW's analysis of Nxaʔamxcín. All segments must be associated with prosodic structure, either in a syllable or in an appendix. Since the syllable structure for Nxaʔamxcín is CVC, in a word-final CC cluster the final C will be an appendix.

3. This generalization is also suggested by CHW.

4. Note that no special formal status is attached to precedence links referred to as "loops." All precedence links are formally the same except for morphological affiliation. In other words, although it is useful for expository reasons to refer to precedence relations that create the surface effect of reduplication as "loops," there is no fundamental distinction between precedence links that cause the surface effects of reduplication, infixation, truncation, or deletion.

5. Linearization in Raimy 2000 is conceptually similar to proposals for linearization made by Mester (1988) and for tier conflation made by McCarthy (1985). As Cook (1994:315) states, linearization is not a reduplication-specific device. Owing to advances in the representation of precedence proposed in Raimy 2000, the formal implementation of linearization is distinct from proposals made in Mester 1988.

6. CHW mention the insertion of the schwa in these forms but do not explain its presence or absence. They do not suggest that the schwa is part of the OOC morpheme, though.

References

Bagemihl, Bruce. 1991. Syllable structure in Bella Coola. *Linguistic Inquiry* 22:589–646.

Chang, M. Laura. 1998. Reduplication in Thao. *Oceanic Linguistics* 37:277–297.

Chomsky, Noam. 1995. *The Minimalist Program*. Cambridge, Mass.: MIT Press.

Cook, Eung-Do. 1994. Against moraic licensing in Bella Coola. *Linguistic Inquiry* 25:309–326.

Czaykowska-Higgins, Ewa, and Marie Louise Willett. 1997. Simple syllables in Nxaʔamxcín. *International Journal of American Linguistics* 63:385–411.

Fitzpatrick, Justin. To appear. A concatenative theory of possible affix types. In *Papers from EVELIN I*, ed. by Andrés Pablo Salanova. Cambridge, Mass.: MIT, MIT Working Papers in Linguistics.

Marantz, Alec. 1982. Re reduplication. *Linguistic Inquiry* 13:435–482.

McCarthy, John J. 1985. *Formal problems in Semitic phonology and morphology*. New York: Garland.

McCarthy, John J. 1986. OCP effects: Gemination and antigemination. *Linguistic Inquiry* 17:207–264.

Mester, Armin. 1988. *Studies in tier structure*. New York: Garland.

Raimy, Eric. 2000. *The phonology and morphology of reduplication*. Berlin: Mouton de Gruyter.

Raimy, Eric. 2005. Prosodic residue in an a-templatic world. Talk presented at University of Delaware Linguistic Colloquium Series, Newark.

Yu, Alan C. L. 2003. The morphology and phonology of infixation. Doctoral dissertation, University of California, Berkeley.

III Metrical Structure

9 Calculating Metrical Structure

William J. Idsardi

9.1 Introduction

This chapter has four main goals: (1) to revise and further simplify the simplified bracketed grid (SBG) theory of metrical computations outlined in Idsardi 1992 and Halle and Idsardi 1995; (2) to relate the parameters of the revised system directly to finite state automata (FSAs), giving a clear, effective, and efficient computational foundation to the theory; (3) to present some short case studies illustrating interesting aspects of the revised theory; and (4) to compare the automata in the present theory with those constructed using recent Optimality Theory (OT; e.g., Prince and Smolensky 2004) proposals for stress (e.g., Hyde 2002, McCarthy 2003) coupled with Karttunen's (1998) proposals for finite state compilation of OT grammars.

9.2 Rules and Machines

The revised SBG theory is largely a response to questions posed by Nigel Fabb about his ongoing collaboration with Morris Halle applying SBG systems to the metrical scansion of poetry (see, e.g., Fabb 2002). Fabb (pers. comm.) asked how the parameterized SBG rules actually worked to scan across a form, and I answered (rather flippantly) that they, like other phonological rules, could be compiled into FSAs, a result known at least since the early 1970s (Howard 1972, Johnson 1972). Formulating the rules as FSAs has certain practical advantages, as many modern (and not-so-modern) programming languages and tools (e.g., Sed, Awk, Perl, Ruby, JavaScript) offer regular expression facilities that can be used to implement FSAs fairly easily. It is particularly fortuitous that the excellent Xerox software for compiling and manipulating FSAs is now available (Beesley and Karttunen 2003). This makes it possible to quickly build and test large FSAs and compare different grammars for their effectiveness and efficiency (see in particular section 9.4). Space restrictions prevent me from providing anything like a comprehensive introduction to the use of

FSAs in understanding the application of phonological rules. Good introductions to the general topic can be found in Kenstowicz and Kisseberth 1977:188ff., 1979:326–327. Textbooks on mathematical linguistics such as Gross 1972 and Partee, ter Meulen, and Wall 1990, or introductions to automata theory such as Hopcroft and Ullmann 1979, offer further information on FSAs; Beesley and Karttunen 2003 is indispensable.

The SBG theory follows Halle and Vergnaud (1987) in viewing the calculation of prosodic structure as being governed by a system of parameterized rules. That is, there exists a set of ordered rules, constituting a derivation. However, not all conceivable rules are allowed; rather, they fall into fairly narrow classifications. Strict ordering of parameterized rule classes was also required in Idsardi 1992; for example, Edge Marking universally preceded Iterative Constituent Construction. Idsardi and Purnell (1997) proposed to derive such ordering from more general principles (rule complexity and the Elsewhere Condition). Although these are interesting and important questions about the nature of rule ordering, I will not address them directly here, as the revisions to the theory generally streamline the analyses in ways that make these questions difficult to assess.

The major changes to the theory are the following: (1) the abandonment of all avoidance constraints, clash resolution being handled by deletion rules, as in Idsardi 1994; (2) the unification of Edge Marking rules with Iterative Constituent Construction rules into a generalized Grouping rule component; (3) the introduction of an iterativity parameter; (4) the direct identification of parameter settings for rules with particular properties of FSAs; and (5) the projection of brackets onto higher grid lines.

With these changes, we can reduce metrical calculations to two basic operations: Projection, which creates a new line of the grid from the current top line, and Grouping, which partitions the current top line of the grid into groups. Formally, this is a calculus over two types of elements: grid marks, notated with "x," and partition junctures, "(" and ")." As with previous versions of the SBG theory, "(" groups marks to its right, and ")" groups marks to its left. A single boundary is sufficient to define a grouping, and in general the groupings do not need to exhaust the elements in the entire form. To project a new grid line, two parameters must be specified indicating which marks and brackets should be projected, summarized in (1).

(1) *Parameters for Projection rules*
    Project the *leftmost/rightmost* element of each group
    Project *left/right/no* brackets

The changes in (1) bring the projection from all grid lines into accord with what was assumed to be possible in projecting syllable information onto line 0. The marking of heavy syllables (and other special syllable configurations such as Dorsey's Law vowels in Winnebago; see below) by projecting brackets onto line 0 is an instance of (1), with a further specification of the context for syllable bracket projection. The ultimate goal of this change is to give an SBG account of syllable structure, by using brackets on the x-tier to indicate a simplified (even impoverished) syllable structure, not unlike that proposed by Clements and Keyser (1983). I do not have space in this chapter to explicate and defend such a theory, but in general we would expect that the x-tier groups would approximate the extent of the moras in Hyman 1985, especially the first mora of a syllable in that theory, although we would also expect nonexhaustive parsing of the x-tier into syllables (i.e., there are more general cases of extrasyllabicity). One such example of nonexhaustive parsing is likely to be the treatment of coda consonants. In particular, in some languages "coda" consonants would simply be unsyllabified, and the groupings for the syllables would then not be exhaustive. The "mora" groups would be right-headed and heavy syllable marking would have the x-tier context x)x, as for example in English heavy syllable marking in forms like *aptitude*, (2).

(2) (x   x (x
      æ)p(ti)(tu)ud

To create regular groups of marks we will employ Grouping rules, using the parameter settings given in (3).

(3) *Parameters for Grouping rules*
    Insert *left/right* brackets
    For every *two/three* elements
    Starting from the *leftmost/rightmost* element
    Iteratively/Noniteratively
    Starting in the *insert/skip* state

This gives a total of 32 possible Grouping rules. Ternary systems are not very well attested in natural language systems (though see Tripura Bangla, below), though there are poetic systems with ternary groupings (e.g., dactylic and anapestic; see Fabb 2002) and many musical examples in triple $\left(\frac{3}{4}\right)$ time (waltz, minuet, etc.). The 16 predicted binary patterns of grouping are given in (4), along with some example languages.

(4)

Bracket	Size	Direction	Iterative/Noniterative	Start	x x x x x x	x x x x x x x	Example languages
a. L (	2	L ⇒	I	Insert	(x x(x x(x x	(x x(x x(x x(x	Maranungku, Auca stems
b. L (	2	L ⇒	I	Skip	x(x x(x x(x	x(x x(x x(x x	Winnebago
c. L (	2	L ⇒	N	I	(x x x x x x	(x x x x x x x	North Kyung-sung Korean
d. L (	2	L ⇒	N	S	x(x x x x x	x(x x x x x x	Tokyo Japanese
e. L (	2	R ⇐	I	I	x(x x(x x(x	(x x(x x(x x(x	Suruwaha?
f. L (	2	R ⇐	I	S	(x x(x x(x x	x(x x(x x(x x	Nengone, Auca suffixes, Garawa
g. L (	2	R ⇐	N	I	x x x x x(x	x x x x x x(x	Turkish?
h. L (	2	R ⇐	N	S	x x x x(x x	x x x x x(x x	Polish, Indonesian, Turkish?
i. R)	2	L ⇒	I	I	x)x x)x x)x	x)x x)x x)x x)	Maranungku?
j. R)	2	L ⇒	I	S	x x)x x)x x)	x x)x x)x x)x	Araucanian
k. R)	2	L ⇒	N	I	x)x x x x x	x)x x x x x x	Tauya
l. R)	2	L ⇒	N	S	x x)x x x x	x x)x x x x x	Garawa
m. R)	2	R ⇐	I	I	x x)x x)x x)	x)x x)x x)x x)	Suruwaha, Tauya
n. R)	2	R ⇐	I	S	x)x x)x x)x	x x)x x)x x)x	Latin, Greek
o. R)	2	R ⇐	N	I	x x x x x x)	x x x x x x x)	Russian, Japanese palatal prosody
p. R)	2	R ⇐	N	S	x x x x x)x	x x x x x x)x	Shingazidja, Latin, Greek clitics

The basic FSA for (4j) is shown in (5). By convention, the FSA starts in state 0.

(5)

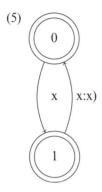

This FSA is R2LIS; it inserts a ")" every two marks, from left to right, iteratively, skipping (not inserting) on the first mark. We read the arcs between states in the following way. Simple arcs (those without :) match and consume the symbols shown on the arc (the labels are to the right of the arcs). Transductions (arcs with :) match the symbol to the left of the : in the input and replace it with the symbols to the right of the :. In state 0, then, the machine accepts "x," outputs "x," and moves to state 1. In state 1, the machine accepts "x," outputs "x)," and moves back to state 0. In the terminology suggested by Nigel Fabb (pers. comm.), in moving from state 0 to state 1 we skip a mark, and in moving from state 1 back to state 0 we insert a bracket. The double circles enclosing the state nodes indicate that the machine can stop in this state (i.e., it is legal to be at the end of the string).

The full machine, which additionally respects preexisting metrical structure (in the sense of Halle 1990), is shown in (6). Notice that the arcs from either state when the machine encounters "(x" always go to state 1, and the arcs for "x)" and "(x)" always go to state 0. That is, preexisting brackets are always treated in the same way, regardless of the current state of the machine.

(6)

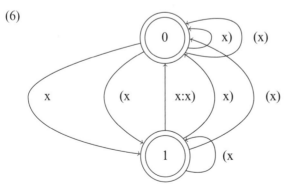

The basic FSA for R2LII, (4i), the one that inserts on the first mark instead, is shown in (7a), and the full machine is shown in (7b).

(7) a.

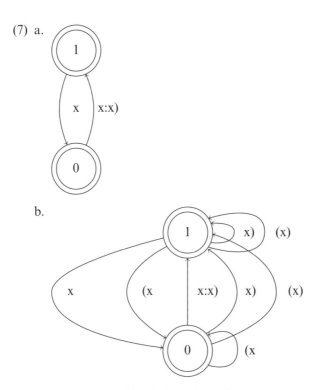

b.

These machines are identical to those for **R2LIS** except for the starting state (recall that the starting state is by convention numbered 0). That is, the state labels in the diagram have been switched. A better method would be to simply annotate the diagram to say which is the starting state, similar to the conventions used for final states (and in fact employed in a minority of FSA studies). In this chapter, I will continue to follow the usual FSA numbering conventions, however.

The basic FSA for L2LII, (4a), is given in (8a), and the full FSA is given in (8b).

(8) a.

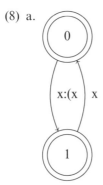

b.

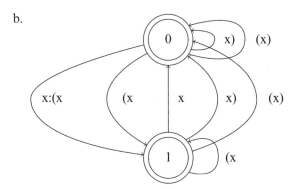

Again, the FSA for L2LIS is the same, with the state labels reversed. That is, the machine starts in the other state. This exhausts the binary machines, as the right-to-left machines simply scan the string starting from the opposite end.

An example of a basic FSA for ternary parsing is shown in (9a), and the full machine is shown in (9b). These are created from the basic binary machines by fissioning the skip state. That is, the ternary machines are mechanically derivable from the binary machines.

(9) a.

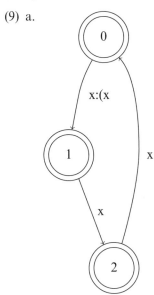

b.

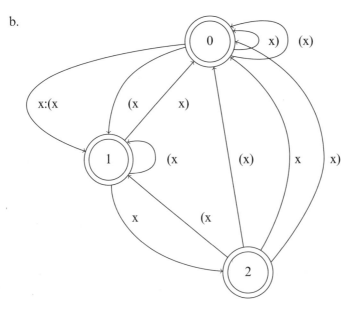

Notice also that the only difference is that the basic ternary parser has two "skip" states but the same two additional rules describe how to elaborate the basic machine to get the full machine. That is, the embellishments needed to derive the full machine from the basic machine are stated in (10).

(10) *Embellishments to augment basic machines to full machines*
  a. If (x go to state 1
  b. If x) go to state 0
  c. If (x) go to state 0

Thus, for iterative machines there is a basic machine, which is elaborated in the same way each time to produce the full machine. In addition, the start state can be specified for a parsing, and the size of the machine (number of skip states: 1 or 2) can be specified. Thus, there is a direct relation between the parameters used here, listed in (3), and the construction of the appropriate FSA.

The machines encountered so far have an interesting property: none of them requires any lookahead. Consider a hypothetical variant of L2LII that would require at least two marks at the end, resulting in a ternary constituent at the far side of odd strings, a mirror image of the Garawa pattern: (xx(xx(xx, (xx(xx(xxx. A machine for this is (11).

(11)

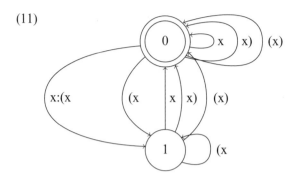

In this machine, state 0 has two arcs for "x." One inserts (outputs "(x") and moves to state 1, the other skips (outputs "x") and stays in state 0. This is a nondeterministic FSA (NDFSA or NFA) because of the choice available in state 0. But, furthermore, state 1 is not an acceptable finishing state. In that way, the output "(xx(xx(xx(x" is not allowed. However, we need to also establish the priority of inserting over skipping in nonfinal cases, which could be done in FSAs by assigning probability values to the arcs. The problem with NDFSAs is that they need additional information to work properly. To ensure that we don't use the skip when we don't need it, we need to make a more complicated machine (i.e., transform the NDFSA into a deterministic FSA). Additionally, "(x" is all right at the end of the grid as long as it is preexisting (in other words, the machine has to respect such a bracket). We can build such a machine, as shown in (12).

(12)

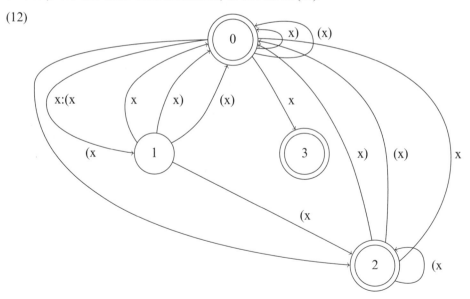

This machine is clearly more complicated than L2LII. Instead of making progressively more complicated elemental machines, we will combine elemental machines to create more complicated machines, as described in Beesley and Karttunen 2003. That is, cases like Garawa will be analyzed by applying two Grouping rules in succession, as proposed in Idsardi 1992 to handle "weak local parsing" (Hayes 1995) effects in Chugach Alutiiq. In particular, Garawa-type cases will have a noniterative footing rule, followed by an iterative one. That is, the footing that (12) would do would be done by L2RNS followed by R2LIS, giving parsings for even-numbered strings like xx)xx)(xx) and for odd-numbered strings like xx)xx)x(xx); see Tripura Bangla, below.

Thus, we need to address at this point what the noniterative machines look like. As a simple example, let us look at L2LNI, diagrammed in (13). In the noniterative case, none of the arcs return to state 0. Once the machine is in state 1, it will consume the rest of the string without changes; one might term this a spin state.

(13)

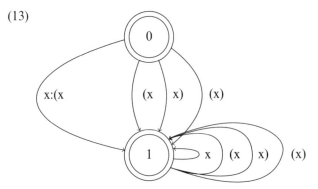

The behavior of noniterative machines that begin with a skip is not quite as clear. I give my proposal for R2LNS in (14). The question at issue is whether we should wait for a successful insertion before consuming the rest of the string, or whether the application should be vacuous under various circumstances. Given the paucity of relevant evidence at the moment, I will simply leave this question open, though (14) assumes a successful eventual insertion, which seems appropriate for Tripura Bangla, below.

(14)

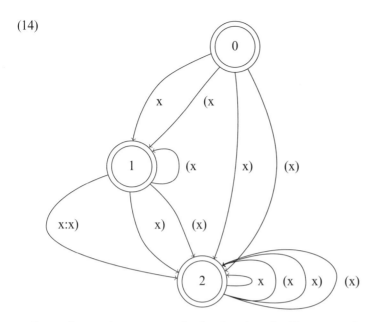

Returning to the parameterized rules given in (3), we see that ternary parsing can be derived from binary parsing by fissioning a state in the binary machine. Similarly, starting in the opposite state changes the "phase" of the parsing, and directing all arcs away from the starting state defines a noniterative machine. The bracket inserted remains a fundamental choice, as does the direction in which the form is scanned. We are left with a small number of fundamental machines, none of them larger than three states, which cover the metrical parsings necessary to analyze counting structures in phonology.

9.3   Case Studies

In this section, I will briefly consider how the revised theory would deal with certain illustrative cases that exercised the older SBG theory in several ways.

9.3.1   Old English

In Idsardi 1994, I offered an SBG account of the stress system of Old English. A translation into the present system is straightforward: heavy syllables begin feet and project two grid marks, the grouping is R2LIS (i.e., the first machine considered above, (5)), and feet project the leftmost element onto line 1. As discussed in Idsardi 1994, there is some dispute about whether sequences of two light syllables following a heavy syllable bore a secondary stress or not. That is, it is not clear from the available evidence whether forms such as *sealfode* 'I anointed' had a secondary stress on the second syllable. In Idsardi 1994, I suggested that this vacillation in secondary stress was due to the open foot, as shown in (15).

(15) (xx) x x)
      sealfode

One of the changes in the present theory—the projection of brackets—allows a more principled answer to the question. If we project left brackets onto line 1, then we can make a further distinction in the stress grid, distinguishing the heads of closed feet from those of open feet, and ultimately only projecting the former onto line 2. That is, on line 0 we will project the leftmost elements of each foot and project left brackets as well. Then on line 1 we will have left-headed feet (L2LNI is vacuous on line 1, as L2LNI applies on line 0 and the bracket will then project), and on line 2 we will again have L2LNI and left-headed feet, giving the parsing in (16).

(16)   x
       (x
       (x   x
       (xx) x x)
       sealfode

Thus, rather than enlarge the number of Projection rules by adding extra conditions to Projection, we will build a little more structure and distinguish these cases by carrying forward certain structures from lower grid lines; in this case, the left brackets from line 0 are carried onto line 1.

9.3.2 Auca

The stress system of Auca (Pike 1964, Hayes 1995:182ff.) is famous for its clashing stress trains. This system was not easy to handle in Idsardi 1992 because the theory adopted there assumed a tight connection between the direction of the scansion and the bracket inserted (right brackets were inserted in scansions beginning from the leftmost element, and vice versa). Stems in Auca have alternating stress on odd-numbered elements counting from the left: #XxXxX...; suffixes have stress on even-numbered elements counting from the right: ...XxXx#. When there is an even number of total marks, the two stress trains are in phase and there are no conflicts and no clash. In words with an odd number of syllables, where the stress trains collide a stress clash results: XxXxX-Xx, XX-xXx. This is handled by computing footing over the stem with L2LII and then reparsing the entire form, including suffixes, with L2RIS, as shown in (17).

(17)   *Stem*   *Word*
      a. 5 + 2   (xx(xx(x   (xx(xx(x-(xx
      b. 2 + 3   (xx   (x(x-x(xx

The important fact is that by using left brackets in the stem parse, we leave the final foot open, and liable to theft of its material by the oncoming suffix parse. That is, the suffix parse can steal the last mark of the last foot of the stem to create a new foot, as in (17b). Notice that if we had used R2LIS on the stem, we would have generated a lapse instead of a clash: xx)xx)x-(xx and xx)-x(xx.

Thus, this account generates the correct stress patterns of Auca without additional machinery beyond the parameterized values for the two scansions. In contrast, Hayes's (1995) account must invoke exceptions to exceptions for Auca. Auca generally allows subminimal feet (unusual according to Hayes), but subminimality is revoked to allow reparsing from the suffix train, and the resulting forms allow subminimal feet that are not located at the edge of the domain, contrary to Hayes's general principles governing subminimal feet. Kim (2003) gives an OT account for Auca, directly stipulating that clash occurs either across the stem-suffix boundary or at the end of the stem.

9.3.3 Winnebago

Halle and Idsardi (1995) use Winnebago as an example of a language employing several avoidance constraints. Here, I offer a reanalysis of Winnebago that employs only one rule of clash resolution, substantially similar to the one proposed for Old English in Idsardi 1994. The parameters for Winnebago are given in (18). I employ two parsings for Winnebago, eliminating the need for the various avoidance constraints used in Halle and Idsardi 1995.

(18) a. Project (x for CRV—then subject to Dorsey's Law, giving CVRV with x(x
    b. L2LIS
    c. Final Clash Deletion: ($\rightarrow \varnothing$ / (x__x#
    d. R2LIS
    e. Project R,)
    f. Project R

Some example parsings are shown in (19). Dorsey's Law vowels are capitalized.

(19) a.
```
          x    x
          x)   x)
      x (x  x)(x  x)  x
      hi rakOroho ni
```
    b.
```
          x
          x) x
      x (x  x)(x
      kErepAna
```

```
c.    x        x        x
     x)   x   x)        x)
  x (x   x) (x (x  x)  (x   x)
  harakishUrujikshAna
```

Form (19c) shows the effect of L2LIS feeding Final Clash Resolution. Cases with interior lapses of three syllables (Halle and Idsardi 1995:438) must be analyzed in the present framework by placing additional left boundaries to create an extra (x group in the form. The exact nature of such a process is not clear; one possibility is to insert left boundaries on syllables before heavy syllables, which themselves get a left boundary and two grid marks. The net effect would be to prevent syllables immediately before heavy syllables from being stressed, as shown in (20). (20a) gives the projection for heavy syllables and the preceding syllable, and (20b) shows the completed parse.

```
(20) a.   x   x   x   (x  (xx   x   x
          waGiGishgapuizhere

     b.        x        x       x
              x)       x)      x)
          x  (x   x) x  (x  (xx   x  x)
          waGiGigishgapuizhere
```

One way to view the net effect of the rules in (18) is that they distinguish binary groups from unary ones. Because of this, Winnebago does not constitute an effective argument against theories employing only a single juncture element (Separator Theory), as outlined by Reiss (this volume). In the case of Winnebago, the effect achieved by R2LIS and Project) can also be achieved by restricting Projection to groups of two or more elements (or, alternatively, a second clash deletion rule could be proposed to handle the nonfinal cases).

9.3.4 Tripura Bangla

In their analysis of Winnebago and other languages, Beasley and Crosswhite (2003) emphasize the use of avoidance constraints, adding Avoid #xx) to Winnebago to achieve ternary parsing at the beginning of the form: #xxx)x .... Instead, in the present proposal, L2LIS parses the beginning of the string as #x(xx(x .... Beasley and Crosswhite go on to analyze a genuinely ternary system, Tripura Bangla (Das 2002), using Avoid)xx to force ternarity, as proposed in Idsardi 1992 for Chugach Alutiiq. The present analysis simply admits the existence of ternary parsing systems (despite their rarity in stress systems). Here, I offer a brief reanalysis of Tripura Bangla under the present proposal. In words consisting only of light syllables, stress falls on the first, fourth, seventh syllables, and so on, but not on the last syllable. Adapting Beasley and Crosswhite's analysis to the present framework, this is equivalent to the two Grouping rules R2RNS and R3LIS with Projection of the leftmost element, as shown for the abstract forms in (21).

(21) a. x   x

      x x x) x) x

   b. x   x

      x x x) x x x) x

Heavy syllables generally attract stress and disrupt the count, but they group with two following light syllables, showing that heavy syllables project a left boundary and only a single mark onto line 0. When there are two heavy syllables in a row, the second is not stressed, which has the effect of applying (22a) iteratively from left to right (the same rule is used in Old English to resolve #LH sequences and was used word-finally in Winnebago, above). The FSA for (22a) is shown in (22b). By the way, the effect of simultaneous application of (22a) as opposed to the iterative application observed in Tripura Bangla can be achieved by having the (x:x arc return to state 1 rather than state 0.

(22) a. (→ Ø / (x__x

   b.

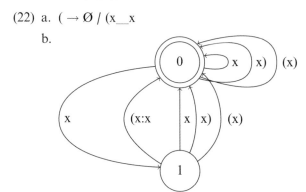

Partial derivations for HHH, LLH, and LLLHH are shown in (23).

(23)

	H H H	L L H	L L L H H
Project (for H	(H (H (H	L L (H	L L L (H (H
R2RNS (see (14))	—	L L)(H	L L L)(H (H
R3LIS	—	—	—
Clash Resolution	(H H (H	—	L L L)(H H
Project leftmost	x x	x x	x x
	(H H (H	L L)(H	L L L)(H H

The present analysis of Tripura Bangla uses the two available brackets to encode different information in feet; left brackets carry forward heavy syllable information. In Separator Theory (Reiss, this volume), where there is only one grouping juncture

|, this cannot be done. This raises problems in Tripura Bangla in distinguishing between final L, which does not bear stress, and final H, which does. Obviously, another rule could be added stipulating that final H projects |x|, whereas nonfinal H projects only |x. This is clearly more complicated than projecting (x for H uniformly, and so we have a trade-off between the complexity of additional representational possibilities and the complexity of additional rules. Likewise, Separator Theory without further adornments will make different predictions for clash resolution in strings like those in (24) (it should be noted that cases like (24b) are not yet attested).

(24)   *SBG theory*   *Separator Theory*
   a. (H (H L) L | H | H L | L
   b. L L L) L (H L) L   L L L | L | H L | L

Two responses are possible in Separator Theory: (1) to state a second Clash Resolution rule for the | L | H sequences, or (2) to apply Clash Resolution before any grouping operations. Since rules must be ordered anyway, ordering Clash Resolution would seem to pose no particular problems, though Clash Resolution would be ordered later in Old English and Winnebago. Thus, although Tripura Bangla does not provide any definitive argument against Separator Theory, it does illustrate the trade-off between additional representational abilities and the necessity of additional rule computations in the absence of representational possibilities.

9.4   Automata for Optimality Theory

Karttunen (1998) demonstrates how to construct FSAs from OT grammars using the lenient composition operator .O. in the Xerox finite state calculus. This operator is available (but not documented) in Beesley and Karttunen 2003, so the main source on the use of lenient composition remains Karttunen 1998. As an exercise, I will construct an FSA using OT and lenient composition to compute R2LIS, (4j), the first machine discussed above. Recall that the basic SBG machine is shown in (5), and the full machine is shown in (6).

The OT equivalent for R2LIS without regard for headedness was constructed using constraints of the form advocated by McCarthy (2003). The constraints, in their ranking order, are given in (25).

(25) a. *FtBinMax*
        No more than two elements per foot
     b. *FtBinMin*
        At least two elements per foot
     c. *Parse2*
        No pairs of unparsed elements

  d. *Parse*
    No unparsed elements
  e. *Unparsed-at-End*
    No initial or medial unparsed elements (compare Lapse-at-End)

This constraint ranking produces parses as in (26).

(26) a. Even: (xx)(xx)(xx)
     b. Odd: (xx)(xx)(xx)x

Leniently composing these constraints using Karttunen 1998 produces the FSA in (27). This machine has 45 states and 90 arcs, compared with the 2 states and 8 arcs of the full machine in (6).

(27)

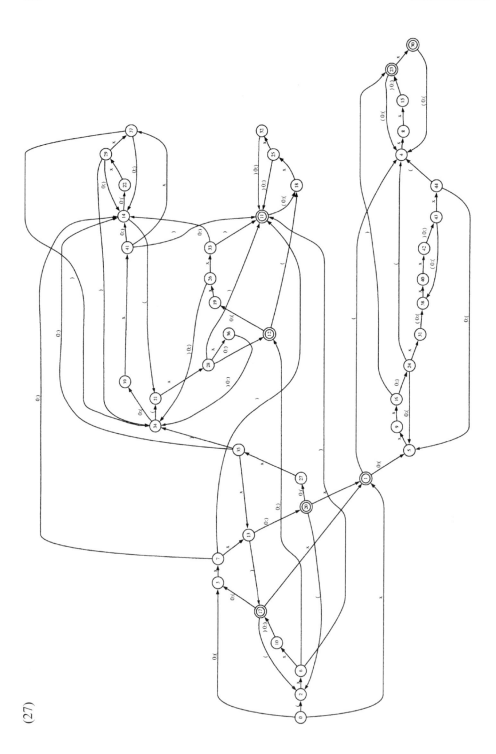

This major difference in the size of the automata raises many questions, some of which cannot be answered at this point. Does the software work properly? That is, is the FSA properly reduced to minimum size? Is lenient composition the wrong way to construct FSAs from OT constraints? Is there a problem with the constraints in (25)? Do certain combinations of constraints cause the explosion in machine size? Most of these questions require additional investigation. One point made by Karttunen is clear, however. The use of constraints with an unbounded number of violations possible is a major source of computational complexity.

It is immediately evident that while we can construct a cascade of constraints that prefer n violations to $n + 1$ violations up to any given n, there is no way in a finite-state system to express the general idea that fewer violations is better than more violations. (Karttunen 1998:11)

But an unbounded number of violations is exactly what McCarthy's (2003) proposal requires. Although it eliminates the gradient evaluation of each violation instance, a given form can have unboundedly many instances of a violation-type, as the following quotation shows:

It is sufficient for any constraint to assign one violation-mark for *each instance* of the marked structure or unfaithful mapping in the candidate under evaluation. (McCarthy 2003:130; emphasis added)

In the present example, all the constraints in (25) can be violated an unbounded number of times by a given candidate. Karttunen goes on to explore the implications of this finding, as follows:

It is curious that violation counting should emerge as the crucial issue that potentially pushes optimality theory out of the finite-state domain thus making it formally more powerful than rewrite systems and two-level models. (Karttunen 1998:11)

Combining Karttunen's findings with those reached here, we see that OT is formally more powerful than rule-based theories; it is also orders of magnitude less efficient in calculating simple parsing problems such as (4j), which rule-based theory can accomplish with the minimal possible machine.

9.5 Conclusions

In this chapter, I have offered some revisions of the SBG theory, eliminating avoidance constraints, combining the mechanisms of Edge Marking and Iterative Constituent Construction into a general Grouping system, and relating the new Grouping system to FSAs. I have shown that the resulting FSAs are small and efficient, orders of magnitude smaller than the corresponding OT machines compiled according to proposals in Karttunen 1998. The revisions allow for simpler accounts of difficult cases in Old English, Auca, Winnebago, and Tripura Bangla, representing a significant improvement in the theory. These cases also highlight the utility of the distinction between open and closed feet, and they demonstrate the utility and efficiency of employing the distinct grouping junctures (and).

References

Beasley, Tim, and Katherine Crosswhite. 2003. Avoiding boundaries: Antepenultimate stress in a rule-based framework. *Linguistic Inquiry* 34:361–392.

Beesley, Kenneth R., and Lauri Karttunen. 2003. *Finite state morphology.* Stanford, Calif.: CSLI Publications.

Clements, G. N., and Samuel Jay Keyser. 1983. *CV phonology.* Cambridge, Mass.: MIT Press.

Das, Shyamal. 2002. Some aspects of the phonology of Tripura Bangla and Tripura Bangla English. Doctoral dissertation, CIEFL, Hyderabad.

Fabb, Nigel. 2002. *Language and literary structure: The linguistic analysis of form in verse and narrative.* Cambridge: Cambridge University Press.

Gross, Maurice. 1972. *Mathematical models in linguistics.* Englewood Cliffs, N.J.: Prentice-Hall.

Halle, Morris. 1990. Respecting metrical structure. *Natural Language and Linguistic Theory* 8:149–176.

Halle, Morris, and William J. Idsardi. 1995. General properties of stress and metrical structure. In *The handbook of phonological theory*, ed. by John Goldsmith, 403–443. Cambridge, Mass.: Blackwell.

Halle, Morris, and Jean-Roger Vergnaud. 1987. *An essay on stress.* Cambridge, Mass.: MIT Press.

Hayes, Bruce. 1995. *Metrical stress theory: Principles and case studies.* Chicago: University of Chicago Press.

Hopcroft, John E., and Jeffrey D. Ullman. 1979. *Introduction to automata theory, languages and computation.* Reading, Mass.: Addison-Wesley.

Howard, Irwin. 1972. A directional theory of rule application in phonology. Doctoral dissertation, MIT.

Hyde, Brett. 2002. A restrictive theory of metrical stress. *Phonology* 19:313–360.

Hyman, Larry. 1985. *A theory of phonological weight.* Dordrecht: Foris.

Idsardi, William J. 1992. The computation of prosody. Doctoral dissertation, MIT.

Idsardi, William J. 1994. Open and closed feet in Old English. *Linguistic Inquiry* 25:522–533.

Idsardi, William J., and Thomas Purnell. 1997. Metrical tone and the Elsewhere Condition. *Rivista di Linguistica* 9:129–156.

Johnson, C. Douglas. 1972. *Formal aspects of phonological description.* The Hague: Mouton.

Karttunen, Lauri. 1998. The proper treatment of optimality in computational phonology. In *FSMNLP'98: Proceedings of the International Workshop on Finite State Methods in Natural Language Processing, June 30–July 1, 1998*, ed. by Lauri Karttunen and Kemal Oflazer, 1–12. Ankara, Turkey: Bilkent University, Faculty of Engineering.

Kenstowicz, Michael, and Charles Kisseberth. 1977. *Topics in phonological theory*. New York: Academic Press.

Kenstowicz, Michael, and Charles Kisseberth. 1979. *Generative phonology*. New York: Academic Press.

Kim, Hyo-Young. 2003. An OT account of Auca stress. *Language Research* 39:337–354.

McCarthy, John. 2003. OT constraints are categorical. *Phonology* 20:75–138.

Partee, Barbara H., Alice ter Meulen, and Robert E. Wall. 1990. *Mathematical models in linguistics.* Dordrecht: Kluwer.

Pike, Kenneth L. 1964. Stress trains in Auca.In *In honour of Daniel Jones: Papers contributed on the occasion of his eightieth birthday, 12 September 1961*, ed. by David Abercrombie, 425–431. London: Longmans, Green.

Prince, Alan S., and Paul Smolensky. 2004. *Optimality Theory: Constraint interaction in generative grammar.* Malden, Mass.: Blackwell.

10   Stress Assignment in Tiberian Hebrew

B. Elan Dresher

10.1   Introduction

The metrical structure of Tiberian Hebrew, as seen through the assignment of main stress and related processes that lengthen and reduce vowels, has long been problematic for theories of metrical structure. The main problem has been that different processes have required apparently incompatible metrical structures. Thus, Tiberian Hebrew has appeared to lack *metrical coherence* (Dresher and Lahiri 1991): incompatible metrical constituents interfere with each other in ways that go beyond what is characteristic of metrical structure in other languages.

The simplified bracketed grid (SBG) theory developed by Idsardi (1992, this volume) and Halle and Idsardi (1995) offers a more elegant alternative to previous analyses of Tiberian Hebrew metrical structure. I will argue that the evidence previously taken as supporting inconsistent metrical constituents does not in fact require the construction of entire constituents; the same evidence can be accounted for by the construction of more minimal single brackets. The marks required by the different processes do not contradict each other; rather, metrical structure is constructed progressively without destroying previous marks.

One characteristic of earlier analyses that is retained in the current proposal is the derivational nature of the construction of Tiberian Hebrew metrical structure. The assignment of aspects of metrical structure interacts with phonological processes in intricate ways that create surface opacity. While these results follow straightforwardly from a derivation, they pose a challenge to nonderivational theories.

10.2   Earlier Approaches: Metrical Overwriting

Tiberian Hebrew is what van der Hulst (1996) has called a "main stress first" language, in that main stress is assigned very early, prior to other metrical structure (Blake 1951, Prince 1975, Malone 1993, Balcaen 1995). For reasons to be made clear below, this early stress is assigned to a word-final syllable if and only if it is closed, and otherwise to the penult. McCarthy (1979) and Hayes (1980) construct a quantity-sensitive left-headed foot (trochee) at the right edge of the word (1); sample forms are shown in (2).

(1) *Main Stress Rule (MSR)*
    Build a quantity-sensitive trochee on the right side.

(2) *Main Stress Rule: Sample forms*

	a. *'slew'*	b. *'slew + 3pl.'*	c. *'word'*	d. *'your m.sg. word'*
Line 2	x	x	x	x
Line 1	(x)	(x)	(x)	(x)
Line 0	x (x)	x (x x)	x (x)	x x (x x)
MSR	ha rag	ha ra guu	da bar	da ba re kaa

The words in (2a) and (2c) end in closed syllables, which count as heavy. Hence, the final trochee consists only of this syllable. In (2b) and (2d), the final syllable is open, allowing a binary foot to be constructed.

The quantity distinctions implied by this patterning classify closed syllables as heavy and open syllables as light. However, word-final vowels in open syllables tend to be long, as in the above examples. It is typologically unusual to count long vowels as light. Moreover, such a classification contradicts that required by vowel reduction, discussed immediately below, as well as by secondary stress and the phrasing indicated by the system of accents (Dresher 1981a,b, 1994).

The earlier accounts of Tiberian Hebrew stress viewed the anomalous definition of quantity required by the MSR as simply one of a number of unusual aspects of the rule. Later analyses have attempted to reconcile the treatment of final long vowels with more usual systems of syllable quantity. In place of (1), Rappaport (1984) constructs a quantity-insensitive left-dominant binary foot at the right edge of each word. To force stress onto final closed syllables, her analysis first assigns them an accent, thereby achieving the same result as a quantity-sensitive foot: stress a final closed syllable, otherwise stress the penult. There is little other motivation, however, for assigning lexical accents in Tiberian Hebrew; moreover, accents here are assigned precisely to syllables that are treated as heavy in the rest of the grammar.

Rather than treat final closed syllables in a special way, Balcaen (1995) proposes to reconsider the underlying quantity of final vowels. Final vowels are predictably long in Tiberian Hebrew, suggesting that a rule of final lengthening applies to underlying short vowels.[1] On this analysis, which I adopt here, long vowels can be considered as heavy syllables throughout the grammar, while allowing the MSR to treat final short vowels as light (3).

(3) *Underlying forms and the Main Stress Rule*

	a. *'slew'*	b. *'slew + 3pl.'*	c. *'word'*	d. *'your m.sg. word'*
Line 0	x x	x x x	x x	x x x x
UR	ha rag	ha ra **gu**	da bar	da ba re k**a**
Line 2	x	x	x	x
Line 1	(x)	(x)	(x)	(x)
Line 0	x (x)	x (x x)	x (x)	x x (x x)
MSR	ha rag	ha ra gu	da bar	da ba re kaa

While the MSR can now be seen as operating on the same quantity distinctions as the rest of the phonology, the placement of main stress in (3) is *opaque* in the sense of Kiparsky 1973, in that main stress does not always surface in the position assigned in (3). In forms (3a) and (3c), main stress surfaces as shown, but this is not the case for (3b) and (3d). In the latter two forms, main stress actually surfaces, in the typical case, on the final syllable, not on the penultimate.

Evidence that the penultimate syllables in these forms are actually stressed at some stage of the derivation comes from the rule of Pretonic Lengthening (PTL).[2] This rule causes a vowel in an open syllable to lengthen when it immediately precedes the main stress. In (5), PTL applies as shown, consistent with the placement of the main stress to this point.

(4) *Pretonic Lengthening*

Lengthen a vowel in an open syllable immediately to the left of main stress.

(5) *Pretonic Lengthening: Sample forms*

	a. *'slew'*	b. *'slew + 3pl.'*	c. *'word'*	d. *'your m.sg. word'*
Line 2	x	x	x	x
Line 1	(x)	(x)	(x)	(x)
Line 0	x (x)	x (x x)	x (x)	x x (x x)
PTL	h**aa** rag	h**aa** ra gu	d**aa** bar	da b**aa** re ka

There is more evidence supporting the above assignment of main stress. Words that are in prominent prosodic positions, usually marked by Masoretic accents that (imperfectly) indicate Intonational Phrases (Dresher 1994), are said to be in *pause* and are called *pausal* forms. Forms that are not in pause are *contextual* forms.

When a word occurs in pause, main stress surfaces on the vowel stressed by the above rules; in many cases, this vowel is also lengthened (6a–c). In (6), the extra grid line represents the main phrasal stress.[3]

(6) *Pausal Stress (PS): Sample forms*

	a. *'slew'*	b. *'slew + 3pl.'*	c. *'word'*	d. *'your m.sg. word'*
Line 3	x	x	x	x
Line 2	…x)	…x)	…x)	…x)
Line 1	(x)	(x)	(x)	(x)
Line 0	x (x)	x (x x)	x (x)	x x (x x)
PS	haa **raag**	haa **raa** gu	daa **baar**	da baa **re** ka

In contextual forms, the original main stress (and the trochaic foot) appear to be overwritten by quantity-sensitive iambic feet built from right to left (7). These feet are known as reduction feet (R-feet) because they give rise to an alternating pattern of vowel reduction/deletion. R-feet are illustrated in (8).[4]

(7) *Iambic feet from right (R-feet)*
    Build quantity-sensitive iambs from the right.

(8) *R-feet: Sample contextual forms*

	a. *'slew'*	b. *'slew + 3pl.'*	c. *'word'*	d. *'your m.sg. word'*
Line 2	x	x	x	x
Line 1	(x x)	(x x)	(x x)	(x x)
Line 0	(x) (x)	(x) (x x)	(x) (x)	(x x) (x x)
R-feet	haa rag	haa ra gu	daa bar	da baa re ka

Vowels in weak position in these iambic feet are reduced; depending on various conditions, some of these reduced vowels are deleted. Affected vowels are represented by *V* in (9).

(9) *Reduction/Deletion (R/D) of weak vowels*

	a. *'slew'*	b. *'slew + 3pl.'*	c. *'word'*	d. *'your m.sg. word'*
Line 2	x	x	x	x
Line 1	(x x)	(x x)	(x x)	(x x)
Line 0	(x) (x)	(x) (. x)	(x) (x)	(. x) (. x)
R/D	haa rag	haa r**V** gu	daa bar	d**V** baa r**V** ka

Additional rules result in the final surface forms of the selected words, shown in (11) and (12). Some of these rules (not necessarily in order) are given in (10).[5]

(10) *Additional rules relevant to sample forms*
  a. *Spirantization*
     Spirantize a nongeminate stop /p, b, t, d, k, g/ following a vowel.
  b. *Final Lengthening*
     Lengthen a word-final vowel.

c. *Tone Lengthening*
Lengthen a vowel that bears main stress under certain conditions; in the examples presented here, stressed /a/ lengthens in nouns (e.g., *dɔːvɔ́ːr*) but not in verbs (e.g., *hɔːrɔ́ɣ*).

d. *Canaanite Rounding*
aː > ɔː

(11) *Surface contextual forms*

a. *'slew'*	b. *'slew + 3pl.'*	c. *'word'*	d. *'your m.sg. word'*
hɔːrɔ́ɣ	hɔːrɣúː	dɔːvɔ́ːr	dəvɔːrxɔ́ː

(12) *Surface pausal forms*

a. *'slew'*	b. *'slew + 3pl.'*	c. *'word'*	d. *'your m.sg. word'*
hɔːrɔ́ːɣ	hɔːrɔ́ːɣu	dɔːvɔ́ːr	dəvɔːréxɔː

The main difficulty in this type of analysis has been the relation between the left-headed feet assigned by the MSR (1) and the right-headed R-feet (7) that govern vowel reduction and deletion. In sample contextual forms (11b) and (11d), the latter overrun the former, causing the previously stressed vowel to reduce and in some cases delete. This kind of interaction has been problematic, aside from the evident lack of metrical coherence in having two such opposed metrical constituents in the same domain.

Rappaport (1984) proposes that the R-feet are not in fact stress feet, but are constructed on a different plane from the stress feet in (1). Vowel reduction and deletion follow the R-foot plane, independent of constituency assigned by the stress feet. On this account, the R-feet do not have to overwrite the stress feet, but coexist with them.

This solution does not really solve the metrical coherence problem, however. It remains the case that two contradictory types of metrical constituents appear to be required in a single domain, whether we call them R-feet or stress feet. On an empirical level, the claim that R-feet are simply independent of the stress plane is incorrect. The crucial cases concern the pausal forms. We have seen that in pause, the R-feet do not reduce the vowel stressed by the MSR and hence do not cause a shift in stress to the right. In cases where the vowel lengthens under pause, one might suppose that this is due to the fact that the stressed syllable has become heavy, so that the normal construction of the R-feet would treat it like any other heavy syllable, which is immune to reduction. An example is (13b).

(13) *Pausal Stress: Two planes*

	a. *'slew'*	b. *'slew + 3pl.'*	c. *'word'*	d. *'your m.sg. word'*
Stress feet				
Line 3	x	x	x	x
Line 2	. . . x)	. . . x)	. . . x)	. . . x)
Line 1	(x)	(x)	(x)	(x)
Line 0	x (x)	x (x x)	x (x)	x x (x x)
	haa **raag**	haa **raa** gu	daa **baar**	da baa **re** ka
Line 0	(x) (x)	(x) (x) (x)	(x) (x)	(x x) (x x)
Line 1	x x	x x x	x x	x x
R-feet				

In (13b), the lengthened pausal vowel is treated as an R-foot and thus avoids reduction and loss of stress.

Such an account does not work for forms like (13d), where the stressed vowel does not undergo pausal lengthening. Nevertheless, it retains its stress and is not reduced. Prince (1975:199) stipulates that the rule of vowel reduction does not affect pausal forms. That is, the extra measure of stress carried by pausal forms is sufficient to make them immune from reduction. While this makes intuitive sense, it is necessary to integrate this explanation into a metrical account. In a biplanar analysis such as (13), construction of R-feet should not be influenced by marks on the stress plane. Evidently, stress does influence construction of the R-feet.

To my knowledge, none of the metrical analyses proposed for Tiberian Hebrew address the question of how pausal forms like (12d) are derived—that is, how the heightened phrasal stress prevents the construction of an iambic R-foot that would put the stressed vowel in a weak position. Rather than speculate about how this fact can be integrated into the above analysis, I will consider it in the context of the revised SBG analysis to be presented in the next section.

10.3   A Simplified Bracketed Grid Analysis

Using unpaired brackets allows for a more elegant derivation in which metrical structure is constructed progressively without destroying previous marks.

The key point concerns the early MSR. I propose that this rule does not assign a stress, or even a metrical constituent, but rather a left bracket. This bracket is assigned to the left of the last vowel of the word that is not absolutely word-final. If the final syllable is closed, the bracket will go to its left (15a,c); if open, it will go to the left of the penult (15b,d).

(14) *Left Bracket Insertion (LBI)*

Insert a left bracket to the left of the last vowel of the word that is not absolutely word-final.

(15) *Underlying representation (UR) and Left Bracket Insertion*

	a. *'slew'*	b. *'slew + 3pl.'*	c. *'word'*	d. *'your m.sg. word'*
	x x	x x x	x x	x x x x
UR	ha rag	ha ra gu	da bar	da ba re ka
	x (x	x (x x	x (x	x x (x x
LBI	ha rag	ha ra gu	da bar	da ba re ka

This rule is followed by PTL, reformulated now to be sensitive to the bracket assigned by LBI, not to a stress.[6]

(16) *Pretonic Lengthening*

Lengthen a vowel in an open syllable immediately to the left of a left bracket.

(17) *Pretonic Lengthening: Sample forms*

	a. *'slew'*	b. *'slew + 3pl.'*	c. *'word'*	d. *'your m.sg. word'*
	x (x	x (x x	x (x	x x (x x
PTL	**haa** rag	**haa** ra gu	**daa** bar	da **baa** re ka

In earlier analyses, vowel lengthening on an unstressed syllable due to PTL was taken as evidence for positing a stress on the immediately following syllable. This evidence does not necessarily point to a stress; all it shows is that it is necessary to distinguish the syllable preceding the lengthened one in some way. The left bracket accomplishes this in a minimal way.

As in the earlier analyses, at this point the derivation can take two different paths, depending on the prosodic position of the word. Let us first consider the pausal forms. Recall that the surfacing of stress in pausal forms was taken as a second type of evidence pointing to the existence of an early main stress on the syllable in question. Unlike the evidence of PTL, pausal evidence does directly indicate an actual stress. Therefore, it is reasonable to suppose that the effect of being the head of a phrase is to cause the assignment of higher-level grid marks to the right of the bracket assigned by LBI. To harmonize with the rest of the analysis, in which heads of constituents are on the right, I will suppose in addition that pausal stress induces a right bracket to the right of the syllable bearing phrasal stress at every level of the grid.

(18) *Pausal Stress (PS)*

Assign a right bracket and a grid mark at every prosodic level up to the Intonational Phrase on a vowel to the right of a left bracket.

On this account, Pausal Lengthening (PL) is a distinct process that applies to certain vowels that have pausal stress.

(19) *Pausal Lengthening*

Lengthen a stressed vowel (with certain exclusions, as in *daba:réka*) in the head of an Intonational Phrase.

(20) *Pausal Stress: Sample forms*

	a. *'slew'*	b. *'slew + 3pl.'*	c. *'word'*	d. *'your m.sg. word'*
Line 3	x)	x)	x)	x)
Line 2	x)	x)	x)	x)
Line 1	x)	x)	x)	x)
Line 0	x (x)	x (x) x	x (x)	x x (x) x
PS	haa rag	haa ra gu	daa bar	da baa re ka

(21) *Pausal Lengthening: Sample forms*

	a. *'slew'*	b. *'slew + 3pl.'*	c. *'word'*	d. *'your m.sg. word'*
Line 3	x)	x)	x)	x)
Line 2	x)	x)	x)	x)
Line 1	x)	x)	x)	x)
Line 0	x (x)	x (x) x	x (x)	x x (x) x
PL	haa **raag**	haa **raa** gu	daa **baar**	da baa re ka

If we choose the contextual path, the process of assigning the R-feet that control vowel reduction and deletion can be decomposed into steps that assign a right bracket to the right of a heavy syllable (22), operating on the output of LBI; insert a right bracket every two syllables, starting from the right (23); and project the rightmost element of each constituent onto line 1 (24).

(22) *Project heavy syllables*
Assign) to heavy syllables.

(23) *Iterative brackets from the right (R-feet)*
Insert) every two syllables from the right.

(24) *Iambic feet*
Project the rightmost element of each line 0 constituent on line 1.

(25) *R-feet: Sample contextual forms*

	a. *'slew'*	b. *'slew + 3pl.'*	c. *'word'*	d. *'your m.sg. word'*
Project H	x) (x)	x) (x x	x) (x)	x x) (x x
	haa rag	haa ra gu	daa bar	da baa re ka
Project R	x x	x x	x x	x x
Insert)	x) (x)	x) (x x)	x) (x)	x x) (x x)
	haa rag	haa ra gu	daa bar	da baa re ka

As before, vowels in the weak position of a foot are reduced or deleted (26).

(26) *Reduction and deletion of weak vowels: Contextual forms*
　　　　　　　a. *'slew'*　　b. *'slew + 3pl.'*　c. *'word'*　　d. *'your m.sg. word'*
Line 1　　　　x　x　　　　x　　　x　　　x　x　　　　　x　　　　x
Line 0　　　　x) (x)　　　x) (.　x)　　x) (x)　　　　.　x) (.　x)
　　　　　　　haa rag　　haa rV gu　　daa bar　　dV baa rV ka

The head of the rightmost foot is assigned main stress (27), (28).[7]

(27) *Main Stress Rule*
　　　a. Insert) at the right edge of line 1.
　　　b. Project the rightmost element of line 1 onto line 2.

(28) *Main Stress Rule: Contextual forms*
　　　　　　　　　a. *'slew'*　　b. *'slew + 3pl.'*　c. *'word'*　　d. *'your m.sg. word'*
Line 2　　　　　　x　　　　　　x　　　　　　x　　　　　　x
Line 1　　　x　x)　　　　x　x)　　　　x　x)　　　　x　x)
Line 0　　　x) (x)　　　x) (.　x)　　x) (x)　　　.　x) (.　x)
　　　　　　haa rag　　haa rV gu　　daa bar　　dV baa rV ka

In the pausal forms, the medial vowel is protected from reduction by the early PS rule (18).

(29)　　　　　　　　　*R-feet: Sample pausal forms*
　　　　　　　　　a. *'slew'*　　b. *'slew + 3pl.'*　c. *'word'*　　d. *'your m.sg. word'*
Line 3　　　　　　x)　　　　　x)　　　　　x)　　　　　x)
Line 2　　　　　　x)　　　　　x)　　　　　x)　　　　　x)
Line 1　　　　　　x)　　　　　x)　　　　　x)　　　　　x)
Line 0 *Proj. H*　　x) (x)　　　x) (x)　x　　x) (x)　　x　x) (x)　x
　　　　　　　　　haa rag　　haa raa gu　　daa baar　　da baa re ka

Line 3　　　　　　x)　　　　　x)　　　　　x)　　　　　x)
Line 2　　　　　　x)　　　　　x)　　　　　x)　　　　　x)
Line 1 *Proj. R*　x　x)　　　x　x)　x　　x　x)　　x　x)　x
Line 0 *Ins.)*　　x) (x)　　　x) (x)　x)　　x) (x)　　x　x) (x)　x)
　　　　　　　　　haa rag　　haa raa gu　　daa baar　　da baa re ka

Applying the other rules in (10) as before, we arrive at the surface forms in (11) and (12).

10.4 The Opacity of Metrical Structure Assignment in Tiberian Hebrew

We have derived two surface forms for our sample verb: [hɔːrɔ́ːɣuː] in pause and [hɔːrɣúː] in context. In the case of pause, there is no possibility of this stress clashing with a following one, since pausal forms by definition are final in their Intonational Phrase. However, a contextual form may be followed in the same Phonological

Phrase by a word with initial stress, and this situation can trigger Stress Retraction. Retraction moves the main stress back to the next full vowel in an open syllable, yielding [hɔːrɣuː] in our example.

(30) *Stress Retraction*
  In clash, retract stress to the next full open syllable.

(31) *Stress Retraction: Sample form*

Line 2		x	x	→	x	x
Line 1	x	x)	x)		x	x)	x)
Line 0	x)	(. | x)	(x)		x)	(. | x)	(x)

        haa rVguu ʔiiš   haa rVguu ʔiiš
        'slew'   'man'   '(they) slew a man' (Gen. 49:6)

The challenge, for a constraint-based theory that selects optimal candidates in a single pass (Prince and Smolensky 2004), is to devise a grammar that obtains all three surface forms—pausal [hɔːrɔ́ːɣuː], unretracted contextual [hɔːrɣúː], and retracted contextual [hɔ́ːrɣuː]—from the single underlying form /harag + u/. Revell (1987:111) interprets the facts diachronically and argues that stress retraction must have developed following vowel reduction; if it did not, retraction would have pulled stress back to the medial vowel, and the retracted form should have been the same as the pausal form.

This argument is actually a synchronic argument about the grammar of Tiberian Hebrew. Since the pausal form shows that the medial vowel is stressable, why is the same form not optimal when a form with nonfinal stress is required? Any nonderivational solution would have to overcome the considerable amount of opacity involved in the derivational approach sketched above.[8]

Notes

I would like to thank Jean Balcaen, Vincent DeCaen, and Bill Idsardi for helpful ideas and discussion over the years. Errors in this account are solely mine. This research was supported in part by grant 410-2003-0913 from the Social Sciences and Humanities Research Council of Canada.

This chapter is a revised version of a paper presented at the City University of New York Phonology Forum Symposium on Architecture and Representation in Phonology, 20–21 February 2004.

1. Some final vowels surface as short, but these can be shown to derive from vowel-consonant sequences.

2. There are certain restrictions on the rule; see Prince 1975:62–66, Malone 1993:85–87.

3. Notice that we must assume that words are already in place in phrases at this point in the derivation. This presupposes that some phrasing has already taken place before the phonological derivation is complete (Dresher 1983).

4. Generative analyses of vowel reduction originate with Prince (1975). Various metrical interpretations are proposed by McCarthy (1979), Hayes (1980), and Rappaport (1984).

5. Khan (1987) argues that Hebrew vowels at the time of completion of the Tiberian notation system were no longer distinguished by quantity. Thus, the transcriptions and grammar presented here refer to an earlier stage of the language.

6. This formulation is inspired by Balcaen 2000. As before, there are restrictions on the rule that I do not discuss here.

7. The Main Stress Rule (27) does not apply in pausal forms, or applies to no effect, as these forms already have the main phrasal stress assigned.

8. On the particular problems caused by the opacity of spirantization, see Idsardi 1997, 1998.

References

Balcaen, M. Jean. 1995. The prosody of Tiberian Hebrew. Master's thesis, University of Saskatchewan, Saskatoon.

Balcaen, M. Jean. 2000. Prosody and syntax in Tiberian Hebrew. Ms., University of Toronto.

Blake, Frank. 1951. Pretonic vowels in Hebrew. *Journal of Near Eastern Studies* 10:243–255.

Dresher, B. Elan. 1981a. Accentuation and metrical structure in Tiberian Hebrew. In *Theoretical issues in the grammar of Semitic languages*, ed. by Hagit Borer and Youssef [Joseph] Aoun, 180–208. MIT Working Papers in Linguistics 3. Cambridge, Mass.: MIT, MIT Working Papers in Linguistics.

Dresher, B. Elan. 1981b. Metrical structure and secondary stress in Tiberian Hebrew. In *Brown University working papers in linguistics 4*, ed. by Carol Chapin, Phil Shinn, and John Ryalls, 24–37. Providence, R.I.: Brown University, Linguistics.

Dresher, B. Elan. 1983. Postlexical phonology in Tiberian Hebrew. In *Proceedings of the West Coast Conference on Formal Linguistics 2*, ed. by Michael Barlow, Daniel P. Flickinger, and Michael T. Wescoat, 67–78. Stanford, Calif.: Stanford University, Stanford Linguistics Association.

Dresher, B. Elan. 1994. The prosodic basis of the Tiberian Hebrew system of accents. *Language* 70:1–52.

Dresher, B. Elan, and Aditi Lahiri. 1991. The Germanic foot: Metrical coherence in Old English. *Linguistic Inquiry* 22:251–286.

Halle, Morris, and William J. Idsardi. 1995. General properties of stress and metrical structure. In *The handbook of phonological theory*, ed. by John Goldsmith, 403–443. Cambridge, Mass.: Blackwell.

Hayes, Bruce. 1980. A metrical theory of stress. Doctoral dissertation, MIT.

Hulst, Harry van der. 1996. Separating primary accent and secondary accent. In *Stress patterns of the world*, ed. by Harry van der Hulst, Rob Goedemans, and Ellis Visch, 1–26. The Hague: Holland Academic Graphics.

Idsardi, William J. 1992. The computation of prosody. Doctoral dissertation, MIT.

Idsardi, William J. 1997. Phonological derivations and historical changes in Hebrew spirantization. In *Derivations and constraints in phonology*, ed. by Iggy M. Roca, 367–392. Oxford: Oxford University Press.

Idsardi, William J. 1998. Tiberian Hebrew spirantization and phonological derivations. *Linguistic Inquiry* 29:37–73.

Khan, Geoffrey. 1987. Vowel length and syllable structure in the Tiberian tradition of Biblical Hebrew. *Journal of Semitic Studies* 32:23–82.

Kiparsky, Paul. 1973. Abstractness, opacity, and global rules. In *Three dimensions of linguistic theory*, ed. by Osamu Fujimura, 57–86. Tokyo: TEC.

Malone, Joseph. 1993. *Tiberian Hebrew phonology*. Winona Lake, Ind.: Eisenbrauns.

McCarthy, John J. 1979. Formal problems in Semitic phonology and morphology. Doctoral dissertation, MIT.

Prince, Alan S. 1975. The phonology and morphology of Tiberian Hebrew. Doctoral dissertation, MIT.

Prince, Alan S., and Paul Smolensky. 2004. *Optimality Theory: Constraint interaction in generative grammar*. Malden, Mass.: Blackwell.

Rappaport, Malka. 1984. Issues in the phonology of Tiberian Hebrew. Doctoral dissertation, MIT.

Revell, E. J. 1987. *Nesiga (retraction of word stress) in Tiberian Hebrew*. Textos y estudios 'Cardenal Cisneros'. Madrid: CSIC (Consejo Superior de Investigaciones Científicas), Instituto de Filología.

11 Brackets and Grid Marks, or Theories of Primary Accent and Rhythm

Harry van der Hulst

11.1 Introduction

In this chapter, I present the outlines of a formal theory of word accent.[1] The theory is nonmetrical in that the account of primary accent location is not based on iterative foot structure. The theory separates the representations of primary and rhythmic accents, the idea being that the latter are accounted for "with reference to" the primary accent location. This means that rhythmic structure is either assigned later (in a derivational sense) or governed by constraints that are subordinate to the constraints that govern primary accent (as is possible in the approach presented in Prince and Smolensky 2004). This approach has been called a "primary-accent-first theory" (see van der Hulst 1984, 1990, 1992, 1996, 1997, 1999, 2000a, 2002, in preparation, van der Hulst and Lahiri 1988, van der Hulst and Kooij 1994 for earlier statements). The theory (presented in sections 11.2 through 11.6) is offered here as an alternative to the approach in Idsardi 1992, this volume. However, it was not developed as an alternative to this theory. Rather, like Idsardi's theory, it was developed as an alternative to standard metrical phonology (Liberman and Prince 1977, Vergnaud and Halle 1978, Hayes 1980, Halle and Vergnaud 1987). In section 11.7, I will point to some parallels and differences between Idsardi's theory and the one presented here.

11.2 Word Accentuation

11.2.1 Standard Metrical Theory

The key insight of standard metrical theory is that syllables (or perhaps subsyllabic constituents such as skeletal positions, rhymes, or moras) of words are organized into a layer of foot structure, each foot having a head. Primary accent is then derived by organizing the feet into a word structure in which one foot is the head. The head of the head foot, being a head at both levels, expresses primary accent. In this view, rhythmic accents are assigned first, while primary accent is regarded as the promotion of one of these rhythmic accents; rhythmic accents form a subset of the secondary accents, the latter notion comprising also so-called cyclic accents ("traces" of primary accents that occur in embedded constituents of complex words).

Here and in the rest of this chapter, I will assume that structures like those delivered by formal algorithms in standard metrical phonology, my own model, and Idsardi's model characterize properties of mental representation of words, but have no intrinsic phonetic content. However, aspects of these structures (in particular, edges and heads) may be cued by various phenomena such as salient phonetic properties (causing the perceptual impression of prominence, i.e., primary "stress" and rhythmic alternation), phonotactics (certain positions allow greater complexity), anchoring of tones (lexical or postlexical), and allophonic processes (such as aspiration in English). There is no necessity for all aspects of these abstract structures to be somehow "audible" in all words in all languages. The fundamental raison d'être of these structures may ultimately be cognitive in that sets of elements can be mentally represented only in certain ways. All the phenomena that signal these structures in one way or another may then simply be parasitic on structures that exist for independent, cognitive reasons (see van der Hulst, in preparation).

11.2.2 Reversing the Order of Things, and Why

In van der Hulst 1984, and subsequently in a number of other works (see above), I proposed that we reverse the order of things by first deriving the primary accent location, making the assignment of rhythmic accent a truly secondary matter.[2] The initial (and, in retrospect, perhaps not the crucial) motivation for this proposal was that in most systems, primary accent seems to fall on the foot that is assigned first in the classical metrical account. Formally, this means that in systems that assign feet from left to right, the word tree would in almost all languages be left-headed, while in right-to-left systems it would almost always be right-headed. I suggested initially that this pattern would be the only possible one if indeed primary accent is universally assigned first, with rhythm echoing (or rippling away); note Garde's (1968) apt term *echo accent* for rhythmic accent. However, problematic for this view is the fact that in a class of accent systems the location of primary word accent depends on the number of syllables that make up the whole word. In classical terms, in such systems the direction of foot assignment would not correlate with the headedness of the word tree in the above manner. Thus, for example, primary accent would be initial in even-numbered words and would fall on the second syllable in odd-numbered words. I termed such systems "count systems," which is perhaps an infelicitous term in that we need not literally count the syllables. Rather, syllables are grouped in binary feet throughout the word, and the last-assigned foot is promoted to head word status. Systems of this sort obviously present a challenge to the strong claim that all primary accents can be derived nonmetrically (i.e., without prior exhaustive foot assignment).

Once the primary-accent-first approach had been proposed, additional (and per-haps better) motivation for it emerged. Six additional lines of support can be distin-guished. On the one hand, it now made sense that the weight criteria for primary and rhythmic accents can differ (see (1a)). After all, the primary-accent-first theory has available two distinct algorithms, one for primary accent, the other for rhythmic ac-cent. Nothing, then, prevents a situation where one is quantity-sensitive while the other isn't, or where both are quantity-sensitive in different ways. Clearly, if such dis-crepancies exist, they are unexpected from the viewpoint of the standard metrical account, which then needs to be amended by allowing two different phases of foot assignment, the one that accounts for primary accent either being noniterative or see-ing most of its feet erased.

A second motivation involves the right- or leftheadedness of the foot structure that is necessary for primary and secondary accent. Cases have been attested in which dif-ferent foot types appear to be necessary (see (1b)). From the viewpoint of classical metrical theory, such systems again form an anomaly.

A third motivation comes from the fact that the edge-orientation of primary and secondary accent can differ in that, for example, primary accent is on the right edge (let us say the penultimate syllable), while the wave of rhythm seems to come from the left (see (1c)). Such a situation also presents a problem for the standard theory. At the same time, these cases show that rhythmic accents are not always echoing away from the primary accent, but rather can display a "polarizing" (i.e., "opposite edge") effect of some sort. Primary-accent-first theory can deal with this phenome-non, but the standard account cannot, at least not straightforwardly. In this case, too, it is of course possible to have two phases of foot assignment: a first foot layer (right to left) of which we erase all but the rightmost foot and then a second assign-ment of foot structure, now from left to right.[3] Or one might suggest that a foot is assigned noniteratively on the right edge, followed by an iterative application from left to right. The point is that such derivations are not expected given the core design of standard metrical theory.

(1)		*Primary accent*	*Rhythmic accent*	
	a. Weight	Weight-sensitive	Weight-insensitive	(English)
		Weight-insensitive	Weight-sensitive	(Finnish)
	b. Foot type	Left-headed	Right-headed	(BigNambas, Marind)
		Right-headed	Left-headed	(Taga, Dari, Uzbek)
	c. Word	Right-edge	Left-edge	(English)
		Left-edge	Right-edge	(Turkish)

A fourth motivation is that there are bounded, weight-sensitive systems that plainly cannot be accounted for by the standard theory, no matter what variant of foot theory one adopts (see (8) and discussion below).

A fifth motivation comes from the fact that, whereas primary accent location can easily be lexically governed to some extent, rhythmic accents never show any trace of being lexically determined. This difference in particular has prompted the suggestion that primary accent is, or at least can be, lexical, while rhythmic accents are post-lexical (see Hurch 1995). All the usual criteria for distinguishing between lexical and postlexical rules seem to square with the differences between primary and secondary rhythmic accent locations.

Finally, a sixth motivation comes from the treatment of so-called unbounded systems. Various approaches to unbounded systems, employing both bounded and un-bounded feet, have been proposed over the years (see van der Hulst 1999, 2000a,b, 2002, 2006 for overviews). Hayes (1995) states that such systems are nonmetrical. He remarks that since "the facts in this area are quite simple and fill out all the logi-cal possibilities, it is hard to develop a theory that goes much beyond just describing the facts" (p. 33). He handles "opposite edge" systems (first/last, last/first; see below) by constructing unbounded weight-sensitive feet (as proposed in the standard theory). "Same edge" systems (first/first, last/last) are handled by "projecting prominence dis-tinctions" (heavy syllables) and directly assigning primary accent to the left- or right-most heavy or (in the absence of a heavy) left- or rightmost syllable. At this point, let me explain the "first/first, first/last, etc." terminology since I will continue to use it: a system is said to be, for example, first/first if primary accent is located in the first heavy syllable within the accentual domain, or, in the absence of heavy syllables, on the first syllable.

In summary, there are many reasons for exploring an alternative framework, that is, one in which primary accents are assigned nonmetrically. With these accents in place, a constituent structure can be erected (almost automatically; see section 11.5) that accommodates the full accentual structure of words.

11.2.3   Primary-Accent-First Theory: How Does It Work?

The key idea is that primary accent is always located on a left- or rightmost syllable within the accentual domain. Representations of primary accent involve the presence of a grid structure as in standard metrical phonology, or more specifically as in Prince 1983. Following Prince 1983, I refer to the relevant constraint as the End Rule. Heavy syllables are projected at level 1 of the grid if the system is weight-sensitive.[4] Syllables that are lexically marked are automatically present at level 1 (i.e., that is how they are marked). If there is no special (i.e., heavy or lexically marked) syllable, level 1 will be provided with a mark by a default rule. Hence, the general scheme for primary accentuation consists of three parameterized constraints (*parameters* for short), as in (2).

(2) a. *Projection*
     Project weight (*yes/no*) to level 1.
  b. *Default Rule*
     Assign a mark to the (*leftmost/rightmost*) syllable in case level 1 is empty.
  c. *End Rule*
     Assign primary accent to the (*leftmost/rightmost*) mark at level 1.

The End Rule can be set only in case the domain can contain more than one level 1 mark. This can easily happen in weight-sensitive systems (whenever more than one heavy syllable is present in the domain), but is probably rare in weight-insensitive systems where only multiple lexical marks can create the required situation. In bounded systems, that situation is much less likely to occur than in unbounded systems (such as Russian; see below). If, for some reason, it is important to represent word accent at level 2 in all cases, we might stipulate that the unspecified End Rule will simply "reinforce" the mark at level 1 by adding an extra grid mark at level 2.

To differentiate between bounded and unbounded systems, we need a domain parameter. The accentual schema in (2) may apply within a two-syllable domain on the left or right side of the word, modulo extrametricality, or within the word as a whole (also modulo extrametricality), as shown in (3).

(3) *Domain setting*
   a. The domain of accent assignment is *left/right/unspecified*.
   b. Extrametricality: *left/right/unspecified*.

In (3), both parameters can be left unspecified, which indicates in the case of (3a) that all syllables are within the accentual domain, and in the case of (3b) that there are no extrametrical elements. Alternatively, to avoid the unspecified "third value," one could adopt additional parameters on which the other parameters depend. For example, one could replace (3) by (4).

(4) *Domain setting (alternative)*
   a. The domain is *unbounded* (the whole word)/*bounded* (two edge syllables).
     a'. The bounded domain of accent assignment is *left/right*.
   b. Extrametricality: *yes/no*.
     b'. Extrametricality: *left/right*.

This alternative is perhaps preferred since we already have other parameters that require dependent subparameters—for example, the parameter in (2a). If weight is relevant, we need to specify which syllabic properties contribute to weight. In addition, we need a further parameter dependent on (4b') that specifies what is extrametrical—

a syllable, a mora, a final consonant, or whatever options are required. An independent issue regarding extrametricality is whether it is an available option on the left side. The virtual absence of systems with accent on the third syllable suggests that extrametricality is (for whatever reason) limited to the right edge.

Let us now turn to a more detailed discussion of bounded and unbounded systems, respectively, still focusing on primary accent. I will deal with secondary rhythmic accent in section 11.5.

11.3 Bounded Systems

The first step in deriving bounded systems is to delimit on the right or left side of the word a domain for primary accentuation of two syllables (modulo extrametricality). The second step is to apply the Default Rule to provide this domain with a mark just in case no other special syllable (heavy or lexically marked) is present at level 1. If primary accent is weight-sensitive, this means that heavy syllables project a mark to level 1 in the two-syllable domain. The account is made complete by setting the value for the End Rule, (2c). I will first discuss weight-sensitive systems, which present a more interesting challenge than weight-insensitive systems.

11.3.1 Weight-Sensitive Bounded Systems

The primary-accent-first approach allows four types of bounded weight-sensitive systems at each edge of the word (modulo extrametricality).

(5) *Right-edge cases*
   a. *Rotuman: Final in case of σh], otherwise penultimate*

x	x	x	x
x	x	x x	x
(h l)]	(l h)]	(h h)]	(l l)]

   "Rightmost heavy, otherwise leftmost (last/first)"
   Domain: bounded, right
   Project: heavy syllable
   Default Rule: left
   End Rule: right

   b. *Yapese: Penultimate in case of hl], otherwise final*

x	x	x	x
x	x	x x	x
(h l)]	(l h)]	(h h)]	(l l)]

   "Rightmost heavy, otherwise rightmost (last/last)"
   Domain: bounded, right

Project: heavy syllable
Default Rule: right
End Rule: right

c. *Aklan: Penultimate in case of hσ], otherwise final*

x		x	x			x	
x		x	x	x		x	
(h	l)]	(l h)]	(h	h)]		(l	l)]

"Leftmost heavy, otherwise rightmost (first/last)"
Domain: bounded, right
Project: heavy syllable
Default Rule: right
End Rule: left

d. *Awadhi: Penultimate except in case of lh]*

x		x	x			x	
x		x	x	x		x	
(h	l)]	(l h)]	(h	h)]		(l	l)]

"Leftmost heavy, otherwise leftmost (first/first)"
Domain: bounded, right
Project: heavy syllable
Default Rule: left
End Rule: left

(6) *Left-edge cases*

a. *Capanahua: Peninitial in case of [σh, otherwise initial*

x		x	x	x
x	x	x	x x	x
[(h	l)	[(l h)	[(h h)	[(l l)

"Rightmost heavy, otherwise leftmost (last/first)"
Domain: bounded, left
Project: heavy syllable
Default Rule: left
End Rule: right

b. *Archi: Initial in case of [hl, otherwise second*

x		x	x	x
x	x	x	x x	x
[(h	l)	[(l h)	[(h h)	[(l l)

"Rightmost heavy, otherwise rightmost (last/last)"
Domain: bounded, left

Project: heavy syllable
Default Rule: right
End Rule: right

c. *Ossetic: Initial in case of [hσ, otherwise postinitial*

```
x           x       x           x
x x         x       x x         x
[ (h  l)    [ (l  h)   [ (h  h)    [ (l  l)
```

"Leftmost heavy, otherwise rightmost (first/last)"
Domain: bounded, left
Project: heavy syllable
Default Rule: right
End Rule: left

d. *Malayalam: Postinitial in case of [lh], otherwise initial*

```
x           x       x           x
x           x x     x           x
[ (h  l)    [ (l  h)   [ (h  h)    [ (l  l)
```

"Leftmost heavy, otherwise leftmost (first/first)"
Domain: bounded, left
Project: heavy syllable
Default Rule: left
End Rule: left

The theory proposed here is completely instantiated for bounded weight-sensitive systems, although there are frequency differences.[5] Note that only those cases in which the domain contains two heavy syllables critically require a setting of the End Rule. Other cases that necessitate this rule would be ones that involve lexical marking.[6]

The four-way distinction that is found on each edge of the word cannot easily be replicated with foot structure, whatever variant one assumes. In the original metrical theory (Vergnaud and Halle 1978, Hayes 1980), two of these four systems require a retraction rule, as shown in (7).[7]

(7) Rotuman: quantity-sensitive trochee
    Yapese: quantity-sensitive iamb
    Aklan: quantity-sensitive iamb, plus retraction rule in the hh] case
    Awadhi: quantity-sensitive trochee, plus retraction rule in the hh] case

A similar situation exists for the left-edge systems. The newer foot theory proposed in Hayes 1995 or Kager 1993 cannot do without retraction rules in some cases. The present account makes no appeal to retraction rules and is thus more restrictive. It allows structure-building rules only, and it is thus compatible with a constraint-based approach. It is not obvious how the retraction analysis (involving structure-changing operations) could be translated into a purely constraint-based grammar formalism.

Additional cases that need attention are so-called broken window cases, in which an accent can "jump outside" through the binary accent window to an antepenultimate position just in case the antepenultimate syllable is heavier than the penultimate syllable. At first sight, extrametricality cannot be invoked easily in those cases since it would be unacceptable (for reasons of locality) to make extrametricality dependent on a relative weight-relationship between σ_3 σ_2, as in (8). A retraction rule is always possible, but it is unattractive given the above criticism of the standard approach to cases like Aklan and Awadhi.

Broken window systems are not unbounded, since no syllable outside the three-syllable window is ever relevant. An example of such a system is Maithili (Hayes 1995:149–162). Primary accent is on the final syllable if this is heavy; otherwise, it is penultimate. However, as shown in (8), if both final and penultimate syllables are light and the antepenultimate is heavy, primary accent goes to the antepenultimate.

(8) *Maithili*

x	x	x	x	x
x	x	x x	x	x
(h l)]	(l h)]	(h h)]	(l l)]	h (l l)]

A possible analysis of this case within the present approach is to analyze the final syllable as extrametrical if and only if it is light. We then set both the Default Rule and the End Rule to the value "right," as in (9).

(9)

x	x	x	x	x
x	x	x x	x	x
(σ h) ⟨l⟩]	(l h)]	(h h)]	(l l) ⟨l⟩]	(h l) ⟨l⟩]

The system of constraints for Maithili is given in (10). It remains to be seen whether all broken window systems can be dealt with in this manner.

(10) *Maithili primary accent*
   a. Domain: bounded, right
   b. Extrametricality: yes, light syllable
   c. Project: heavy syllable
   d. Default Rule: right
   e. End Rule: right

11.3.2 Weight-Insensitive Bounded Systems

Let us now briefly turn our attention to weight-insensitive bounded systems. Weight-insensitive systems differ from the systems in (5) and (6) in that no special syllables are designated for projection to level 1. Initial, second syllable, antepenultimate,

penultimate, and final accent all depend on the choice of domain edge, extrametricality, and the default rules. Many systems of this type have exceptions, however.
Exceptions can be marked in lexical representations in two ways, the choice depending on the type of exception: either words are marked for extrametricality, or syllables are marked with what I have elsewhere called "diacritic weight" (van der Hulst
1999). Lexically marked syllables behave just like heavy syllables and, in a diachronic sense, often are remnants of a weight system (as in various Romance languages; see Roca 1999). Other sources for lexical marking are unadapted loanwords
with accent patterns that deviate from the pattern of the receiving language.

The algorithm for Polish, a weight-insensitive penultimate system allowing words
to have exceptional penultimate or final accent, is depicted in (11) and exemplified in
(12).

(11) *Polish primary accent*
   a. Domain: bounded and right
   b. Extrametricality: no
   c. Project weight: no
   d. Default Rule: left
   e. End Rule: (not set)

(12) a. x   b. x   c. x   Rule (11e)
         x   **x**   x   Rules (11c), (11d)
         (σ σ)]   (σ **σ**)]   (σ σ) ⟨σ⟩]   Rules (11a), (11b)
         Penultimate   Final   Antepenultimate

(12a) represents the regular case. In (12b), there is a lexical mark on the final syllable,
shown in boldface, whereas (12c) requires the final syllable to be lexically marked as
extrametrical. If there is no lexically marked syllable, (11d) inserts a level 1 mark on
the leftmost syllable as in (12c). It stands to reason that no accentual domain will
contain more than one lexically marked syllable, unless the domain would include
(parts of) more than one morpheme, in which case, in principle, two lexical marks
could be present. Unless this is the case, the End Rule cannot be set. It was suggested
earlier that we might assume that in such a case the End Rule reinforces the grid
mark of level 1, as was done in (12).

11.4 Unbounded Systems

A uniform characterization of bounded and unbounded systems is possible in the
present approach. In unbounded systems, accent locations are not restricted to a syllable near the left or right edge of the word. Rather, primary accent is assigned to the
left- or rightmost special syllable, taking into account the whole word (modulo extra-

metricality). Syllables can be special by virtue of being heavy and/or being diacritically marked. In the present approach, the four types of unbounded systems quite simply arise from cross-classifying the options of the Primary Accent Rule and the Default Rule; see (13).

(13) a. *Classical Arabic, Huasteco, Eastern Cheremis*

```
                x          x
        x       x          x
   (l l l h l l l h l l)   (l l l l l)
```

"Rightmost heavy, otherwise leftmost (last/first)"
Domain: unbounded
Project: heavy syllable
Default Rule: left
End Rule: right

b. *Komi, Kwak'wala, Golin*

```
                x                      x
        x       x                      x
   (l l l h l l l h l l)    (l l l l l)
```

"Rightmost heavy, otherwise rightmost (last/last)"
Domain: unbounded
Project: heavy syllable
Default Rule: right
End Rule: right

c. *Aguacatec, Western Cheremis*

```
        x                              x
        x       x                      x
   (l l l h l l l h l l)    (l l l l l)
```

"Leftmost heavy, otherwise rightmost (first/last)"
Domain: unbounded
Project: heavy syllable
Default Rule: right
End Rule: left

d. *Indo-European, Murik*

```
        x                      x
        x       x              x
   (l l l h l l l h l l)   (l l l l l)
```

"Leftmost heavy, otherwise leftmost (first/first)"
Domain: unbounded

Project: heavy syllable
Default Rule: left
End Rule: left

Thus, unbounded systems assign primary accent to the rightmost or leftmost heavy syllable, assuming furthermore that the Default Rule is independent and may select the same or the opposite edge of the word. Goldsmith (1990:180ff.) proposes an approach of this type, which in the present theory is applied to bounded and unbounded systems alike. In both types of systems, primary accent is located in terms of the same parameters except for the parameter that determines the size of the accentual domain.

In most of the examples in (13), special syllables are heavy. There are also so-called unbounded lexical accent systems (like Russian) in which morphemes may contain lexically marked syllables. If morphemes are put together to form words, primary accent is placed in accordance with the schemes shown in (14). For further discussion, see van der Hulst 1999, in preparation.

(14) a. Last/First: (vacancy)
     b. Last/Last: Modern Hebrew
     c. First/Last: Turkish
     d. First/First: Russian

The unbounded nature of Turkish (which in most cases has final accent) is revealed by the fact that a lexical accent on any morpheme followed by any number of other morphemes will emerge as bearing the primary accent (see van der Hulst 1999:60–64). In both examples in (15), a suffix is added to a stem carrying a lexical accent. This marked syllable rather than the (regular) final syllable carries primary accent.

(15) a. akşám - leyin 'at evening'
     b. şévrole - la 'with Chevrolet'

There is no formal reason why unbounded systems should be weight-sensitive or use lexical accents. The present theory allows unbounded, weight-insensitive systems as well. Such a system would have initial or final accent, or—with extrametricality—second syllable or penultimate accent. This implies that, strictly speaking, only antepenultimate weight-insensitive systems (like Macedonian) are outside the reach of the unbounded-domain treatment. However, as soon as a system has lexical exceptions, we learn from their locations whether a system is bounded or unbounded. To see this clearly, let us consider how Polish, for example, could at first sight be analyzed as an unbounded system with the rules in (16), yielding the metrical structures in (17).

(16) *Polish primary accent*
   a. Domain: unbounded
   b. Extrametricality: yes (unless marked)
   c. Project weight: no
   d. Default Rule: right
   e. End Rule: (not set)

(17) a. x   b. x   c. x   Rule (16e)
         x   x   x   Rules (16c), (16d)
        (σ) ⟨σ⟩]   (σ σ)]   (σ σ) ⟨σ⟩]   Rules (16a), (16b)
      Penultimate   Final   Antepenultimate

Exceptional final and penultimate accent location would have to be marked with di-acritic weight. Such a treatment is possible, but it would not account for the fact that no lexical marks lead to unbounded accent effects in Polish (as does happen in Turk-ish, for example). It would appear, then, that the types of exceptions that occur in a system reveal the nature of the system.

11.5   Constituent Structure

In the proposed model, primary accent selection is determined by a procedure that attributes minimal internal structure to words. In bounded systems, a binary domain is postulated adjacent to one edge of the word or, in case of extrametricality, removed from the edge by one syllable or an even smaller unit. In unbounded sys-tems, we postulate no word-internal structure at all, except when excluding a periph-eral extrametrical unit. In both cases, whatever word-internal structure is postulated could merely exist for the purpose of computing the location of primary accent and nothing else. What kind of additional word-internal structure is needed, if any, and for what reason? Taking issue with the idea of needing exhaustive binary foot struc-ture to account for rhythmic structure, Prince (1983) showed that the relevant pat-terns could be generated in terms of procedures that place alternating marks in the grid (perhaps with strength differentiation among these to account, for example, for the strongest rhythmic initial beat in languages such as English). The model pre-sented here is compatible with this proposal and therefore it offers a refinement on Prince's grid-only approach in the sense that it adds a special procedure for selecting the head of the word. Others writers, however, have argued that word-internal con-stituency is necessary, at least in bounded systems, in part to account for phenomena of accent shift; see Vergnaud and Halle 1987. For reasons of space, I will remain neutral with respect to this issue. My proposal for primary accent location can also be combined with a procedure for erecting a word-internal prosodic constituent structure. Constituent structure, if indeed needed, would have to respect the heads that are assigned by primary accent placement. It is reasonable to expect that algorithms for additional structure (whether grid-only or involving feet) can be fairly simple given that the apparent complexities of such procedures in the traditional metrical approach were largely caused by the intricacies of primary accent location, which we have factored out from the account of rhythmic accents. As stated at the beginning of this chapter, procedures for rhythmic organization not only follow primary accent assignment, but in most cases are lexical postcyclic, postlexical, or part and parcel of phonetic implementation.

11.6   Count Systems

The proposed domain-based theory covers all discussed cases of primary accent location in a maximally simple fashion. Once assigned, primary accents form the controlling force behind the construction of word-internal rhythmic structure. The present theory, then, is "backward" in two ways: first, it derives primary accent before secondary rhythmic accent; and second, it derives heads (of words) before erecting word-internal constituent structure if such structure turns out to be needed. Before concluding that all matters of primary accent location are nonmetrical, we have to deal with cases in which the location of primary accent has been claimed to depend on the number of syllables in the whole word (modulo extrametricality). For example, in some languages, in words with an even number of syllables primary accent is penultimate, while in words with an odd number of syllables it is final. See (18).

(18) Right-headed   x   x
     Left-to-right   (x   x)   (x   x   x)
                      (x x) (x x)   (x x) (x x) (x)
                       1 2   3 4   1 2   3 4   5

   Such systems do not seem compatible with the view that the location of primary accent takes priority over the creation of rhythmic (foot) structure. How can we treat systems of this type? In count systems, it would seem that primary accent is crucially based on an exhaustive "perfect gridding" (or foot parsing) of the whole word. If this is indeed so, count systems make it impossible to claim that all primary word accents are nonmetrical. In van der Hulst 1997, I have discussed in some detail that it is probably too early to give up on this strong claim and therefore premature to conclude that count systems represent a real "metrical residue" of primary accent systems. Much is at stake here, because if we were to accept a standard metrical account of count systems, we would have to accept that noncount bounded systems (except the most complicated cases where primary accent must precede secondary accent assignment for a variety of reasons; Hayes (1995:116–117) calls these "top-down systems") are ambiguous, since these then could be derived as in the present model ("primary accent first"), or in the standard way as in the classical metrical theory ("secondary rhythmic accent first"). The strong claim that all primary accent is non-metrical can be maintained if we can demonstrate that the metrification in count systems, applied without guidance of the primary accent routine that takes precedence over it, simply fails to deliver primary accents. This would be the case if we can show that words in such systems have word-internal rhythmic structure but no word-level primary accent. This is, in essence, what I have tried to argue in van der Hulst 1997, on which the remainder of this section draws.

First let us note that some languages have indeed been reported to lack the notion of primary word accent. Hayes (1995) refers to a number of languages in which words have several equally strong accents. Whatever the appropriate treatment of such systems may turn out to be, they do not refute the claim that all primary accentuation is nonmetrical, simply because they lack "primary accent." However, I strongly suspect that the claim that words in some languages lack primary accent refers to cases in which the choice of a word head depends on phrasal matters. In such cases, there would be no lexical rule for primary word accentuation. Here I refer to a parallel situation in English, where many adjectival or attributive words have two different patterns depending on whether they are used phrase-finally (*thirTEEN*) or before a noun with initial stress (*THIRteen men*). Traditionally, such cases have been dealt with in terms of rules that change the primary word accent location, but it seems equally feasible (and preferred within the present approach) to say that such words lack a primary accent at the lexical level. The location of primary stress is then fully taken care of by the phrasal accentuation rules. This approach is supported by the fact that in traditional analyses, the so-called Rhythm Rule seems to duplicate the effect of independently needed phrasal rhythm rules.

In this section, I will try to show that there is some plausibility to the conjecture that count systems fall in the class of systems that lack primary word accent, and that the "primary word accent" mentioned in the descriptions of such languages is really a phrasal accent, possibly signaled in terms of an intonational tone. If this conjecture can be maintained, count systems cease to be counterexamples to the non-metrical approach to primary accent.

In van der Hulst 1997, I suggest that "lacking primary accent" may have two sources. First, a situation of this type may indicate a historical accentual change involving a shift of primary accent from one side of the word to the other. In such cases, the location of a "primary accent" is perhaps entirely dependent on the position of words in the phrase. I show why, in this stage of development, a system may come across as a word-level count system.

To illustrate this point, in van der Hulst 1997 I refer to an account of the development from "early" Latin (with initial accent) to Classical Latin (with (ante)penultimate accent), and to accentual variation in Arabic languages that include initial accent, (ante)penultimate accent, and (trochaic and iambic) count systems. I also apply this line of reasoning to Australian count systems, although in these cases the lack of word accent may also be the result of a second source for the absence of primary accent. For reasons of space, I refer the reader to van der Hulst 1997 for details.

The second source for "lacking word accent" can lie in the morphosyntactic structure of a language. In languages with a richly developed polysynthetic morphology, and therefore with words of considerable length, it is not uncommon to avoid a unique word-level primary accent. One reason for this may be that very long words do not "fit" a single prosodic word template and behave prosodically more like phrases, with the result that phrasal accentuation is responsible for what might be described as "primary word accent." A second, more fundamental reason may be that such languages, with their dependence on highly productive morphology (often at the "expense" of a rich syntactic system) rely much less on the notion of word as a lexical entity and thus have much less opportunity to establish a lexical accent pattern.

As with systems that are in historical transition, such morphology-dependent systems may create the impression of a count system if, for example, the word-level rhythm is left to right, while phrasal accent occurs on the right edge of the phrase. With respect to this class of count systems, there is another noteworthy tendency, which also points to the relevance of phrasal accentuation: several descriptions explicitly mention that the location described as having "primary word accent" is identified by a "tonal accent," which is sometimes explicitly referred to as part of the intonational system. In this case, the identification of count systems with systems that are explicitly reported as lacking primary word accent is further supported by the observation that both types of systems are reported for languages that occur within the same language families. Hayes (1995:sec. 6.3) offers several examples of these types of cases, which are more fully discussed in van der Hulst 1997. If deeper investigation of the relevant cases supports my conjectures, it may turn out that "count" systems do not exist as word-level primary accent types, simply because these systems do not involve the notion of primary word-level accent. This would mean that there is no metrical residue with respect to primary accent location.

11.7 Simplified Bracketed Grid Theory

Standard metrical theory has evolved, via Halle and Vergnaud's (1987) bracketed grid theory, into the theory of metrical structure assignment that was developed in

Idsardi 1992; see Halle and Idsardi 1995. The most recent presentation of this model can be found in Idsardi, this volume. In this section, I will make some comments on this theory, which I have characterized elsewhere (van der Hulst 2000b:319) as being preoccupied with the notational system (in terms of the manipulation of brackets) without consideration of the "semantics" of this notation. In my understanding of the bracketed grid notation, brackets are supposed to be notational devices that represent constituent structure, that is, a purely graphic variant of tree structure graphs. As such (as in syntactic representations that use brackets), a left bracket or a right bracket by itself doesn't "mean" anything. Hence, the idea of formulating algorithms that insert left or right brackets (forming "open constituents") struck me as incoherent and only possible by assigning a different sort of "meaning" to these symbols. Note that the "open constituents" are present not only in intermediate representations; final representations still have them. I understand that so-called open constituents can do some work (e.g., in the case of incorporating "clitic material"), but I fail to grasp what kind of constituent an open constituent is. This caused and causes my concern that perhaps brackets in Idsardi's model are not graphic devices for constituent structure at all. Rather than characterizing constituent structure (in the traditional sense), Idsardi's brackets function more like boundary (or juncture) symbols of some sort. In fact, this possible "meaning" of these symbols is brought out in the open in Reiss's discussion of the model in this volume. Reiss proposes to further develop (i.e., simplify) Idsardi's model by replacing the left and right brackets by a single symmetrical divider symbol ("|"). I believe that Reiss's proposal is a logical step, given the way in which Idsardi uses the left and right brackets, which is indeed more like divider (boundary, juncture) symbols than as notational devices for constituent structure.

Taking the model that Idsardi proposes in this spirit, and leaving aside the question of what kind of constituent structure is being assigned (if any), it is easy to see that a laudable attempt is being made to develop fully explicit algorithms that deliver representations for all possible word accent systems, making use of the smallest number of rule types. This goal is, of course, what all models ought to strive for, but— and here I agree with Idsardi—this appears to be nonobvious to those who have been working on accent systems within the framework of Optimality Theory. It does seem to be the case that there has been reduced concern with articulating the representations that are employed.

Naturally, I believe that my own enterprise is very much concerned with the same goals that drive Idsardi's. To the extent that Idsardi's model is closer to standard metrical phonology (particularly in adopting a rigid bottom-up approach), it may very well be that some of my criticism of the standard metrical approach applies to his model as well. Thus, Dresher (this volume) points out that the arguments for giving priority to assigning primary accent (at least in some critical cases like Tiberian

Hebrew) are valid. It would seem to me that a consistent bottom-up approach cannot account for this phenomenon in a straightforward way. Thus, the major thing that may be "wrong" (from my perspective) with Idsardi's model is its inability to deal with the primary-accent-first syndrome that is the essential phenomenon motivating my own model. But I could be wrong about that aspect of Idsardi's model. Perhaps it can deal with primary accent first. In fact, I have no doubt that it can—but I have not seen a full demonstration of all the relevant cases. And this is a very relevant point: both models need to be applied to a wide(r) variety of cases before we can embark on a detailed comparative study. So far, we both have provided some hints of how our systems will cover the array of word accent systems, leaving aside numerous details and complications that might force either model to add machinery. True, Idsardi has provided several analyses in his earlier work (Idsardi 1992) and several others (including revisions) in his contribution to this volume. My own approach has formed the basis for analyzing over 500 accent systems within the context of the StressTyp database (Goedemans, van der Hulst, and Visch, 1996a,b, Goedemans and van der Hulst 2005a–d). It seems to me that both models need to be exemplified in a longer work (comparable, let us say, to Hayes 1995) in which there will be ample opportunity to cover a wide variety of systems, including all their "dirty details" (see van der Hulst, in preparation). Whereas systems in which primary accent cannot or need not be based on prior assignment of rhythmic structure form a challenge for Idsardi's model, count systems are potentially problematic for my model if they truly exist (recall section 11.6).

Another factor that prevents detailed comparison at this point is that Idsardi's model accounts for both primary accents and secondary rhythmic accents, whereas I have so far accounted only for primary accents.

I do not believe that Idsardi's proposed formalization in terms of finite state automata presents an advantage as such. There are no inherent restrictions on accentual structure that follow from this formalization, as far as I can see. For example, given the possibility of building in two "skip states" to derive ternary systems, there are no formal objections to designing automata that have more than two skip states. Abstracting away from the finite state formalization, it would seem that both models appeal to somewhat similar formal devices such as projecting grid marks to a higher level and forming constituents by inserting brackets. The theories are similar in another respect as well; they both aspire to be monotonic, that is, to make use of structure-building operations only, banning rules that change structure by deleting or moving elements. However, it is not clear to me how Idsardi's model can handle systems like those of Aklan and Awadhi that rely on retraction rules in traditional metrical approaches.

Rather than spending much time on tedious out-of-context, isolated comparisons, it seems to me that both models need to be further developed and applied to a wide range of cases. We will thus gain useful insight into the nature of accent systems and into the workings (and possible shortcomings) of these models. It may well be that a fuller development will show that the models are less different than they initially appear to be. So much the better.

11.8   Conclusions

The main goal of this chapter has been to outline an approach to word accent systems that deviates from the standard metrical account (including descendants like Idsardi's model) in separating the treatment of primary accent from the assignment of rhythmic accents and, if necessary, the construction of word-internal constituency. I supplied an array of reasons for this deviation. I then considered a treatment of so-called count systems (elsewhere called "the metrical residue") that is consistent with the model. Finally, I briefly compared my model with Idsardi's, concluding that both models are viable approaches to the phenomenon in question, albeit that Idsardi's model faces some of the same problems that motivated me to develop an alternative to standard metrical phonology.

Notes

1. All languages mentioned in this chapter are analyzed in StressTyp, a database system that provides information (extracted from the literature) about more than 500 languages. This database, which provides parametric analyses of all systems and references to sources that have been used, has been developed by the author and various other scholars, in particular Rob Goedemans (see Goedemans, van der Hulst, and Visch 1996a–c, Goedemans and van der Hulst 2005a–d for details and online availability).

2. A similar claim has been made in other studies, usually with reference to specific systems; see Harms 1981, Roca 1986, Hayes 1995, Hurch 1995. In his book, Hayes refers to primary-accent-first systems as "top-down systems," suggesting that the word tree is built first while foot structure is "tucked in" later. How this works formally has never been clear to me. Apparent top-down systems were used in the early Optimality Theory literature (Prince and Smolensky 2004) as an argument against the possibility of accounting for all accent systems derivationally.

3. This comes close to Halle and Vergnaud's (1987) account of English, a language displaying polar rhythm in that the initial syllable is typically rhythmically strong (as long as primary accent is not on the second syllable).

4. To deal with more than two degrees of weight, if such a situation exists, the projection rules must be applied more than once.

5. Supporting information for these claims comes from StressTyp.

6. This approach predicts that a lexical mark could overwrite weight in causing an hl domain to have second syllable accent in a system like Archi or final accent in a system like Rotuman by providing a lexical mark to the light syllable. At this point, I do not have data that either confirm or disconfirm this prediction.

7. An alternative for Yapese (as found in Hayes 1980) in this case would be to invoke a so-called quantity-determined foot type, a trochee in this case. This would leave the sequence ll] unfooted, and the final syllable would be stressed by the word tree.

References

Garde, Paul. 1968. *L'Accent*. Paris: Presses Universitaires de France.

Goedemans, Rob, and Harry van der Hulst. 2005a. Fixed stress locations. In *The world atlas of linguistic structures*, ed. by Martin Haspelmath, Matthew Dryer, David Gil, and Bernard Comrie, 62–65. New York: Oxford University Press.

Goedemans, Rob, and Harry van der Hulst. 2005b. Weight-sensitive stress. In *The world atlas of linguistic structures*, ed. by Martin Haspelmath, Matthew Dryer, David Gil, and Bernard Comrie, 66–69. New York: Oxford University Press.

Goedemans, Rob, and Harry van der Hulst. 2005c. Weight factors in weight-sensitive stress systems. In *The world atlas of linguistic structures*, ed. by Martin Haspelmath, Matthew Dryer, David Gil, and Bernard Comrie, 70–73. New York: Oxford University Press.

Goedemans, Rob, and Harry van der Hulst. 2005d. Rhythm types. In *The world atlas of linguistic structures*, ed. by Martin Haspelmath, Matthew Dryer, David Gil, and Bernard Comrie, 74–77. New York: Oxford University Press.

Goedemans, Rob, Harry van der Hulst, and Ellis Visch. 1996a. *The organization of StressTyp*. In *Stress patterns of the world*, ed. by Rob Goedemans, Harry van der Hulst, and Ellis Visch, 27–68. The Hague: Holland Academic Graphics.

Goedemans, Rob, Harry van der Hulst, and Ellis Visch. 1996b. *StressTyp manual*. Leiden: Holland Institute of Generative Linguistics (HIL).

Goedemans, Rob, Harry van der Hulst, and Ellis Visch. 1996c. StressTyp: A database for prosodic systems in the world's languages. *Glot International* 2 (1/2): 21–23.

Goldsmith, John. 1990. *Autosegmental and metrical phonology*. Oxford: Blackwell.

Halle, Morris, and William J. Idsardi. 1995. General properties of stress and metrical structure. In *The handbook of phonological theory*, ed. by John Goldsmith, 403–443. Cambridge, Mass.: Blackwell.

Halle, Morris, and Jean-Roger Vergnaud. 1987. *An essay on stress*. Cambridge, Mass.: MIT Press.

Harms, Robert T. 1981. A backwards metrical approach to Cairo Arabic stress. *Linguistic Analysis* 7:429–451.

Hayes, Bruce. 1980. A metrical theory of stress. Doctoral dissertation, MIT.

Hayes, Bruce. 1995. *Metrical stress theory: Principles and case studies*. Chicago: University of Chicago Press.

Hulst, Harry van der. 1984. The diminutive suffix and the structure of Dutch syllables. In Hans Bennis and W. U. S. van Lessen Kloeke, eds., *Linguistics in the Netherlands 1984*, 73–83. Dordrecht: Foris.

Hulst, Harry van der. 1990. The book of stress. Ms., Department of General Linguistics, Leiden University.

Hulst, Harry van der. 1992. The independence of main stress and rhythm. Paper presented at the Krems Phonology Workshop.

Hulst, Harry van der. 1996. Separating primary accent and secondary accent. In *Stress patterns of the world*, ed. by Harry van der Hulst, Rob Goedemans, and Ellis Visch, 1–26. The Hague: Holland Academic Graphics.

Hulst, Harry van der. 1997. Primary accent is non-metrical. *Rivista di Linguistica* 9:99–127.

Hulst, Harry van der. 1999. Word accent. In *Word prosodic systems in the languages of Europe*, ed. by Harry van der Hulst, 3–116. Berlin: Mouton de Gruyter.

Hulst, Harry van der. 2000a. Issues in foot typology. In *Issues in phonological structure*, ed. by S. J. Hannahs and Mike Davenport, 95–127. Amsterdam: John Benjamins. Originally published in *Toronto working papers in linguistics* 16, 77–102. Toronto: University of Toronto, Toronto Working Papers in Linguistics.

Hulst, Harry van der. 2000b. Metrical phonology. In *The first Glot International state-of-the-article book*, ed. by Lisa Cheng and Rint Sybesma, 307–326. Berlin: Mouton de Gruyter. Originally published in *Glot International* 1 (1): 3–6.

Hulst, Harry van der. 2002. Stress and accent. In *Encyclopedia of cognitive science, vol. 4*, ed. by Lynn Nadel, 246–254. London: Nature Publishing Group.

Hulst, Harry van der. 2006. Word stress. In *Encyclopedia of language and linguistics*, ed. by Keith Brown, 3:451–458. 2nd ed. Oxford: Elsevier.

Hulst, Harry van der. In preparation. Word accentual systems. Ms., University of Connecticut.

Hulst, Harry van der, and Jan Kooij. 1994. Two modes of stress assignment. In *Phonologica*, ed. by Wolfgang Dressler and John Rennison, 107–114. Turin: Rosenberg and Sellier.

Hulst, Harry van der, and Aditi Lahiri. 1988. On foot typology. In *Proceedings of North East Linguistic Society (NELS) 18*, ed. by James Blevins and Juli Carter, 286–309. Amherst: University of Massachusetts, Graduate Linguistic Student Association.

Hurch, Bernhard. 1995. Accentuations. In *Natural Phonology: The state of the art on Natural Phonology*, ed. by Bernhard Hurch and Richard A. Rhodes, 73–96. Berlin: Mouton de Gruyter.

Idsardi, William J. 1992. The computation of prosody. Doctoral dissertation, MIT.

Kager, René. 1993. Alternatives to the Iambic-Trochaic Law. *Natural Language and Linguistic Theory* 11:381–432.

Liberman, Mark, and Alan Prince. 1977. On stress and linguistic rhythm. *Linguistic Inquiry* 8:249–336.

Prince, Alan S. 1983. Relating to the grid. *Linguistic Inquiry* 14:19–100.

Prince, Alan S., and Paul Smolensky. 2004. *Optimality Theory: Constraint interaction in generative grammar*. Malden, Mass.: Blackwell.

Roca, Iggy M. 1986. Secondary stress and metrical rhythm. *Phonology Yearbook* 3:330–341.

Roca, Iggy M. 1999. Stress in the Romance languages. In *Word prosodic systems in the languages of Europe*, ed. by Harry van der Hulst, 659–812. Berlin: Mouton de Gruyter.

Vergnaud, Jean-Roger, and Morris Halle. 1978. Metrical structures in phonology. Ms., MIT.

12 Long-Distance Dependencies and Other Formal Issues in Phonology

Charles Reiss

12.1 Introduction

In general, I favor the Halle and Idsardi approach to stress computation because it explicitly aims to reduce to a bare minimum the set of primitives needed in the model—most significantly, the foot types (iambs, trochees, etc.) that constitute the primitives of other models are epiphenomena arising from the foot construction algorithms in the Halle and Idsardi model. In section 12.2 of these comments, I discuss Idsardi's appeal to finite state automata (FSAs), suggesting that his accompanying critique of Optimality Theory (OT) may not be compelling. In section 12.3, I address the use of directed brackets in the model presented by Idsardi in this volume and its predecessors.

12.2 Idsardi's Appeal to Finite State Automata

12.2.1 Neutral Vowels and Finite State Automata

One of Idsardi's stated goals is "to relate the parameters of [the system presented in this volume] directly to finite state automata (FSAs), giving a clear, effective, and efficient computational foundation to the theory" (p. 191). In particular, he proposes "the direct identification of parameter settings for rules with particular properties of FSAs" (p. 192).[1] Idsardi's examples are quite clear, and it is interesting to note that phonological rules can be related to FSAs. However, it may be worth considering that doing so raises several problems, at least when we leave the domain of stress.

Consider the form of an FSA that would either compute or accept vowel harmony strings in a language like Finnish, which has the transparent neutral vowel [i]. Schematically, using "+" to mark a morpheme boundary, a back vowel word might have a string of vowels like [a-i + a], whereas a front vowel word might have [æ-i + æ]. In other words, the harmony from a low vowel in the root appears to pass through the phonetically front [i]. This [i] may be part of the root or part of a suffix. The problem is that there is a long-distance dependency between the first vowel and the last vowel in the two schematic examples, and FSAs are notorious since *Syntactic Structures* (Chomsky 1957) for their inability to generate strings with long-distance dependencies.

Now, it is trivial to design an FSA that can deal with the Finnish facts, but doing so requires the use of two different transitions corresponding to phonetic [i]: one that falls on the path through the machine that corresponds to the front vowel word, and one that falls on the path of the back vowel word. We can see the problem by comparing an FSA that will generate both and only the two schematic forms [a-i + a] and [æ-i+æ], in (1), with one that will generate these two forms, but also the ill-formed *[æ-i + a] and *[a-i + æ], in (2).

(1) *An FSA that generates a sample of Finnish*

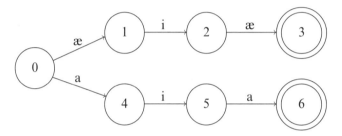

(2) *An FSA that overgenerates for the Finnish sample*

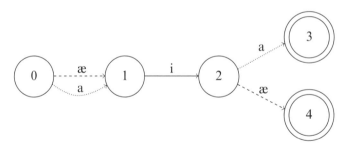

The problem with the FSA in (2) is that there is no way to guarantee that if the dashed transition with [æ] is taken from state 0 to state 1, then the dashed path is also taken from state 2 to state 4, and similarly, that if the dotted transition with [a] is taken from state 0, then the dotted transition from state 2 to state 3 will be taken. An FSA does not have memory to keep track of how it arrived at a particular state, so the history of a transition chosen from state 0 is not accessible at state 2.

For these reasons, we need something like the FSA in (1). If we believe, however, that there is a single underlying vowel that surfaces as [i] in both front and back vowel words, then this FSA fails to capture this generalization. Instead, it encodes two transitions for [i], treating the [i] of [a-i + a] and [æ-i + æ] as different entities.

For the sake of concreteness, let us look at the following Finnish forms that show neutral [i] vowels in both the root and a suffix:

(3) *Finnish vowel harmony data*

	Surface form	Underlying form	Gloss
a.	værttinæ		'distaff, spinning wheel part'
b.	værttinællænihæn	/værttinæ-llA-ni-hAn/	'with my distaff!' (emphatic)
c.	palttina		'thin linen'
d.	palttinallanihan	/palttina-llA-ni-hAn/	'with my thin linen!' (emphatic)

The root in the (3a,b) forms contains just the [−back] vowel /æ/, as well as the neutral /i/. The root in the (3c,d) forms contains just the [+back] vowel /a/, as well as the neutral /i/. In presenting these data, I adopt a standard position that the suffixes /llA/ and /hAn/ contain a low unrounded vowel, unspecified for [±back], denoted /A/. The suffix /ni/ contains neutral /i/. Of course, building an FSA to generate forms with these alternating suffixes will also lead to the kind of duplication we are discussing relative to the neutral [i]: each alternating suffix will have to be listed multiple times in a finite state grammar to reflect the environment where each alternant appears.

In general, to generate Finnish forms, we need an FSA with a loop that accepts [+back] vowels and a loop that accepts [i]. We then need another FSA with a loop that accepts [−back] vowels and a loop that accepts [i]. These FSAs can be written in various ways, even collapsed into one complex machine, but the point remains that [i] will have to be represented twice—once for [+back] words and once for [−back] words. Thus, it appears that the foregoing constitutes a valid criticism of the practice of understanding phonological rules as FSAs, at least under well-accepted assumptions about the lexicon and feature representations.

12.2.2 Natural Classes and Finite State Automata

If phonological rules are to be interpreted as FSAs, then we might expect the FSAs to make reference to the same representational primitives as are used in standard phonology. Of course, this is not a logical necessity, since we may just want to show that any computation done using Idsardi's stress model has a weakly equivalent FSA. This does not appear to be Idsardi's intention, however, since he limits his FSA transitions to rewrite rules of the kind familiar from earlier versions of his theory, and compatible with standard generative phonology. In fact, the contrast that he offers to FSAs whose transitions relate to an OT account of stress computation is predicated on the assumption that each FSA model sticks to the representational primitives of its non-FSA correspondent. For this reason, it is again instructive to consider segmental phonology.

Because the transitions from a state in an FSA are not ordered or ranked like standard phonological rules or constraints, it is not possible to constrain which path is followed in the transition from a state with multiple exiting transitions. Any transition whose input statement matches the string undergoing processing can be followed.

Now consider what would happen if we expressed a rule affecting only voiced stops in an FSA. One transition of the machine would have to accept voiced stops and, say, turn them into fricatives. Another transition would have to do nothing to the current symbol if it were not a voiced stop. In a rule-based framework, this is achieved by having a rule affecting voiced stops that applies if and only if its structural description is met. The absence of an effect on other segments (those that are not voiced stops) when such a rule applies is modeled in rule-based frameworks by *not* having a rule, by doing nothing. (The need for a null transition in the FSA is reminiscent of the need for Faithfulness constraints in OT—both contrast with the *absence* of a rule in traditional generative phonology.)

So, in addition to the transition changing a voiced stop at the current state into a fricative, there has to be a transition out of the current state for segments that are not voiced stops. The problem is that this set of segments is not a natural class; it cannot be defined by a conjunction of features. In the literature on FSA phonology (e.g., van der Beek et al. 2002:182ff.), standard practice appears to be to use sets of segments and their complement sets in the statements of phonological transductions. I am not claiming that Idsardi would not be able to enrich FSAs with a mechanism to mimic rule ordering and elsewhere conditions, and I am not claiming that the traditional generative insistence that phonological statements refer to natural classes is correct. However, I am raising the point that model comparison and translation from one framework to another are not as straightforward as Idsardi suggests.

I turn now to an issue that arises in Idsardi's model, as well as in all its direct ancestors.

12.3 Directionality and Foot Boundaries

In work by Halle and others predating Idsardi's (1992) thesis (e.g., Halle and Vergnaud 1990), it was assumed that the marks on lines of metrical grids were parsed into feet by matched brackets. A foot was defined as a sequence of marks between a left and a right bracket: (* *). It was also assumed that brackets always appeared immediately matched on each line. For example, the following were not possible grid lines: (* * (*) and (* (*) *). In other words, scanning a line from left to right, there had to be alternating left and right brackets. Feet did not contain other feet, and feet did not overlap with each other.

One innovation of Idsardi's thesis was to allow unmatched brackets. In Idsardi 1992 and Halle and Idsardi 1994, a foot is defined as a string of marks to the right of a left bracket, up to any other bracket or the end of the string; or to the left of a right bracket, up to any other bracket or the beginning of the string. The strings in (4) are well-formed in this framework.

(4) a. # (* * * #
      b. # (* *) #
      c. # (* * (* #
      d. # (* * * #
      e. # * *) #

Because the brackets are not labeled like those used in syntactic structures, the system does not allow for containment relations among feet. And because the "outside" (the convex side) of a bracket implicitly defines an edge of the foot it is adjacent to (which must have a concave side of a bracket at its other edge), the system does not allow for interlocking feet. If it is the case that either the first bracket to the left of every grid mark in a line is a left bracket, or the first to the right is a right bracket (or both), then the grid line is exhaustively footed. This situation obtains in all the representations in (4), but it is not a necessary property of grid lines, as we will see.

I propose simplifying the representational scheme even further by assuming just one, nondirected foot boundary marker, "|." This approach was briefly explored by Idsardi (1992), who calls it "Separator Theory," and also in unpublished work by Daniel Currie Hall (2000, 2005) and myself (Reiss, ongoing research). It appears to be conceptually simpler to have an inventory containing just |, than one containing (and).[2] A further suggestive argument is that the Halle and Idsardi system actually has directionality built into it in at least three other ways, potentially making the directionality encoded in (and) redundant.

A first way in which the Halle and Idsardi model refers to directionality is in its use of parameterized rules, such as the Iterative Constituent Construction rules that, depending on the setting, scan a string from right to left and insert left brackets (ICC:L in Halle and Idsardi 1994) or scan from left to right and insert right brackets (ICC:R). If direction of scanning and type of insertion were independently needed parameters, we might expect to find attested versions of Iterative Constituent Construction that scan left to right and insert left brackets, as well as versions that scan right to left and insert right brackets. Apparently these are not found.

In addition to the parameterized rules, Halle and Idsardi allow for language-specific rules affecting brackets. These rewrite rules, like rules of segmental phonology, encode directionality in their structural descriptions. For example, (5) deletes a left bracket crucially to the right of certain grid marks.

(5) $(\rightarrow \emptyset / \# (* \underline{\ \ }$

A third encoding of directionality is found in the rules for projecting heads of feet to the next higher grid line. These rules can refer either to the leftmost element of a foot or to the rightmost element. So, the first foot in a string like (6a) might project either of its marks, depending on the language; the fact that a string of marks is "inside" a left bracket, but not a right one, say, is not relevant to the question of which element projects. If head projection has the setting R(ight), then (6a) projects (6b). With head projection set to L(eft), we get (6c).

(6)   *   *   *   *

    a. (* * (* *)   b. (* * (* *)   c. (* * (* *)

12.4   Nondirected Foot Boundary Markers

I propose as a working definition that a foot consists of all marks between two boundary markers or between a boundary marker and the beginning or end of a string. It thus follows that a string of marks will be exhaustively parsed into feet if and only if it contains at least one foot boundary marker. Compare the completely footed (7a) in this system with the incompletely footed (7b) in Halle and Idsardi notation.

(7) a. * * | * *
    b. * * (* *

The two notational systems differ in principle, since the Halle and Idsardi system can be used to represent incompletely footed lines. However, note that any string that is exhaustively footed in the Halle and Idsardi system will also be footed in the system proposed here if the Halle and Idsardi brackets are replaced by |, since any string with at least one | is exhaustively footed. Furthermore, I now show that any string that is exhaustively footed in the Halle and Idsardi system has the same foot structure in the system here, if we replace each directed boundary marker by a nondirected one.

Let X represent a nonnull string of grid marks (*'s) in a grid line L. Assuming L to be exhaustively parsed into feet in the Halle and Idsardi system, there are five possible contexts in which X can occur, shown in (8).

(8) a. (X #
    b. # X)
    c. (X (
    d.) X)
    e. (X)

A string of *'s may be final (8a), initial (8b), between two left brackets (8c), between two right brackets (8d), or between a left and a right bracket (8e). There are no other possibilities if the *'s of L are exhaustively parsed. If we replace the directed brackets of (8) with the nondirected boundary marker |, we get the structures in (9). The translation does not affect any of the foot edges, and thus it does not affect any of the foot structure of L.

(9) a. | X #
    b. # X |
    c. | X |
    d. | X |
    e. | X |

12.5   Undesirably Footed Marks

So far, I have shown that a notational system that uses only a nondirected boundary marker can represent every foot structure of a string that is fully footed using the directed brackets of the Halle and Idsardi model. Since the single-marker system is less powerful, yet allows all apparently necessary representational distinctions considered thus far, it is tentatively to be preferred on theoretical grounds. Let us now investigate whether this success can be extended to strings that are not fully footed in the Halle and Idsardi system.

In addition to the structures in (8), the only other contexts in which an X can be represented in the Halle and Idsardi model are between the outsides of two brackets—that is, with a right bracket to the left and a left bracket to the right (10a)—or between the outside of a bracket and a line edge marker (10b,c). In the Halle and Idsardi model, such structures correspond to grid lines that are not exhaustively parsed into feet. The *'s that constitute X in (10a–c) do not belong to any foot. Replacing the brackets of (10) with nondirected markers as in (11) gives structures that are equivalent to those in (8), ones that are exhaustively parsed in the proposed model.

(10) a.) X (
     b. # X (
     c.) X #

(11) a. | X |
     b. # X |
     c. | X #

We have now located the different empirical predictions made by the Halle and Idsardi directed bracket theory and the model proposed here. If we accept the claim that footing can be partial, then we must accept the representational complexity of directed brackets. Taking a partially footed line like (12), suppose that we project the rightmost element of each foot to the next grid line, as in (13). The middle * on the lower line is not footed and thus does not project.

(12) * *) * (* *

(13)   *   *
       * *) * (* *

Translating (12) into the proposed system yields (14), with three feet.

(14) * * | * | * *

The next higher grid line's *'s are projected from the rightmost member of each line foot, yielding (15), with ^ representing the problematic grid mark. Now, the middle * is footed on the lower line, and since it qualifies as rightmost in its foot, it projects to the higher line.

(15)   *   ^   *
       * * | * | * *

   To facilitate comparison, consider unfooted marks with the case of right projection to the next line (16a) and left projection (16b). Translating (16) into nondirected boundary notation and projecting appropriate heads results in (17). Again, the symbol ^ represents the offending marks.

(16)   *   *
      a. Project R: ... *) * (* ...   b. Project L: ... *) * (* ...

(17)   * ^   ^ *
      a. Project R: ... * | * | * ...   b. Project L: ... * | * | * ...

   There is, however, a way to avoid having such offending grid marks appear in the final stress grid. This is to invoke a kind of rule proposed by Idsardi (1992), a rule of bracket deletion, like (5).[3] If we posit rules like (18a,b), we can generate the desired structures from the lower grid lines of (17).

(18) a. | $\rightarrow$ $\emptyset$ / * | * __ *   b. | $\rightarrow$ $\emptyset$ / * __ * | *

   Rule (18a) turns the string * | * | * into * | * *, thus grouping the mark that is unfooted in (16) with the foot to its right. This grid line will project as in (19a). Similarly, rule (18b) turns the string * | * | * into * * | *, thus grouping the unfooted mark of (16) with the foot to its left. This grid line will project as in (19b). The underlined *'s may also project, depending on whether or not they are at a foot edge.

(19)   *   *
      a. Project R: ... * | * *...   b. Project L: ... * * | *...

What is crucial is that we have generated line 1 representations like those in (17), even though we used only exhaustively footed grid lines generated with nondirected boundary markers and a bracket deletion rule of the type standardly used in the Halle and Idsardi system. Once we saw that we can work with fully footed grid lines, we combined this with the result that directed and nondirected boundary markers do not give distinct footings of exhaustively footed lines. This allowed us to simplify the theoretical apparatus by using just nondirected markers.

Two objections should arise at this point. The first is that the proposed solution appears to work only for single unfooted marks in medial position. I deal with this issue in work in progress. The second is that a derivation requiring a bracket deletion rule is apparently more complex than one that does not require such a rule, ceteris paribus. However, since I am assuming that the goal is to find the most elegant model of stress computation for *all* languages, I invoke the argument made by Chomsky (1986:38).

Because evidence from Japanese can evidently bear on the correctness of a theory of S_0, it can have indirect—but very powerful—bearing on the choice of the grammar that attempts to characterize the I-language attained by a speaker of English.

In other words, getting rid of directed brackets may appear to complicate the account of stress in a particular language, but it appears to simplify our Universal Grammar, the theory of S_0, the initial state of the human language faculty. If bracket deletion rules are required by some languages, then they are available to all languages.[4]

Various empirical problems need to be addressed before adopting Separator Theory, and some of these problems are pointed out by Idsardi himself in writing (1992) or in personal communication. Hall (2005) addresses one of Idsardi's main empirical objections. Clearly, this brief discussion is not intended to be a demonstration of the sufficiency of separators, since a theory of stress must ultimately be able to account for the wide array of data addressed, for example, by Halle and Idsardi. Here, I adopt the methodological practice of attempting to defend the proposal for the simplest cases. If this initial attempt seems promising, more complex data sets can be pursued in the future.

12.6 Conclusions

For the reasons developed in section 12.2, I am not convinced by Idsardi's critique of OT based on the complexity of the FSA he derives by translating a rule-based analysis and an OT analysis into FSAs. In particular, it is not clear that standardly accepted generalizations about representations in rule-based phonology can survive the translation to FSAs. As I mentioned, there are at least two unresolved issues in the nature of the translation from rule-based phonology alone: the question of long-distance dependencies and the question of natural classes. Given the lack of proposals in the literature concerning representations in OT, the task of theory comparison is even more obscure.

More generally, it remains unclear just what Idsardi means by "relating" his model and an OT model to FSAs. Even if one model is actually more amenable to an FSA "translation," it does not follow that such a model is inherently simpler. This point is particularly relevant given the well-known inadequacy of FSAs for other aspects of language, as shown by Chomsky in *Syntactic Structures*.

I also suggested that various versions of Idsardi's stress computation theory encode directionality in several ways and that this apparent redundancy can perhaps be eliminated by using nondirected brackets, separators. Some apparent empirical problems remain (as Idsardi has pointed out), but I look forward to further work addressing these problems.

Finally, I would like to reiterate the point that Idsardi's work in the domain of stress computation is, to my mind, very attractive for its ongoing search for a minimal set of primitives. This most recent attempt, in which Idsardi no longer appeals to avoidance constraints, is yet another step in the right direction, one that I generally endorse as part of a program of developing a purely procedural theory of phonology.

Notes

I am grateful to Alan Bale, Chuck Cairns, Sean Koo, Fred Mailhot, and especially Peter Liem and Bill Idsardi for discussion of the issues addressed here.

1. Following Idsardi, I will gloss over the distinction between finite state automata for generating or accepting strings and finite state transducers, which can convert strings into other strings. The distinction is orthogonal to the points I raise.

2. Although, as Peter Liem (pers. comm.) points out, it is not obvious how to define conceptual simplicity.

3. As another example, Idsardi (1992:33) proposes a rule to delete unmatched left brackets.

4. It is also possible to avoid projecting particular marks by complicating the nature of projection rules. If the rules can be made more specific than merely "Project * at the left/right edge of a foot" by specifying that the asterisks are, say, next to a | to the left and a * to the right, we can prevent unary feet from projecting.

References

Beek, Leonoor van der, Gosse Bouma, Jan Daciuk, Tanja Gaustad, Robert Malouf, Gertjan van Noord, Robbert Prins, and Begoña Villada. 2002. Algorithms for linguistic processing. NWO PIONIER Progress Report. Rijksuniversiteit Groningen: Graduate School for Behavioral and Cognitive Neurosciences.

Chomsky, Noam. 1957. *Syntactic structures*. The Hague: Mouton.

Chomsky, Noam. 1986. *Knowledge of language.* New York: Praeger.

Hall, Daniel Currie. 2000. Prosodic representations and lexical stress. In *Proceedings of the 2000 CLA Annual Conference*, ed. by John T. Jensen and Gerard van Herk, 49–60. Ottawa: University of Ottawa, Cahiers Linguistiques d'Ottawa.

Hall, Daniel Currie. 2005. Chugach Alutiiq in a separator theory of prosodic structure. Presented at the Montréal-Ottawa-Toronto Phonology Workshop, McGill University, February 2005. Available at http://www.chass.utoronto.ca/~danhall/.

Halle, Morris, and William J. Idsardi. 1994. General properties of stress and metrical structure. In *Language computations*, ed. by Eric Sven Ristad, 37–69. Providence, R.I.: American Mathematical Society. Also in *The handbook of phonological theory*, ed. by John Goldsmith, 403–443. Cambridge, Mass.: Blackwell, 1995.

Halle, Morris, and Jean-Roger Vergnaud. 1990. *An essay on stress.* Cambridge, Mass.: MIT Press.

Idsardi, William J. 1992. The computation of prosody. Doctoral dissertation, MIT.

IV Architecture

13 Markedness Theory versus Phonological Idiosyncrasies in a Realistic Model of Language

Andrea Calabrese

13.1 Introduction

One goal of this chapter is to propose an architecture for phonological theory that reconciles the "conventional" aspect of phonology with the "natural" one by building a theory of phonology that combines a substantive notion of markedness, part of Universal Grammar (UG), with language-specific rules and constraints. In this way, I aim to solve the "paradox" that Anderson (1985:78) said is faced by any theory trying to define what constitutes a "possible phonological rule in a natural language":

On the one hand, most rules are tantalizingly close to being explicable (or 'natural') in terms of phonetic factors [i.e., explainable in terms of markedness theory in the framework proposed here], while, on the other hand, rules show no tendency at all to stick close to this phonetic explicability, and instead often become 'crazy' rules (Bach and Harms 1972).

The phonological system of a language produces a complex set of output phonological representations derived from lexical representations by phonological operations, some of which are of historical origin and others due to UG. Phonological theory must have an architecture such that processes involving universal markedness considerations and purely language-specific processes interact with each other smoothly and efficiently. I assume that the theory separates these processes into distinct components.

The components referred to in the preceding paragraph must traffic in representations that can interface properly with relevant body/brain components. For example, the motor system must be able to articulate representations that are the output of the phonology, and the sensory system must also be able to process them. Furthermore, the long-term memory system must be able to encode them.

One component of the architecture proposed here is the markedness module (MM), with an internal structure described below. The MM is the repository of all the interface properties between the phonology and the sensorimotor processes external to the phonology proper. The architecture proposed here also contains a component with language-specific rules, to handle the wide range of phonological phenomena that cannot plausibly be analyzed as the activity of markedness considerations. The internal structure of this component and its interaction with the MM is also described below.

This chapter assumes a realistic approach to language such as that advocated in Bromberger and Halle 1992, 1997, 2000; see also Halle 2002. This view of language is based on two indisputable facts: given an utterance, (1) there must be a long-term representation of the elements occurring in it; (2) there is an articulatory representation of it before actual muscular implementation. Phonology investigates the system of knowledge that is responsible for the computational steps that convert the memorized representation of the utterance into its articulatory representation. This knowledge involves representations and computations that have a concrete spatiotemporal occurrence, allow the production of concrete articulatory events, and are part of the workings of an actual brain with all its limitations. "Competence" is therefore the system of knowledge that allows the production of these articulatory representations and is distinct from "performance," which involves the "contingencies" of this production (see Bromberger and Halle 2000:35).

The chapter is organized as follows. Section 13.2 briefly sketches the MM, one component of the architecture of phonological theory. It shows how the interaction between markedness statements and repairs accounts for phenomena such as glide insertion in French and sonorant metathesis in Bulgarian. Section 13.3 argues that in addition to negative instructions such as the markedness statements, positive instructions are needed to account for phonological phenomena in an adequate manner. These positive instructions are implemented like the rules of classical generative phonology. A model of the complete architecture of phonological theory is outlined in this section. Section 13.4 focuses on the composition of the MM and its internal structure. It will be shown that in addition to markedness statements, other theoretical devices such as prohibitions, correlation statements, and natural rules are needed to account for markedness effects across languages. Visibility theory is the topic of section 13.5. This theory, first proposed in Calabrese 1995, is intended to replace underspecification theory. It is assumed that featural representations are fully specified. Phenomena previously accounted for by underspecification can now be accounted for by "spotlighting" either contrastive or marked specifications. Section 13.6 deals with derivations. It argues that the extrinsic rule ordering characterizing classical generative phonology can be reproduced in a model containing rules and negative constraints like the one proposed here by assuming that the checking of instructions can be ordered. Section 13.7 deals with historical sound changes, and specifically with how these changes give rise to the particular architecture of the phonological model proposed in this chapter.

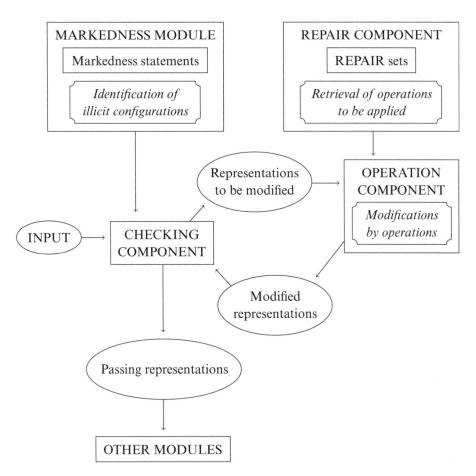

Figure 13.1
Structure of the markedness module

13.2 The Markedness Module

A first approximation of the structure of the markedness module is given in figure 13.1. Later in this chapter, I will both elaborate the internal structure of the MM and sketch its interaction with other modules in a more complete architecture (see figure 13.4).

Each markedness statement (MS) is a negative constraint, part of UG. For each language, some MSs are active and the others are inactive; if an MS is active, then representations that violate it are absolutely prohibited. MSs are ranked in UG, so that some MSs may not be active unless certain other ones have also been made inactive.

The input representation is checked by each MS in the checking component. If the input does not violate any MS, it passes and goes on to further modules. However, if an MS marks a configuration in the input as illicit, it must be modified and the input is sent to the repair component, along with information about which MS is violated. The repair component consists of a number of repair sets, one for each MS; I use the term *REPAIR set* for each such set. Each REPAIR set typically contains a set of ranked repair operations. UG supplies the operations and their order; some of the operations, however, may be absent on a language-specific basis. Using the highest-ranked operation is to be considered the best, or preferred, way to repair a given illicit configuration. The other operations indicate less preferable repairs that are to be used when the derivation started by the next-higher-ranked operation fails to generate a licit output. The highest-ranked operation is always the first to apply to repair the relevant illicit configuration,[1] amending the input and generating a revised configuration. The representation with the revised configuration then goes back to the checking component for further evaluation. Although the representation with the revised configuration now satisfies the MS that triggered the revision, it may in fact violate another MS as a consequence of this revision. If it does, it goes back to the repair component, where the newly created illicit configuration is fixed up by the highest-ranked operation of the REPAIR set associated with this MS. This revised representation is sent back to the checking component to determine whether the revision violates still another MS. If it does, the repair process starts again and goes through the stages described above; if it does not, the revised representation is licensed and passes on to other modules. Thus, the repair of an input illicit configuration may begin a derivation involving several other REPAIR sets. Figure 13.2 illustrates the case in which all of the REPAIR sets intervening in the derivation from an input contain at least one repair operation.

Crucially, some REPAIR sets may be empty; the violation of the associated MS is therefore unrepairable. If the derivation encounters such an empty REPAIR set, it crashes. When a derivation crashes, a new derivation starts by applying the second-ranked operation of the REPAIR set associated with the first-violated MS. This process repeats until a licit configuration is generated and the revised licit representation is sent to other modules. Figure 13.3 illustrates the case in which one of the REPAIR sets intervening in the derivation from an input is empty.[2]

13.2.1 French Hiatus

French hiatus resolution illustrates the interaction between MSs and REPAIRs. In French, a high vowel before another vowel becomes a glide (1a) unless it is preceded by a tautosyllabic consonant cluster, in which case a glide is inserted between the high front vowel and the following vowel (1b). Of course, it would be possible to posit two rules, one of which applies in the environment for (1a) and the other in

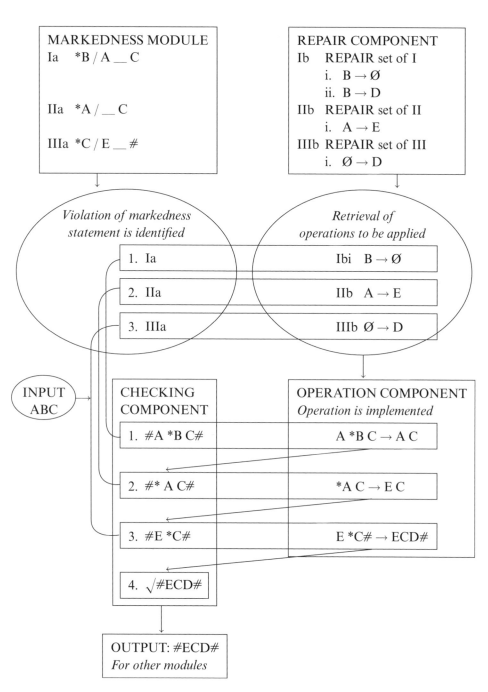

Figure 13.2
Example derivation

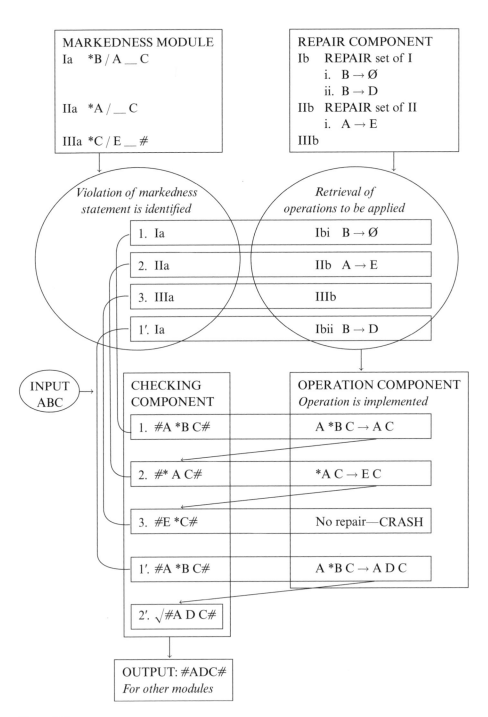

Figure 13.3
Example derivation with empty REPAIR set

the environment for (1b). However, this would be missing the generalization that the two processes "conspire" to ensure hiatus resolution.

(1) *French hiatus resolution*
    a. /lu + e/ → [lwe]
       /li + e/ → [lje]
    b. /kri + e/ → [krije], *[krje]
       /pli + e/ → [plije], *[plje]

The glide formation process illustrated in (1a) is arguably simpler than the glide insertion process in (1b); the former involves only resyllabification, whereas the latter entails both inserting a skeletal position and resyllabification. However, the simpler process would yield an illicit output if applied in the (1b) environment, as illustrated by the asterisked forms in (1b); these forms violate the language's canonical syllable structure. This, then, is another "conspiracy": the language employs the more complex process for resolving hiatus just in case it is required to ensure licit syllable structure.

To illustrate how these insights are captured within the architecture proposed here, I first posit two MSs in UG. NoHiatus, in (2), prohibits a succession of two vowels separated by a syllable boundary, and NoTriCon, in (3), marks as illicit a triconsonantal sequence in a syllable's onset. Both of these MSs are contained in the MM, and both are active in French. (See Calabrese 2005 for a more complete account of the French facts and the relevant MSs and REPAIR sets.)

(2) *NoHiatus*
    * ... V.V ... (No heterosyllabic, adjacent vowels)

(3) *NoTriCon*
    *($_\sigma$ CCCV ...

UG supplies the ordered REPAIR set for (2) in (4). There is no REPAIR specified for (3).

(4) *REPAIR set for NoHiatus (supplied from UG, in the MM)*
    a. Nucleus Removal (= glide formation)
    b. Line Addition (= glide insertion)

A REPAIR always begins with the highest-ranked operation of the REPAIR set. In the case of the constraint in (2), two strategies are widely used across languages: glide formation (4a) and glide insertion (4b). The process of glide formation (4a) can be accounted for by a process that removes the syllabic nucleus node of the first vowel, leaving the melody and the timing slot; the rhyme node above the first vowel is also automatically deleted, as is the syllabic structure for the onset. This is followed by further resyllabification REPAIRs, not described in this chapter, which incorporate the consonants left unsyllabified by the first operation; I assume, of course, that the only difference between a high vowel and a glide is that the former occupies a syllabic nucleus and the latter does not. This is depicted in (5); see Calabrese 2005:207ff. for further elaboration.

(5)

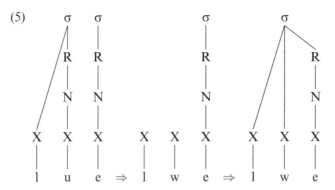

The resyllabification repair operations that follow (4a) ultimately incorporate a skeletal position into the onset: the onset in the input in (5) consists of one consonant, and the onset in the output consists of two consonants. The application of (4a) and its subsequent resyllabification repairs to a bisegmental onset would then yield an illicit result, because French does not allow trisegmental onsets, as mentioned above. It is a challenge to provide a unified and simple account for both the prohibition against trisegmental onsets and the failure of (4a) to apply to bisegmental onsets. The architecture described here meets this challenge, as follows.

Consider an input with a bisegmental onset, as in (6). If we were to apply (5a), we would remove the syllabic nucleus of the high vowel, rendering the first two consonants and the vocoid unsyllabified. Incorporation of the three unsyllabified segments into the onset (by means of the resyllabification REPAIR operations mentioned above) would create the derivation in (6). When the final step of (6) is sent back to the MSs for evaluation, it fails on NoTriCon, a failure that is unrepairable. This derivation crashes. Accordingly, the original input is sent back to the repair component to be modified by the next-highest-ranked operation of the REPAIR set of NoHiatus (2), which is Line Addition, (4b).

(6)

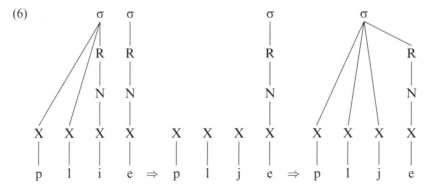

The configuration produced by Line Addition, the second stage of the derivation in (7), is disallowed by a prohibition against ambisyllabic nuclei. This illicit configuration is repaired by fission (see Calabrese 2005:96, and below in connection with Bulgarian liquid metathesis), creating the rightmost form in (7). Fission inserts a new skeletal position but not a new melody; the latter is borrowed from the segment undergoing fission, /i/. This new skeletal position dominates a high palatal vocoid but is not a nucleus, so it is phonetically [j].

(7)

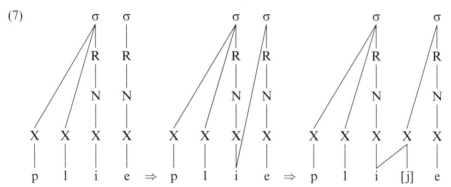

13.2.2 Bulgarian Liquid Metathesis

Bulgarian liquid metathesis offers a more complex example of repair operations (Scatton 1975, Zec 1987, Petrova 1994, Barnes 1997, Hermans 1998, Lambova 2000). Bulgarian liquid metathesis involves alternations in the sequence of liquid plus schwa in inflectionally and/or derivationally related forms of the same root: *grəb* [grəp] 'back, n.sg.' ~ *gərbove* [gərbove] 'back, n.pl.' ~ *grəbnak* [grəbnak] 'backbone'. The distribution of the liquid plus schwa sequences appears to be characterizable in terms of syllable structure as in (8) (the so-called Maslov-Aronson generalization; see Maslov 1956, Aronson 1968, Stojanov 1980, Tilkov et al. 1982, Lambova 2000).

(8) *Bulgarian syllable structure*
   a. The sequence [Lə] (where L = Liquid) occurs before a consonant followed by another consonant or word boundary (i.e., a tautosyllabic consonant):
      grəbnak [grəb.nak] 'backbone'
   b. The sequence [əL] (where L = Liquid) occurs before a consonant followed by a vowel (i.e., a heterosyllabic consonant):
      gərbove [gər.bo.ve] 'back, n.pl'

(9)	vrəx	'top, sg.'	vərxove	'top, pl.'	vərxar	'top leafage'
	krəv	'blood, sg.'	kərvi	'blood, pl.'	krəvta	'blood, def.sg.'
	gləč	'clamor'	gəlča	'(I) scold'		

The alternating stems in (9) are to be contrasted with the nonalternating stems in (10).

(10) a. krəg   'circle, sg.'   krəgove   'circle, pl.'
         prəč   'male goat, sg.'   prəčove   'male goat, pl.'
         pləx   'rat, sg.'   pləxove   'rat, pl.'
     b. kərt   'mole, sg.'   kərtove   'circle, pl.'
         sərp   'sickle, sg.'   sərpove   'sickle, pl.'
         tərg   'auction, sg.'   tərgove   'auction, pl.'

The difference between the alternating and nonalternating stems can be accounted
for by assuming that the nonalternating stems have the vowel /ə/ in the underlying
nucleus (11), whereas the alternating stems have a liquid in the underlying nucleus (13).

(11) *Underlying forms of nonalternating stems*
        a. /krəg/ 'circle'   b. /kərt/ 'mole'
            /prəč/ 'male goat'   /sərp/ 'sickle'
            /pləx/ 'rat'   /tərg/ 'auction'

(12) *Formal structure of roots in (11)*

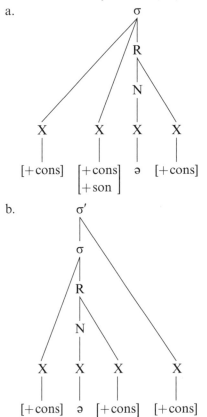

Bulgarian disallows complex codas; second consonant of a final cluster is an appendix, (12b) (Calabrese 2005).

It is crucial to the analysis that the nucleus vowel be missing in the alternating stems, as illustrated in the list of underlying forms in (13); their formal structure is illustrated in (13b) (see Calabrese 2005 for a slightly different analysis of alternating roots).

(13) *Underlying forms of alternating stems*
    a. /vrx/ 'top'
       /krv/ 'blood'
       /glč/ 'clamor'

    b.

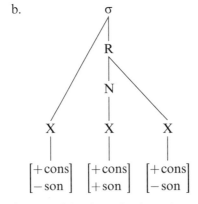

Before we delve into the formal structure of these underlying forms, consider the following observation by Trubetzkoy:

In Serbo-Croatian and also in Bulgarian the *r* is often found with a syllabic function. Usually this involves the combination of *r* plus a vocalic glide of indeterminate quality which sometimes occurs before and sometimes after the *r*, depending on the environment. In Serbo-Croatian such an "indeterminate vowel" does not occur in any other position. The indeterminate vocalic glide that occurs before or after the *r* cannot be identified with any phoneme of the phonemic system, and the entire sequence of *r* plus (preceding or following) vocalic glide must be considered a single phoneme. Bulgarian, on the other hand, has an "indeterminate vowel" which occurs also in other positions. . . . The transitional vowel to syllabic *r* in this case is considered a combinatory variant of the indeterminate vowel, and the entire sequence is regarded as polyphonematic (as *ər* or *rə*). (1939:59)

Let us put aside the issue of the monophonematic or polyphonematic analysis of the syllabic /r/ in Bulgarian and Serbo-Croation, which was important for Trubetzkoy but is not important here. What *is* important here is that in both languages, and in other languages as well, a syllabic sonorant becomes a sequence of a vocalic element plus the sonorant. This is a common change; syllabic sonorants were eliminated historically in many languages (e.g., the ancient Indo-European languages; see Watkins

1993) and replaced by sequences of a vowel plus the nonsyllabic counterpart of the sonorant. The same process is found synchronically in languages such as Armenian (Vaux 1998) and several varieties of English such as Scottish English (Catford 1977).

I propose that this process is due to a repair triggered by an active constraint against sonorants in nucleus position, (14).

(14) $*(_\sigma \ldots (_R (_N [+\text{son}, +\text{cons}])_N \ldots)_R)_\sigma$

The inputs to this constraint are syllabic sonorants like the one in (13b), which typically occur in an interconsonantal context. If (14) is active in a language, a structure like (13b) must be repaired. The principle of Last Resort (15) restricts the range of repairs possible in the case of violations of (14). This principle follows from the principle of Economy, which governs the use of means and resources in all human praxis, of which language is a part. I formulate it as in (16), with the assumption that each human activity and its outputs can be decomposed into elementary units. For phonology, the principle of Economy requires that phonological manipulation of a string can take place only if there is an instruction to do so; see (15).

(15) *Last Resort*
      Use a maximally relevant operation minimally.

(16) *Economy*
      Use the minimal number of maximally relevant units.

Under (15), we might minimally delete the feature [+sonorant], creating a syllabic [−sonorant] consonant. These consonants are extremely marked and disallowed in most (but not all) languages. This repair would therefore crash. Another possibility is to delete the feature [+consonantal]. After this deletion, the feature specification [−consonantal] would be automatically inserted. This would create the vocalic feature bundle in the nucleus in (17), whose feature specifications must then be inserted.

(17)

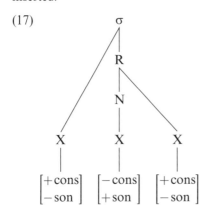

Such a change from a syllabic sonorant to a vowel is attested: for example, syllabic [n] to [a] in Sanskrit or syllabic [r] to [a] in Berber (see Dell and Tangi 1993). However, this is not the preferred treatment of these segments. The preferred repair is replacement with a vowel plus sonorant sequence. The model presented here provides a simple account of this change: it involves the other operation available in this case, feature insertion. Thus, we can correct the disallowed configuration in (13) by adding the feature [−consonantal], creating the structure in (18).

(18)

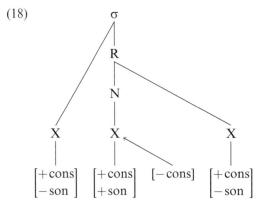

Insertion of [−consonantal] is the only operation in the REPAIR set of (14) in Bulgarian. Insertion of [−consonantal] in the feature bundle of the sonorant in (18) creates a disallowed branching structure that must be repaired by fission, which involves automatic splitting and cloning of the disallowed branching structure (see above and Calabrese 1988, 1995, 2005 for details). The illegal branching we observe in (19) is repaired by splitting the single skeletal position into two, one associated with the specification [+consonantal] and the other with the specification [−consonantal]. The latter skeletal position is associated with the nucleus position. The cloned skeletal slot is depicted in a square. The position of the clone will be discussed shortly.

(19)

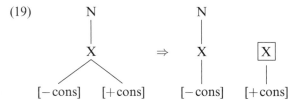

Observe that once fission applies to an input such as that in (18), there are two possible positions for the fissioned skeletal position: it can appear either to the right (20a) or to the left (20b) of the original.

(20) a. *Fission I*

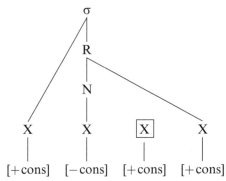

   b. *Fission II*

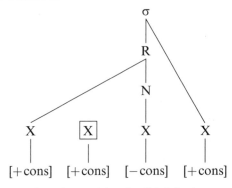

   I assume that the position in (20a) is the unmarked position—one can speculate that it is such because this position preserves rhyme identity in the sense that the inserted sonorant remains a component of the rhyme. We can now state the set of ranked repairs for the constraint against a branching structure as in (21).

(21) *REPAIR set for the constraint against branching X*
      Fission:
      a. (20a)
      b. (20b)

   Resyllabification triggered by the constraint against unsyllabified segments will produce (22a) in the case of (20a) and (22b) in the case of (20b).

(22) a. *(20a) resyllabified*

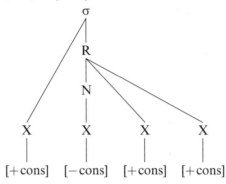

b. *(20b) resyllabified*

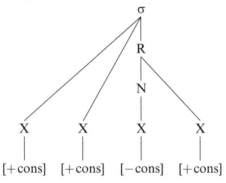

The ranking in (21) accounts for the development of syllabic sonorants as vowel plus sonorant sequences in the history of the Indo-European languages. The development of syllabic liquid consonants is sampled in (23) and (24) (see Watkins 1993). Whereas Indo-Iranian preserved the original syllabic liquids, other Indo-European languages such as Latin, Germanic, and Baltic replaced them with the sequence vowel plus corresponding liquid (the different qualities of the vowels are not discussed here).

(23) | *PIE* | *Indo-Iranian* | *Latin* | *Germanic* | *Lithuanian* |
|---|---|---|---|---|
| *r̥ | r̥ | or, ur | ur | ir/ur |
| *l̥ | r̥ | ol, ul | ul | il/ul |

(24) IE *kr̥d 'heart': Lat. cor, Goth. hairtō, Lit. širdis
    IE *dhr̥s 'to dare': Skt. dhr̥snoti, Goth. gadaursan

The marked treatment in (20b), although less common, is also found in Greek, Old Irish, and Slavic (Watkins 1993), as shown in (25).

(25) IE *dhr̥s 'to dare':   Gr. tʰrasús (but IE *kr̥d, Gr. kardía)
                               Old Ir. cride (from IE *kr̥dyom)
      IE *wl̥kʷos 'wolf':   Old Church Slavonic vlĭku

We can now return to Bulgarian. Here I assume that in the case of alternating
roots, the nucleus is underlyingly syllabic as in (13b). Consider the form [vrəx] 'top',
underlying /vrx/.³ It contains a structure like that in (13b). This violates the constraint against syllabic sonorant consonants, (14). It is repaired by feature insertion
followed by fission. If the cloned skeletal position is inserted in its unmarked position
as in (20a), we will obtain a structure with a complex coda. However, as I argue in
Calabrese 2005, complex codas are not allowed in Bulgarian. Furthermore, the RE-
PAIR set of the MS disallowing them is empty. Therefore, the structure produced by
(20a) is disallowed, and unrepairable. The derivation crashes. In the new derivation,
after the insertion of [−consonantal] to repair the disallowed syllabic liquid, the next
available ranked repair is (20b), which applies. This produces a structure with the /r/
in a complex onset, which is allowed in Bulgarian. We now have an account of the
form [vrəx]. This is shown in (26).

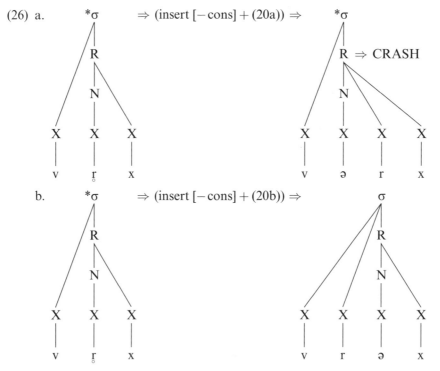

Now consider the form [vərxove]. Syllabification produces a representation like
that in the left-hand diagram in (27), again violating constraint (14). In this case,

there is no problem applying the preferred repair in (20b), since no complex coda is produced. Hence, we obtain the right-hand diagram in (27). The different treatments of the root sonorants in Bulgarian are now accounted for.

(27)

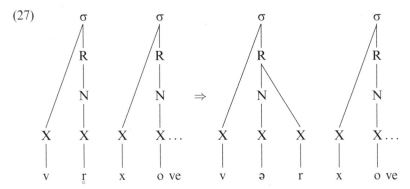

13.3 The Rule Component

I have now sketched how MSs and REPAIRs interact within the MM. I will have more to say about the MM below, but first let us explore what an adequate theory of phonology requires in order to account for language-particular phonological phenomena. Clearly, a theory of phonology must accommodate generalizations that neither are plausibly due to UG nor seem to involve repairs intended to remove violations of MSs. In fact, there seems no way around positing basically dressed-up *SPE*-type rules (Chomsky and Halle 1968) to handle many kinds of phenomena. Consider, for example, the Polish data in (28), which require a rule that raises vowels that immediately precede a final voiced nonnasal consonant: /bor/ → [bur] 'forest', /swob/ → swub → [swup] 'crib'. (Note that in the latter example, a subsequent rule devoices the final obstruent; we will revisit this below.) This raising rule, given in (29), is not plausibly phonetically motivated in contemporary Polish.

(28) | *Noun sg.* | *Noun pl.* | *Gloss* |
|---|---|---|
| a. swub [swup] | swobi | 'crib' |
| b. bur | bori | 'forest' |
| c. dzvon | dzvoni | 'bell' |
| d. snop | snopi | 'sheaf' |

(29) [−high, +round] → [+high] / __[+cons, +voi, −nas] #

It is, of course, easy to see what happened historically: Polish once had an active "natural" process that lengthened vowels before voiced consonants. Although this lengthening was then due to interactions of MSs and REPAIRs, it eventually became "phonologized" in the sense that it acquired some lexical exceptions and other gaps, such as failure to operate before a nasal. When the vowel lengthened in the forms in (28a,b), the result was the representations /swo:b/ and /bo:r/. Now, it is known that long mid (or low) vowels are more marked than long high vowels. Therefore, there is an MS against long mid vowels, and this presumably became active at some time after the vowel-lengthening process became phonologized. The default REPAIR for long mid vowels is to raise to high, so /swo:b/ and /bo:r/ became /swu:b/ and /bu:r/. Finally, Polish lost all its long vowels; that is, it made active a previously inactive MS against long vowels in general, so the vowels that once raised because they were long are now short.

The synchronic grammar of Polish now has the brute force rule in (29), a telescoped vestige of the extinct MS-driven processes in (30) causing lengthening, raising, and subsequent shortening.

(30) a. Lengthening of vowels before voiced coda consonants
     b. Context-free raising of long vowels
     c. Shortening of long vowels

Each of these is a natural process that characterizes similar changes in many languages, but no longer in Polish. The historical shortening of long vowels removed all evidence for the presence of long vowels in Modern Polish, so that now there is no way of motivating any of the processes in (30) synchronically. Thus, we are left with the telescoped rule in (29), which is a genuine rule of Polish phonology.

It follows from the preceding discussion that the architecture of phonological theory must countenance two types of instructions: *positive instructions* and *negative instructions*. Positive instructions are formally implemented as rules, like (29). Negative instructions are formally implemented as negative constraints like the MSs illustrated above for French, each of which is coupled with a unique REPAIR set. The model in figure 13.4 is a first approximation of the overall architecture; it is a minimal revision of the model in figure 13.1. The box labeled *instructions component* contains both MSs and rules. This model, in particular the internal structure of the instructions component, will be substantially elaborated upon later in this chapter, especially in section 13.5.

13.4   More on the Markedness Module

In this section, I will describe the markedness module (MM) in more detail as part of the overall architecture of phonological theory. The MM contains, among other subcomponents, two kinds of universal negative constraints, prohibitions and MSs. Prohibitions identify configurations that are never possible for articulatory and/or acoustic/perceptual reasons; for example, a vowel may not be simultaneously [+high] and [+low]. MSs, as we have seen, identify phonologically complex configurations

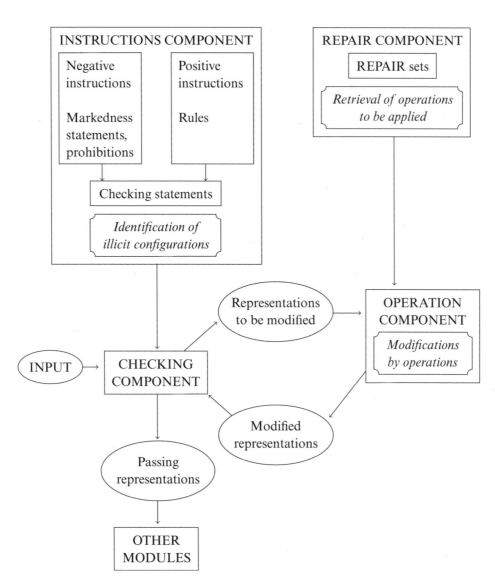

Figure 13.4
Detailed structure of the markedness module

that may be found in some, but not all, phonological inventories. They can be active or deactivated. If an MS is deactivated in a given language, the relevant complex configuration appears in the language. Otherwise, the MS is active (the default condition), and the relevant complex configuration is missing. As argued in Calabrese 1988, 1995, 2005, MSs are universally ranked. This accounts for generalizations about the structure of phonological inventories. (See Calabrese 1995, 2005 for more discussion of this issue.)

13.4.1 Correlation Statements

Correlation statements are also part of the MM. They are the positive counterparts of MSs insofar as they govern the structure of segments. They are universal positive instructions that have the internal structure of segments as their only scope.

Correlation statements differ from MSs and prohibitions. The latter two may govern the structure of segments as well as sequential constraints, and they target configurations that are difficult or impossible. Correlation statements, on the other hand, are positive statements characterizing certain secondary, noncontrastive aspects of the production of a sound. In particular, they require the presence of certain noncontrastive secondary articulatory configurations in the context of other primary articulatory configurations.

An example from Tulu (based on Sagey 1986) may serve to illustrate correlation statements. It is common for labial consonants to cause rounding in adjacent vowels. In Tulu, /i/ becomes /u/ when preceding either a rounded vowel or a labial consonant. The former process is simply a case of assimilation; the latter cannot be classified this way, because the consonant itself is not rounded. This may be accounted for by the correlation statement in (31), which means that [+round] expresses any involvement of the lips in vocoids.

(31) Lips → [$_{lips}$ +round] / [__, −cons]

This is natural given the degree of constriction characterizing nonconsonantal sounds; any constrictions formed with the lips in such sounds can only result in lip rounding. UG bestows (31) on the grammar of Tulu; languages without this correlation statement are more complex in that they must contain a statement suppressing it. We have illustrated that correlation statements account for the presence of noncontrastive secondary articulatory configurations in the context of a primary articulatory configuration, or—as in the case in Tulu—the way a certain articulator must behave in a given stricture environment.

13.4.2 Natural Rules

Natural rules differ from correlation statements in that they characterize the interaction of segments with their environment. Natural rules are rules that belong to UG.

They account for processes that tend to recur across languages, like final devoicing (e.g., the devoicing of the final consonant in [swup] (28)). They can also be active or deactivated. As in the case of MSs, I assume that their default condition is "active" and that they must be deactivated—suppressed like the natural processes discussed in Stampe 1972—in the acquisition process.

A typical natural rule is the one that accounts for devoicing in coda position postulated in (32). As in the case of MSs, I assume that there is a universally fixed ranking of natural rules. Natural processes in the higher positions of the hierarchy are more likely to be active than those in the lower positions. An example of a top-ranked natural rule is the one that fronts a velar consonant before a front vowel. Another is word-final devoicing, as in (32).

(32)

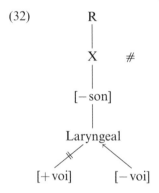

If there is a conflict between a natural rule and an MS, which of them is deactivated must be decided on a language-specific basis, although there appears to be a tendency to deactivate the natural rule. Here is a case in point. The aspiration of stops is a common sound change. In many languages (e.g., Armenian (Vaux 1998), southern Italian dialects), the voiceless series became aspirated by a context-free change. I postulate that this process is due to the natural rule in (33).

(33) [−stiff voc cords] → [+spr glot] / [__, −cont]

The natural rule in (33) conflicts with MS (34), which characterizes aspirated stops as marked.

(34) *[−cont, +spr glot]

In most languages, voiceless stops are unaspirated (Maddieson 1984). To account for this fact, we have to hypothesize that in the conflict between (33) and (34), it is (33) that is deactivated. What are the conditions under which (33) is able to win and (34) is deactivated? This is again tantamount to asking why we find a certain pattern of deactivation of MSs in one language and not in another. It is a case of language-particular stipulation.

Assimilation processes are examples of natural rules. To account for language-particular variation in assimilation, I propose that the MM contains the general rule schema in (35). C in (35a) is a terminal feature or a set of terminal features dominated by the same node C. (35b) is the parameter stating the direction in which C spreads.

(35) a.

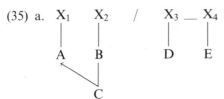

b. Rule schema (35a) applies right to left/left to right.

In (35), the node B assimilates the features C of the node A. For (35a) to be active, the different variables in (35) as well as the direction of the operation must be specified. Rule (35) cannot apply if these variables are not set. Acquisition of assimilation thus consists of determining what, if anything, assimilates to what else, in what environment, and in which direction. This involves establishing new settings for the variables in (35).

The assimilation process in the English past tense is illustrated in (36).

(36) a. No effect: blame-d, derive-d, clogg-ed, close-d
       [+stiff voc cords]: usurp-ed, clock-ed, replace-d, brief-ed
    b. No effect: bough-t, knel-t, dwel-t
       [+stiff voc cords]: lef-t (leave), los-t (lose)

Assuming, as is standard, that the exponent of the unexceptional English past tense is /d/, we see that it assimilates the feature [+stiff vocal cords] from the final phoneme of the verb stem if that phoneme is voiceless, (36a). By contrast, the /t/ exponent of the past tense, which is taken by about 40 English verbs, transmits its [+stiff vocal cords] feature to the stem-final obstruent (from Calabrese and Halle 1998). We can capture this with the rules in (37).

(37) a. $[-\text{son}]$ $+$ $[-\text{son}]$

       [+stiff voc cords]

    b. $[-\text{son}]$ $+$ $[-\text{son}]$

          [+stiff voc cords]

Both rules are language-specific instances of the natural rule schema in (35), and in this sense they are perfectly "natural" rules that are commonly found across languages.

These components of the MM (active MSs, prohibitions, REPAIRs, active natural rules, and correlation statements) belong to the grammar; they are grammatical statements about phonological representations. From the point of view of deriving outputs from inputs, they are not different from language-specific idiosyncratic rules. Unlike rules, however, they are also interface conditions—that is, the means through which the linguistic computational system is able to interpret and read the properties of the sensorimotor system. All these components of the MM represent the sensorimotor system in the linguistic computational system.

To clarify the nature of the MM, it is worth noting that the relationship between the MM and the sensorimotor system differs from grounding in Archangeli and Pulleyblank's (1994) sense. Grounding simply indicates the presence of a reason for statements within the MM. Here, I argue for a closer relationship: the MM is the means by which the grammatical system interprets and categorizes the physiological, articulatory, or acoustic properties of the sensorimotor system. The speaker does not have access to these phonetic properties other than through the MM, just as in our perception of color we do not have access to the intrinsic properties of light. Obviously, the nature and function of these properties in language can be explained by the phonetician in the same way as the nature of our perception of color can be explained by the physicist or the psychologist. However, these phonetic explanations are external to our linguistic behavior in the same way as the physicist's or the psychologist's explanations of our perception of color are external to our experience of color. Phonetic explanations are extragrammatical: only MSs play a role in the grammatical system.

13.4.3 Context-Free Changes

A common objection against markedness theory is that there appear to be exceptions to markedness where marked segments are produced by context-free changes (see, e.g., Dressler 1974). The prototypical example of such a change is the context-free fronting of rounded back vowels that occurred in languages such as Gallo-Romance and Classical Greek, among others. This fronting affects the unmarked vowels [u] and [o] and produces the vowels [ü] and [ö], respectively, which according to any markedness criteria are marked. In the theory presented here, these vowels would be disallowed by the MS in (38). Such cases of fronting appear to involve a spontaneous change from the unmarked to the marked, a change that should be forbidden if markedness theory is correct.

(38) *[−back, +round]

In Calabrese 2000, I proposed the following explanation for a process of this type that occurred in the southern Italian dialect of Altamura (Loporcaro 1988), as shown in (39). In this dialect, [+advanced tongue root] ([+ATR]) rounded vowels are fronted (see (39a,b)), whereas [−ATR] ones are not (see (39c)).

(39) a. [+ATR] /u/   /ursə/ → [yrsə]   'bear'
                        /nuvelə/ → [nyvelə]   'cloud'
     b. [+ATR] /o/   /ommə/ → [ømmə]   'man'
                        /nottə/ → [nøttə]   'night'
     c. [–ATR] /ɔ/   /dɔltʃ/ → *[døltʃ]   'sweet'
                        /kanɔʃʃə/ → *[kanøʃʃə]   'know'

In Calabrese 2000, I proposed that the fronting in (40a,b) involves a repair due to the MS in (40), which characterizes the feature configuration [+back, +ATR] as phonologically complex. The MS in (40) is active in this dialect and triggers the RE-PAIR in (41). As I explain more fully in Calabrese 2005, deletion of the feature [+back] triggers insertion of the feature [–back], fronting /u, o/ to [y, ø], respectively. We thus have an account for the spontaneous fronting of rounded back vowels.

(40) *[+ATR, +back]

(41) Input: *[+ATR, +back]
     REPAIR: Deletion of [+back]

Cases of this type are by no means rare. Many other cases display emergence of the marked: for example, syncope gives rise to complex syllabic structures; vowel assimilation such as umlaut gives rise to marked vowels such as [ü, ö, ä]; vowel-consonant interactions (e.g., palatalization) give rise to marked consonants such as palatoalveolar affricates; and so on. All these cases involve a conflict between an active instruction, be it a natural rule or an MS, and an MS disallowing the marked configuration produced by the process triggered by that instruction. The historical change leading to the emergence of the marked involves activation of the instruction that leads to a violation of the latter MS, which is deactivated.

The crucial issue in all of these cases—including the back vowel fronting discussed above—is that the violated MS is deactivated instead of being repaired. When a phonological operation generates a configuration—featural, syllabic, or involving some other prosodic structure—that is normally not admitted in a language (i.e., illicit because of an MS)—the language has two options: (1) to repair the disallowed configuration, or (2) to deactivate the relevant MS, thereby admitting the previously excluded configuration. Under this option, the language accepts paying the cost of deactivating the relevant MS and enlarging its phonological inventory.

13.5 Visibility Theory and Spotlighting

Following conclusions in Calabrese 1995 (see also Mohanan 1991), I propose that underlying featural representations are fully specified. It is known that some constraints/rules are sensitive only to marked feature specifications, others to all contrastive specifications, and still others to noncontrastive specifications as well. This asymmetry can be accounted for by assuming that rules can be characterized as being sensitive to three classes of feature specifications, as in (42).

(42)
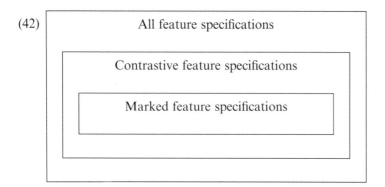

Underspecification is then not a property of representations, but actually a property of constraints/rules. Some phonological constraints/rules have access only to marked feature specifications; others are restricted to dealing exclusively with contrastive feature specifications; still others are sensitive to all types of feature specifications (for analyses based on the same ideas, see Halle 1995, Halle, Vaux, and Wolfe 2000, Vaux 2000). This is visibility theory, illustrated by Kinande vowel harmony. Kinande has the vowel system /i, ɪ, u, ʊ, e, ɛ, o, ɔ, a/; note that all the vowels except /a/ exhibit [ATR] contrast. Schlindwein (1987) describes a vowel harmony process in this language that spreads [+ATR] leftward onto high and mid vowels. /a/ is transparent to this process, illustrating the asymmetry between contrastive and noncontrastive values of [ATR]. The Kinande harmony rule is thus characterized as accessing only contrastive features; therefore, the noncontrastive [−ATR] of the low vowel is not visible to it, and the rule simply disregards it.

Steriade (1987) has shown many cases where contrastive features can either trigger or block a process, whereas redundant features are frequently transparent and fail to trigger or be targets. This was one of the major motivations for underspecification theory. However, the compelling criticisms of this theory (Clements 1987, 2000, Steriade 1987, 1995, Christdas 1988, Mohanan 1991, Odden 1992, Calabrese 1995) suggest that an alternative is in order; visibility theory achieves the aims of underspecification theory while not incurring the liabilities.

Evidence for feature visibility is provided by cases in which a certain feature F is invisible to a process X but is required in order to state the environment of another process Y that applies before X. Coronals in English are a typical case. English has a process of postlexical place assimilation in which coronals may succumb to velars and labials (*hot cakes* → *ho[k k]akes*). Processes of this type have been accounted for by assuming coronal underspecification. The problem is that coronals must be referred to in early levels of phonology to rule out onset clusters such as */tl/, */dl/ or to state a constraint on /yu/ in stressed syllables in American English (e.g., *butte* [byut], *cute* [kyut], *mute* [myut], but *tune* [tun], *[tyun]). (See Mohanan 1991, McCarthy and Taub 1992, Calabrese 1995 for further discussion of coronals in English.) As proposed in Calabrese 1995, the simplest solution to this problem is to state that whereas postlexical place assimilation in English is sensitive only to marked place features (which will thus spread at the expense of the unmarked coronal), syllabification constraints such as those mentioned above are sensitive to all place features including the unmarked coronal.

I propose that accessing a given set of feature specifications involves a process of spotlighting. Suppose that the checking and operation systems of phonology have a limited computational capacity. If so, they will work much more efficiently if their domains of application are restricted or prioritized. Spotlighting only certain aspects of the phonological representations would achieve this. Checking the satisfaction of an instruction clearly involves identifying the relevant representational units in the representation. These units are spotlighted and the instruction is checked against what is spotlighted. The minimal assumption is that all the units mentioned in the instruction are spotlighted. The further assumption is that spotlighting one feature on a tier involves spotlighting all other features on the same tier.

Let us also assume that spotlighting may be restricted by two parameterized conditions. The first parameter, if set to its unmarked state, "on," restricts spotlighting to contrastive features. If we assume that contrastive features are the most salient aspect of the representations, the spotlighting of these features is naturally explained. The other parameter limits spotlighting to marked features; its unmarked state is also "on." Spotlighting of marked features is more restrictive, but more costly insofar as only a subset of the salient features is selected, an operation that requires more "focusing." Thus, the least marked state would be for the contrastive feature parameter to be on, in which case the setting for the marked feature parameter is irrelevant. However, accessing all features is the most costly option of all because of the expenditure of computational capacity that is required to check all features. This is the marked setting of both parameters, "off."

By tying visibility to the independently required notion of markedness, the theory proposed here is highly constrained: a visible feature specification must be either marked or contrastive, a notion that follows directly from the notion of markedness. The range of units that can be checked and in particular disregarded is extremely limited and follows from the active MSs, which are independently needed and assumed to belong to UG.

The theory presented here rejects the classical hypothesis that in memorizing (the sound of) a morpheme, speakers store only the idiosyncratic properties of the base form so that predictable properties are unspecified. There is no evidence or need to assume this. Rather, it is derivational efficiency that governs the construction of underlying representations: given the processes characterizing the language, the underlying representation of a morpheme must contain all the information needed to account for the surface pronunciation of the morpheme efficiently and with minimal effort. The success of the derivation is the fundamental criterion used to establish which sound or set of sounds is underlying and which sound or set of sounds is derived. The segment or set of segments that allows one to predict all the variants by a process in the simplest and most efficient way is chosen as underlying. Full specification of segmental features allows this successful derivation, once we introduce REPAIRs to account for the interaction between the structure of a phonological system and the differing effects of phonological processes. In this case, redundant feature specification in the underlying representation of morphemes could actually be helpful for memory retrieval (see Derwing 1973, Meyer and Schvaneveldt 1971, Newman, Sawusch, and Luce 1997, Vaux 2003:94). However, derivational efficiency also requires that underspecification in some cases must be allowed in underlying representations. This occurs in the case of syllable structure, as well as in the case of other prosodic structures, where one wants to avoid wasteful destruction and rebuilding of structure, something that would be extremely costly from the point of view of an efficient derivation.

13.6   Derivations

Cases involving phonological opacity are successfully treated in a derivational framework. This is accomplished in the current model by specifying, on a language-particular basis, the order in which representations are checked for the application of instructions, either positive or negative. This can be depicted by means of the flowchart in figure 13.4, which is a more complete version of the flowchart in figure 13.1.

13.6.1   Checking

Checking is an operation that scans a string to identify whether or not the conditions for the application of an instruction (rule or constraint) are met. Checking parses a string to identify possible violations of the constraint or to identify configurations that meet the structural description of the rule. I assume that, ceteris paribus, given a set of instructions, the operations triggered by these instructions will tend to apply in a feeding relationship until fully licit outputs are created. To account for bleeding/counterfeeding/counterbleeding interactions between operations, I propose that the checking of instructions in a given input can be extrinsically specified on a language-particular basis: checking of a specified instruction can be delayed until after another instruction has been checked. That is, the grammar may contain special statements, as in (43), that specify when a given instruction X must be checked with respect to certain other instructions. In this way, a phonological derivation like those of classical generative grammar can be produced.

(43) The checking of instruction X follows the checking of instruction Y.

Input representations are first sent to the checking component in figure 13.4 to determine whether they meet the requirements for an instruction (either an MS or a rule). Any representation that meets these requirements is parsed by the operator component, which stores the list of the operations associated with the instruction so that the appropriate operations can be retrieved. These operations are then implemented in the operation component. (43) says that some checking statements are extrinsically ordered with respect to one another.

With regard to order, the following logical possibilities exist. First, checking statements may require positive instructions to be ordered with respect to each other. This is simply the familiar order of idiosyncratic rules. For example, the checking statement for the Polish raising rule in (29) must precede the one for the natural rule that devoices word-final obstruents. Second, a checking statement may require the checking of a positive instruction to precede the checking of a negative instruction; this is illustrated below for Icelandic. Third, a checking statement may require a negative instruction to precede a positive instruction; for example, in the Yawelmani dialect of Yokuts, a language-particular rule of vowel harmony is implemented after vowel epenthesis, which is triggered by an MS governing syllable structure. Fourth, checking statements may require negative instructions to be ordered with respect to each other; a case of this type is again found in the Yawelmani dialect of Yokuts, where vowel epenthesis (which, as mentioned above, is triggered by an MS governing syllable structure) must be implemented before vowel shortening (which is again due to a constraint on syllable structure, specifically rhyme structure).

In addition to these ordering possibilities, the model of grammar described here allows for cyclic rule application. This will be illustrated in the course of the Icelandic example below.

13.6.2 Icelandic

As is well-known, Modern Icelandic has an epenthesis process that occurs when consonant-final stems are followed by the suffix [-r] of the nominative. Examples are shown in (44a), and the process is described in (44b) (Oresnik 1972, Anderson 1974, Kiparsky 1984, Kenstowicz 1994).

(44) a. Nom. sg.   dal-ur   hest-ur   hatt-ur   stað-ur
         Acc. sg.   dal   hest   hatt   stað
                 'valley'   'horse'   'hat'   'place'

     b. $\emptyset \rightarrow u \;/\; C\_\_r\,\#$

This process of epenthesis is in a counterfeeding relationship with /u/-umlaut, which rounds and fronts a low vowel before the vowel [u], (45b). The /u/ inserted by the epenthesis rule in (44b), however, never causes umlaut, as is evident from the nominative singular of the words for 'valley', 'hat', and 'place' in (44). These words are not exceptions to the umlaut rule; they have the dative plural forms *döl-um*, *höt-um*, and *stöð-um*, respectively.

(45) a. Nom. sg.   barn   baggi   1sg.   kalla
       Dat. pl.   börn-um   bögg-ull   1pl.   köll-um
                 'child'   'parcel'   'call'

   b. a → ö / __ C_0 u

In a derivational approach, this situation is simply accounted for by assuming that the *u*-umlaut process applies before epenthesis, as in (46). (UR = underlying representation)

(46) UR   dal + r   dal + um
    u-umlaut   döl-um
    epenthesis   dal-ur

As in the earlier Polish example, the reason for this ordering is basically diachronic: epenthesis was introduced later in Icelandic than *u*-umlaut. Synchronic alternations can frequently be analyzed in terms of a set of ordered processes that resemble historical changes. It is reasonable to assume that speakers perform similar operations. But how do we implement this in the current proposal?

Ordering in the application of rules (i.e., "positive instructions") is straightforward. However, it is not obvious how to account for the interaction between rules and negative constraints in an extrinsically ordered derivation. If a negative constraint were active in a grammar, we would expect it always to be active and trigger a REPAIR. Hence, a REPAIR could only be in a feeding relationship with a rule; no counterfeeding or counterbleeding relationship is possible here. As we will see, the Icelandic example does require such an order; that is why I propose the notion of checking.

To see this, let us start by examining the epenthesis data in (44b). Here, epenthesis is an instance of a REPAIR triggered by the constraint in (47), which disallows unsyllabified skeletal positions such as that of the suffixal [-r]. (48) is the REPAIR associated with (47); (49) shows the derivation for *dal-ur* 'valley, nom. sg.'.

(47) Unsyllabified skeletal positions (= X′) are not allowed.

(48) *REPAIR for (47)*
    1. *Syllabic incorporation (line insertion)*
       a. Attach X′ to onset of adjacent σ;
       b. Attach X′ to coda of adjacent σ;
       c. Attach X′ as appendix of adjacent σ.

2. *Syllable insertion*

   Insert σ and attach X′ to
   a. the nucleus of σ;
   b. i. the coda of σ if X′ is word-final;
       ii. the onset of σ;
       iii. the coda of σ.

(49) a.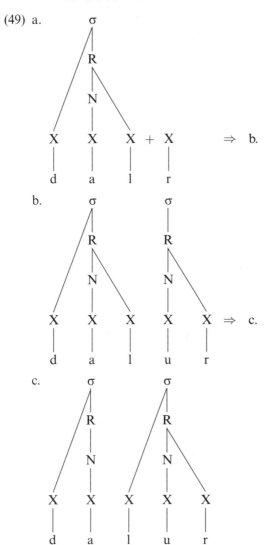

We begin with the underlying representation in (49a). Here, the suffixal /-r/ is unsyllabified in violation of (47), so the representation is sent to (48). (48,1a) is inapplicable, because there is no adjacent syllable to which the offending segment can be adjoined as an onset. Application of (48,1b) would generate the coda [lr], which is impossible because it would violate the Sonority Sequencing Principle. Because Modern Icelandic allows only /s/ as an appendix (see below), we must resort to syllable-insertion, as in (48,2). No syllabic sonorants are allowed in Icelandic, so (48,2a) crashes. Next, we try (48,2b). A syllable is inserted by anchoring its margin to the unsyllabified segment. The unsyllabified [r] of (49a) is word-final; therefore, it is syllabified as a coda, as in (49b). The nucleus of the inserted syllable is filled in with the feature specification of the vowel [u], an idiosyncratic operation that I will not discuss here. In (49b), there is a bad syllable contact between the epenthetic [u] and the preceding coda consonant; the coda consonant /l/ precedes a nucleus. This problem is fixed by resyllabifying the consonant as the onset of the following syllable, as in (49c). The derivation is successful.

Turning next to *u*-umlaut, we note that it is an idiosyncratic process that can only be formulated as the rule in (50), which spreads the feature [+round] of [u] onto a preceding low vowel and deletes [+low] and [+back], while replacing them with their opposite-valued correspondents, [−low] and [−back].

(50) u-*umlaut rule*

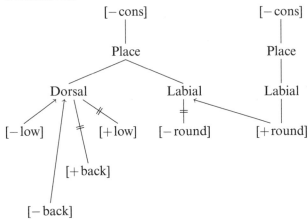

The rule in (50) applies to /dalum/ to create [dölum]. We must ensure that it does not apply to /dalur/, the result of epenthesis, which is the REPAIR operation in (48). For this, we invoke (43) and stipulate that checking of the constraint in (47) is delayed until after the checking of (50), as in (51). This sequence of operations creates derivations essentially like those in (46), except that "epenthesis" is really RE-PAIR (47).

(51) The checking of (47) follows the checking of (50).

This analysis is a simple solution to the Icelandic case. The grammar assigns a special status to the idiosyncratic rule of *u*-umlaut and at the same time characterizes epenthesis as repair of an illicit syllabic sequence. Crucially—and this is the main point of this section—I have illustrated the order between checking of negative instructions and the checking of positive instructions. The point is that derivations are created by stipulating the ordering of when instructions are checked.

As another example of this ordering, let us consider the interaction of high-vocoid deletion and epenthesis in Modern Icelandic. High-vocoid deletion deletes a postconsonantal high vocoid preceding another consonant or in word-final position; see the rule in (52). Interestingly, the epenthetic [-u-] appearing before the suffixal [-r] of the nominative behaves as if it were not there. The entire array of facts is exemplified in (53).

(52) $[-\text{cons}, +\text{high}] \rightarrow \emptyset \, / \, C \_\_ \, \{\#, C\}$

(53) Nom. sg.   lyf-ur   byl-ur   beð-ur   söng-ur
     Acc. sg.   lyf   byl   beð   söng
     Gen. sg.   lyf-s   byl-s   beð-s   söng-s
     Dat. pl.   lyfj-um   bylj-um   beðj-um   söngv-um
     Gen. pl.   lyfj-a   bylj-a   beðj-a   söngv-a
                 'medicine'   'storm'   'bed'   'song'

A derivational framework captures these facts very simply, by assuming that high-vocoid deletion applies before epenthesis; see (54).

(54) UR   /#bylj-um#/   /#bylj-s#/   /#bylj#/   /#bylj-r#/
     high-vocoid   —   byl-s   byl   byl-r
     deletion
     epenthesis   —   —   —   byl-ur

An explanation for this state of affairs is again to be found in history. In particular, there was a stage of Icelandic where suffixal [-r] was allowed in word-final position after consonants, as shown in (55) (see Noreen 1970). We can assume that this was due to the fact that Old Icelandic allowed a special appendix position for /r/ as well as /s/ (e.g., *nið-r/nið-s* 'kinsman, son, nom. sg./gen. sg.').

(55) *Some Old Icelandic forms*
     niðr   'kinsman, son'
     vegr   'way, road'
     harmr   'skin'
     stelr   'steals'

High-vocoid deletion was already implemented at this stage, as shown by the alternations in (56).

(56) *Old Icelandic*

Nom. sg.	nið-r
Acc. sg.	nið
Gen. sg.	nið-s
Dat. pl.	niðj-um
Gen. pl.	niðj-a

The alternation involving the high vocoid was due to a process of syncope affecting short high thematic vowels in unstressed final syllables (compare *nið-r* with *hirði:r* 'herdsman') (see Noreen 1970; see also Calabrese 1994). The precise conditions under which this syncope occurred are not investigated here. The syncope process is stated in (57).

(57) *Syncope*

$$\text{N}$$
$$|$$
$$\text{X} \rightarrow \emptyset \text{ in the relevant morphophonological context}$$
$$|$$
$$[-\text{cons}]$$

This syncope process applies to underlying /nið-i-r/ and changes it to [nið-r], as shown in (58).

(58) /nið-i-r/ → (57) → nið_r → (48,1) → [niðr]

The crucial change leading to Modern Icelandic was the restriction of the special appendix position only to /s/. Thus, /r/ could no longer be syllabified as an appendix, and a configuration containing /r/ in that position had to be repaired by syllable insertion, (48,2). This is shown in (59).

(59) /nið-i-r/ → (57) → nið_r → (48,2) → [niður]

I assume that this diachronic change is reanalyzed in the synchronic grammar of Icelandic as the recent inclusion of the special statement in (60). The surface word /bylur/ would then be derived as depicted in (54).

(60) The checking of (47) follows the checking of (57).

Let us go back to the interaction between *u*-umlaut and epenthesis. The Icelandic data display some interesting complications that will allow us to further the analysis and consider the issue of cyclic application of REPAIRs. Icelandic has another process of syncope, shown in (61) (see Anderson 1974, Kenstowicz 1994). The nominative singular suffix [-r] assimilates to a preceding sonorant, and stress falls on the initial syllable.

(61) Nom. sg.   hamar   fifil-l   morgun-n
     Dat. sg.   hamr-i   fifl-i   morgn-i
                  'hammer'   'dandelion'   'morning'

This process interacts with *u*-umlaut as shown in (62).

(62) Nom. sg.   ketil-l   Nom. pl.   regin   Nom. sg.   bagg-i
     Dat. sg.   katl-i   Gen. pl.   ragn-a   Dimin.   bögg-ul-i
     Dat. pl.   kötl-um   Dat. pl.   rögn-um   Dat. sg.   bögg-l-i
                 'kettle'   'gods'   'parcel'

Forms such as *kötl-um* show that syncope feeds *u*-umlaut, as in (63a); the /i/ must be deleted for the structural description of *u*-umlaut to apply. At the same time, forms such as *bögg-l-i* suggest that *u*-umlaut precedes syncope (63b), because the /u/ that is eliminated by syncope causes *u*-umlaut.

(63) UR   a.   /katil + um/   b.   /bagg + ul + i/
          syncope   katl-um   *u*-umlaut   bögg-ul-i
          u-umlaut   kötl-um   syncope   böggl-i

This paradox is readily resolved in a classical derivational framework if both rules are applied cyclically and syncope precedes *u*-umlaut, as stated in (64); the cyclic derivations are shown in (65).

(64) The checking for *u*-umlaut follows the checking for syncope.

(65) UR   a. /katil + um/   b. /bagg + ul + i/
     Cycle 1   katil + um   bagg + ul
     syncope   katl-um   —
     u-umlaut   kötl-um   bögg-ul
     Cycle 2   —   bögg-ul-i
     syncope   —   böggl-i
     u-umlaut   —   —

We can import the basic features of the traditional analysis into the model presented here. The syncope process that applies in (62) must be analyzed as involving a rule removing "reduced" vowels, that is, vowels occurring in special prosodic situations. I will not investigate here the conditions under which syncope occurs in Icelandic; therefore, I will not state the conditions under which vowels are "reduced." Basically, the syncope rule is the same as the rule in (57).

The operation triggered by syncope is shown in (66).

(66) a.

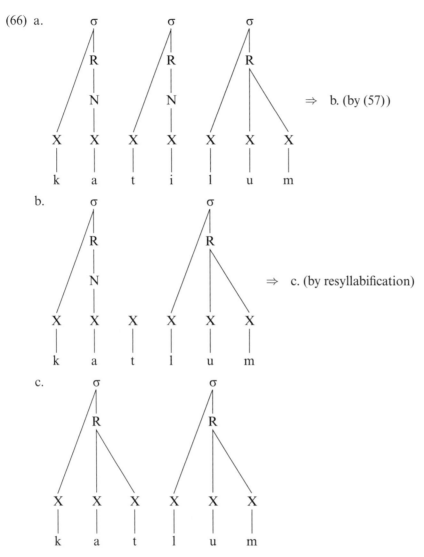

⇒   b. (by (57))

⇒   c. (by resyllabification)

The output produced by (57) is disallowed by the constraint against unsyllabified segments, and it is repaired as shown in (66c). This representation contains only licit configurations, so the derivation is successful. Halle and Vergnaud (1987) proposed that cyclicity is a property of morphemes. Morphemes can be divided into two types, cyclic and postcyclic. Cyclic processes apply in cyclic morphemes, postcyclic processes in postcyclic ones. We can translate this idea into the present framework by saying that the checking for instructions follows the morphological structure of the word. Some instructions are checked cyclically, others noncyclically. We can thus say that *u*-umlaut and syncope are checked cyclically in Icelandic and that the stem is a cyclic domain. Crucially, in each cycle the checking for *u*-umlaut follows the checking for syncope. The derivation in (65) can thus be reformulated in the model presented here.

13.7   Historical Changes

I will conclude with some speculations on historical change. Adopting a Jakobsonian perspective on language (see Jakobson 1941), I assume that markedness also plays a fundamental role in explaining sound change. In the realistic view developed here, sound changes due to markedness involve a decrease in the complexity allowed in a language;[4] representations must then be adjusted in order to be articulated. In phonological terms, this means that certain MSs that were deactivated become active and that a repair adjusts the representations that have thus become disallowed, or that a natural rule that was deactivated becomes active again. Under this interpretation, a sound change is an innovative repair. This innovative repair is then grammaticalized and becomes part of the grammar of a linguistic community.

How does such an innovative repair become part of a grammar so that there is an actual change in the grammar? It is fundamental at this point to clarify what I assume about grammar. I assume that grammar has a double identity: it is not only (1) a computational system (i.e., a set of symbols) and a set of computations using these symbols, but also (2) an institution along the lines suggested by Sperber (1995)—that is, a system of mental representations (and computations) shared by speakers of a given linguistic community. Thus, from the latter point of view, it is at the same time a cultural institution dictating norms of acceptability and an individual speaker's concrete mind/brain state insofar as this individual speaker shares the mental representations of the other members of the same community. In learning a language, speakers must adjust their internal representations through the adjustment of parameter settings, deactivation of MSs, and so on, in such a way that they become similar to those of other members of the community.

Under this view, grammaticalization is the process by which a given individual linguistic innovation/representation becomes "public," that is, shared by the members of the community. This sharing probably has its basis in mimetic behavior, an important characteristic of the human species (Hauser, Chomsky, and Fitch 2002). Once a representation is shared by the members of a linguistic community, it acquires a coercive value of its own. It becomes the "norm" of the group: "You say so!" In this sense, a "realistic" phonology is about concrete mental representations/states that are, however, by definition shared by all the members of a given linguistic community.

If this is correct, each sound change involves three parts (Labov 1994, 2001, Hale 2007): an innovation performed by an individual speaker, the transmission of this innovation from this speaker to other speakers in a linguistic community, and finally, the adoption of this innovative feature in the grammar of the community. Only the first part is properly linguistic; the other two parts are controlled by sociolinguistic or fully social factors.[5] Let us consider the removal of hiatus configurations like the one found in the development from Latin to Romance. Such innovative simplification involves a novel pronunciation: in the present example, the Spanish pronunciation [mu.lyer] instead of Classical Latin [mu.li.er].[6] The next crucial step is the transmission of the innovative pronunciation to other members of the speech community who may adopt it. How this transmission occurs and why is the object of study not of linguistics but of sociology and sociolinguistics (Labov 1994, 2001).[7]

It is important to observe that in the realistic approach proposed here, this transmission must occur between concrete individuals in a real time and a real space. This excludes sudden spreading of changes throughout a community and throughout the vocabulary of this community—such spreading could occur only through divine intervention, something like the reverse of the tower of Babel. In a realistic perspective, there must be a concrete individual who produces the innovative pronunciation (a repair triggered by an MS or the application of a natural rule), and obviously there must be a spatiotemporal contact between the innovator and those who adopt the innovation. The new pronunciation must affect an actual form—ideally, a single form. Other individuals must—consciously or unconsciously—observe this innovative form, parse the innovation, and analyze it as the application of a repair or a rule. Once this is done, they may adopt it and spread it to other forms. At this point, this innovative pronunciation may become associated to certain lexical or grammatical classes. However, if the transmission of the innovation is totally successful, it will spread throughout the words of the language and the speech community and thus become a characteristic feature of the language of this community.[8] Once this occurs, the innovation becomes grammaticalized and thus a feature of the language's grammar. A change in the language's grammar results, and if this change produces phonological alternations, we can speak of adding a rule to the grammar in Halle's (1962) sense. This explains why the formal apparatus of a given synchronic grammar coincides in part with that of the changes leading to it. A synchronic grammar is also the product of the complex crystallization of all the changes leading to it.

Observe that once a process/representation becomes shared as a norm by the members of a community, it becomes arbitrary insofar as its intrinsic properties are fixed in the public representation. The same mechanisms that govern fashion play a role here (see Postal 1967 on this point). In the same way that wearing a certain piece of clothing, which could have at first had a particular motivation, becomes established as representing a certain group identity or social status, when one person's new pronunciation of a word is adopted by other members of a group, the intrinsic motivation that led to the first usage is lost, and the new pronunciation is preserved as a conventional property of group identity. A process that is traditional in this sense can still be transparently motivated by the markedness considerations that led to its origin, but it is at the same time conventional and arbitrary. Being conventional, the process is open to the inclusion of arbitrary statements such as those accounting for the extrinsic ordering of instructions, those involved in idiosyncratic rules, and those accounting for exceptions as argued above. These arbitrary statements have a motivation in history. Still, markedness may play a role in the process, accounting for how it interfaces with the sensorimotor system and thus allowing more efficient and economical derivation of the surface phonological forms of a language—such efficiency and economy being the main goal of synchronic phonology. Anderson's paradox mentioned at the beginning of the chapter is therefore explained.

13.8   Conclusion

To summarize what has been discussed in this chapter: The synchronic phonology of a language is both natural and conventional. It is natural because sound changes are motivated by markedness considerations. An analysis based on considerations of this type has an advantage in terms of economy and efficiency and will tend to be preserved in the language. But phonology is also conventional because of the way in which language is transmitted in a social group. Because of the conventional nature of human language, the effects of idiosyncratic accumulation of historical changes and events can be encoded in a given language's surface shape. These effects introduce arbitrariness into the synchronic phonology of languages: they therefore display exceptions, idiosyncratic rules, and extrinsically ordered processes in derivations, all of which may obscure the natural side of phonology.

Notes

Thanks to Chuck Cairns Morris Halle, Sylvain Bromberger, Ellen Kaisse, Keren Rice, Gabriele Usberti, and the audience at the CUNY Phonology Forum Symposium on Architecture and Representation in Phonology for helpful comments and suggestions.

1. This set of ranked operations can also be viewed as a set of disjunctively ordered rules.

2. See Calabrese 2005 for a more detailed discussion of how repairs are implemented. See the same volume for a discussion of the case in which no other repair operation is available after a crash (this is the case in which so-called blocking takes place).

3. A yer is in fact part of the lexical form of this word, as shown in Calabrese 2005:189ff.

4. Markedness obviously does not need to be the only factor in innovation: mistaken reanalysis of inputs in the transmission process (see Ohala 1981, 1990, 1993, Hale 2007) or even play

can also be factors. Here I am interested in what happens when markedness is a factor. In the model presented here, this type of change is due to the decrease in phonological complexity allowed by the speaker—in other words, to the activation of a markedness constraint.

5. If changes may also occur during transmission owing to mistaken reanalysis of inputs (see Ohala 1981, 1990, 1993, Hale 2007), then transmission is an object of linguistic analysis.

6. Notice that here I am questioning the traditional—Neogrammarian—view of sound change, which assumes that sound changes involve gradual, unnoticed phonetic increments that are later "phonologized" (see Hyman 1975, 2001, Anderson 1985). It is unclear to me what "phonologization" means and how it is supposed to occur. If we assume that morphemes and words are represented in terms of features, any change affecting them must by definition be implemented through a manipulation of features and therefore must be discrete. Thus, I am submitting here that changes are always discrete—phonological *ab origine*. Obviously this is quite a strong statement and much more theoretical work is needed to support it. Still, I do not see much evidence for the Neogrammarian point of view. We do not have evidence for the small variations that eventually should lead to the phonological changes. Undoubtedly there are individual phonetic variations, but how do we know that they have anything to do with actual phonological changes? I think that in stating that changes are gradual, the Neogrammarian scholars were simply influenced by the classical Darwinian framework, which assumed that all changes leading to speciation are gradual and not observable. But as Stephen Jay Gould argues (see Gould and Eldredge 1971, Gould 2002), evolutionary changes may be abrupt: there are discrete changes, jumps in speciation. If repairs are behind many changes, as I would like to argue, we are forced to say that the same is true in the case of phonological changes.

7. But see note 5.

8. If my proposal is on the right track, there should not be an a priori difference between a Neogrammarian type of change that spreads fast and without exceptions throughout the vocabulary of a linguistic community and the "lexical diffusion" type of change spreading slowly word by word (see Labov 1981, 2001, Kiparsky 1988, 1995; see also Chen and Wang 1975, Wang and Cheng 1977, Wang 1979 specifically on lexical diffusion). The same mechanism of transmission should underlie both types of changes: (1) an individual produces an innovation; (2) another individual analyzes the innovation as involving the application of an instruction to manipulate the phonological representation of the innovation; (3) this individual applies the innovative instruction to the phonological representation of other forms; (4) other individuals do the same. It seems to me that the best way to characterize the difference between the Neogrammarian and the "lexical diffusion" type of change is in terms of the epidemiological model of cultural change proposed by Sperber (1995). The innovative instruction is like a virus or germ that can be more or less infectious. Neogrammarian-type changes are caused by "highly infectious" instructions that spread fast, to all individuals and to all possible words, without exceptions. "Lexical diffusion"–type changes are instead caused by "less infectious" instructions that spread slowly, to fewer individuals and fewer words. Kiparsky's (1988, 1995) proposal that Neogrammarian-type changes are postlexical processes involving noncontrastive aspects of representations, whereas "lexical diffusion"–type changes are lexical processes involving contrastive aspects of representations, could be captured by assuming that the former are "highly infectious," whereas the latter are not.

It is fair to say that instructions leading to the simplification of a marked structure should be more infectious than instructions simply leading to "crazy changes."

References

Anderson, Stephen R. 1974. *The organization of phonology*. New York: Academic Press.

Anderson, Stephen R. 1985. *Phonology in the twentieth century*. Chicago: University of Chicago Press.

Archangeli, Diana, and Douglas Pulleyblank. 1994. *Grounded Phonology*. Cambridge, Mass.: MIT Press.

Aronson, Howard. 1968. *Bulgarian inflectional morphology*. The Hague: Mouton.

Bach, Emmon, and Robert T. Harms. 1972. How do languages get crazy rules? In *Linguistic change and generative grammar*, ed. by Robert Stockwell and Ronald Macaulay, 1–21. Bloomington: Indiana University Press.

Barnes, Jonathan. 1997. Bulgarian liquid metathesis and syllabification in Optimality Theory. In *Formal Approaches to Slavic Linguistics 6: The Connecticut Meeting*, ed. by Željko Bošković, Steven Franks, and William Snyder, 38–53. Ann Arbor: University of Michigan, Michigan Slavic Publications.

Bromberger, Sylvain, and Morris Halle. 1992. The ontology of phonology. In Sylvain Bromberger, *On what we know we don't know*, 209–228. Chicago: University of Chicago Press.

Bromberger, Sylvain, and Morris Halle. 1997. The content of phonological signs: A comparison between their use in derivational theories and in optimality theories. In *Derivations and constraints in phonology*, ed. by Iggy M. Roca, 93–122. Oxford:. Oxford University Press.

Bromberger, Sylvain, and Morris Halle. 2000. The ontology of phonology (revised). In *Phonological knowledge: Conceptual and empirical issues*, ed. by Noel Burton-Roberts, Phillip Carr, and Gerard Docherty, 19–37. Oxford: Oxford University Press.

Calabrese, Andrea. 1988. Towards a theory of phonological alphabets. Doctoral dissertation, MIT.

Calabrese, Andrea. 1994. Sievers' Law in Gothic: A synchronic analysis with some notes on its diachronic development. *The Linguistic Review* 11:149–194.

Calabrese, Andrea. 1995. A constraint-based theory of phonological markedness and simplification procedures. *Linguistic Inquiry* 26:373–463.

Calabrese, Andrea. 2000. The fronting of ū and the status of ATR in Romance. In *Phonological theory and the dialects of Italy*, ed. by Lori Repetti, 59–88. Amsterdam: John Benjamins.

Calabrese, Andrea. 2005. *Markedness and economy in a derivational model of phonology*. Berlin: Mouton de Gruyter.

Calabrese, Andrea, and Morris Halle. 1998. Grimm's and Verner's Law: A new perspective. In *Mir Curad: A festschrift in honor of Calvert Watkins*, ed. by Jay Jasanoff, H. Craig Melchert, and Lisi Oliver, 47–62. Innsbrucker Beiträge zur Sprachwissenschaft. Innsbruck: Universität Innsbruck, Institut für Sprachen und Literaturen.

Catford, John C. 1977. *Fundamental problems in phonetics*. Bloomington: Indiana University Press.

Chen, Matthew Y., and William S.-Y. Wang. 1975. Sound change: Actuation and implementation. *Language* 51:255–281.

Chomsky, Noam, and Morris Halle. 1968. *The sound pattern of English*. New York: Harper and Row.

Christdas, Prathima. 1988. The phonology and morphology of Tamil. Doctoral dissertation, Cornell University.

Clements, G. N. 1987. Toward a substantive theory of feature specification. In *Proceedings of North East Linguistic Society (NELS) 18*, ed. by James Blevins and Juli Carter, 79–83. Amherst: University of Massachusetts, Graduate Linguistic Student Association.

Clements, G. N. 2000. In defense of serialism. *The Linguistic Review* 17:181–199.

Dell, François, and Ouae Tangi. 1993. On the vocalization of /r/ in Ath-Sidhar Rifian Berber. *Linguistica Communicatio* 5 (1–2): 5–53.

Derwing, Bruce. 1973. *Transformational grammar as a theory of language acquisition*. Cambridge: Cambridge University Press.

Dressler, Wolfgang. 1974. Diachronic puzzles for Natural Phonology. In *Papers from the Parasession on Natural Phonology*, ed. by Anthony Bruck, Robert Allen Fox, and Michael W. La Galy, 95–116. Chicago: University of Chicago, Chicago Linguistic Society.

Gould, Stephen Jay. 2002. *The structure of evolutionary theory*. Cambridge, Mass.: Harvard University Press.

Gould, Stephen Jay, and Niles Eldredge. 1971. Speciation and punctuated equilibria: An alternative to phyletic gradualism. *Geological Society of America Annual Meeting*. Washington, D.C. Abstracts with program.

Hale, Mark. 2007. *Theory and method in historical linguistics*. Cambridge, Mass.: Blackwell.

Halle, Morris. 1962. Phonology in generative grammar. *Word* 18:54–72. Reprinted in *The structure of language*, ed. by Jerry A. Fodor and Jerrold J. Katz, 89–94. Englewood Cliffs, N.J.: Prentice-Hall, 1964.

Halle, Morris. 1995. Feature geometry and feature spreading. *Linguistic Inquiry* 26:1–46.

Halle, Morris. 2002. *From memory to speech and back: Papers on phonetics and phonology 1954–2002*. Berlin: Mouton de Gruyter.

Halle, Morris, Bert Vaux, and Andrew Wolfe. 2000. On feature spreading and the representation of place of articulation. *Linguistic Inquiry* 31:387–444.

Halle, Morris, and Jean-Roger Vergnaud. 1987. *An essay on stress*. Cambridge, Mass.: MIT Press.

Hauser, Marc, Noam Chomsky, and W. Tecumseh Fitch. 2002. The faculty of language: What is it, who has it, and how did it evolve? *Science* 298:1569–1579.

Hermans, Ben. 1998. Opaque insertion sites in Bulgarian. In *Formal Approaches to Slavic Linguistics 7: The Seattle Meeting*, ed. by Katarzyna Dziwirek, Herbert Coats, and Cynthia M. Vakareliyska, 167–183. Ann Arbor: University of Michigan, Michigan Slavic Publications.

Hyman, Larry. 1975. *Phonology: Theory and analysis*. New York: Holt, Rinehart and Winston.

Hyman, Larry. 2001. On the limits of phonetic determinism in phonology: *NC revisited. In *The role of speech perception in phonology*, ed. by Elizabeth Hume and Keith Johnson, 141–185. San Diego, Calif.: Academic Press.

Jakobson, Roman. 1941. *Kindersprache, Aphasie, und allgemeine Lautgesetze.* Uppsala: Almqvist & Wiksell.

Kenstowicz, Michael. 1994. *Phonology in generative grammar.* Oxford: Blackwell.

Kiparsky, Paul. 1984. On the lexical phonology of Icelandic. In *Nordic prosody III*, ed. by Claes-Christian Elert, Irene Johansson, and Eva Strangert, 135–164. Stockholm: Almqvist & Wiksell.

Kiparsky, Paul. 1988. Phonological change. In *Linguistics: The Cambridge survey*, ed. by Frederick Newmeyer, 1:363–415. Cambridge: Cambridge University Press.

Kiparsky, Paul. 1995. The phonological basis of sound change. In *The handbook of phonological theory*, ed. by John Goldsmith, 640–670. Cambridge, Mass.: Blackwell.

Labov, William. 1981. Resolving the Neogrammarian controversy. *Language* 57:267–308.

Labov, William. 1994. *Principles of linguistic change.* Vol. 1, *Internal factors.* Cambridge, Mass.: Blackwell.

Labov, William. 2001. *Principles of linguistic change.* Vol. 2, *Social factors.* Oxford: Blackwell.

Lambova, Mariana. 2000. The relevance of economy to phonological derivations and representations. Paper presented at the 23rd GLOW Colloquium, University of the Basque Country and University of Deusto.

Loporcaro, Michele. 1988. *Grammatica storica del dialetto di Altamura.* Pisa: Girardini.

Maddieson, Ian. 1984. *Patterns of sounds.* Cambridge: Cambridge University Press.

Maslov, I. 1956. *Ocherk bolgarskoj grammatiki* [An essay on Bulgarian grammar]. Moscow: Izdatel'stvo literatury na inostrannyx jazykax.

McCarthy, John, and Alison Taub. 1992. Review of *The special status of coronals: Internal and external evidence*, ed. by Carole Paradis and Jean-François Prunet. *Phonology* 9:363–370.

Meyer, David, and Roger Schvaneveldt. 1971. Facilitation in recognizing pairs of words: Evidence of a dependence between retrieval operations. *Journal of Experimental Psychology* 90:227–234.

Mohanan, K. P. 1991. On the bases of radical underspecification. *Natural Language and Linguistic Theory* 9:285–326.

Newman, Rochelle, James Sawusch, and Paul Luce. 1997. Lexical neighborhood effects in phonetic processing. *Journal of Experimental Psychology: Human Perception and Performance* 23:873–889.

Noreen, Adolf. 1970. *Altisländische und altnorwegische Grammatik (Laut- und Flexionslehre) unter Berücksichtigung des Urnordischen.* Alabama Linguistic and Philosophic Series 19. University: University of Alabama Press.

Odden, David. 1992. Simplicity of underlying representation as motivation for underspecification. In *Papers in phonology*, ed. by Elizabeth Hume, 85–100. OSU Working Papers in Linguistics 41. Columbus: Ohio State University, Department of Linguistics.

Ohala, John. 1981. The listener as a source of sound change. In *Papers from the Parasession on Language and Behavior*, ed. by Carrie S. Masek, Roberta A. Hendrick, and Mary Frances Miller, 178–203. Chicago: University of Chicago, Chicago Linguistic Society.

Ohala, John. 1990. The phonetics and phonology of assimilation. In *Between grammar and the physics of speech: Papers in laboratory phonology I*, ed. by John Kingston and Mary Beckman, 258–275. Cambridge: Cambridge University Press.

Ohala, John. 1993. The perceptual basis of some sound patterns. In *Phonology and phonetic evidence: Papers in laboratory phonology IV*, ed. by Bruce Connell and Amalia Arvaniti, 87–94. Cambridge: Cambridge University Press.

Oresnik, Janez. 1972. On the epenthesis rule in Modern Icelandic. *Arkiv för Nordisk Filologi* 87:1–32.

Petrova, Rossina. 1994. Prosodic theory and schwa metathesis in Bulgarian. In *Formal Approaches to Slavic Linguistics 2: The MIT Meeting*, ed. by Sergey Avrutin et al., 319–340. Ann Arbor: University of Michigan, Michigan Slavic Publications.

Postal, Paul. 1967. *Aspects of phonological theory*. New York: Harper and Row.

Sagey, Elizabeth. 1986. The representation of features and relations in nonlinear phonology. Doctoral dissertation, MIT.

Scatton, Ernest. 1975. *Bulgarian phonology*. Columbus, Ohio: Slavica.

Schlindwein, Deborah. 1987. P-bearing units: A study of Kinande vowel harmony. In *Proceedings of North East Linguistic Society (NELS) 17*, ed. by Joyce McDonough and Bernadette Plunkett, 115–150. Amherst: University of Massachusetts, Graduate Linguistic Student Association.

Sperber, Dan. 1995. *Explaining culture: A naturalistic approach*. Oxford: Blackwell.

Stampe, David. 1972. A dissertation on Natural Phonology. Doctoral dissertation, University of Chicago.

Steriade, Donca. 1987. Redundant values. In *Proceedings of Chicago Linguistic Society (CLS) 23*. Vol. 2, *Parasession on Autosegmental and Metrical Phonology*, ed. by Anna Bosch, Barbara Need, and Eric Schiller, 339–363. Chicago: University of Chicago, Chicago Linguistic Society.

Steriade, Donca. 1995. Underspecification and markedness. In *The handbook of phonological theory*, ed. by John Goldsmith, 114–174. Cambridge, Mass.: Blackwell.

Stojanov, Stojan. 1980. *Gramatika na bâlgarskija knizhoven ezik* [Grammar of Standard Bulgarian]. 3rd ed. Sofia: Sofia University Press.

Tilkov, Dimitâr, Stojan Stojanov, and Konstantin Popov, eds. 1982. *Gramatika na sâvremennija bâlgarski knizhoven ezik 1: Fonetika* [Grammar of Modern Standard Bulgarian 1: Phonetics]. Sofia: Bâlgarska Akademija na Naukite (BAN).

Trubetzkoy, Nikolai S. 1939. Grundzüge der Phonologie. Travaux du cercle linguistique de Prague VII. Reprinted, Göttingen: Vandenhoeck und Ruprecht, 1967. Citations from the English translation by Christiane A. M. Baltaxe. Berkeley and Los Angeles: University of California Press, 1969.

Vaux, Bert. 1998. *The phonology of Armenian*. Oxford: Oxford University Press.

Vaux, Bert. 2000. Disharmony and derived transparency in Uyghur vowel harmony. In *Proceedings of North East Linguistic Society (NELS) 30*, ed. by Masako Hirotani, Andries Coetzee, Nancy Hall, and Ji-yung Kim, 671–698. Amherst: University of Massachusetts, Graduate Linguistic Student Association.

Vaux, Bert. 2003. Syllabification in Armenian, Universal Grammar, and the lexicon. *Linguistic Inquiry* 34:91–125.

Wang, William S.-Y. 1979. Language change: A lexical perspective. *Annual Review of Anthropology* 8:353–371.

Wang, William S.-Y., and Chin-Chuan Cheng. 1977. Implementation of phonological change. In *The lexicon in phonological change*, ed. by William S.-Y. Wang, 86–100. The Hague: Mouton.

Watkins, Calvert. 1993. Il Proto-Indo-Europeo: Comparazione e ricostruzione. In *Le lingue indoeuropee*, ed. by A. Giacalone and P. Ramat. Bologna: Il Mulino.

Zec, Draga. 1987. Bulgarian ə epenthesis: A case for moraic structure. In *Proceedings of North East Linguistic Society (NELS) 18*, ed. by James Blevins and Juli Carter, 553–567. Amherst: University of Massachusetts, Graduate Linguistic Student Association.

14 Comments on Diachrony in Calabrese's "Markedness Theory versus Phonological Idiosyncrasies in a Realistic Model of Language"

Ellen M. Kaisse

There is very little in Calabrese's excellent chapter with which I would take issue. My disagreements all center on his views on Neogrammarian sound change and lexical diffusion, which are presented in section 13.8 under the rubric of "Historical Changes."

As the reader knows, one of Calabrese's overall goals in this chapter is to present a balanced, "realistic" view of phonology—one in which the natural and the conventional both hold a place. When he turns his attention to diachronic matters, he therefore takes the unexceptionable view that sound change involves both natural and conventional components. Seen within his theory of markedness and repairs, the natural portion of a sound change involving markedness consists of an individual's activation of a markedness constraint and a concomitant application of a repair that was previously not needed. The conventional portion of change consists of the transmission of the change and its adoption by the rest of the speech community. Once the change is grammaticalized via this adoption, it may (but need not) come to include nonnatural features that speakers adopt because the community says to, not because they are inherently natural. Thus, not all phonology will be natural.

So far, so good. But Calabrese takes a step in this argument whose motivation eludes me. He says that ideally the individual speaker's change and the community's adoption of that change will be initiated with an individual word whose pronunciation others copy, and will proceed through the community word by word. For Calabrese, then, lexical diffusion is the primary method of historical change. And lexical diffusion is by its nature phonetically abrupt (Wang and Cheng 1977). Gradient, incremental phonetic developments, the stuff of Neogrammarian theory, are not, he says, the mechanism of sound change. Gradient variability may exist, yes, but Calabrese denies that it is the method by which language change is effected. Rather, all changes are discrete and treat the word rather than the sound as the unit of change. Neogrammarian change is only apparent and probably never primary. It is the result of lexical diffusion that has extended through the entire lexicon.

I take issue with this claim for several reasons. First, I do not think that it reflects the empirical state of the art, as it was arrived at, for instance, in Labov's (1994) critical distillation. Second, it ignores the theoretical motivation for the two kinds of sound changes distinguished by Kiparsky (1988, 1995), which I find compelling. And third, I do not see a clear connection between Calabrese's claim here and his more general and persuasive claim, namely, that phonology has conventional and natural aspects. Language change, it seems to me, can be perfectly compatible with that view without insisting that lexical diffusion be the primary mechanism of change.

Let us begin with the question of gradualness. In note 6, Calabrese says:

I do not see much evidence for the "Neogrammarian" point of view. We do not have evidence for the small variations that eventually should lead to the phonological changes. Undoubtedly there are individual phonetic variations, but how do we know that they have anything to do with actual phonological changes? ... If repairs are behind many changes, as I would like to argue, we are also forced to say that the same is true in the case of phonological changes.

I find this statement puzzling enough that I suspect I do not understand what Calabrese intends here. Are not the hundreds of pages published by Labov, by Shuy, Wolfram, and Riley (1966), and by many other authors on the Northern Cities, Martha's Vineyard, and Philadelphia vowel shifts precisely long-term documentations of gradual sound changes leading to wholesale movements in the vowel space? And those variations are neither individual nor random, but are constrained, rule-governed, and socially significant. We will look at some characteristics of the Northern Cities Shift in a moment. But first let us look at the likely motivation for Calabrese's anti-Neogrammarian stance.

The key, as I understand it, is that phonological change is due to repairs and that Calabrese conceives of repairs as by their nature categorical. In note 6, we read that "if ... morphemes ... are represented in terms of features, any change affecting them must by definition be implemented through a manipulation of features and therefore must be discrete." An illustrative example given comes from section 13.7, where a marking statement against hiatus became active in the development of Spanish from Latin. Latin [mu.li.er] thus became intolerable and was repaired to [mu.lyer].

But why could a repair not begin in a gradual and variable fashion, with the high vowel gradiently shortened, especially in fast speech, in more intimate speech settings, and among younger speakers, until at last it was interpreted phonologically as a glide rather than a short syllable nucleus? This is the sort of situation I found in studies on hiatus in Modern Greek a generation ago (Kaisse 1977). Failure to resolve hiatus was often an option, especially in slow or monitored speech, but more often, speakers would shorten a high vowel, sometimes to the extent of desyllabifying it, sometimes not. Speaking more directly to the Latin-to-Spanish example, Mercado (1981) found the same gradient treatment of high vowels in hiatus between words in

Puerto Rican Spanish. Just as we have variable and gradient phonetic implementation of what eventually come to be regular phonological rules, could we not have similar implementation of what eventually come to be exceptionless, categorical repairs? Similarly, must a markedness statement become activated in an all-or-nothing fashion? Could it not be active in certain less formal styles, among younger speakers, and gradually become inviolable? I do not see the necessary connection between Calabrese's view of the architecture of phonology and his rejection of Neogrammarian sound change as a primary mechanism.

Let us look more closely at the empirical evidence for Neogrammarian sound change. Labov (1981, 1994) documents Neogrammarian sound change in progress (as well as lexical diffusion in progress), mainly through documenting "apparent time" in instrumental analyses of speakers of different age groups. Chapters 15–18 of Labov 1994 are devoted to an extremely detailed discussion of many of the cases supporting Neogrammarian sound change and many ostensibly supporting lexical diffusion. His conclusion, to the extent that it may be stated in a few words, is found on page 501:

[Lexical diffusion] is far overshadowed by phonetic conditioning. There is no evidence here [i.e., even in dialect geography, on which rested all the early claims that each word has its own history] that lexical diffusion is the fundamental mechanism of sound change.... Once the data of dialect geography are examined with the appropriate mathematical tools, they are thoroughly consistent with the Neogrammarian view that sound change affects word classes and phonemes.

Examining only one of Labov's and others' elaborately documented cases, consider Northern Cities Shift, "one of the most vigorous sound changes now in progress in the United States" (Labov 1994:178). The cities in question run in a band from northern New York State (including Rochester and Buffalo) through Detroit, to Chicago. The development of this fronting and raising movement of /æ/ and the concomitant fronting of /a/ to take its place has been documented across both real and apparent time. By sampling over the course of several years and by sampling speakers of different ages at a single time, Labov finds ample evidence for gradient factors in the movement of /æ/: a following nasal consonant produces the most raised, fronted allophones (e.g., [iᵊnd] 'and'); a preceding obstruent-initial cluster inhibits raising and fronting (e.g., [klɛᵊsifay] 'classify'); and so forth. Speakers from larger cities are ahead of those from rural areas in the vowel shift. In fact, younger, urban speakers fail to show any allophones of /æ/ in the low front position—all have moved up to mid or high and are followed by a central glide. In the meantime, /a/ has shifted to the position formerly occupied by /æ/, so that speakers of other dialects may think a Northern cities speaker is saying *lacks* when he or she intends *locks*. No lexical conditioning is found; that is, vowels front and raise according to their phonetic environment, not word by word.

In addition to analyzing ongoing changes in American English, Labov reevaluates some of the most celebrated cases that were originally put forward as examples of lexical diffusion. Serious challenges had already been brought to Wang and Cheng's (1977) treatment of Chaozhou tone split, which even Wang himself later recognized to be due to dialect borrowing rather than lexical diffusion. Labov reanalyzes the shift in Atalyalic (a group of Austronesian languages of Taiwan) from final labials to velars. He shows that it is not a case of lexical diffusion, as it was previously argued to be, but of variable, fine phonetic conditioning of a sound change. As the above quotation from Labov indicates, few genuine cases of lexical diffusion are left standing.

We see, then, that lexical diffusion did not emerge as a common mechanism of change either in Labov's own work or in his survey and reanalysis of the work of others. Let us turn now to the best explanation given to date for why there should be two apparent types of sound change, the common Neogrammarian type and the more unusual lexical diffusion. Kiparsky (1988) conjectures that lexical diffusion comes from a change in a lexical rule while Neogrammarian change is a change in (or, I imagine, an addition of) a postlexical rule.[1] Rules gradually move up through the grammar, becoming more opaque, grammaticalized, and categorical.

I reproduce in (1) the chart of counterposed characteristics of Neogrammarian versus lexically diffused changes that Labov compiled and that Kiparsky argues were predicted by the theory of Lexical Phonology.

(1) *Neogrammarian versus lexically diffused changes (from Labov 1981, quoted in Kiparsky 1988:398)*

	"Neogrammarian" change	*Lexical diffusion*
Discrete	no	yes
Phonetic conditioning	fine	rough
Lexical exceptions	no	yes
Grammatical conditioning	no	yes
Social affect	yes	no
Predictable	yes	no
Learnable	yes	no
Categorized	no	yes
Dictionary entries (neutralizing)	1 (no)	2 (yes)

Kiparsky's representative example from Labov's work is the Neogrammarian Northern Cities /æ/-tensing I discussed above. To exemplify a lexically diffusing sound change, Kiparsky chooses to analyze Labov's data on Philadelphia /æ/-tensing, with some additions of his own. This lexically conditioned split of */æ/ is one of the most robust cases remaining after Labov's dissection of the classical lexical diffusion examples, one on which Labov and his students worked for many years.

Kiparsky's central point is that the two kinds of sound change are a consequence of the fact that there are two kinds of rules: lexical and postlexical. Postlexical rules are exceptionless, have no grammatical conditioning, and can be gradient and non-discrete. Though Kiparsky does not say so explicitly, this kind of postlexical rule is what we might well call a phonetic rule. Changes in such rules of course look like Neogrammarian sound change. However, once a rule has become lexical, it can have exceptions and must be categorical, not gradient. In Philadelphia, unlike the Northern Cities, there already was a tensed, raised vowel in the system (the output of the old British English broad /ɑ/ rule), so when the raising sound change was acquired, it merged with the lexical rule. Kiparsky then shows that the Philadelphia tensing rule has the five characteristics of a lexical rule: among them, it is sensitive to the morphological structure of a word, it does not occur in words belonging to non-lexical categories (no tensing in the auxiliary verb *can*, but tensing in the noun *can*), and it has exceptions—the hallmark of a lexically diffusing change.[2] This explains the "unlearnability" of the rule. Payne (1976) found that children who moved late to a Philadelphia suburb were able to acquire many phonological characteristics of the dialect, including the fronting of /uw/, which is proceeding gradiently across all words. But they could not acquire the arbitrary splits in the lexicon, such as *mad* with a tense vowel and *sad* with a lax vowel.

Since lexical rules tend to be chronologically old processes in the history of a language, while postlexical rules are typically the newer rules of the phonology, Calabrese's claim that changes start as changes in the pronunciation of an individual word and spread through the lexicon as they spread to new speakers requires us to believe that most sound changes are not additions and expansions of newer rules, but changes in lexical rules. But this is not how I read the testimony of historical sociolinguistics.

More recent work on the phonetics-phonology interface also supports the idea that gradient processes and phonological rules are made of the same stuff. Calabrese states (note 6) that "we do not have evidence for the small variations that eventually should lead to the phonological changes." If the Labovian evidence is not sufficient, consider Flemming's (2001) demonstration of the profound crosslinguistic resemblances between phonological rules and phonetic processes. To mention only one of his many examples, the phonological, neutralizing shortening of vowels in closed syllables in Turkish is strikingly like phonetic closed-syllable shortening in Finnish. The latter applies to both phonemically short and phonemically long vowels without neutralizing the contrast between them. To judge by Flemming's catalogue of processes, there hardly seem to be any phonological rules that do not have close parallels in well-attested phonetic rules.[3] True, authors cannot or do not always take the step of tying earlier variable states of a language to later, fully phonologized ones, but I believe ample cases can be found in the sociolinguistic literature.

Notes

1. Kiparsky (1995) extends this proposal, describing lexical diffusion as the analogical extension of an already established lexical rule. In later work on stratal Optimality Theory, Kiparsky maintains the distinction between lexical and postlexical strata. However, he does not discuss how the insights the Lexical Phonology and Morphology model provided into the characteristics of lexical and postlexical processes might be transferred into a constraint-based theory, let alone how stratal Optimality Theory might account for the two types of sound change.

2. Note 8 of Calabrese's chapter is a response to my remarks presented at the CUNY Phonology Forum Symposium on Architecture and Representation in Phonology in 2004. In that note, he allows that Neogrammarian change may exist, but that it is simply a more rapid, infectious version of the social adaptation of an individual change, while lexical diffusion involves a slower, less infectious spread. But I do not see that this concession helps us understand why postlexical rules should be subject to rapid spread while lexical ones are not.

3. It should be noted that Flemming does not present his examples as instances of grammaticalization. Rather, he argues that both apparently phonetic and apparently phonological processes are all part of the phonology of a language and should not be stated in two components of the grammar.

References

Flemming, Edward. 2001. Scalar and categorical phenomena in a unified model of phonetics and phonology. *Phonology* 18:7–44.

Kaisse, Ellen M. 1977. Hiatus in Modern Greek. Doctoral dissertation, Harvard University.

Kiparsky, Paul. 1988. Phonological change. In *Linguistics: The Cambridge survey*, ed. by Frederick Newmeyer, 1:363–415. Cambridge: Cambridge University Press.

Kiparsky, Paul. 1995. The phonological basis of sound change. In *The handbook of phonological theory*, ed. by John Goldsmith, 640–670. Cambridge, Mass.: Blackwell.

Labov, William. 1981. Resolving the Neogrammarian controversy. *Language* 57:267–308.

Labov, William. 1994. *Principles of linguistic change*. Vol. 1, *Internal factors*. Cambridge, Mass.: Blackwell.

Mercado, Ismael. 1981. Vowel sandhi in a Spanish dialect. Master's thesis, University of Washington.

Payne, Arvilla. 1976. The acquisition of the phonological system of a second dialect. Doctoral dissertation, University of Pennsylvania.

Shuy, Roger, Walt Wolfram, and William Riley. 1966. *A study of social dialects in Detroit.* Final report, Project 6–134. Washington, D.C.: Office of Education.

Wang, William S.-Y., and Chin-Chuan Cheng. 1977. Implementation of phonological change. In *The lexicon in phonological change*, ed. by William S.-Y. Wang, 86–100. The Hague: Mouton.

15 Nuancing Markedness: A Place for Contrast

Keren Rice

15.1 Overview of "Markedness Theory versus Phonological Idiosyncrasies in a Realistic Model of Phonology"

Calabrese (this volume), in an elaboration and refinement of Calabrese 2005, presents an impressive overview of what he terms a "realistic theory of phonology." Such a theory embodies several properties. First, and crucially, he views a realistic theory as one that meets an important criterion set out by Bromberger and Halle (2000:21): "Phonology is about concrete mental events and states that occur in real time, real space, have causes, have effects, are finite in number." This theory treats economy as a response to scarcity of time and resources and markedness as a theory of linguistic costs. It is, overall, Calabrese argues in his 2005 book, a Saussurean view of phonology.

This view of phonology encompasses several subcomponents, all of which find their congeners in the theory laid out in *The Sound Pattern of English* (Chomsky and Halle 1968): derivations, economy, rules and constraints as procedural instructions, and markedness theory. In these brief remarks, I focus on substance and markedness, two closely related components of the theory, considering them with respect to contrast.

15.2 Substance and Markedness in Phonology

The roles of substance and markedness in phonological theory are somewhat controversial. In Calabrese's work, substance and markedness both have key roles to play; however, others have argued that substance is not important in phonological theory (e.g., Hale and Reiss 2000) and that phonological markedness is subject to variation (e.g., Rice 2002) and should not be considered part of phonological theory (e.g., Hume and Tserdanelis 2002).

Hale and Reiss (2000) take a strong position on the role of substance. For instance, they assert that "the substance of phonological entities is *never* relevant to how they are treated by the computational system" (Hale and Reiss 2000:162; emphasis original). Explicitly in his book and implicitly in his contribution to this volume, Calabrese contradicts this position, arguing that there is no evidence for the existence of these pure forms other than as abstractions in a mathematical world.

Referring to markedness constraints such as *DORSAL, *VOICE that are commonly found in Optimality Theory (OT) analyses, Hale and Reiss (1998:7) state that "positing the type of universal substantive constraints found in the OT literature adds nothing to the explanatory power of phonological theory." Calabrese takes a rather different position on markedness, arguing that it is a core component of phonological theory, with markedness constraints playing an active role in ruling out complex actions.

15.3 Substance and Markedness in Sound Change

What are the expectations of a theory in which substance and universal markedness constraints play an active role? Calabrese makes clear predictions about sound change due to markedness, stating (p. 296) that they "involve a decrease in the complexity allowed in a language; representations must then be adjusted in order to be articulated. In phonological terms, this means that certain MSs [marking statements] that were deactivated become active and that a repair adjusts the representations that have thus become disallowed, or that a natural rule that was deactivated becomes active again. Under this interpretation, a sound change is an innovative repair. This innovative repair is then grammaticalized and becomes part of the grammar of a linguistic community."

A major implication of this view is that substance will play an important role in sound change, with the presence of a more marked segment implying the presence of the less marked one. But is this always the case? In what follows, I examine two instances where marked segments have been introduced into an inventory, presumably involving deactivation of a markedness statement. A new contrast is introduced in one case, but not in the other.

Consider first the introduction of the front rounded vowel /ü/ into the inventory of Spoken Manchu and Xibe, Manchu languages of China. The following analysis is drawn from work by Zhang (1996). Zhang proposes the inventory in (1) for Written Manchu, the language he takes to be the direct parent of Spoken Manchu and Xibe:

(1) *Written Manchu vowel inventory*

    i   u

          ʊ

     ə

     a   ɔ

The inventories of Spoken Manchu and Xibe are given in (2).

(2) *Spoken Manchu   Xibe*
   i   ü   u   i   ü   u
   ε   a   o   ε   ö a o

The inventories differ in several ways; what is critical for the discussion here is that Written Manchu has no high front rounded vowel, while Spoken Manchu and Xibe do. Some cognates are given in (3) and (4).

(3) *Written Manchu   Spoken Manchu*
   niŋggun   nüŋŋun   'six'   (Zhang 1996:111)
   tugi   tügu   'cloud'   (Zhang 1996:111)

(4) *Written Manchu   Xibe*
   niŋggun   nüŋun   'six'   (Zhang 1996:124)
   ʃumin   cümin   'deep'   (Zhang 1996:124)

In both Spoken Manchu and Xibe, the high front rounded vowel derives historically from a process of vowel harmony, whereby the first vowel of a word became high front rounded when the first two vowels of the word were /i/ and /u/, in either order. Note that this harmony is not a synchronic process in either language. In Spoken Manchu, /ü/ is pretty much restricted to the first syllable of the word, where it contrasts with all other vowels in appearing before both /i/ and /u/ (Zhang 1996:114). In Xibe, /ü/ contrasts with all other vowels when the following vowel is /i/ and with all vowels except /ε/ when the following vowel is /u/ (Zhang 1996:128). There is thus every indication that this vowel has become part of the system of Spoken Manchu and Xibe.

This change adds to the complexity of the system in introducing a new sound, a front rounded vowel. Such a change runs counter to Calabrese's proposal, which allows only sound changes that decrease the complexity found in a language. When this change is examined with greater care, however, one can see why it might have occurred. Zhang (1996) argues that the change is motivated: it accompanied a shift of stress to the first syllable of the word. Concomitant with this was an increase in the allowed segmental complexity of the first syllable, presumably brought about by deactivating a markedness statement. Such a change is not likely a true counterexample to Calabrese's proposal, as the circumstances under which the front rounded vowel is found are very limited. It nevertheless shows the complexity of sound change, and that a simple statement that sound changes are due to innovative repair is insufficient to account for the subtleties of sound change, as Calabrese recognizes in his chapter.

The next example of the introduction of a front rounded vowel illustrates another way in which front rounded vowels can become part of a system. Some dialects of

South Slavey, an Athapaskan language of northern Canada (Rice 1989), have introduced such a vowel. The standard South Slavey vowel inventory is shown in (5)
(Rice 1989:39–43).

(5) *South Slavey vowel inventory*

    i   u   (plus nasalized vowels)

    e   o

      a

The examples in (6) show forms from two dialects (examples from Rice 1989:41); I
label one *conservative* and the other *innovative*.

(6)   *Conservative*   *Innovative*
    a. de-h-su̱ gha   de-h-sṳ gha   'I will pull it out'
    b. g-ú̱-h-ʔǫ   g-ǘ-h-ʔǫ   'she/he found it'
    c. hu̱-ne-h-ch'oh   hṳ-ne-h-ch'oh   'I am angry'
    d. m-u̱-de-ndi   m-ṳ-de-ndi   'it is easy'

Notice the innovation: where the conservative dialect has a high back rounded vowel
[u], the innovative dialect has replaced this with a high front rounded vowel [ü]. This
replacement occurred in both stems (6a) and prefixes (6b–d).

    Taking Calabrese's description of sound change into account, this change seems to
represent a true counterexample to the claim that sound changes are due to a decrease in the complexity allowed in a language: the high front rounded vowel is considered to be more complex than the high back rounded vowel that it replaces in
the innovative dialect. Why might such a change occur, introducing a clearly more
marked element? Calabrese discusses a somewhat similar case, in the Altamura dialect of Italian, where [+ATR] rounded vowels are fronted while [−ATR] rounded
vowels are not. For this case, he proposes that back advanced tongue root vowels
are marked, triggering a repair strategy that deletes the feature [+back], leading to
fronting of the back round vowel. While such an argument might work for the shift
in South Slavey, there is no evidence that the feature [ATR] plays any role in the
grammar of this language. It thus appears here that substance truly does not matter,
as Hale and Reiss argue; nor does markedness appear to play a role.

    Consider the nature of the South Slavey vowel inventory, a prototypical five-vowel
system. The substitution of [ü] for [u] involves no fundamental change in the South
Slavey vowel system; the two dialects differ only by the phonetic realization of the
high rounded vowel as back or front. What we see is a change that is likely motivated by nonphonological factors, where the phonological contrasts underdetermine
the exact phonetic output. The replacement of [ü] by [u] could have a variety of
sources—one possibility is that it is motivated by social factors, another that it represents the first stage in merging the high vowels to a front vowel (as occurred in the

closely related language Dogrib). Basically, in the absence of a contrastive front rounded vowel in the system, the high rounded vowel is free to vary between front and back.

One might draw two conclusions from this discussion of front rounded vowels. First, it appears that phonological change can involve the deactivation of markedness statements as well as their activation, suggesting that, as Hale and Reiss argue, substance is not important in phonology. Second, it appears that universal substantive markedness is not as important a concept in phonological theory as has often been argued, in that markedness seems to play no role in the phonetic realization of the South Slavey vowel inventory.

15.4   Substance, Markedness, and Contrast in Phonology

In the remainder of this response, I examine the roles of substance and markedness in grammar, asking if they can truly be dispensed with, as the discussion of historical change might indicate. My answer, developed more fully in Rice, to appear (see also Rice 1999, 2002, 2007), is that in the absence of contrast universal substantive markedness basically plays no role, and that the substance of phonological entities is, as Hale and Reiss say, not relevant to how a phonological entity is treated by the computational system. However, as contrasts in an inventory increase, both substance and markedness become relevant in interesting ways.

I begin by considering the laryngeal realizations of word-final obstruents. Although it is often assumed that under neutralization, obstruents will be realized as voiceless unaspirated (e.g., Lombardi 1994), a language survey suggests this generalization is not valid. Word-final consonants can indeed be realized as voiceless unaspirated, a common pattern. However, they are also realized as voiceless aspirated, glottalized, or even voiced, depending on the language. Examples of languages with each of these properties are shown in (7); if a language is listed in more than one row, within-language variation occurs.

(7) *Word-final obstruents: Laryngeal realizations under neutralization*

T	T^h	T'	D	Languages
x				Ahtna (after VV), German, Jamul Tiipay, Kiowa, Kisar, Maidu, Sekani, Wiyot
	x			Ahtna (after VV), German, Klamath, Koyukon, Misantla Totonac (San Marcos dialect), Takelma, Tunica, Zoque
		x		Acehnese, Dumi, Limbu, Misantla Totonac (Yecuatla dialect), Nenets
			x	Lezgian (certain classes), Somali
		x	x	?

In the case of laryngeal features, one might be tempted to say that aspiration and glottalization are simply release features and that the crosslinguistic variation illustrated in (7) is not relevant for phonology. When one examines possible places of articulation found in word-final position, however, similar facts are found. (8) shows languages with systems that have labial, coronal, and velar stops. In conditions where place of articulation is neutralized—word-final position is illustrated here—any place of articulation is possible, depending on language.

(8) *Word-final stops: No contrast for place of articulation*

p	*t*	*k*	*Languages*
x			Godoberi, Nimburan, Lhasa Tibetan
	x		Alawa, Finnish
		x	Fuzhou, East Finnmark Saami (Karasjok dialect)

While it is statistically more likely that coronal stops will appear in word-final position, nevertheless languages are found in which only labials or only velars can occur. Thus, crosslinguistic variation in neutralization positions seems to be the norm.

What might such crosslinguistic variation be due to? First, it could possibly arise from structural considerations. For instance, it might be the case that one class of sounds occurs in a rhyme, another in a coda, and still another in the onset of an empty-headed syllable. While such an analysis is possible, I believe it is unlikely that it can account for the variation in languages presented here. Other factors might also play a role. Different languages might make different choices because they place different weights on factors such as ease of articulation and perceptual salience. Historical factors could be involved (see, e.g., Hyman 2001), as could social factors. Substance and markedness simply do not seem to be important under conditions of neutralization since any member of a feature class is possible in a particular position crosslinguistically under this condition, albeit with very different frequencies (for more detail, see Rice 1999, 2002, 2007, to appear). Taken by themselves, such facts point in favor of Hale and Reiss's position that substance has no explanatory role in phonological theory and that markedness constraints add nothing to the theory's explanatory power. On their own, these facts likewise provide an argument against Calabrese's position that phonology involves substance and that markedness plays a critical role. Before we reject substance and markedness as important factors in phonological theory, however, it is worthwhile to consider some further characteristics of elements that are considered to be unmarked.

In work on semantic markedness, Battistella (1990:27) compares properties of marked and unmarked elements: "Indeterminateness refers to the semantic criterion that marked elements are characteristically specific and determinate in meaning while the opposed unmarked elements are characteristically indeterminate, a factor that follows from the definition of semantic markedness as having both a general meaning and a meaning opposite from that of the marked term." This claim that unmarked elements are characteristically indeterminate in semantics is echoed in work by Avery and myself on unmarked elements in phonology (e.g., Rice 1996, 1999, 2002, 2007, to appear, Rice and Avery 1995) as well as by many other authors. Avery and I argue that in the absence of contrast, the phonetic realization of a segment is phonologically underdetermined; see also Dresher 2003 for similar claims. Thus, in the absence of contrast, substance and markedness appear to play no role in phonology. The neutralization facts suggest that this claim is correct; it is also borne out when we look at assimilation.

One common diagnostic for markedness comes from asymmetric assimilation (e.g., Rice 1999, 2002, 2007, Rice and Avery 2004). In this type of assimilation, given elements F_1, F_2, and F_3, F_1 can be said to be unmarked with respect to F_2 and F_3 if F_1 assimilates to F_2 and F_3, and if F_2 and F_3 fail to assimilate to F_1. Consider place-of-articulation assimilation when there is no contrast with respect to place features of the target. Under such conditions, any place of articulation is subject to assimilation. Some of the languages that show this for nasal assimilation are listed in (9).

(9) *Target of assimilation*   *Language*
     Labial   Manam dialect, Sentani dialect
     Coronal   Spanish (Castilian), Harar Oromo preverbs
     Velar   Japanese, Selayarese

Again we see that the substance of the phonological entity is not relevant to how it is treated by the computational system: whether the target consonant is labial, coronal, or velar in place of articulation, it functions as an assimilation target when it is the only segment of its manner available in the target position, regardless of its place of articulation.

Now consider place-of-articulation assimilation as the contrasts in place of articulation in the target position increase. The facts are sketched briefly in (10); see Rice and Avery 2004 and Rice, to appear, for more in-depth discussion of the relationship between assimilation targets and markedness.

(10) *Targets of nasal place assimilation*
      a. No place contrast in nasal target:
          any place of articulation can be the target of assimilation.
      b. Two-way place contrast in nasal target:
          either place can be the target of assimilation.
      c. Labial plus distinctive coronals in nasal target:
          labial is the target of assimilation.
      d. Larger contrast, no placeless segment, no coronal contrasts:
          coronal is the target of assimilation.

(10) illustrates that a theory that abandons substance totally is no more empirically adequate than one that embraces substance indiscriminately. On the one hand, substance effects are absent in the absence of contrast: neutralization illustrates that any feature of a class can emerge in a position of neutralization; assimilation targets show that in the absence of contrast, any possible place of articulation can serve as a target. However, the facts change as inventories grow: for instance, (10c)—pointing out that when an inventory includes labials and distinctive coronals, only the labial can be the target of neutralization—illustrates that substance in the form of contrasts does play a role in phonological theory.

15.5   Conclusions

What is the lesson here? It appears that a position somewhere between that argued by Calabrese and that espoused by Hale and Reiss is required. Substance has little, if any, role to play in the absence of contrast: more marked segments can arise out of language change (as in the creation of [ü] in South Slavey), any feature of a class can arise as a result of neutralization (laryngeal neutralization, place-of-articulation neutralization in word-final position), and any feature of a class can be submerged in assimilation. Languages are thus rife with exceptions to markedness statements and an apparent lack of appeal to substance. However, as the contrasts in an inventory increase, substance increases in importance and, likewise, crosslinguistic markedness as measured by possible assimilation targets emerges. Thus, added to Calabrese's list of essential components in phonological theory is an additional property, contrast. When the role of contrast in phonology goes unrecognized, languages appear to admit a wide range of idiosyncrasy in terms of both diachrony and synchrony, idiosyncrasy that yields to systematicity when the critical role of contrast is understood.

Note

This work is supported by funding from the Social Sciences and Humanities Research Council of Canada to Elan Dresher and Keren Rice and by Keren Rice's Canada Research Chair in Linguistics and Aboriginal Studies. Thank you to the participants at the CUNY Phonology Forum Symposium on Architecture and Representations in Phonology and to the students at the University of Toronto and to Andrea Calabrese for thoughtful discussion.

References

Reference works for languages mentioned in this chapter are marked with *.

*Anceaux, Johannes Cornelius. 1965. *The Nimboran language*. The Hague: Martinus Nijhoff.

*Barker, Muhammad Abd-al-Rahman. 1964. *Klamath grammar*. Berkeley and Los Angeles: University of California Press.

Battistella, Edwin. 1990. *Markedness: The evaluative superstructure of language*. Albany, N.Y.: SUNY Press.

Bromberger, Sylvain, and Morris Halle. 2000. The ontology of phonology (revised). In *Phonological knowledge: Conceptual and empirical issues*, ed. by Noel Burton-Roberts, Phillip Carr, and Gerard Docherty, 19–37. Oxford: Oxford University Press.

Calabrese, Andrea. 2005. *Markedness and economy in a derivational model of phonology*. Berlin: Mouton de Gruyter.

Chomsky, Noam, and Morris Halle. 1968. *The sound pattern of English*. New York: Harper and Row.

*Christensen, John, and Sylvia Christensen. 1992. Kisar phonology. In *Phonological studies in four languages of Maluku*, ed. by Donald A. Burquest and Wyn D. Laidig, 33–65. University of Texas, Arlington and Pattimura University: Summer Institute of Linguistics.

*Cowan, Hendrik Karel Jan. 1965. *Grammar of the Sentani language*. The Hague: Martinus Nijhoff.

*Denwood, Philip. 1999. *Tibetan*. Amsterdam: John Benjamins.

Dresher, B. Elan. 2003. Contrast and asymmetry in inventories. In *Asymmetry in grammar*. Vol. 2, *Morphology, phonology, acquisition*, ed. by Anna Maria Di Sciullo, 237–259. Amsterdam: John Benjamins.

*Driem, George van. 1987. *A grammar of Limbu*. Berlin: Mouton de Gruyter.

*Driem, George van. 1993. *A grammar of Dumi*. Berlin: Mouton de Gruyter.

*Durie, Mark. 1985. *A grammar of Acehnese: On the basis of a dialect of North Aceh*. Dordrecht: Foris.

*Eulenberg, Alexander. 1996. *Godoberi*. Munich: Lincom Europa.

*Haas, Mary R. 1941. Tunica. In *Handbook of American Indian languages*, vol. 4. New York: Augustin Publishers.

Hale, Mark, and Charles Reiss. 1998. Some more misconceptions about Optimality Theory. Ms., Concordia University.

Hale, Mark, and Charles Reiss. 2000. "Substance abuse" and "dysfunctionalism": Current trends in phonology. *Linguistic Inquiry* 31:157–169.

*Hargus, Sharon. 1988. *The Lexical Phonology of Sekani*. New York: Garland.

*Harris, James. 1984. Theories of phonological representation and nasal consonants in Spanish. In *Papers from the XIIth Linguistic Symposium on Romance Languages*, ed. by Philip Baldi, 153–168. Amsterdam: John Benjamins.

Hume, Elizabeth, and George Tserdanelis. 2002. Labial unmarkedness in Sri Lankan Portuguese Creole. *Phonology* 19:441–458.

Hyman, Larry. 2001. On the limits of phonetic determinism in phonology: *NC revisited. In *The role of speech perception in phonology*, ed. by Elizabeth Hume and Keith Johnson, 141–185. San Diego, Calif.: Academic Press.

*Jessen, Michael, and Catherine Ringen. 2002. Laryngeal features in German. *Phonology* 19:189–218.

*Jetté, Jules, and Eliza Jones. 2000. *Koyukon Athabaskan dictionary*. Fairbanks, Alaska: Alaska Native Language Center.

*Kari, James. 1990. *Ahtna Athabaskan dictionary*. Fairbanks, Alaska: Alaska Native Language Center.

*Karlsson, Fred. 1999. *Finnish: An essential grammar*. London: Routledge.

*Lichtenberk, Frantisek. 1983. *A grammar of Manam*. Honolulu: University of Hawaii Press.

Lombardi, Linda. 1994. *Laryngeal features and laryngeal neutralization*. New York: Garland.

*MacKay, Carolyn J. 1999. *A grammar of Misantla Totonac*. Salt Lake City: University of Utah Press.

*Miller, Amy. 2001. *Jamul Tiipay*. Berlin: Mouton de Gruyter.

*Mithun, Marianne, and Hasan Basri. 1986. The phonology of Selayarese. *Oceanic Linguistics* 25 (1–2): 210–254.

*Nielson, Konrad. 1926. *Lærebok i lappisk*. Oslo: Brøgger.

*Norman, Jerry. 1988. *Chinese*. Cambridge: Cambridge University Press.

Rice, Keren. 1989. *A grammar of Slave*. Berlin: Mouton de Gruyter.

Rice, Keren. 1996. Aspects of variability in child language acquisition. In *Proceedings of the UBC International Conference on Phonological Acquisition*, ed. by Barbara Bernhardt, John Gilbert, and David Ingram, 1–14. Somerville, Mass.: Cascadilla Press.

Rice, Keren. 1999. Featural markedness in phonology: Variation. Part 1. *Glot International* 4 (7): 3–6. Part 2. *Glot International* 4 (8): 3–7.

Rice, Keren. 2002. Featural markedness in phonology: Variation. In *The second Glot International state-of-the-article book*, ed. by Lisa Cheng and Rint Sybesma, 387–427. Berlin: Mouton de Gruyter. (Slightly revised version of Rice 1999.)

Rice, Keren. 2007. Markedness. In *The Cambridge handbook of phonology*, ed. by Paul de Lacy, 79–97. Cambridge: Cambridge University Press.

Rice, Keren. To appear. *Featural markedness*. Cambridge: Cambridge University Press.

Rice, Keren, and Peter Avery. 1995. Variability in a deterministic model of language acquisition: A theory of segmental elaboration. In *Phonological acquisition and phonological theory*, ed. by John Archibald, 23–42. Hillsdale, N.J.: Lawrence Erlbaum.

Rice, Keren, and Peter Avery. 2004. The representational residue: The role of contrast in phonology. Paper presented at the 12th Manchester Phonology Meeting, Manchester.

*Saeed, John. 1999. *Somali*. Amsterdam: John Benjamins.

*Salminen, Topani. 1998. Nenets. In *Uralic languages*, ed. by Daniel Abondolo, 516–547. London: Routledge.

*Sapir, Edward. 1912. The Takelma language of southwestern Oregon. Reprinted in *The collected works of Edward Sapir*. Vol. 8, *Takelma texts and grammar*, ed. by Victor Golla. Berlin: Mouton de Gruyter, 1990.

*Sharpe, Margaret C. 1972. *Alawa phonology and grammar*. Canberra: Australian Institute of Aboriginal Studies.

*Shipley, William F. 1964. *Maidu grammar*. Berkeley and Los Angeles: University of California Press.

*Teeter, Karl V. 1964. *The Wiyot language*. Berkeley and Los Angeles: University of California Press.

*Vance, Timothy J. 1987. *An introduction to Japanese phonology*. Albany, N.Y.: State University of New York Press.

*Watkins, Laurel. 1984. *A grammar of Kiowa*. Lincoln: University of Nebraska Press.

*Wonderly, William L. 1951. Zoque II: Phonemes and morphophonemes. *International Journal of American Linguistics* 17:105–123.

*Yu, Alan C. L. 2004. Explaining final obstruent voicing in Lezgian: Phonetics and history. *Language* 80:73–97.

Zhang, Xi. 1996. Vowel systems of the Manchu-Tungus languages of China. Doctoral dissertation, University of Toronto.

V Interactions

16 Phonetic Explanations for Recurrent Sound Patterns: Diachronic or Synchronic?

Juliette Blevins

16.1 Sources of Similarity

Phonology is the study of sound patterns of the world's languages. In all spoken languages, we find sound patterns characterizing the composition of words and phrases. These patterns include overall properties of contrastive sound inventories (e.g., vowel inventories, consonant inventories, tone inventories), as well as patterns determining the distribution of sounds or features of sounds (stress, tone, length, voicing, place of articulation, etc.) and their variable realization in different contexts (alternations).

Of great interest in phonology is the study of *recurrent* sound patterns. These are patterns that occur with greater than chance frequency across the world's languages. Recurrent sound patterns are found with respect to sound inventories (e.g., the recurrent three-vowel system /i, u, a/), the distribution of segments and features (e.g., recurrent limitation of geminates to intervocalic position), and alternations in sound patterns that may characterize related words (e.g., recurrent word-final devoicing of voiced obstruents).

Many phonologists and phoneticians agree that the majority of recurrent sound patterns in the world's languages have sound phonetic explanations grounded in aspects of speech articulation and perception. However, there is some disagreement about where these phonetic explanations belong. One extreme position is that phonetic explanations are aspects of diachronic modeling of sound change and can be excised altogether from synchronic grammars (e.g., Blevins 2004a, 2006b). Another position is that markedness constraints encoding phonetic knowledge of articulatory and perceptual ease are active components of synchronic phonologies (e.g., Hayes and Steriade 2004). Before we assess the arguments for these diverse positions, a general overview of potential sources of similarity will be useful.

Within biological systems, there are at least five distinct sources for observed similarities, as listed in (1).

(1) *Sources of similarity for biological (and linguistic) characteristics*
  a. Direct genetic inheritance
  b. Parallel evolution
  c. Physical constraints on form/function
  d. Convergence or chance
  e. Nonnatural factors

A biological characteristic, like hair or eye color, may be due to direct genetic inheritance (1a). A second source for similarities is parallel evolution (1b). In the history of the lizard family, toepads have evolved independently at least three times, in *Iguanidae, Scincidae*, and *Gekkonidae*. In each case, the evolution of toepads correlates with a shift to arboreal habitats, supporting the view that toepads are an adaptive feature (Larsen and Losos 1996). A third source for shared characteristics is physical constraints on form (1c). For example, there are recurrent similarities in patterns of spots and stripes on cats and seashells that stem from biochemical processes that occur in the course of development (Stewart 1998). Similar characteristics may also be only superficially similar, arising from distinct developments, with distinct functions and structures (1d). A well-studied example of this involves the eyes of vertebrates and the eyes of cephalopods. A final category (1e) includes nonnatural factors that result from human manipulation of biological organisms: these include older methods of grafting and hybridization, as well as new forms of genetic modification.

  Parallel sources of similarity can be identified for recurrent sound patterns. Similar sound patterns can be the result of direct genetic inheritance within language families (1a). For example, the existence of closed syllables and complex onsets and codas in both English and German can, in many cases, be seen as features inherited from Proto-Germanic (Blevins 2006a). Final obstruent devoicings in German, Catalan, and Indonesian, on the other hand, are cases of parallel evolution (1b). Final devoicing was not inherited from Proto-Germanic, Proto-Romance, or Proto-Austronesian, but evolved independently in these unrelated language families because of parallel phonetic factors (Blevins 2006b). Categorical perception in humans is one physical constraint (1c) that plays a role in the determination of similar feature and segment category boundaries crosslinguistically. And, as with biological traits, linguistic similarities may be a consequence of chance or independent convergence (1d). In both Japanese and Gilbertese, two unrelated languages, the only consonants that can end words are nasals. In earlier stages of both languages, though, it appears that all syllables were open. While the evolution of word-final nasals in Japanese was due to contact with Chinese, final nasals in Gilbertese result from a regular sound change of word-final voiceless high vowel loss after nasals. Finally, linguistic parallels to grafting, hybridization, and genetic modification include change through direct language contact, language mixing, and second language learning (1e). Note that the only category that requires direct reference to the architecture of grammar is (1c). All other explanations for recurrent similarities in linguistic systems are external to the grammar itself.

16.2 Phonetic Explanation

Having reviewed these general sources of similarity, let us return to the two different positions regarding phonetic explanation noted earlier. Within Evolutionary Phonology (Blevins 2004a, 2005b, 2006a,b, 2008), the majority of recurrent sound patterns are attributed to parallel evolution. Common phonetically based sound changes give rise to recurrent sound patterns, and phonetic explanation is attributed to diachronic processes, with phonetically based markedness principles excised from synchronic grammars. Within other approaches, like that proposed by Hayes and Steriade (2004), phonetically based markedness constraints are active components of synchronic grammars.

Before we look at empirical arguments for each position, let us review a general point concerning the architecture of grammar. If historical explanations from direct genetic inheritance, parallel evolution, or convergent evolution can be shown to account for sound patterns within one language, a group of related languages, or (in the case of parallel evolution) a group of unrelated languages, then there is no explanatory role for synchronic rules or constraints enforcing the same sound patterns. The same general principle can be stated in terms of a simplicity metric. All else being equal, simpler grammatical models are preferred to more complex ones. A model that duplicates explanation within or across domains is in some basic sense more complex than one that does not. Therefore, if we can demonstrate that principled diachronic explanations exist for particular sound patterns, and that diachronic explanations are needed in any case, considerations of simplicity dictate that explanations for the same sound patterns should not be duplicated in synchronic accounts. This general point features prominently in Evolutionary Phonology (Blevins 2004a), where principled diachronic explanations for sound patterns replace, rather than complement, synchronic explanations, unless independent evidence demonstrates, beyond reasonable doubt, that a separate synchronic explanation is warranted.

Within phonetic markedness accounts, however, there appears to be duplication of phonetic explanations across the diachronic and synchronic domains. Hayes and Steriade (2004:26) believe there is clear empirical support for the view that "diachrony helps explain some aspects of phonological naturalness." Nevertheless, they attempt to justify their position that phonetically based markedness constraints are active components of synchronic phonologies with three brief arguments. In the remainder of this section, I evaluate these three arguments and show that data from all three domains are consistent with the view that the domain of phonetic explanation in phonology is diachronic, not synchronic.

The first argument presented by Hayes and Steriade (2004:26–27) is that child phonology shows "many phonological phenomena that could not originate as innocent misapprehensions." In fact, this view is not contested by proponents of historical phonetic explanations. A wealth of data illustrates that the majority of recurrent features of child phonology (e.g., CV syllable stage, cluster reduction stage, consonant harmony, sibilants produced as stops) are reflections of articulatory developmental stages, reflecting developmental constraints on performance, not on language competence (see, e.g., Locke 1983, Vihman 1996). Three strong arguments that these recurrent stages are performance effects independent of grammar are (1) the fact that they are distinct from common phonetically motivated sound changes and recurrent sound patterns; (2) the use of multiple strategies for avoiding sounds a child has not yet mastered (e.g., to avoid /l/, a child might use consonant harmony, pronounce [l] as [j], or simply avoid words with /l/); and (3) the use of context-dependent local strategies in the course of segment acquisition that are also performance-based (Berg 1995).

The second objection that Hayes and Steride raise is the doubt that "innocent misapprehension is capable of driving systematic phonological change" (Steriade 2001:232–233, Hayes and Steriade 2004:27). The particular example they mention is regressive nasal place assimilation. Place assimilation of a nasal stop to a following oral stop is a common sound change; it is also reflected by alternations in many of the world's languages. Perception studies (e.g., Fujimura, Macchi, and Streeter 1978, Ohala 1990) *do* show a match between misapprehension and sound change, with CV transition as opposed to VC transition dominating the percept, giving rise to a single homorganic interpretation of place for a medial heterorganic sequence. In Fujimura, Macchi, and Streeter's experiment, homorganicity correlated with duration of consonantal interlude, while in Ohala's experiment 1, nonhomorganic sequences were judged as homorganic 93% of the time. Where, then, is the mismatch between experimental results and attested sound change?

Steriade (2001) cites the results of an experiment by Hura, Lindblom, and Diehl (1992). In this experiment, where heterorganic VNCV sequences were presented to English speakers, nasals showed an error rate of 6.9%, significantly higher than the 3% error rate for fricatives in the same position. The result of interest to Steriade was that most errors were *nonassimilatory*. In particular, 76.1% of all incorrect nasal responses were /n/. If listeners' responses were based on the place of articulation of the following stop, she argues, responses would be balanced among the three distinct places of articulation. Steriade takes these results as rejecting the general hypothesis that regressive nasal-place assimilation has a perceptual basis, concluding that misperception of nasal place in VNCV may have a perceptual origin, but that assimilation in this context is the consequence of optimizing assimilation that characterizes synchronic grammars.

Steriade's interpretation is surprising, since Hura, Lindblom, and Diehl are careful to note that, because of the longer VC_1C_2V intervals used in their study, it would be a mistake to reject Ohala's hypothesis of perceptually based assimilation. Not only were intervocalic consonantal intervals long in this study—in addition, the stimuli were made from a set of nonsense names, with N##C sequences spanning the end of the first name and the beginning of the last name. In Blevins 2007, I suggest that specific facts about the English lexicon, namely, the fact that disyllabic first names with initial stress ending in lax vowel $+$ /n/ are more frequent than those ending in velar or labial nasals, may provide a better explanation of these results.

Steriade's objection also involves a simplification of the actual assumed mechanisms of change. Certain sound changes, like $*\theta > f$, are arguably primarily perceptual, with no obvious role for articulation. But in the case of other well-studied changes like vocalization and elision of velarized laterals (Recasens 1996), $*p > f > h$ changes (Foulkes 1997), and velar palatalization (Guion 1998), perception is demonstrated to be just one component of a historical change that also involves significant articulatory weakening and/or coarticulation.

Steriade's final argument for integrating phonetic explanations into synchronic grammars comes from the study of stop-sibilant metatheses (Steriade 2001, Hayes and Steriade 2004:27). The general structure of the argument is as follows. Metathesis between sibilants and stops can arise through listener error. Confusability is, in principle, symmetric. Therefore, if asymmetries in observed patterns of stop-sibilant metathesis exist, they suggest that optimization is at work. The fallacy in this argument should be immediately apparent, given the discussion of nasal-place assimilation above. Confusability is not, in principle, symmetric. The fact that cues in CV transitions dominate those in VC transitions where consonantal intervals are relatively short shows that perception can give rise to inherent asymmetries in sound patterns. In principle, then, it is possible that the claimed asymmetries in stop-sibilant metathesis have perceptual explanations as well.

However, the most explanatory account for the majority of regular sound changes involving sibilant metathesis is based on the role of dominant ambient patterns in the language being acquired. The general suggestion is that sound changes with sources in perceptual ambiguity, like stop-sibilant metathesis, are more frequent when their output already exists as an unambiguous sound pattern in the language at large than they are otherwise (Blevins 2004a:247ff.). All cases of stop $+ s$ and $s +$ stop metathesis cited by Steriade are cases where output clusters are cluster types that already exist in the language (Hume 2004). This generalization does not follow from a model in which misperception identifies the target of change, with reversal occurring only in cases where perception is optimizing. Consider, for example, what the two models predict for a language like Taba (also known as East Makian), a South Halmahera language (Bowden 2001). In this language, nonderived word-initial clusters include /ps/, /ss/, and /ns/, and there are no nongeminate clusters with /s/ as the first member. Under Steriade's account, prevocalic clusters like /ps/, /ts/, and /ks/ may pose perceptual difficulties with respect to the position of the sibilant noise. If this occurs, resolution of this ambiguity could result in stop-sibilant metathesis, whose output optimizes the perception of the stop, placing it in prevocalic position. However, many derived stop-sibilant clusters occur (/t-sobal/ 'we incl. sail', /k-sobal/ 'I sail', etc.), but metathesis does not take place. If this were an isolated example, it would be unremarkable. However, there is no language where preexisting *s*T clusters cannot be seen to "prime" metathesis. To summarize, a model in which stop-sibilant metathesis is both perceptually based and primed by preexisting sound patterns makes better overall predictions regarding attested stop-sibilant metatheses than a model where perceptual ambiguity is resolved by synchronic perception-optimizing ambiguity alone.

Finally, Steriade's approach to stop-sibilant metathesis has empirical weaknesses. Following the general approach of Grammont (1933) and Hume (1998), Steriade (2001:234) views stop-sibilant metathesizing sound changes (in, e.g., Latin, Ancient Greek, and Old Dutch) as optimizing place contrasts for the stop: "the stop moves to a position where it will have CV transitions, the preferred source of place information for major place distinctions." However, not all stop-sibilant metatheses have the effect of optimizing the cues for the stop consonant.

(2) *Stop-sibilant metathesis* $*t \ldots s > s \ldots t$ *in some Malayo-Polynesian languages*

    a. *Northern Philippines* $*t \ldots s > s \ldots t$

Proto-Malayo-Polynesian	Ilokano	
*Ratus	gasut	'hundred'
*Retas	gessat	'to snap, of string'
*utas	usat	'open a road, clear a path'
*tebus	sambut	'redeem'

    b. *Southern Philippines, Sulawesi* $*t \ldots s > s \ldots t$

Proto-Sangiric	Sangir	Sangil	Talaud	Bantik	
*Ratus	hasuʔ	rasuʔ	ʒasutta	hatusuʔ	'hundred'
*bitis	bisiʔ	ʔisiʔ	bisitta	bitisiʔ	'calf of leg'
*taŋis	saʔiʔ	saʔiʔ	saʔitta	taŋisiʔ	'to cry'
*tages	saʔeʔ	saheʔ	sahatta	tageseʔ	'reef'

Sneddon (1984:31–33) documents metathesis of *t* and *s* within the Sangiric subgroup (southern Philippines, northern Sulawesi), and parallel cases are found in Northern Philippine languages, including Ilokano, Bontok, and Pangasinan. As illustrated in (2a), the change is restricted to inversion of *t* and *s*, occurs across intervening consonants and vowels, and results, in Ilokano, in forms with word-final *t*. What is interesting about the recurrent sound change in (2) is that a stop that was once prevocalic ends up in word-final position, where, under Steriade's model, cues for place of articulation are weakest. Data of this sort, then, do not support her claim that "only certain types of reversal, which can be identified as perception-optimizing, are frequent and systematic."

Historical phonetic explanations for recurrent sound patterns find strong support in the experimental and typological literature (Blevins 2004a). Straightforward historical phonetic explanations exist for the majority of lenitions, fortitions, deletions, assimilations, dissimilations, and metatheses, eliminating the need for synchronic markedness constraints. The existence of rare recalcitrant cases of recurrent sound change like low-vowel dissimilation (Lynch 2004) or context-free *$t > k$ (Blust 1990, 2004) does not suggest that this research program is misguided. Rather, these examples demonstrate the need for detailed studies of the perception and production of *aCa* in contrast to other VCV sequences in Austronesian languages, and salient acoustic and perceptual similarities of *t*, *k* in contrast to *p*, in sound systems where *t* and *k* do not contrast. Furthermore, recurrent sound patterns like antigemination that defy sound phonetic explanations illuminate the model further, by demanding integration of phonetically based sound change with paradigmatic contrast (Blevins 2005b). Finally, the historical phonetic approach to recurrent sound patterns makes predictions about the rate of sound change in different domains, and their synchronic consequences. If, as many authors argue, contextually predictable material is more likely to undergo lenition than nonpredictable material, leniting sound changes should happen faster in reduplicated strings than in nonreduplicated strings, with synchronic consequences for the form of reduplicated affixes. This prediction is supported by a range of sound patterns in Oceanic languages (Blevins 2005a).

16.3   Modeling Phonological Knowledge

Once well-documented diachronic explanations are excised from synchronic grammars, what explanatory domains remain? What architecture most accurately characterizes phonological knowledge, and what types of experimental evidence are most likely to shed light on its content? General and language-specific phonetic knowledge has been amply demonstrated experimentally, but what is the status of knowledge determining the patterns most commonly accounted for by phonological rules, constraints, or descriptions?

Answers to these questions are only beginning to come into focus, and some are quite surprising. Consider, for example, the type of phonological knowledge determining alternations between voiced and voiceless obstruents in languages with final devoicing sound patterns. Recent studies show that this knowledge may have a very different character from structuralist, generativist, and optimality conceptions. Ernestus and Baayen (2003) show that Dutch speakers interpret neutralized final devoiced segments in Dutch as voiced or voiceless by making use of phonological/ phonetic similarity patterns in the lexicon, interpreting new words in such a way as to conform to these learned patterns. A synchronic grammar of Dutch should be able to characterize knowledge of phonological/phonetic similarity in the sense that it is used by speakers in this particular experiment. The resulting grammar will be highly descriptive, since word-forms are the apparent basis of analogical generalizations. Studies of this sort highlight the extent to which knowledge of phonetics and phonology is learned knowledge of language, since the basis of emergent analogical generalizations is learned sound patterns of individual words.

At the same time, experimental paradigms also reveal that language-specific phonetic knowledge is used in unexpected ways in word recognition tasks. Kemps et al. (2005) show that Dutch listeners use subphonemic prosodic cues early in a word to optimize morphological processing of contrasts expressed later in the word via suffixation. Experiments of this type suggest that a standard phonological analysis localizing the contrast between Dutch *boek* 'book' and *boeken* 'books' after the stem is misguided, or in need of substantial enrichment. The lexical representations evidenced in lexical processing are extremely rich, with speakers (as far as has been tested) using all perceptually salient systematic phonetic cues available to disambiguate word forms.

Finally, we can turn to recent tests regarding the validity of certain types of opacity and neutralization in phonological rule or constraint systems. Sanders (2001) presents experimental data suggesting that the Polish [o]~[u] alternation, well-known from the problem set in Kenstowicz and Kisseberth's classic textbook (1979:72–73), is not synchronically productive. And the famous vowel neutralization between /u:/ and /o:/ in Yawelmani Yokuts, discussed at length in the same text, must be reanalyzed when it is acknowledged that long-vowel lowering and vowel harmony are both morphologically restricted processes, not general sound patterns of the language as a whole (Blevins 2004b).

What models of synchronic phonology have this degree of descriptive phonetic detail, adopt learning as a primary mechanism, allow for probabilistic generalizations over the lexicon, treat phonetic explanations as primarily historical, and posit analogy as the primary mode of generalization? Phonetic detail is guaranteed in phonetic exemplar models, where lexical representations consist of stored "memories" of auditory stimuli (Johnson 1997, 2007, Pierrehumbert 2001, 2003), with phonetic details intact. Within such models, frequencies of sound patterns play a crucial role in the acquisition of phonological and phonetic competence, and it is precisely this competence that linguists attempt to model. At the phonetic level, exemplar theory provides one model of how probability distributions over cognitive maps may be used in speech perception and production. Modeling of the lexicon is viewed in terms of stronger and weaker connections between words with more and fewer shared properties. The grammar provides a very concrete tracking of generalizations over the lexicon, resulting in wide-ranging probabilistic generalizations. The form and content of these generalizations are addressed in work on analogical modeling. This ranges from formal studies (e.g., Skousen 1989, 1992) to experiments probing lexical organization (e.g., Ernestus and Baayen 2003) and simulations probing emergent analogical generalizations in the production/feedback loop (e.g., Wedel 2004). As summarized by Pierrehumbert (2001:202), the lexical network and the cognitive map each explain "a large and diverse battery of findings about implicit knowledge of speech, and no viable alternative has been proposed for either concept." Given this, it is not surprising that the only testable theories of grammar take lexical networks and cognitive maps as architectural starting points for characterizing phonetic and phonological knowledge.

16.4   Concluding Remarks

These brief remarks highlight four important architectural issues at the phonetics-phonology interface that need to be addressed before importing the entirety of phonetic knowledge into synchronic phonologies. First, in the search to *explain* recurrent sound patterns, one should give equal consideration to all potential sources of similarity, including direct inheritance and parallel evolution, to counter the bias toward synchronic explanations that characterizes modern phonological theory. Second, where historical phonetic explanations can be documented for recurrent sound patterns, synchronic explanations are at best redundant and at worst useless. Synchronic grammars can be greatly simplified once the weight of explanation is lifted. The majority of markedness constraints can be eliminated from synchronic grammars, and feature systems (Mielke 2008), syllable structure (Blevins 2003), and regular exceptions to regular alternations (Blevins 2005b) may also be emergent properties of grammar. Third, the match between diachronic phonetic explanations and attested data is better than that between synchronic phonetic explanations and attested data. The evidence before us strongly suggests that synchronic phonologies are not the domain of phonetic explanation. And finally, by locating phonetic explanations in the historical domain, we neither deny phonetic knowledge as part of linguistic knowledge nor sacrifice descriptive adequacy. On the contrary, frameworks incorporating phonetic exemplar modeling and general analogical mechanisms integrate cognitive maps for detailed low-level phonetic encoding with complex lexical networks. The architecture relating these two components is a fertile area of ongoing inquiry.

References

Berg, Thomas. 1995. Sound change in child language: A study of inter-word variation. *Language and Speech* 38:331–363.

Blevins, Juliette. 2003. The phonology of Yurok glottalized sonorants. *International Journal of American Linguistics* 69:371–396.

Blevins, Juliette. 2004a. *Evolutionary Phonology: The emergence of sound patterns*. Cambridge: Cambridge University Press.

Blevins, Juliette. 2004b. A reconsideration of Yokuts vowels. *International Journal of American Linguistics* 70:33–51.

Blevins, Juliette. 2005a. The role of phonological predictability in sound change: Privileged reduction in Oceanic reduplicated substrings. *Oceanic Linguistics* 44:455–464.

Blevins, Juliette. 2005b. Understanding antigemination. In *Linguistic diversity and language theories*, ed. by Zygmunt Frajzyngier, David Rood, and Adam Hodges, 203–234. Amsterdam: John Benjamins.

Blevins, Juliette. 2006a. New perspectives on English sound patterns: 'Natural' and 'unnatural' in Evolutionary Phonology. *Journal of English Linguistics* 34:6–25.

Blevins, Juliette. 2006b. A theoretical synopsis of Evolutionary Phonology. *Theoretical Linguistics* 32:117–165.

Blevins, Juliette. 2007. Interpreting misperception: Beauty is in the ear of the beholder. In *Experimental approaches to phonology*, ed. by Maria-Josep Solé, Patrice Speeter Beddor, and Manjari Ohala, 144–154. Oxford: Oxford University Press.

Blevins, Juliette. 2008. Consonant epenthesis: Natural and unnatural histories. In *Language universals and language change*, ed. by Jeff Good, 79–107. Oxford: Oxford University Press.

Blust, Robert. 1990. Three recurrent changes in Oceanic languages. In *Pacific island languages: Essays in honour of G. B. Milner*, ed. by J. H. C. S. Davidson, 7–28. London: University of London, School of Oriental and African Studies.

Blust, Robert. 2004. *t to k: An Austronesian sound change revisited. *Oceanic Linguistics* 43:365–410.

Bowden, John. 2001. *Taba: Description of a South Halmahera language*. Pacific Linguistics 521. Canberra: Australian National University.

Ernestus, Mirjam, and R. Harald Baayen. 2003. Predicting the unpredictable: Interpreting neutralized segments in Dutch. *Language* 79:5–38.

Foulkes, Paul. 1997. Historical laboratory phonology: Investigating /p/ > /f/ > /h/ changes. *Language and Speech* 40:248–276.

Fujimura, Osamu, Marian J. Macchi, and Lynn A. Streeter. 1978. Perception of stop consonants with conflicting transitional cues: A cross-linguistic study. *Language and Speech* 21:337–346.

Grammont, Maurice. 1933. *Traité de phonétique*. Paris: Delagrave.

Guion, Susan G. 1998. The role of perception in the sound change of velar palatalization. *Phonetica* 55:18–52.

Hayes, Bruce, and Donca Steriade. 2004. Introduction: The phonetic bases of phonological markedness. In *Phonetically based phonology*, ed. by Bruce Hayes, Robert Kirchner, and Donca Steriade, 1–33. Cambridge: Cambridge University Press.

Hume, Elizabeth. 1998. The role of perceptibility in consonant/consonant metathesis. In *WCCFL 17: The proceedings of the Seventeenth West Coast Conference on Formal Linguistics*, ed. by Kimary N. Shahin, Susan Blake, and Eun-Sook Kim, 293–307. Stanford, Calif.: CSLI Publications.

Hume, Elizabeth. 2004. The indeterminacy/attestation model of metathesis. *Language* 80:203–237.

Hura, Susan L., Björn Lindblom, and Randy L. Diehl. 1992. On the role of perception in shaping phonological assimilation rules. *Language and Speech* 35:59–72.

Johnson, Keith. 1997. Speech perception without speaker normalization. In *Talker variability in speech processing*, ed. by Keith Johnson and John W. Mullennix, 145–166. San Diego, Calif.: Academic Press.

Johnson, Keith. 2007. Decisions and mechanisms in exemplar-based phonology. In *Experimental approaches to phonology*, ed. by Maria-Josep Solé, Patrice Speeter Beddor, and Manjari Ohala, 25–40. Oxford: Oxford University Press.

Kemps, Rachel, Mirjam Ernestus, Robert Schreuder, and R. Harald Baayen. 2005. Prosodic cues for morphological complexity: The case of Dutch plural nouns. *Memory and Cognition* 33:430–446.

Kenstowicz, Michael, and Charles Kisseberth. 1979. *Generative phonology: Description and theory*. New York: Academic Press.

Larson, Allan, and Jonathan B. Losos. 1996. Phylogenetic systematics of adaptation. In *Adaptation*, ed. by Michael R. Rose and George V. Lauder, 187–220. San Diego, Calif.: Academic Press.

Locke, John L. 1983. *Phonological acquisition and change*. New York: Academic Press.

Lynch, John. 2004. Low vowel dissimilation in Vanuatu languages. *Oceanic Linguistics* 42:359–406.

Mielke, Jeff. 2008. *The emergence of distinctive features*. Oxford: Oxford University Press.

Ohala, John J. 1990. The phonetics and phonology of aspects of assimilation. In *Papers in laboratory phonology I*, ed. by John Kingston and Mary Beckman, 258–275. Cambridge: Cambridge University Press.

Pierrehumbert, Janet. 2001. Stochastic phonology. *Glot International* 5 (6): 195–207.

Pierrehumbert, Janet. 2003. Probabilistic phonology: Discrimination and robustness. In *Probability theory in linguistics*, ed. by Rens Bod, Jennifer Hay, and Stefanie Jannedy, 177–228. Cambridge, Mass.: MIT Press.

Recasens, Daniel. 1996. An articulatory-perceptual account of vocalization and elision of dark /l/ in the Romance languages. *Language and Speech* 39:63–89.

Sanders, Nathan. 2001. Preserving synchronic parallelism: Diachrony and opacity in Polish. In *Proceedings of CLS 37*, ed. by Mary Andronis, Christopher Ball, Heidi Elston, and Sylvain Neuvel, 501–516. Chicago: University of Chicago, Chicago Linguistic Society.

Skousen, Royal. 1989. *Analogical modeling of language*. Dordrecht: Kluwer.

Skousen, Royal. 1992. *Analogy and structure*. Dordrecht: Kluwer.

Sneddon, James N. 1984. *Proto-Sangiric and the Sangiric languages.* Pacific Linguistics B-91. Canberra: Australian National University.

Steriade, Donca. 2001. Directional asymmetries in place assimilation: A perceptual account. In *The role of speech perception in phonology*, ed. by Elizabeth Hume and Keith Johnson, 219–250. San Diego, Calif.: Academic Press.

Stewart, Ian. 1998. *Life's other secret*. New York: Wiley.

Vihman, Marilyn May. 1996. *Phonological development: The origins of language in the child*. Oxford: Blackwell.

Wedel, Andrew. 2004. Self-organization and the origin of higher-order phonological patterns. Doctoral dissertation, University of California, Santa Cruz.

17 Phonetic Influence on Phonological Operations

Thomas Purnell

17.1 Introduction

The core tenet that phonology is abstract has been challenged on the basis of the gradience and temporality of speech (Port and Leary 2005). Moreover, newer proposals about the relation between phonology and phonetics (Steriade 1995, 1997, Blevins 2004, Hayes, Kirchner, and Steriade 2004) have argued against the autonomy of phonology. The primary concern of this chapter is the phonetics-phonology interface generally, and whether phonetic knowledge actively participates in the phonological module.

One theme running through this chapter is that the problem facing scientists working with sounds is largely a problem of demarcation. Such a theme resonates with Goldsmith (1993), who observes that defining levels is difficult and the most important issue facing linguistics. To see the various ways the demarcation problem has played out, let us assume for a moment that there exists a continuum of operations or representations of sounds between the levels of phonology and phonetics located at either end.[1] This assumption may be temporary, but it allows us to see how representative researchers understand differences between phonetic and phonological knowledge. First, to Morris Halle the line distinguishing phonology from phonetics is somewhere between abstract contrasts and gradience, early rules inserting idiosyncratic distinctive features and late default rules inserting the unmarked values of features.[2] This position is built on earlier notions that phonetics is just a general implementation of all the heavy lifting done by phonological rules. In other words, the phonological knowledge a speaker possesses includes the idea of how a phonetically well-formed sequence of phonemes is defined. To scientists operating in this framework, the line between phonetics and phonology must be further away from the phonology end of the continuum.[3] Second, reacting to the position that "phonology is supposed to specify the language-specific properties of speech, while the phonetic inventory and its implementation is supposed to be universal" (Port and Leary 2005:943), Robert Port positions the demarcation line as close to the phonological end of the continuum as possible (Port 2007). In this view, most (if not all) processes involving sounds are due to probabilistic gesticulation of the minimally specified morphosyntactic units (i.e., minimal pairs). Although claiming to be "against formal phonology," Port allows for minimal pairs and the statistical actuation of lexical items and therefore must conceive of some systematicity among human language sounds. Third, John Ohala (e.g., 1900) argues against specifying any distinct point of demarcation between phonetics and phonology. Ohala, in his many articles on this topic, attempts to account for why sound changes appear to move seamlessly from a superficial change to an allophonic change to a phonemic change.

Two "weaker" spin-off (and at times antagonistic) positions have emerged recently from Ohala's work. The first, Juliette Blevins's Evolutionary Phonology, holds that perception is the primary source of sound change; specifically, "common sound patterns typically result from common phonetically motivated sound change" (Blevins 2004:23). What is important here is that Blevins does not claim that the perceptual system affects sound change; rather, she claims that misperception—and not, for instance, autonomous social factors of identity (Labov 1972)—lead to sound change.[4] The point I raise here about Blevins's privileging of the historical analysis of language (Blevins 2004:63) is that phonetics offers only one type of potential sound change, understood only in retrospect and lacking anticipatory predictive power, as explained in section 17.2.[5] The second spin-off from Ohala's work is the view that phonetic knowledge is active inside phonology. This view results when the boundaries between phonetics and phonology are removed, as in Optimality Theory (McCarthy and Prince 1993, Prince and Smolensky 2004).[6] The active-phonetic-knowledge model is also evident in proposals by Donca Steriade (Steriade 1997, Hayes and Steriade 2004) regarding perceptual salience of certain syllabic and prosodic positions. General support for this position has been provided by Kingston and Diehl (1994), who argue that phonetic knowledge regarding the perception of the family of acoustic cues signaling voicing is active in phonology. While I will address Kingston and Diehl's position only in part, in section 17.3 I will advocate that the complexity of information passed between articulation and phonology argues against phonetic transparency in phonology.

While each position offers a unique answer to similar problems and thus informs our understanding of where the demarcation line falls, the views related to Ohala's work are particularly interesting because they seek to clarify how speakers come by active perceptual knowledge in phonology. Specifically, since both Steriade's synchronic position and Blevins's diachronic position use perception foundationally in their arguments, in this chapter I address the effect of perception within phonology and appeal to the oft-used criterion of predictability to argue against phonetic transparency. As a result, this chapter contributes to the defense of a neogenerative abstract phonology, because whatever knowledge we have in phonology, it must be predictive; phonetic knowledge (read, perceptual knowledge based on acoustic variability) is inherently unpredictable.

Although there are a number of ways of responding to the perceptual knowledge positions, I argue here primarily against the position of Hayes, Kirchner, and Steriade (2004) (henceforth HKS). HKS question whether the covariation of auditory or articulatory patterns with phonological patterns constitutes active knowledge or merely informs our understanding of language variation and change. Their answer is that auditory and articulatory behaviors constitute phonetic knowledge active in speakers' productive phonological grammars because of an asymmetry between devoicing in geminates and singletons. That is, speakers know that the gradient difference between a long voiced stop and a voiceless one is articulatorily more complex than the difference between voiced and voiceless singletons. Consequently, because voiced geminate obstruents are easier to devoice than singletons, they indeed devoice them. Assuming that the processes of devoicing and modification in this context are phonological processes and not phonetic processes, I confess that I fail to see how any analysis like HKS's has predictive power, how the principles upon which their analysis rests are more axiomatic than other principles, and how the alleged knowledge is necessarily active. In the remainder of this chapter, I will discuss the insufficient predictive power of phonetic knowledge generally (section 17.2) and specifically how, under HKS's analysis, the arbitrary selection of layered perceptual cues prohibits a direct link between phonetics and phonological constraints (section 17.3).

17.2 Predictive Power

The notion of predictability is assumed to be essential in formulating any scientific theory. Phonological operations need to be predictable in nature because any formal statement reflecting a speaker's knowledge must be accurate and replicable in order to pass scientific muster. In particular, I take issue with incorporating phonetic knowledge (i.e., acoustic characteristics in speech) into phonological knowledge precisely because phonetic knowledge is unpredictable. In this chapter, I will put forth several reasons for acknowledging the difficulty in reliably predicting phonological categories from acoustic characteristics. Central to much of the discussion is the general concept of voicing, or VOICING using Docherty's (1992) method of using uppercase letters to signal a general concept. The reason for casting the discussion in terms of a general concept of VOICING instead of with a phonetic term related to vocal fold vibration or an abstract phonological feature such as [voice] is the large number of acoustic characteristics beyond glottal pulsing related to such phonological notions of voicing as [voice], [stiff] and [slack], or fortis and lenis. I stake out a position in contrast to others (e.g., Stevens and Blumstein 1981, Kingston and Diehl 1994, 1995) by arguing that the relation between the percepts of VOICING and the acoustic characteristics of VOICING is more variable than previously thought (Purnell et al. 2005). Thus, predictability of VOICING within phonology does not derive universally from any one acoustic characteristic, but from a prephonological evaluation of the strength or weight of the characteristics against each other. The apparently systematic knowledge that speakers have about sound relations in their language cannot be reliably determined through transparent processing of acoustic detail—or, as Halle (1962) puts it, by staying too close to the "phonetic ground."[7] In this chapter, I address instances where phonetic knowledge has been explicitly claimed to be active in synchronic phonological processes. (NB: Having made the point that the latent or underlying concept of VOICING entails considerably more phonetically than mere glottal pulsing, I will cease using the uppercase notation.)

In paraphrasing Blevins's claim that "common sound patterns typically result from common phonetically motivated sound change" (2004:23) by stating that the perception of acoustic variability causes phonological change, we need to understand the related notions of causation and explanation because they underscore the idea that levels of understanding are vital to correctly characterizing the phonetics-phonology interface. Sober (1984), like Davidson (1963) before him, makes useful distinctions about causation and explanation parallel to our demarcation problem. To make a point about separation (or demarcation) of levels of representation, Sober considers the case of a simple sugar cube dissolving in water. First, Sober notes that claiming that the cube dissolves because it is soluble is unsatisfactory without knowing the composition of the cube. Moreover, because the act of submerging the sugar cube in water does not cause the cube to dissolve, it is unsatisfactory to claim that the cube dissolves because it is placed in water. Instead, the cause of dissolution is the interaction of the molecular structure (i.e., a standing condition) of the cube with the molecular structure (another standing condition) of the water. In other words, understanding the cause of a sugar cube's dissolution is possible only by understanding (1) two standing conditions and (2) the process that takes place when the two standing conditions meet. Moreover, processes are defined by the causal standing conditions and the effect. Thus, just stating that something is soluble will not indicate the properties of the effect. To be soluble means to be able to melt or dissolve. In other words, dropping a sugar cube in water will not produce the same kind of effect as dropping an ice cube into water.

Consider how the example of sugar cube dissolution extends by analogy to the phonetics-phonology interface. Port and Halle share an understanding of both standing conditions in the syntax-to-acoustics relation: morphosyntactic units (minimal pairs with linearly ordered "somethings")[8] and temporal actuation of speech in a conversation. Our task, then, is to explain the process used to produce the effect of acoustic characteristics. Port's characterization of abstract phonology (Port and

Leary 2005:947) need not be the only one. Port assumes first that abstract phonology has as its goal phonetic output and second that phonetic implementation within the concept of abstract phonology is universal. For example, Port assumes that abstract phonologists argue only for phonetic transparency and not for an implementational grammar as well where an additional linguistic component must be engaged in the actuation of temporally arranged abstract units into temporal acoustic characteristics. Just as stating that something is soluble does not indicate the properties of the effect of dissolution, neither does stating that there is variability in voice onset times indicate the distinctive feature [voiced]. Port misses the point raised by Iverson and Salmons (1995, 1999, 2003) that obstruent voicing in onset positions (e.g., voice onset time) and obstruent voicing in coda positions (e.g., devoicing or fortition) are typologically related in the systematic implementation of the distinctive features [spread glottis] and [slack vocal cords]. The similarity in coda and onset patterns among obstruents argues for at least a single abstract representation underlying the observed surface pattern. In the acoustics-to-syntax relation, given multitudinous acoustic characteristics as the standing conditions, what is the process yielding the effect of morphosyntactic unit activation? Presumably the complexity necessary to implement obstruent voicing distinctions implies minimally two processes and sets of standing conditions under what we call "perception." The demarcation problem is centered on our ability to state the processes (most likely more than one) that must arise from multiple temporally arranged acoustic characteristics.

So, how would incorporating phonetic knowledge into phonological knowledge increase the ability of theoretical phonology to make empirically accurate predictions, in order to reach a deeper understanding of conditions and processes in phonology? I argue that the power of phonetics does not lie in its predictive abilities. Indeed, it has no such power. Although theoretical phonology is based on well-described phonetic data (usually referred to as "phonetic grounding"; Archangeli and Pulleyblank 1994), its goal is not identical to that of descriptive phonology, which is interested in identifying and taxonomizing crosslinguistic contrasts. The goal of a linguistic theory is to posit a formal system whose statements predictably support a consistent analysis of novel forms (Halle 1962). Even by assuming only a trifle of modularity, one can maintain that the goal of theoretical phonology is not to model articulation, acoustic structure, or auditory input to the perceptual system, but to model the input to articulation. Phonetic analysis, in contrast, is restricted to providing only a natural retrospective on how changes might have occurred by what Joseph (2001:110) among others terms a "postdict" or "retrodict" analysis. Phonology and articulation operate over elements that differ not only in degree (contrast/gradience), but also in identity (abstract phonemes and allophones/nerves, bones, muscles, and soft tissue). Obviously, the phonological model must have boundaries established by articulatory and perceptual constraints past which the articulation module would find the phonological information it receives entirely incoherent. Nothing compels those boundaries, however, to operate obligatorily inside the model.

If a model permits the commingling of operations over gradient and abstract elements, then we should expect gradience and not contrasts to govern the actuation of all sounds in human language. The theoretical task, then, is to articulate how a phonological model predicts commingling and under what conditions it occurs. However, both strong and weak models fail to do this. The strongest view is that phonetics exerts direct control over phonology: all phonetic knowledge, then, is phonological knowledge, and all phonological knowledge is phonetic knowledge. Ohala, for one, has made such claims (Ohala 1974, 1986, 1990, 1992a,b, 1997). Even if the relation can be characterized as a continuum with contrastiveness at one end and gradience at the other, and even if phonetic and phonological markedness are two distinct motivators of linguistic change and operations, phonetic markedness (defined here as articulatory least effort or perceptual salience) is potentially unconstrained in its control over contrastiveness. The second, and less strong, claim is that phonetics only exerts indirect control over phonology. Phonetic grounding (a speaker's knowledge about phonetic markedness) is obtained through synchronic knowledge, and projects a fragment of the phonetics into the phonology. This claim is not as strong as Ohala's continuum view because the phonetic control this knowledge exerts is somehow constrained. Since proponents of the weak view acknowledge that "each factor geometrically increases the space of logical possibilities that must be considered in formulating constraints" (HKS 2004:15), they nevertheless must be espousing the requirement that no piece of phonetic information be left behind. In the absence of a clear algorithm for allowing certain pieces of phonetic information into phonology but excluding other pieces of phonetic information, the distinction between the weak and strong views is superficial. Any approach such as HKS's that argues for little to no separation between phonetics and phonology assumes a type of phonological knowledge that is phonetic in nature, and recognizes the gradient evaluation of categorical data and a speaker's awareness of phonetic goodness of fit. The result, then, is the abolition of all semantic distinctiveness between the terms *phonology* and *phonetics*. In particular, *contrast* no longer implies oppositional states.[9]

However, if we allow for gradient evaluation of categorical data, and if there is no way of knowing what phonetic information is prohibited from being used in this evaluation, then we have no way of predicting instances of acoustic or phonological independence. Let us look at two examples. The first is related to voicing—specifically, to tonogenesis and the connection between tones and voicing. If speakers of languages with obstruent voicing contrasts are exposed sufficiently to the contrast, then by HKS's reasoning, we must claim that all humans are aware of the effectiveness that voicing has with respect to tones. However, Matisoff (1973) and Kingston and Solnit (1989), among others, report that the advent of tones as a reflex of onset and coda consonant voicing is not unidirectional. For instance, it is not the case that all voiceless consonants have a high tone reflex. Voiced consonants in Chi wei, for example, induce tone lowering while voiced consonants in Shan induce tone raising (Kingston and Solnit 1989:267). Thus, if phonetic knowledge is deep inside phonology and not mediated by some intermediate implementation level introducing the directionality variation, then HKS's account should predict tonogenesis to work in exactly one way. However, in some languages speakers must relate the phonetic evidence and the phonetics of voicing in different ways.

A second example, unrelated to voicing, is the unpredictable expression of vowel splits and mergers (e.g., Labov 1994, Thomas 1995). One vowel shift, the Northern Cities Shift, is described by Labov as a chain shift without a uniform pull or push sequence of events. The first step, the raising of [æ] as the head of the shift, should begin a pull but instead is historically followed by the lowering of [ɪ] and [ɛ] as the chain tail. While the vowel raising is more robust, the lowering of the chain tail qualities, the directionality of [ɛ] (Gordon 2000), and the shifting of shift-medial vowels [ʌ, ɔ, a] may or may not be active in speakers with a rising [æ]. More important, the shifts often place the rising front vowel in contention for vowel space with the falling front mid lax vowel. This clash and the open gaps left by nonshifting low and back vowels in many speakers' grammars is unpredicted by such phonetic theories as adaptive dispersion (Liljencrants and Lindblom 1972, Lindblom and Engstrand 1989, Johnson, Flemming, and Wright 1993, Johnson 2000), which predict vowel space equilibrium and retrodict the idea of push and pull chain shifts. It might be suggested that other issues in perceptual salience are at work in predicting phonological variation and change in vowel shifts. Polka and Bohn (2003) document perceptual asymmetries whereby humans, cats, and birds are better able to distinguish contrasts when nonperipheral vowels are synthesized to a peripheral position than when the situation is reversed. In other words, at one level of hearing, listeners display a preference for peripheral vowels. Yet, the fact that the Northern Cities Shift is not complete among all speakers within its region and is avoided by speakers coming in regular contact with them suggests that while peripherality may be a preferred listening state, it has a lesser, and less predictive, role in speech than some (see, e.g., Blevins 2004) would claim.

But now we need to look at whether standing conditions of phonology are mirrors of standing conditions of phonetics. *Supervenience* is the term Sober (1984) uses for a property that is not physical, but that may characterize various states. Two items can share the supervening property yet be distinct. Supervenience is perhaps reflected in phonology by two segments' sharing the same distinctive feature and by that feature's relation to a latent factor underlying various physical properties. Sober, citing Fisher (1930), notes that "fitness, although measured by a uniform method, is qualitatively different for every different organism, whereas entropy, like temperature, is taken to have the same meaning for all physical systems" (1984:49). The parallel in phonology is this. We might expect that there are phonological properties that can be directly traced from the articulatory gesture to acoustic characteristics to perceptual cues that are uniform across all human languages. At the same time, we should expect to find phonological properties that supervene over several acoustic characteristics; for example, the general phonological property of voicing (as opposed to some distinctive feature [voiced]) is represented by a family of different acoustic characteristics, and these characteristics are not equally selected or weighted across a speech community or a language. While it was once thought that acoustic characteristics interact in a universal fashion (Kingston and Diehl 1994, 1995), the acoustic characteristics and perceptual cues of voicing are perhaps not uniform even across dialects and time (Purnell, Salmons, and Tepeli 2005, Purnell et al. 2005).

Moreover, we should expect—if phonetic knowledge were active—a greater alliance between typological frequency and phonetic gestures. Ohala (1983, 1997) and Westbury and Keating (1986) are often cited as observing the difficulty in maintaining glottal pulsing throughout long voiced obstruents. From Ohala's pellucid explanation, lowering the larynx to maintain voicing potentially leads to the formation of implosives (e.g., [bb] > [ɓ] in Sindhi; Ohala 1997). Kingston and Diehl, citing Ohala's Sindhi example, state that the development of voiced implosives "exemplifies minimal exertion of phonetic control" (1994:424). However, if the Sindhi case represents a minimal articulatory simplification and if acoustic significance implies perceptual significance, then the phonetic explanation must provide some understanding of the relative rarity of voiced implosives, and theories must adjust for the disharmonic relation between ease of articulation and typological frequency.

Finally, there is more to the problem than the fact that acoustic information is unable to make predictions regarding observed sound patterns. Often, generalizations regarding acoustic characteristics lead to theoretical indeterminacy, as has been proven in the case of the Norwegian [ʃl] cluster. Ohala (1974, citing Foley 1973) provided a very reasonable retrospective of sound change whereby [sl] devoiced so that the sounds now surface as [ʃl] (e.g., [oʃlo] 'Oslo'; cf. [sn] as in [sn]akke 'talk'). According to Ohala's proposal, the [l] in the [sl] cluster underwent some degree of devoicing, and since the [l̥] spectrally resembles an [ʃ], the alveolar fricative retracted to a postalveolar position (see also Haugen 1942, Fant 1960). Lass (1980) countered with other instances of voiceless laterals failing to cause a shift from [s] to [ʃ] (instead changing to [f] or [θ]), and Ohala (1984) acknowledged that voiceless [l̥] to [ʃ] was just one of many possible changes.[10] So in the end Ohala was unable to use phonetic knowledge to predict the rise of novel forms. What makes the situation even less favorable for a phonetic explanation is the presence of a phonological alternative, meaning that the phonetic analysis is indistinguishable from a phonological one.

Kristoffersen (2000:104) provides a synchronic rule capturing the spreading of an apicality feature rather than relying on diachronic phonetic knowledge. What we take away from this example and the above discussion is that formalizing phonetic knowledge as active in a productive, synchronic phonological grammar is too ambitious because the data are overly variable, the output is unpredictable, and the facts can often be accounted for by appealing to traditional synchronic and diachronic notions of phonology.

17.3 Layering and Selection of Phonetic Cues

In addition to the general problems HKS's proposal faces by building on Ohala's indeterminate demarcation between phonetics and phonology, HKS's specific argument, summarized by the phrase "Acoustic exposure necessitates perceptual import," is invalid. Consider this principle, stated as follows:

(1) a. A speaker observes substantial geminate devoicing.
    b. Therefore, the speaker knows the effectiveness of the closure voicing contrast.

In light of the layering of articulatory characteristics per cognitive category and the variable selection of those acoustic characteristics as perceptual cues, I argue in this section that the conclusion (1b) is invalid given that the outcome of the premise of phonetic observation (1a) is not necessarily an understanding of the perceptual value of acoustic characteristics, and that the perceptual value of an acoustic characteristic (1b) is not necessarily determined just by the observation of that characteristic (1a).

If a devoiced geminate is observed by the perceptual system, the output will be a valid linguistic category. What is unclear is the category that will be identified. The direct result of hearing the strongest members of the family of acoustic characteristics for a substantially undervoiced geminate is more likely to be a recategorized geminate even though a possible perception of the undervoiced geminate is ambiguously a voiced or a voiceless geminate. Following experimental convention, the outcome of (1a) could be tested among speakers of a language with both voiced and voiceless geminates using a forced-choice perceptual paradigm where glottal pulsing and duration of the ambiguously voiced stop gap are systematically modified in order to determine the percentage of correct identification at some point in the continuum between fully not voiced and fully voiced tokens. Given the widely held view that consonants are perceived categorically, a crossover point should occur somewhere along the continuum for each acoustic characteristic involved in signaling voicing. Regardless of where this crossover point occurs, its very existence indicates that subjects are able to categorize at a rate greater than chance time and time again. This categorization ability (we should eschew the word *knowledge* in this context) should always prevent a constraint of the kind HKS propose, where a complex gradient acoustic comparison leads to categorical perception of a sound. HKS predict gradient, not categorical, perception. We can be confident that the findings of our thought experiment would show that speakers who have a voiced geminate in their inventory robustly perceive a voiced geminate. This would be contrary to HKS's prediction that substantial loss of glottal pulsing in the closure period of a geminate would lead to perception of a voiceless token. This experiment would also most certainly confirm another pattern, namely, bidirectionality or final fortition in certain languages (Iverson and Salmons 1995, 2003).[11] We expect that in a novel setting, like a perception experiment, subjects will display a categorical discernment of voicing and length. Even allowing for an asymmetrical pattern where the crossover points for voiced and voiceless geminates occur in different locations, phonetic sensitivity is still bidirectional and the knowledge is parochial, not universal. The most generous interpretation of HKS's claim is that it is a statement about the increased frequency with which a voiced geminate is devoiced with respect to a voiceless geminate in a free variation setting. But, as the Sindhi example above suggests, there is no direct relation between typological frequency and articulation; the same should hold for perception and typological frequency.

The layering of acoustic cues, or the multiplex of articulatory-acoustic-auditory relations, argues against concluding that listeners know perceptual value (1b) just by observation (1a). Lisker (1986) observed the stabilizing effect of a many-to-one relation holding between phonetic cues and contrasts, which others have shown to hold across different inputs (Miller 1981a,b, Nearey 1989). Geminates, like all other human language sounds, are subject to cue layering. Ladefoged and Maddieson (1996:91) note that while the chief measure of long stops is closure duration (the short-to-long ratio crosslinguistically is 1:1.5 to 1:3), it is not the only cue to consonantal length. Prosody appears to play a role as well in geminate preservation. Geminates most often occur word-medially, and the first member is syllabified as a coda (Maddieson 1985). Acoustic characteristics under phonological organization preserve categorical distinctions such as voicing. Other cues to gemination may include secondary stress (as in Estonian and Sami; Ladefoged and Maddieson 1996), utterance-initial stop burst intensity, the rate of formant transitions, F0, or the relative amplitude of a following vowel (as in Pattani Malay; see below).

If acoustic exposure necessitates perceptual import, then we expect all acoustic characteristics to be perceptually significant since speakers will be exposed to these characteristics. Abramson (1986) suggests that the ability of Pattani Malay speakers to produce long geminate stops word-initially—which ought to be a highly marked occurrence—comes from four cues. The importance of the Pattani Malay acoustic findings in 1986 came to light only because of perceptual data reported by Abramson

(1991). As it turns out, Abramson found amplitude differences on the following vowel to be the perceptually salient feature of consonant gemination for Pattani Malay speakers. What is important here is that there are acoustic characteristics that are not important for the perception of segments and that are not predicted by a model conflating the phonetic with the phonological. For HKS, conclusion (1b) is one of several possible conclusions from premise (1a). The reason this acoustic/perceptual mismatch in Pattani Malay is possible lies in the relative independence of the categorization module to select (or be told how to select from the speech community) which features are given which value. Not only are some acoustic characteristics (e.g., low-frequency characteristics) omitted from use in the perception of segments, as is the case in Pattani Malay; in fact, acoustic characteristics can trade off, conveying a latent percept rather than a superficial one (Repp 1982), and the perceptual weighting of the acoustic characteristics can vary (Purnell, to appear).

Japanese geminates also exhibit layering of acoustic characteristics and perceptual cues. Although duration appears to be the primary acoustic characteristic for the perception of geminates (e.g., Beckman 1982, Port, Dalby, and Odell 1987, Kubozono 1989, Han 1992, Otake et al. 1993, Sato 1993, Cutler and Otake 1994), there are other phonetic cues covarying with consonantal length. Han (1994) found that the duration of vowels before and after geminates in Japanese (with the exception of [tt] compared to [t]) is modified slightly (V_1 is lengthened by 11% and V_2 is shortened by 9%). Brighenti and Homel (1993) found that Italian and Japanese are alike in many ways including variability in syllabic duration, suggesting that factors other than the usual syllabic weight units play a role. For Japanese, this would mean showing the relevance of subsyllabic units other than the ubiquitous unit of weight, the mora. Findings by Cutler and Otake (2002) suggest that for CV portions of Japanese words, the segments rather than the moras play a role in initial stages of perception. This research suggests that Japanese speakers perceive weight independently of the usual unit of syllabic weight (i.e., the moras).

Once the stops are organized in terms of the syllable, certain acoustic characteristics of voicing in specific syllabic positions become less important (notably any characteristic coinciding with the constriction such as glottal pulsing). Assuming that syllabification will turn the first segment of a geminate into a coda (Maddieson and Emmorey 1985), glottal pulsing in the coda consonant does not have to be pervasive. Glottal pulsing need only last longer in a voiced coda than a voiceless one. For example, voicing can be conveyed by lengthening of the vowel before the coda obstruent. Moreover, glottal pulsing does not even have to be encoded in the onset consonant. Pulsing in the onset just needs to start before, at, or soon after the burst to be perceived as voiced, depending on the distribution of voiced and voiceless aspirated obstruents. Therefore, the voicing ratio is variable and can be changed by positional adaptation. Since the (phonological) prohibition against voiced geminates is tied to (phonetic) passive devoicing, a problem arises because many languages (e.g., English) do not use persistent vocal cord vibration as the only or even primary perceptual cue for voicing. HKS's prohibition against voiced geminates must be about more than just length or voicing since geminate stops are not impossible to preserve in a language. Not only the layering of acoustic characteristics is important, but also the selection of acoustic characteristics as perceptual cues. For example, Kingston and Diehl (1994, 1995) suggest that generally in American English, voicing of coda obstruents is signaled by one of four cues: preceding vowel duration, glottal pulsing in the stop gap, changes in F1, and changes in F0. Recently, these four cues to voicing in coda obstruents were found to hold a different acoustic status among speakers of a dialect of Wisconsin English such that vowel duration and glottal pulsing are in a trading—not enhancement—relation, while changes in F1 and F0 differ negligibly by obstruent coda voicing (Purnell, Salmons, and Tepeli 2005, Purnell et al. 2005, Salmons, Tepeli, and Purnell, to appear). The relative perceptual salience of cues in American English dialects and Pattani Malay argues against the conclusion (1b) following from (1a); the only way for a speaker to know the value of a phonetic feature comes from networks within a speech community. A speaker will only learn a lot about the phonetics of geminate devoicing, not about the place of geminate devoicing in the phonological system.

17.4   Conclusion

In this chapter, I have looked at the degree to which phonetic knowledge is active in the phonology and not simply filtered by the perceptual system. I have argued that the power of phonetic knowledge to directly influence phonology is restricted by an indirect relation between acoustic characteristics and perceptual cues. Since we cannot make wholly accurate predictions from phonetic details, positing active phonetic knowledge within phonology does not satisfy a necessary requirement for a phonological theory. This failure to make reasonably accurate predictions leads to three conclusions. First, the main premise of HKS 2004 is invalid. Second, the evidence discussed here reaffirms the contention that the field of phonology needs to keep some distance from the phonetic "ground" (Halle 1962). Although phonologists often describe the distance between phonetics and phonology as a smooth continuum, it is more likely that both levels are by and large autonomous and that a demarcation distinguishes one level from the other. With further study, we may find that what has long been conceived of as a continuum is in fact a transfer of informational packets through a series of operational states, including an abstract representational state and a neuromotor state governed by boundary conditions governing skilled movements. Third, and most important, the relation between phonetics and phonology is no doubt more complex than we know and are able to articulate. For example, Stevens discusses the relation between phonetics and phonology through a description of distinctive features that (1) "define which articulators are to be controlled" and (2) "provide a broad specification of how these articulators are to be manipulated" (1998:244). Moreover, other works echo this focus on the "acoustic and articulatory realization" of distinctive features (Clements and Hume 1995). However, this characterization of distinctive features is no doubt limited by our vague understanding of the territory between abstract representations, gestures, and percepts. The issue is that in the region between the output of phonology and the input to articulation, as well as in the complex region between acoustics and phonology, there are nonlinear changes or processes that influence the two standing states at the end of the processes.

Although the presentation of HKS's argument is problematic, the pursuit of experimental evidence may assist in refining the premise. What is lacking in our collective knowledge right now is experimental studies verifying perceptual voicing cues in Japanese and the relation of these cues to the gemination cues. We need to understand how listeners arrive at various degrees of geminate voicing strength, especially given the phonetic variability in geminate length and the encoding of voicing with alternate phonetic cues.

In the end, we must reject Ohala's lack of distinction between phonetics and phonology as unexplanatory. Despite what we learn by investigating the past, the problem with historical phonetics is that it only explains known facts; that is, it is a theory of accommodation. My argument here has been that phonetics explains nothing in phonology partly because of the nonlinear relation between phonetics and phonology. We must also reject Steriade's active-phonetic-knowledge model (Steriade 1997, Hayes, Kirchner, and Steriade 2004) as irrelevant; that is, there is no way to address epistemological problems because there are no limits on phonetic knowledge.

Notes

I appreciate comments on various drafts of this chapter by Chuck Cairns, Bill Idsardi, Andrea Menz, Marianne Milligan, Eric Raimy, Joe Salmons, and Laura Smith. All errors are my own.

1. Alternatively, we could cast the discussion in terms of parallel modules.

2. See, among many articles and books spanning the mid 1960s and the late 1990s, Halle 1962, Chomsky and Halle 1968, Halle and Mohanan 1985, the *fin du siècle* writings of Patricia Keating (1996, 1991), and syntax-phonology interface discussions like the one in Inkelas and Zec 1990.

3. This includes any proposal that relegates phonetics to its own narrowly defined domain, such as, the morphophonemic, word, and phonetic levels in Harmonic Phonology (Goldsmith 1993).

4. It is important to note that Blevins does admit that the attention members of a speech community give to Labovian variables may also contribute to language change (2004:31). It is not

clear that one can present a comprehensive theory of sound system restructuring without taking into account the extensive social forces behind nonperceptual patterns. In other words, there can be no adequate answer to Blevins's question ("Why do sound systems pattern the way they do, and not otherwise?"; 2004:78) absent some account of production (Labov 1994) and identity (Labov 2001).

5. For references, see Blevins 2004:78–81.

6. There are a number of variations on the theme of phonetic transparency related to Optimality Theory; see *Phonology* 18, issue 1, 2001 for some of them. It is noteworthy that McCarthy (2003) argues against gradience in phonology.

7. This statement does not prohibit knowledge about acoustic characteristics from influencing prephonological operations, such as adaptation to perceptual boundaries (e.g., Repp and Liberman 1987).

8. For the time being, we can be vague about whether "something" equates with distinctive features, actual gestures, and so on, in order to avoid unnecessary distractions.

9. It is not clear that writers proposing strong or weak positions can deliver on any proposal involving contrastive gradience or gradient contrastiveness. More often than not, evaluation of gradience is reducible to oppositional contrast—generally, that is, to standard distinctive features. For example, although Côté claims that some segments are "more contrastive" than others (2004:2), the evaluation of gradience is based on oppositional contrastive distinctive features (2004:5).

10. Nor can Ohala's position be used to make predictions about phonetic restitutions—that is, the case where a sound is eliminated by a particular process, only to reappear in later generations.

11. Final fortition is the active use of [spread glottis] in certain coda positions. This contrasts with the characterization of devoicing as being the loss of the [voiced] feature.

References

Abramson, Arthur S. 1986. The perception of word-initial consonant length: Pattani Malay. *Journal of the International Phonetic Association* 16:8–16.

Abramson, Arthur S. 1991. Amplitude as a cue to word-initial consonant length: Pattani Malay. In *Proceedings of the 12th International Congress of Phonetic Sciences*, 98–101. Aix-en-Provence: Université de Provence.

Archangeli, Diana, and Douglas Pulleyblank. 1994. *Grounded Phonology*. Cambridge, Mass.: MIT Press.

Beckman, Mary. 1982. Segment duration and the mora in Japanese. *Phonetica* 39:113–135.

Blevins, Juliette. 2004. *Evolutionary Phonology: The emergence of sound patterns*. Cambridge: Cambridge University Press.

Brighenti, Laura, and Peter Homel. 1993. Syllable duration in Italian and Japanese. Paper presented at the 126th meeting of the Acoustical Society of America.

Chomsky, Noam, and Morris Halle. 1968. *The sound pattern of English*. New York: Harper and Row.

Clements, G. N., and Elizabeth Hume. 1995. The internal organization of speech sounds. In *The handbook of phonological theory*, ed. by John Goldsmith, 245–306. Cambridge, Mass.: Blackwell.

Côté, Marie-Hélène. 2004. Syntagmatic distinctness in consonant deletion. *Phonology* 21:1–41.

Cutler, Anne, and Takashi Otake. 1994. Mora or phoneme: Further evidence for language-specific listening. *Journal of Memory and Language* 33:824–844.

Cutler, Anne, and Takashi Otake. 2002. Rhythmic categories in spoken-word recognition. *Journal of Memory and Language* 46:296–322.

Davidson, Donald. 1963. *Essays on actions and events*. Oxford: Oxford University Press.

Docherty, Gerard J. 1992. *The timing of voicing in British English obstruents*. Berlin: Foris.

Fant, Gunnar. 1960. *Acoustic theory of speech production*. The Hague: Mouton.

Fisher, Ronald A. 1930. *The genetical theory of natural selection*. Oxford: Clarendon Press.

Foley, James. 1973. Assimilation of phonological strength in Germanic. In *A festschrift for Morris Halle*, ed. by Stephen R. Anderson and Paul Kiparsky, 51–58. New York: Holt, Rinehart and Winston.

Goldsmith, John. 1993. *The last phonological rule*. Chicago: University of Chicago Press.

Gordon, Matthew J. 2000. *Small-town values and big-city vowels: A study of the Northern Cities Shift in Michigan*. Durham, N.C.: Duke University Press.

Halle, Morris. 1962. Phonology in generative grammar. *Word* 18:54–72.

Halle, Morris, and K. P. Mohanan. 1985. Segmental phonology of Modern English. *Linguistic Inquiry* 16:57–116.

Han, Mieko S. 1992. The timing control of geminate and single stop consonants in Japanese: A challenge for nonnative speakers. *Phonetica* 49:102–127.

Han, Mieko S. 1994. Acoustic manifestations of mora timing in Japanese. *Journal of the Acoustical Society of America* 96:73–82.

Haugen, Einar. 1942. Analysis of a sound group: *sl* and *tl* in Norwegian. *Proceedings of the Modern Language Association* 57:879–907.

Hayes, Bruce, Robert Kirchner, and Donca Steriade. 2004. *Phonetically based phonology*. New York: Cambridge University Press.

Hayes, Bruce, and Donca Steriade. 2004. Introduction: The phonetic bases of phonological markedness. In *Phonetically based phonology*, ed. by Bruce Hayes, Robert Kirchner, and Donca Steriade, 1–33. Cambridge: Cambridge University Press.

Inkelas, Sharon, and Draga Zec. 1990. *The phonology-syntax connection*. Chicago: University of Chicago Press.

Iverson, Gregory K., and Joseph C. Salmons. 1995. Aspiration and laryngeal representation in Germanic. *Phonology* 12:369–396.

Iverson, Gregory K., and Joseph C. Salmons. 1999. Glottal spreading bias in Germanic. *Linguistische Berichte* 178:135–151.

Iverson, Gregory K., and Joseph C. Salmons. 2003. Laryngeal enhancement in early Germanic. *Phonology* 20:43–74.

Johnson, Keith. 2000. Adaptive dispersion in vowel perception. *Phonetica* 57:181–188.

Johnson, Keith, Edward Flemming, and Richard Wright. 1993. The hyperspace effect: Phonetic targets are hyperarticulated. *Language* 69:505–528.

Joseph, Brian D. 2001. Historical linguistics. In *The handbook of linguistics*, ed. by Mark Aronoff and Janie Rees-Miller, 105–129. Oxford: Blackwell.

Keating, Patricia A. 1991. On phonetics/phonology interaction. *Phonetica* 48:221–222.

Keating, Patricia A. 1996. The phonetics-phonology interface. In *Interfaces in phonology*, ed. by Ursula Kleinhenz, 262–278. Berlin: Akademie Verlag.

Kingston, John, and Randy Diehl. 1994. Phonetic knowledge. *Language* 70:419–454.

Kingston, John, and Randy Diehl. 1995. Intermediate properties in the perception of distinctive feature values. In *Phonology and phonetic evidence: Papers in laboratory phonology IV*, ed. by Bruce Connell and Amalia Arvaniti, 7–27. Cambridge: Cambridge University Press.

Kingston, John, and David Solnit. 1989. The inadequacies of underspecification. In *Proceedings of North East Linguistic Society (NELS) 19*, ed. by Juli Carter and Rose-Marie Déchaine, 264–278. Amherst: University of Massachusetts, Graduate Linguistic Student Association.

Kristoffersen, Gjert. 2000. *The phonology of Norwegian*. Oxford: Oxford University Press.

Kubozono, Haruo. 1989. The mora and syllable structure in Japanese: Evidence from speech errors. *Language and Speech* 32:249–278.

Labov, William. 1972. *Sociolinguistic patterns*. Philadelphia: University of Pennsylvania Press.

Labov, William. 1994. *Principles of linguistic change*. Vol. 1, *Internal factors*. Cambridge, Mass.: Blackwell.

Labov, William. 2001. *Principles of linguistic change*. Vol. 2, *Social factors*. Oxford: Blackwell.

Ladefoged, Peter, and Ian Maddieson. 1996. *The sounds of the world's languages*. Oxford: Blackwell.

Lass, Roger. 1980. *On explaining language change*. Cambridge: Cambridge University Press.

Liljencrants, Johan, and Björn Lindblom. 1972. Numerical simulation of vowel quality systems: The role of perceptual contrast. *Language* 48:839–862.

Lindblom, Björn, and Olle Engstrand. 1989. In what sense is speech quantal? *Journal of Phonetics* 17:107–121.

Lisker, Leigh. 1986. "Voicing" in English: A catalogue of acoustic features signaling /b/ versus /p/ in trochees. *Language and Speech* 29:3–11.

Maddieson, Ian. 1985. Phonetic cues to syllabification. In *Phonetic linguistics: Essays in honor of Peter Ladefoged*, ed. by Victoria A. Fromkin, 203–211. Orlando, Fla.: Academic Press.

Maddieson, Ian, and Karen Emmorey. 1985. Relationship between semivowels and vowels: Cross-linguistic investigations of acoustic difference and coarticulation. *Phonetica* 42:163–174.

Matisoff, James. 1973. Tonogenesis in South-East Asia. In *Consonant types and tone*, ed. by Larry M. Hyman, 71–96. Los Angeles: University of Southern California.

McCarthy, John J. 2003. OT constraints are categorical. *Phonology* 20:75–138.

McCarthy, John J., and Alan Prince. 1993. Prosodic Morphology I: Constraint interaction and satisfaction. Ms., University of Massachusetts, Amherst, and Rutgers University.

Miller, Joanne L. 1981a. Effects of speaking rate on segmental distinctions. In *Perspectives on the study of speech*, ed. by Peter D. Eimas and Joanne L. Miller, 39–74. Hillsdale, N.J.: Lawrence Erlbaum.

Miller, Joanne L. 1981b. Some effects of speaking rate on phonetic perception. *Phonetica* 38:1–3.

Nearey, Terrance M. 1989. Static, dynamic, and relational properties in vowel perception. *Journal of the Acoustical Society of America* 85:2088–2113.

Ohala, John J. 1974. Phonetic explanation in phonology. In *Papers from the Parasession on Natural Phonology*, ed. by Anthony Bruck, Robert Allen Fox, and Michael W. LaGaly, 251–274. Chicago: University of Chicago, Chicago Linguistic Society.

Ohala, John J. 1983. The origin of sound patterns in vocal tract constraints. In *The production of speech*, ed. by Peter F. MacNeilage, 189–216. New York: Springer-Verlag.

Ohala, John J. 1984. Explanation in phonology: Opinions and examples. In *Phonologica 1984*, ed. by Wolfgang U. Dressler, Hans C. Luschutzky, Oskar E. Pfeiffer, and John R. Rennison, 215–225. Cambridge: Cambridge University Press.

Ohala, John J. 1986. Against the direct realist view of speech-perception. *Journal of Phonetics* 14:75–82.

Ohala, John J. 1990. There is no interface between phonology and phonetics: A personal view. *Journal of Phonetics* 18:153–171.

Ohala, John J. 1992a. What is the input to the speech production mechanism? *Speech Communication* 11:369–378.

Ohala, John J. 1992b. What's cognitive, what's not, in sound change. *Lingua e Stile* 27:321–362.

Ohala, John J. 1997. The relation between phonetics and phonology. In *The handbook of phonetic sciences*, ed. by William J. Hardcastle and John Laver, 674–694. Oxford: Blackwell.

Otake, Takashi, Giyoo Hatano, Anne Cutler, and Jacques Mehler. 1993. Mora or syllable: Speech segmentation in Japanese. *Journal of Memory and Language* 32:258–278.

Polka, Linda, and Ocke-Schwen Bohn. 2003. Asymmetries in vowel perception. *Speech Communication* 41:221–231.

Port, Robert F. 2007. How are words stored in memory? Beyond phones and phonemes. *New Ideas in Psychology* 25:143–170.

Port, Robert F., Jonathan Dalby, and Michael Odell. 1987. Evidence for mora timing in Japanese. *Journal of the Acoustical Society of America* 81:1574–1585.

Port, Robert F., and Adam P. Leary. 2005. Against formal phonology. *Language* 81:927–964.

Prince, Alan S., and Paul Smolensky. 2004. *Optimality Theory: Constraint interaction in generative grammar*. Malden, Mass.: Blackwell.

Purnell, Thomas C. To appear. Phonetic detail in the perception of ethnic varieties of US English. In *Studies in Sociophonetics*, ed. by Dennis Preston and Nancy Niedzielski. Berlin: Mouton de Gruyter.

Purnell, Thomas C., Joseph C. Salmons, and Dilara Tepeli. 2005. German substrate effects in Wisconsin English: Evidence for final fortition. *American Speech* 80:135–164.

Purnell, Thomas C., Joseph C. Salmons, Dilara Tepeli, and Jennifer Mercer. 2005. Structured heterogeneity and change in laryngeal phonetics: Upper Midwestern final obstruents. *Journal of English Linguistics* 33:307–338.

Repp, Bruno H. 1982. Phonetic trading relations and context effects: New experimental evidence for a speech mode of perception. *Psychological Bulletin* 92:81–110.

Repp, Bruno H., and Alvin M. Liberman. 1987. Phonetic category boundaries are flexible. In *Categorical perception: The groundwork of cognition*, ed. by Stevan Harnad, 89–112. Cambridge: Cambridge University Press.

Salmons, Joseph C., Dilara Tepeli, and Thomas C. Purnell. To appear. Deutsche Spuren im amerikanischen Englischen. In *Deutsche Sprachinseln heute*, ed. by Nina Berend and Elisabeth Knipf-Komlósi. Frankfurt a.M.: Peter Lang.

Sato, Yumiko. 1993. The durations of syllable-final nasals and the mora hypothesis in Japanese. *Phonetica* 50:44–67.

Sober, Elliott. 1984. *The nature of selection: Evolutionary theory in philosophical focus*. Cambridge, Mass.: MIT Press.

Steriade, Donca. 1995. Positional neutralization. Ms., UCLA.

Steriade, Donca. 1997. Phonetics in phonology: The case of laryngeal neutralization. Ms., UCLA.

Stevens, Kenneth N. 1998. *Acoustic phonetics*. Cambridge, Mass.: MIT Press.

Stevens, Kenneth N., and Sheila E. Blumstein. 1981. The search for invariant acoustic correlates of phonetic features. In *Perspectives on the study of speech*, ed. by Peter D. Eimas and Joanne L. Miller, 1–38. Hillsdale, N.J.: Lawrence Erlbaum.

Thomas, Erik R. 1995. Phonetic factors and perceptual reanalyses in sound change. Doctoral dissertation, University of Texas at Austin.

Westbury, John R., and Patricia A. Keating. 1986. On the naturalness of stop consonant voicing. *Journal of Linguistics* 22:145–166.

18 Rule Application in Phonology

Morris Halle and Andrew Nevins

18.1 Introduction

The purpose of this chapter is to outline and defend a theory of phonology employing ordered rules, by illustrating how the theory accounts for certain complex phenomena central to the phonologies of the Slavic languages Russian, Czech, and Serbo-Croatian. We focus on three important principles of phonological rule application:

(1) The application of phonological rules is subject to the principle that when more than one rule applies to a given string, the interaction is determined by rule order. Counterfeeding opacity results from the fact that rules do not get a "second chance" to apply.

(2) Phonological rules are organized into two blocks: cyclic and postcyclic. Cyclic rule application respects morphological constituency and applies to each nested constituent of the word in turn. Postcyclic rules apply once to the entire word, after all cyclic rules.

(3) If a lexical item is an exception to a particular rule R_k, this exceptionality only affects application of R_k; all rules $R_{1...k-1}$ and $R_{k+1...n}$ apply as usual.

We assume that morphological structure building precedes phonological rule application, and specifically that all Slavic nouns have the tripartite form Root + Theme + Case-Number, although the phonological exponent of some of the parts may be subsequently deleted by various rules. For instance, even when traditional methods of surface analysis do not reveal three distinct morphemes in a word such as Czech *žen* 'woman, gen. pl.', we assume that there are in fact three underlying morphemes here, but that both the theme and the case-number suffix are deleted by rules of the phonology, which obscure this structure. As we discuss below, adopting this approach—which sharply distinguishes underlying representations from their surface manifestations—makes it possible to bring out clearly the regularity both of the morphological structure of a word and of the phonological rules that relate its underlying and surface representations.

That a word such as Czech or Russian genitive plural *žen* is underlyingly composed of a root plus two suffixes (one the theme vowel, and one the case ending), of which neither surfaces in this particular environment, is in part a consequence of the discovery by Jakobson (1948) that Russian (and Slavic generally) is subject to a rule of Vowel Truncation. This rule deletes a vowel immediately preceding another vowel and explains why the noun theme vowel /a/, which surfaces in the instrumental plural *žen + a + mi*, is absent in the accusative singular *žen + u*, from underlying /žen + a + u/. Jakobson's rule, originally formulated to account for facts of the Russian conjugation, thus explains a number of facts in the declension of nouns as well as other aspects of the phonology of Czech and other Slavic languages (see Lightner 1972, Gussmann 1980, Rubach 1993).[1]

One main focus of attention of the chapter is the genitive plural form of nouns in the Slavic languages. Historically, the phonetic exponent of the genitive plural in Common Slavic was the short vowel /u/, commonly referred to as *back yer* and represented below with a capital *U*. As noted above, the case endings of all nouns in Slavic consist of a theme vowel followed by the case-number suffix. Since in the genitive plural this gives rise to a sequence of two vowels, Jakobson's rule of Vowel Truncation applies and deletes the theme vowel, leaving the short /U/ as the phonetic marker of the genitive plural. Having caused the deletion of the theme, the short /U/ is itself deleted by a subsequent rule. The genitive plural thus surfaces as the bare stem for many nouns. Russian examples of such genitive plurals are *žen* 'women's', *fabrik* 'factories'' (fem.), *mest* 'places'' (neut.), *volos* 'hairs'' (masc.).

Not all nouns have the bare stem form in the genitive plural. In Russian, for example, certain nouns are subject to a readjustment rule in the genitive plural, which inserts a glide—either /j/ or /w/—between the theme vowel and the case ending. The insertion of the glide between these two vowels has the effect of blocking Vowel Truncation in these forms. In this way, genitive plural forms like Russian /stol + ov/ 'tables'' and /car, + ej/ 'tsars'' are generated (for discussion, see Halle 1994, Bailyn and Nevins 2008).

West and South Slavic display yet another treatment of the genitive plural, which also involves blocking of Vowel Truncation. As explained below, Vowel Truncation in Czech and Serbo-Croatian is blocked not by Glide Insertion, but by marking the genitive plural forms of nouns as exceptions to Vowel Truncation. Since systematic marking of forms as exceptions to a particular rule has rarely, if ever, been invoked as a mechanism of phonological change, we make the case for it below at some length. One result of the discussion is that the development of the genitive plural in the different Slavic languages divides all nouns into three classes: a class where the genitive plural is directly generated from the underlying representation, and two classes where the rule of Vowel Truncation is blocked. In one class, it is blocked by Glide Insertion, and in the other—and far more interesting—class, it is blocked by marking genitive plural forms as exceptions to Vowel Truncation. As we show, this marking has no effect on the operation of any of the other rules of the phonology.

18.2   The Regularity of Morphological Structure (and How It May Be Obscured)

We begin with a problem that arises in the inflection of verbs in Modern Russian like those in (4a–c). A comma following a consonant indicates that it is palatalized ([−back]); the effects of stress and vowel reduction (ikan'e) have been disregarded.

(4)   *Sg. fem. past*   *1pl. pres.*   *1sg. pres.*
    a. l,ez + l + a   l,ez, + e + m   l,ez + u   'climb'
    b. laja + l + a   laj + e + m   laj + u   'bark'
    c. zna + l + a   znaj + e + m   znaj + u   'know'

The first form in (4a), /l,ez + l + a/, is composed of three morphemes: /l,ez/, the stem meaning 'climb'; /l/, the past tense morpheme; and /a/, the feminine singular agreement suffix. Each of these pieces has its own motivated semantic and syntactic role. The same three pieces—stem, tense, agreement—appear in the second form in (4a), the first person plural present /l,ez, + e + m/, except that in this form tense and agreement have different exponents: /e/ is the present tense morpheme, and /m/ stands for first person plural. The third form in (4a) has only two pieces: the stem and the suffix /u/. Semantically and syntactically, however, the form is completely parallel to the other two forms. The fact that the first person singular form has only two pieces clearly needs an explanation.[2]

In his 1948 paper, Jakobson relied on a distinction that would now be viewed as one between underlying and surface representations. Jakobson was not the originator of this distinction; in a footnote (p. 156), Jakobson credited this important distinction to the American linguist Leonard Bloomfield (see Bloomfield 1933:218).[3]

Jakobson's discovery communicated in the 1948 paper was that in order to account for the relation between underlying and surface forms of Russian verbs, it is necessary to assume that Russian is subject to the two truncation rules stated informally in (5).[4]

(5) a. *Vowel Truncation*
       V → ∅ / __ + V
   b. *Glide Truncation*
       j,w → ∅ / __ + C

These rules affect vowels and glides that may be present in the underlying morphological structure of a word. Vowel Truncation (5a) provides an answer to the question that was raised above in connection with (4). The first person singular /u/ in /l,ez + u/ is a person-number suffix, just like the first person plural /m/ in /l,ez, + e + m/, but because the first person singular suffix begins with a vowel, Vowel Truncation (5a) applies in this form and deletes the present tense marker /e/, as shown in (6).

(6) l,ez + e + u   ⇒   l,ezu (by Vowel Truncation)
   (cf. l,ez + l + a   ⇒   l,ezla
        l,ez + e + m   ⇒   l,ezem)

This analysis also accounts for the forms of the verb in (4b), as shown in (7).[5] The last form in (7) shows two applications of Vowel Truncation (5a). As we will discuss below, Vowel Truncation (5a) is a cyclic rule. Finally, as shown in (8), Glide Truncation (5b) is required for the past tense forms of the verb in (4c).

(7) laj + a + l + a   ⇒   lajala
   laj + a + e + m   ⇒   lajem (by Vowel Truncation (5a))
   laj + a + e + u   ⇒   laju (by Vowel Truncation (5a) twice)

(8) znaj + l + a   ⇒   znala (by Glide Truncation (5b))
   znaj + e + m   ⇒   znajem
   znaj + e + u   ⇒   znaju (by Vowel Truncation (5a))

The rules in (5) make possible accounts of great morphological transparency and uniformity for verb forms of different tenses and inflectional combinations. In particular, they make possible accounts where there is only one verbal stem in both past and present tense: the exponent of the present tense is /-e-/ (and, for a second well-defined class of verbs, /-i-/), and all finite verbs have the uniform morphological structure Stem + Theme + Tense + Agreement. These properties of our account reflect the basic working hypothesis of our theory—the *Principle of Morphological Consistency*—which states that, as far as possible, all verbs have the same underlying morphological constituency and that phonological rules are responsible for surface divergences. In other words, we take the position that in the "storage versus computation" trade-off, speakers opt for minimizing storage, and in so doing they opt for uniform morphological structure and a single underlying lexical entry, which is the main locus of unpredictable information.

The existence of truncation rules in the phonology of a language highlights one of the most difficult problems in the study of speech perception: once truncation rules are admitted, a given output is compatible in principle with any number of underlying representations. For example, [laju] could in principle derive not only from /laj + a + e + u/ as in (7), but also from /laj + e + u + e + a + u/ or any other sequence of heteromorphemic vowels. Assuming the uniformity of underlying morphological structure based on an informed theory of morphology is thus crucial to constraining the representations onto which surface [laju] can map.

Another striking phenomenon found throughout Slavic is a pattern of vowel/zero alternations. These vowel/zero alternations derive historically from the fact that the two short high vowels became susceptible to deletion at a late stage in Common Slavic (see Townsend and Janda 1996). These vowels are called *yers* in the philological tradition, and we use the term *yer* here as a synchronic description of abstract vowels that undergo vowel/zero alternations under the specific conditions explained below.[6]

As an example, consider the Russian words in (9). In the genitive singular (9a), the two masculine nouns have stems of the same form, but their nominative singular forms are different (9b).

(9) a. *Gen. sg.*   b. *Nom. sg.*
     park + a   park   'park'
     turk + a   turok   'Turk'

The existence of numerous pairs of this type makes it apparent that, unlike cases of vowel/zero alternations encountered in other languages, those in Slavic cannot be handled by epenthesis, as there is no distinction between the phonological environment of the nominative singular forms of *turk* and *park* that might trigger such a rule. Since the two stems appear in identical contexts, their different behaviors can be attributed only to differences in their underlying representations. Specifically, we propose that in its underlying representation, *turk* contains a yer, but *park* does not. We propose in addition that the nominative singular suffix of these nouns is yer, rather than zero. We illustrate this in (10), where U stands for the [+high, +back] yer. (The [+high, −back] yer is represented by I.)

(10) a. *Gen. sg.*   b. *Nom. sg.*
      park + a   park + U
      turUk + a   turUk + U

These underlying forms with their "abstract" yer vowels are subject to the rules in (11) and (12).

(11) *Yer Lowering*
     Yer → [−high] / __ C_0 Yer

(12) *Yer Deletion*
     Yer → $\varnothing$

The difference between the nominative and genitive singular of *park* and *turk* is thus captured by the presence or absence of a yer in the underlying form. In (13), we show the application of Yer Lowering (11) and Yer Deletion (12) to the underlying forms of the minimal pair from (9).[7]

(13) a. park + U   ⇒   park (by Yer Deletion (12))

        park + a   ⇒   parka

    b. turUk + U   ⇒   turokU (by Yer Lowering (11))   ⇒   turok (by Yer

                                                      Deletion (12))

        turUk + a   ⇒   turka (by Yer Deletion (12))

The important point about the behavior of yers, then, is that vowel/zero alternations arise from a simple and regular sequence of computations: when there are two yers in adjacent syllables, the first one surfaces as a mid vowel, and the second one deletes, and so do all yers that have not undergone Yer Lowering.

The same behavior is found in the verbal system. The verbs /tolUk/ 'pound' and /polz/ 'crawl' show alternations like those in (14).

(14) a. tolUk + e + u   ⇒   tolku (by Vowel Truncation (5a), Yer Deletion (12))

        tolUk + l + a   ⇒   tolkla (by Yer Deletion (12))

        tolUk + l + U   ⇒   tolokl (by Yer Lowering (11), Yer Deletion (12))

    b. polz + e + u   ⇒   polzu (by Vowel Truncation (5a))

        polz + l + a   ⇒   polzla

        polz + l + U   ⇒   polzl (by Yer Deletion (12))

The forms in the last lines of (14a) and (14b) surface as *tolok* and *polz* owing to an additional rule of word-final *l*-deletion whereby the past tense *l* deletes in the context C + ___#, yielding masculine/feminine past tense pairs such as *čital/čitala* 'read' but *l̦ez/l̦ezla* 'climbed', as well as *tolok/tolkla* and *polz/polzla*. In sum, the underlying difference between the verbs *tolUk* and *polz* exactly parallels that between the nouns *turUk* and *park*.

At this point, an important question arises: what happens to an underlying sequence of several consecutive syllables that have yers in their nuclei? For example, what happens in the mapping of three or more yers in consecutive syllables from underlying to surface form? A simplistic interpretation of Yer Lowering (11) and Yer Deletion (12) might lead us to expect that an alternating pattern such as /U...U...U/ might surface as [∅ o ∅]. As it turns out, there is no "pure" answer to this question. In particular, Yer Lowering (11) and Yer Deletion (12) do not apply in alternating fashion, for example, lower-delete-lower-delete. Rather, the application of these rules is governed by an important principle, the cyclic character of rule application, introduced into the theory of phonology by Chomsky, Halle, and Lukoff (1956).

Given a bracketed morphological structure [[X Y] Z], the principle of cyclic rule application dictates that if [X Y] and [[X Y] Z] are cyclic constituents and interact with respect to a cyclic phonological rule such that Y is the trigger for a rule affecting X, and Z is the trigger for a rule affecting Y, the rule affecting X will apply before the rule affecting Y. Cyclic application thus determines a principle of rule-application ordering based on morphological structure.

The Russian noun *ogon,* 'fire' and its derivative *ogon,ek* 'small light' provide an opportunity to consider the interaction of three adjacent yers as determined by the principle of cyclic rule application. Like *turok, ogon,* has an underlying form containing a yer.

(15) a. ogUn, + U ⇒ ogon, (by Yer Lowering (11),   (Nom. sg.)
                              Yer Deletion (12))
      b. ogUn, + a ⇒ ogn,a (by Yer Deletion (12))   (Gen. sg.)

The addition of the derivational suffix -*Ik,* with a front yer, generates a nominative singular form with the nested structure [[X Y] Z], that is, [[ogUn, + Ik] + U] 'small light'. While (15a) makes it evident that Yer Lowering (11) applies before Yer Deletion (12), applying these rules in this order would not generate the correct output for [[ogUn, + Ik] + U]. In particular, the innermost constituent [ogUn, + Ik] would undergo both Yer Lowering (11) and Yer Deletion (12), resulting in *ogon, + k.* This sequence would serve well on the next cycle if the case ending were genitive singular -*a,* yielding *ogon,ka.* It would fail, however, in the nominative singular, where the output is not *ogon,k* but *ogon,ek.* The yer of the diminutive suffix, which lowers the yer of the stem, is in turn lowered by the yer of the case ending. Crucially, each application of Yer Lowering (11) created by considering successively larger morphological constituents will occur before the application of Yer Deletion (12).

To account for this fact, we propose that for [[ogUn, + Ik] + U] to be computed successfully, the rules of the phonology must be organized into two blocks, one cyclic and one postcyclic, as proposed in Halle and Mohanan 1985, Halle and Vergnaud 1987, and Halle and Matushansky 2006 (for an overview, see Kenstowicz 1994:chap. 5). The rules of the cyclic block apply to each nested constituent of the word in turn. After all constituents have undergone cyclic rule application, the rules of the postcyclic block apply once to the entire word, without regard to morphological constituency. Our specific proposal is that Vowel Truncation (5a) and Yer Lowering (11) are cyclic rules, while Yer Deletion (12) is a postcyclic rule.

Consider the cyclic application of Yer Lowering (11) for the derivationally complex form /ogUn, + Ik/ 'small light' in the nominative and genitive singular. As morphological constituency is crucial for application of cyclic rules, we indicate it in (16). Recall that Yer Lowering (11) applies cyclically, constituent by constituent, and that once this cyclic application is done, the postcyclic block of rules, including Yer Deletion (12), applies. We indicate cyclic application by a set of brackets that denote the current immediate constituent undergoing rule application at each step.[8]

(16) a. Cyclic rule application

      ogUn, + Ik + U ⇒ [ogon, + Ik] + U   Derivational affix cycle, Yer
                                                  Lowering (11) applies

      [[ogon, + Ik] + U] ⇒ [[ogon, + ek] + U]   Case cycle, Yer Lowering (11)
                                                  applies

      End of cyclic rule application
      ogon,ekU ⇒ ogon,ek   Postcyclic block, Yer Deletion
                                                  (12) applies

   b. Cyclic rule application

      ogUn, + Ik + a ⇒ [ogon, + Ik] + a   Derivational affix cycle, Yer
                                                  Lowering (11) applies

      [[ogon, + Ik] + a] ⇒ [[ogon, + Ik] + a]   Case cycle, Yer Lowering (11)
                                                  does not apply

      End of cyclic rule application
      ogon,Ika ⇒ ogon,ka   Postcyclic block, Yer Deletion
                                                  (12) applies

Importantly, the sequence of three yers in (16a) yields [o ... e ... ∅], resulting from cyclic application of Yer Lowering (11). To better grasp how cyclic application operates, consider the diminutive /ogUn, + Ik + Ik + U/, which has four consecutive yers in the nominative singular and surfaces as *ogon,eček*. All but the last of these four yers lower under cyclic application. In the genitive singular /ogUn, + Ik + Ik + a/, again all but the last of the yers lower under cyclic application, yielding *ogon,ečka*.[9] In both forms, the postcyclic rule of Yer Deletion (12) eliminates the last yer in the sequence.

We now turn to an important consequence of cyclic rule application, resulting from the fact that *not every immediate constituent of a word undergoes it*. That is, affixation of certain morphemes generates constituents that are not subject to the cyclic rules of the phonology. When such a constituent (termed a postcyclic constituent) is encountered in the derivation, it is simply skipped, and the cyclic rules then apply to the next constituent in the structure.

In many languages, including Russian, prefixes are postcyclic constituents.[10] Evidence for the postcyclic nature of constituents with prefixes in Russian comes from the fact that prepositions are not subject to the cyclic rule of Vowel Truncation (5a), as shown in (17).

(17) [[na + uk] + a]   'science'
     [[[[pro + igr] + a] + l] + a]   'lost, past fem.'
     [[[[po + obed] + aj] + e] + mU]   'we (shall) have dinner'

The fact that Vowel Truncation (5a) does not apply in the prefixed forms in (17) is formally accounted for by assuming that Vowel Truncation (5a) is a rule in the cyclic block and that constituents formed with a prefix are postcyclic. More precisely, as cyclic application proceeds from the most deeply embedded constituent outward, the constituent [prefix + root] will never undergo cyclic application. Moreover, the application of cyclic rules is subject to the principle of Strict Cyclicity (e.g., Mascaró 1976). This principle prevents Vowel Truncation (5a), which has been skipped on the innermost constituent, from applying during a subsequent pass through the cyclic rules. In accordance with this principle, a rule that had a chance to apply on an earlier cycle, but was skipped because the earlier constituent was postcyclic, may not apply to any part of the earlier constituent on a later cycle.

The effects of these principles are well illustrated by comparing the derivation in (18) with that in (16a). In both cases, three yers appear in sequence in a left-branching syntactic structure. However, the innermost constituent in (16a) is cyclic like the rest, whereas the innermost constituent in (18), consisting of the prefix /sU/ and the root /žIg/, is postcyclic and therefore not subject to the rules of the cyclic block.

The fact that Russian prefixes are postcyclic makes a prediction about the behavior of three consecutive yers in this context, namely, that the yer in the prefix will not undergo cyclic lowering. Examples may thus be found in which there are three yers in adjacent syllables: one from a prefix, one within a monosyllabic verb stem, and one in the masculine past ending. (18), adapted from Halle and Vergnaud 1987, illustrates the skipping of Yer Lowering (11) in the postcyclic prefix in the masculine past tense for the verb *sU-žIg* 'burn'.[11]

(18) Cyclic rule application

sU + žIg + l + U ⇒ [sU + žIg] + l + U	Skipped as prefix is postcyclic
[sU + žIg + l]	Past tense /l/ is cyclic, but Yer Lowering (11) does not apply because of strict cyclicity
[sU + žIg + l + U] ⇒ [sU + žeg + l + U]	Next cycle, Yer Lowering (11) applies
End of cyclic rule application	
sU + žeg + l + U ⇒ s + žeg + l	Postcyclic block, Yer Deletion (12) applies twice
s + žeg + l ⇒ žžok	By other postcyclic rules

The result of derivation (18) is quite different from that of derivation (16a), where all three morphemes are cyclic. In (16a), the sequence /U...I...I/ surfaces as [o...e...∅], whereas in (18), with an innermost constituent that is postcyclic, /U...I...U/ surfaces as [∅...o...∅].

When a morpheme contains a yer, it serves as a diagnostic for telling whether a given morphological constituent is cyclic or not. Yers that are in postcyclic constituents never undergo cyclic lowering and never cause cyclic lowering. As we argue extensively in the next section, and as anticipated in the Principle of Morphological Consistency, all Slavic nouns have the structure Root + Theme + Case-Number suffix. These sequences are subject to phonological rules that are assigned to either one or both of the cyclic and postcyclic blocks. In the unmarked case, all constituents of a word are subject to rules of both blocks, with the cyclic rules applying to each immediate constituent in turn, followed by a single pass through the postcyclic rules. In marked cases, specific morphemes—for instance, the Russian prefixes—are exempt from the rules of the cyclic block and are subject only to the postcyclic rules. The postcyclic status of a given morpheme is thus one mechanism that languages use to avoid the application of an otherwise regular rule of the phonology. In the next section, we examine another such mechanism: the marking of a morpheme sequence as an exception to a specific rule.

The highly specific theory developed here imposes severe constraints on how a particular fact is to be accounted for. We take it as evidence supporting the theory that it has made possible a motivated account of the above data, which are quite complex. We conclude this section by reiterating the importance of adopting Morphological Consistency for all nouns and verbs and by pointing out that the immediate explanatory unification afforded by separating rules into cyclic and postcyclic blocks, whose application is determined by morphological status and by falsifiable diagnostics of whether a given morpheme is cyclic or not.

18.3   Exceptional Rule Nonapplication in the Czech Declension

The facts of literary (*spisovná*) Czech (Havránek and Jedlička 1981) discussed in this section argue compellingly for the proposition that there can be exceptions to a particular phonological rule, and that these exceptions are narrowly constrained so they affect that rule only, while all other rules apply normally. The narrow focus of such exceptions sheds interesting light on both the rules and the derivations to which they give rise.

Czech forms are represented below in a mixed orthography that deviates from the official orthography in that vowel length is represented by a colon after the vowel rather than by an acute accent over it. *U* and *I* represent the abstract yer vowels in underlying representations. Following standard Czech orthography, *y* represents a vowel that is phonetically identical to [i] on the surface but differs from /i/ in the contexts in which it occurs. After palatal consonants, only /i/ occurs; but after other consonants, /y/ occurs. We use *E* for the *e-háček* grapheme of Czech that represents /e/, /je/, or /ňe/ (as in *mEst*, which has the phonetic form [mňest]).

Jakobson's rule of Vowel Truncation (5a) also applies in Czech, as shown by the examples in (19), which are all but identical to the Russian examples in (4).

(19)   *Fem. sg. past*   *1pl. pres.*   *1sg. pres.*
    a. lez + l + a   lez + e + me   lez + e + u   'creep'
       [lezla]   [lezeme]   [lezu]
    b. kyp + E + l + a   kyp + E + i: + me   kyp + E + i: + m   'boil'
       [kypEla]   [kypi:me]   [kypi:m]

In (19), we illustrate the first conjugation verb *lez* 'creep' and the second conjugation verb *kyp-E* 'boil'. Comparison of (19a) and (19b) shows that the former retains the present tense vowel in the first person plural while the latter does not, as a result of Vowel Truncation (5a). The forms in (19) also show that Czech differs from Russian in having long and short vowels. Moreover, in Czech all verbs of the second conjugation and some verbs of the first conjugation take *m* as the first person singular present exponent; the remaining verbs of the first conjugation take the exponent *-u*.

Having shown in (19) that, like the phonology of Russian, the phonology of Czech includes the rule of Vowel Truncation (5a), we turn to a set of vowel/zero alternations in Czech that demonstrate that, as in Russian, the underlying form of a morpheme may contain a yer vowel, yielding minimal pairs.

(20) a. kapsa   kapes   'pocket'   (Nom. sg./Gen. pl.)
      ři:msa   ři:ms   'edge'   (Nom. sg./Gen. pl.)
    b. posel   posla   'envoy'   (Nom. sg./Gen. sg.)
      nesl   nesla   'carried'   (Past part. masc./fem.)
    c. rez   rzi   'rust'   (Nom. sg./Gen. sg.)
      mez   meze   'limit'   (Nom. sg./Gen. sg.)

The examples in (20) show that certain word-final consonant clusters are admitted in some words, yet the same clusters trigger vowel insertion in other words. We assume that, as in Russian, this difference is due to the presence of a yer in the underlying representation. Czech differs from Russian in that all yers become [e] under lowering.

Rule (11) in Russian thus corresponds to (21) in Czech.

(21) *Yer Lowering*
    Yer → [−high,−back] / __ C$_0$ Yer

The postcyclic rule of Yer Deletion (12) is the same in both languages. As in Russian, the exponents of the nominative singular and of the masculine past tense in Czech are yers; these trigger rule (21), which lowers the preceding yer, as illustrated in (20).

As in Russian, we assume that all nouns in Czech (and in other Slavic languages) have three parts: a stem, a theme vowel, and a case-number ending. The character of the theme vowel is determined jointly by several factors: semantic animacy, the declension class of the noun, the consonant with which the stem ends, and the inflectional features of the case morpheme. An overriding regularity is that after stems ending with one of the palatal consonants [š, č, ž, j, ř, ň]—that is, after [−anterior] coronal consonants—the theme vowel is /e/ for all classes of nouns. There are 12 distinct patterns of nominal inflection in Czech once all the case-number combinations are considered. The 12 classes of nouns are listed in (22).

(22) a. hrad 'castle' (masc.)
     b. mEst 'city' (neut.)
     c. žen 'woman' (fem.)
     d. kost 'bone' (fem.)
     e. pi:sUň 'song' (fem.)
     f. muž 'man' (masc.)
     g. moř 'sea' (neut.)[12]
     h. ru:ž 'rose' (fem.)
     i. stroj 'machine' (masc.)
     j. pa:n 'gentleman' (masc.)
     k. soudUc 'judge' (masc.)
     l. předsed 'chairman' (masc.)

Certain vowel length alternations in the Czech nominal declension are of special interest to phonological analysis.[13] We begin by considering the plural forms of the feminine noun žen + a 'woman', with theme vowel -a-, in the plural cases.[14]

(23)   *Surface form*   *Root + Theme + Case*
      Inst. pl.   ženami   žen + a + mi
      Dat. pl.   žena:m   žen + a + mU
      Loc. pl.   žena:ch   žen + a + xU
      Gen. pl.   žen   žen + a + U
      Nom. pl   ženy   žen + a + y
      (Acc. = Nom.)

As shown in (23), the theme vowel -a- is present in the underlying representation of all cases, but its presence is obscured on the surface by the operation of Vowel Truncation (5a). In particular, the theme vowel is deleted before both the nominative/accusative plural case ending -y and the genitive plural -U (yer). The deletion of the theme vowel before yer shows that yer behaves like any other vowel with respect to Vowel Truncation (5a). Since in the genitive plural the yer is also word-final, it is subject to the postcyclic rule of Yer Deletion (12).

Of special note is that in the dative and locative plural the theme vowel is long, but in the instrumental plural it is short. We assume that the theme vowel is underlyingly short, and we account for the lengthening by positing that the dative and locative plural case exponents end with a yer. It is the presence of this yer that induces lengthening in a preceding vowel, thus motivating the rule in (24).[15]

(24) *Pre-Yer Lengthening*

$V_{[-high]} \rightarrow V: / \_\_ C_0$ Yer

The operation of Pre-Yer Lengthening (24) is thus responsible for the lengthened theme vowel in the dative and locative in (23). In principle, Pre-Yer Lengthening (24) will lengthen a nonhigh theme vowel whenever one occurs before a yer-containing suffix; thus, we might surmise that even the theme vowel in the genitive plural has the potential of being lengthened (and perhaps is lengthened at an intermediate level of representation though we do not see it because of the operation of Vowel Truncation (5a)).

The genitive plural is of particular interest here since it provides evidence for the ordering of Pre-Yer Lengthening (24) and Vowel Truncation (5a). As shown in (25a), the stem vowel of the noun would be incorrectly lengthened if Vowel Truncation applied before Pre-Yer Lengthening. The correct order of application, shown in (25b), is the counterfeeding order of Pre-Yer Lengthening before Vowel Truncation.

(25) *Rule ordering in genitive plural*
  a. žen + a + U   Vowel Truncation (5a)
   žen + U   Pre-Yer Lengthening (24)
   že:n + U   Yer Deletion (12)
   že:n   *Incorrect output*
  b. žen + a + U   Pre-Yer Lengthening (24)
   žen + a: + U   Vowel Truncation (5a)
   žen + U   Yer Deletion (12)
   žen   *Correct output*

Since Pre-Yer Lengthening (24) precedes Vowel Truncation (5a), as shown in (25b), the model thus far implies that if one could have access to an intermediate level of representation or perhaps a situation in which Vowel Truncation (5a) was not operative, one would find an underlyingly short theme vowel that had been lengthened in the genitive plural (see the intermediate representation *žen + a: + U* in (25b)), in addition to being lengthened in the dative and locative plural.

Just this scenario actually holds for a large group of Czech nouns. In fact, 10 out of the 12 inflectional classes of nouns in (22)—that is, all of them except for the *žen* and *mEst* classes—are subject to an exceptional marking, operative *only in the genitive plural*, that renders these forms exceptions to Vowel Truncation (5a).

(26) *Czech exceptional marking*
  The genitive plural of the 10 inflectional classes in (22a,d–l) is exempt from Vowel Truncation (5a).

The statement in (26) is cast in a very specific way: it mentions that these forms are exceptions to Vowel Truncation (5a). They are not exceptional in any other manner; that is, Pre-Yer Lengthening (24), Yer Lowering (11), Yer Deletion (12), and all other segmental rules of Czech phonology apply to them as would normally be expected.

In (27), we illustrate with plural case forms of the noun *ru:ž-e* 'rose' the consequences of the exceptional marking in (26) as it interacts with the application of otherwise normally operative rules in the Czech declension. (*UR* = underlying representation)

(27)

	UR	*Surface form*
Inst. pl.	ru:ž + e + mi	ru:žemi
Dat. pl.	ru:ž + e + mU	ru:ži:m
Loc. pl.	ru:ž + e + xU	ru:ži:ch
Nom./Acc. pl.	ru:ž + e + ∅	ru:že
Gen. pl.	ru:ž + e + U	ru:ži:

The case endings in (27) are all the same as the case endings in (23), except for the nominative plural, which is ∅ in the five inflectional classes represented by *mož + e*, *ruž + e*, *stroj + e*, and *pi:sUň + e*. Pre-Yer Lengthening (24) applies as expected in the dative and locative, yielding a long theme vowel. In Czech, lengthened mid vowels surface as high vowels, owing to a rule of Mid Vowel Raising (28) that turns long [−high, −low] vowels into their [+high] counterparts,[16] thus accounting for the long *i:*/short *e* alternation in the theme vowel.

(28) *Mid Vowel Raising*
     [−low] V: → [+high]

This raising rule applies to the [+back] theme vowel /o/ after it has been lengthened in the dative plural forms of the masculine and neuter nouns in classes (22a,b,f,i,j), generating *hradu:m*, *pa:nu:m*, *mužu:m*, *stroju:m*, and *mEstu:m*.

In the genitive plural, only a subset of Czech nouns exhibit the behavior illustrated in (25). In addition to the feminine nouns of the *žen* class, the neuter nouns of the *mEst* class show no surface ending in the genitive plural. The nouns of the other 10 classes of (22) have a long high vowel suffix in the genitive plural, as shown in the surface forms in (29).

(29) hrad + u: ru:ž + i:
     kost + i: stroj + u:
     pi:sň + i: pa:n + u:
     muž + u: soudUc + u:
     mor̆ + i: předsed + u:

The distribution of endings in (29) is straightforward: masculine nouns take long /u:/ whereas feminine and neuter nouns ending with a palatal consonant take long /i:/. These are derived from /o:/ and /e:/ by application of Mid Vowel Raising (28).

The forms in (29) differ from those in (25). Because of the exceptional marking (26), the genitive plural ending -*U* in (29) does not induce Vowel Truncation (5a). We illustrate this with the derivations in (30).

(30) a. ru:ž + e + U

        ru:ž + e: + U   Pre-Yer Lengthening (24)

        ru:ž + e: + U   Vowel Truncation (5a): *does not apply* because of (26)

        ru:ž + e: Yer Deletion (12)

        ru:ž + i   Mid Vowel Raising (28)

    b. hrad + o + U

        hrad + o: + U   Pre-Yer Lengthening (24)

        hrad + o: + U   Vowel Truncation (5a): *does not apply* because of (26)

        hrad + o: Yer Deletion (12)

        hrad + u: Mid Vowel Raising (28)

It is important to note that the ordering solution works without added complexity: *each of the four rules in (30) is independently motivated; and when properly ordered, these rules account for the genitive plural facts.* Other treatments of the genitive plural of the 10 classes that are subject to the exceptional marking in (26) require additional machinery because they view the long suffix vowel as a morphological idiosyncrasy or as the result of a templatic effect (e.g., Scheer 2002). Our proposal for the genitive plural employs the same rules as those for all other inflected forms of the Czech nouns.

(31)		UR	Surface forms	Rules applied
a.	Nom. pl.	mEst-o-a	mEsta	Vowel Truncation (5a)
b.	Dat. pl.	mEst-o-mU	mEstu:m	Pre-Yer Lengthening (24), Yer Deletion (12), Mid Vowel Raising (28).
c.	Gen. pl.	mEst-o-U	mEst	Vowel Truncation (5a), Yer Deletion (12)
d.	Loc. pl.	mEst-U-xU	mEstech	Theme vowel replacement (32a), Yer Lowering (21), Yer Deletion (12)

In (31), we illustrate the derivations of the different plural forms of the neuter noun *mEst + o* 'city'. We note that the theme vowel in the locative plural is /U/ rather than /o/. We assume that this is due to a readjustment rule, by which the theme vowel that appears in most of the case-number combinations undergoes a change in its phonetic exponent. Readjustment rules, by hypothesis, are locally determined morphological operations that apply prior to any rules of the cyclic block. In (32), we list the readjustment rules that apply to the theme vowel of Czech nouns.

(32) *Czech theme vowel replacement*
  a. Theme vowel → yer in locative plural of *hrad, mEst, pa:n, předsed* classes (22a,b,j,l)
  b. Theme vowel → /o/ in dative plural and genitive plural of *stroj* class (22i)
  c. Theme vowel → /e/ in genitive plural of *kost* class (22d)
  d. Theme vowel → yer in instrumental singular of *hrad, mEst, muž, mor̆, stroj, pa:n,* and *soudUc* classes (22a,b,f,g,i,j,k)

As a consequence of the readjustment rule of "yer replacement" in (32a), the theme vowel in these locative plural forms exhibits special behavior.[17] Specifically, as Pre-Yer Lengthening (24) does not apply to high vowels, it will not affect the yer theme vowel in (31d), since yer is a high vowel at that point in the derivation.

Rule (32a) applies to the locative plural of the noun stems of the *hrad* class. Consider next the plural forms of the nouns of the *kost* class (22d), shown in (33).

(33)

	UR	Surface form	Rules applied
Inst. pl.	kost + I + mi	kostmi	Yer Deletion (12)
Dat. pl.	kost + I + mU	kostem	Yer Lowering (21), Yer Deletion (12)
Loc. pl.	kost + I + xU	kostech	Yer Lowering (21), Yer Deletion (12)
Nom./Acc. pl.	kost + I + i	kosti	Yer Deletion (12)
Gen. pl.	kost + e + U	kosti:	Theme vowel replacement (32c), Pre-Yer Lengthening (24), Yer Deletion (12)

As a result of the change in the theme vowel induced by (32c), the theme vowel in the genitive plural is subject to Pre-Yer Lengthening (24) and subsequently raises to become the long high vowel /i:/.

Of additional interest is the fact that in none of these forms does Pre-Yer Lengthening (24) apply on the stem cycle. If Pre-Yer Lengthening, a cyclic rule, were to apply to the constituent [root + theme], it would apply to the root vowel in *kost*, incorrectly yielding **ku:stmi* for the instrumental plural. The fact that this does not occur provides evidence, by way of the diagnostic established in section 18.2, that theme vowels are postcyclic.[18] As a postcyclic constituent, then, the [root + theme] constituent does not undergo the cyclic rule of Pre-Yer Lengthening (24).

This completes the inventory of the rules involved in the computation of underlying-to-surface forms in the declension of Czech nouns. In table 18.1, we indicate the theme vowel by a hyphen next to the nominal root (-*o*- is the theme vowel for the root *hrad*, -*a*- is the theme vowel for the root *žen*, etc.). In each cell, we supply the underlying form of the case-number suffix. The surface forms of course diverge from the underlying forms as a result of both the readjustment rules and the phonological rules reviewed above.

As noted throughout the chapter, *U* and *I* represent yers. Accusative cells marked *Nom* or *Gen* are those in which the accusative is syncretic with either the nominative or genitive form (depending on animacy and gender).[19] The neuter noun *kuř-e*, not included in the table, inflects like *moř-e* in the singular and like *mEst-o* in the plural.

A parenthesized form in a cell (e.g., the locative plural of *mEst*) indicates a theme vowel that undergoes readjustment, as described above (see (32)). Each shaded cell marks a form that is an exception to Vowel Truncation (5a) (see (26)). As the reader can verify, only the genitive plural is an exception to rule (5a). Importantly, genitive plural forms that are exceptions to Vowel Truncation (5a) do not constitute exceptions to Pre-Yer Lengthening (24).

Table 18.1
Czech nominal declensions

	hrad-o sg.	hrad-o pl.	mEst-o sg.	mEst-o pl.	žen-a sg.	žen-a pl.
Nom.	U	y	null	a	null	y
Acc.	nom.	nom.	nom.	nom.	u	nom.
Gen.	u	U	a	U	y	U
Dat.	u	mU	u	mU	E	mU
Loc.	u	(U) + xU	u	(U) + xU	E	xU
Inst.	(U) + mU	y	(U) + mU	y	-ou	mi

	muž-e sg.	muž-e pl.	moř-e sg.	moř-e pl.	ru:ž-e sg.	ru:ž-e pl.
Nom.	U	i	null	null	null	null
Acc.	null	null	null	nom.	i	nom.
Gen.	null	(o) + U	null	U	null	U
Dat.	i	(o) + mU	i	mU	i	mU
Loc.	i	xU	i	xU	i	xU
Inst.	(U) + mU	y	(U) + mU	y	i:	mi

Table 18.1
(continued)

	stroj-e sg.	stroj-e pl.	pa:n-o sg.	pa:n-o pl.	soudUc-e sg.	soudUc-e pl.
Nom.	U	null	U	i	null	i
Acc.	nom.	null	gen.	y	null	null
Gen.	null	(o) + U	a	U	null	(o) + U
Dat.	i	(o) + mU	u	mU	i	(o) + mU
Loc.	i	xU	u	(U) + xU	i	xU
Inst.	(U) + mU	y	(U) + mU	y	(U) + mU	y

	předsed-o sg.	předsed-o pl.	pi:sUň-e sg.	pi:sUň-e pl.	kost-I sg.	kost-I pl.
Nom.	a	we:	U	null	U	i
Acc.	u	y	nom.	nom.	U	nom.
Gen.	y	U	null	U	i	(e) + U
Dat.	wi	mU	i	mU	i	mU
Loc.	wi	(U) + xU	i	xU	i	xU
Inst.	w	y	i:	mi	i:	mi

18.4   Cyclic and Postcyclic Rule Interaction in the Serbo-Croatian Genitive Plural

The Serbo-Croatian genitive plural resembles that of Czech. In particular, as in a
subset of Czech nouns (e.g., *ru:ži:* and *hradu:*), the genitive plural form of the majority of Serbo-Croatian nouns ends with a long vowel: for example, *ora:la:* 'eagle, gen.
pl.'.[20] On the plausible assumption that the lengthened vowel in the genitive plural is
to be accounted for in the same way in Serbo-Croatian as in Czech, we posit (1) that
the exponent of the Serbo-Croatian genitive plural is also yer and (2) that, as in
Czech (see (26)), genitive plural forms constitute marked exceptions to Vowel Truncation (5a).

(34) *Serbo-Croatian exceptional marking*
     The genitive plural is exempt from Vowel Truncation (5a).

Since the case ending is a yer, the long vowel of the genitive plural in Serbo-Croatian is the theme vowel, and its length is due to Pre-Yer Lengthening (24), which is triggered by the case ending. The derivation thus proceeds exactly as in Czech (see (30)).

The next question concerns the nature of the theme vowel: as its surface appearance is [a:], one might suppose that it is underlyingly /a/, lengthened by Pre-Yer Lengthening (24). This analysis, while close to the surface, falls short in an important way, to be described below. Instead, our solution takes advantage of the fact that Yer Lowering in Serbo-Croatian generates the low back vowel /a/, formally represented in (35) as the Serbo-Croatian counterpart of the Czech rule (21) and the Russian rule (11).

(35) *Yer Lowering (Serbo-Croatian)*
        Yer → [+low, +back] / __ C_0 Yer

We propose that the theme vowel yielding the surface ending [a:] in the genitive plural is an underlying yer. Like its Czech counterpart (21), rule (35) feeds Pre-Yer Lengthening (24); thus, an underlying yer surfaces as [i:] in Czech and as [a:] in Serbo-Croatian.

Perhaps the most interesting fact about the Serbo-Croatian genitive plural is that the final vowel of the noun stem is always lengthened. This fact has puzzled linguists for well over a century. For example, Leskien (1914:416) remarked that there was in his day already an entire literature on the Serbo-Croatian genitive plural, none of which he found convincing. Leskien was especially puzzled by the treatment of stem-final vowels preceding the genitive plural suffix. He asked "why an old sestUrU surfaces not as *sestra: but as sestára: (= sesta:ra:)" (p. 416).[21]

Since the stem vowel in question precedes the yer theme vowel, the length of the stem-final vowel follows automatically from the operation of Pre-Yer Lengthening (24). We thus propose that the theme vowel of the genitive plural of Serbo-Croatian nouns becomes a yer as the result of a readjustment rule, like that proposed for Czech (see (32)). The readjustment rule for Serbo-Croatian that yields a yer as the theme vowel in the genitive plural, and its effect of lengthening the stem-final vowel, are shown in (36) and (37).

(36) *Serbo-Croatian theme vowel replacement*
        Theme vowel → yer in genitive plural

(37) *Partial derivation of Serbo-Croatian genitive plural*
        [sestUr + U]   [root + theme] constituent
        sestar + U   Yer Lowering (35)
        sesta:r + U   Pre-Yer Lengthening (24)

However, the suggestion that the theme vowel of the genitive plural is a yer that induces Pre-Yer Lengthening (24) of the stem-final vowel is incompatible with our proposal above that theme vowels are generally postcyclic. The partial derivation in (37) tacitly assumes that theme vowels are cyclic. If the genitive plural theme vowel were postcyclic, Pre-Yer Lengthening (24) would not be applicable to the innermost [root + theme] constituent. After application of Yer Lowering (35) and Pre-Yer Lengthening (24) in the next constituent, the result would be as shown in (38), where brackets denote immediate constituents.

(38) *Incorrect derivation of Serbo-Croatian genitive plural*

[sestUr + U] + U	No cyclic rules apply if [root + theme] constituent is postcyclic
[sestUrU + U]	Next constituent
[sestUra + U]	Yer Lowering (35)
[sestUra: + U]	Pre-Yer Lengthening (24)
[sestUra: + U]	Marked exception to Vowel Truncation (5a); see (34)
sestUra:U	End of cyclic block
sestra:	Postcyclic Yer Deletion applies; *incorrect output*

The incorrect output in (38) is what one would expect if the [root + theme] constituent were postcyclic, and it is this expectation that led to Leskien's question cited above.

An answer appears once it is assumed that in the genitive plural the theme vowel constituent is cyclic. In other words, in Serbo-Croatian a special readjustment rule assigns cyclic status to the innermost constituent of genitive plural words. This rule is included in a general summary of the cyclic status of constituents in (39).

(39) a. Affixal morphemes are marked as cyclic by default.

b. Slavic prefixes and theme vowels are marked as postcyclic.

c. The theme vowel of the Serbo-Croatian genitive plural is marked as cyclic.

As the derivation in (40) shows, (39c) allows the correct output to be generated.

(40) *Correct derivation of Serbo-Croatian genitive plural*

[sestUr + U] + U	*Innermost constituent is cyclic*
[sestar + U] + U	Yer Lowering (35)
[sesta:r + U] + U	Pre-Yer Lengthening (24)
[sesta:rU + U]	Next constituent
[sesta:ra + U]	Yer Lowering (35)
[sesta:ra: + U]	Pre-Yer Lengthening (24)
[sesta:ra: + U]	Marked exception to Vowel Truncation (5a); see (34)
sesta:ra:U	End of cyclic block
sesta:ra:	Postcyclic Yer Deletion applies; *correct output*

A yer theme vowel that is cyclic triggers the cyclic rule of Pre-Yer Lengthening (24). In other words, the rules and the ordering in (38) did not capture the facts correctly because they did not incorporate (39c). The correct derivation in (40) requires no new idiosyncratic rule of stem-vowel lengthening in order to derive the lengthened stems.

An aspect of the architecture of cyclic and postcyclic rule application that has not yet been discussed is described in (41).

(41) A phonological rule *R* may be assigned to *both* the cyclic and the postcyclic blocks.

We explore the consequences of (41) for Serbo-Croatian with the orderings and the assignment to blocks shown in (42). Notice that one rule is assigned only to the cyclic block, one rule is assigned only to the postcyclic block, and two rules are assigned to both blocks.

(42) *Cyclic block rule application order*
   Yer Lowering (35)
   Pre-Yer Lengthening (24)
   Vowel Truncation (5a)

   Postcyclic block rule application order
   Yer Lowering (35)
   Pre-Yer Lengthening (24)
   Yer Deletion (12)

The assignment of rules to the two blocks in (42) has consequences for stems that have yer in their last syllable. In a number of such stems, the vowel preceding the yer is lengthened in case forms where the yer is deleted, but not in case forms where the yer is subject to Yer Lowering (35), as illustrated in (43).

(43) | | Surface form | UR |
|----------|--------------|----|
| Nom. sg. | jarac | jarUc + o + U |
| Gen. sg. | ja:rca | jarUc + o + a |
| | 'male goat' | |

This postcyclic lengthening is distinct from the lengthening in *sesta:ra:*, which is cyclic. As shown in (42), we assume that Pre-Yer Lengthening (24) is assigned to the postcyclic block as well as the cyclic block. As a result of the ordering, Yer Lowering (35) bleeds Pre-Yer Lengthening (24), and hence any yer that lowers (such as a stem yer in the nominative singular of masculine *o*-stem nouns) will not induce lengthening of the preceding vowel. Unlike the cyclic variant of Pre-Yer Lengthening, the postcyclic variant does not apply when the triggering yer is word-final; if it did, the nominative singular (and genitive plural) forms would surface with an incorrect long vowel in the last syllable. We state the noncyclic rule of Pre-Yer Lengthening in (44), and in (45) we illustrate the application of both the cyclic and the noncyclic rules to the nominative and genitive singular of *jarUc*.

(44) *Nonfinal Pre-Yer Lengthening (postcyclic)*

$V_{[-high]} \rightarrow V\text{:} \ / \ \_\_ \ C_0 \ Yer \ C_0 \ V$

(45)		jarUc + o + U	jarUc + o + a
Cyclic block			
Yer Lowering (35)		inapplicable	inapplicable
Pre-Yer Lengthening (24)		jarUc + o: + U	inapplicable
Vowel Truncation (5a)		jarUc + U	jarUc + a
Postcyclic block		jarUcU	jarUca
Yer Lowering (35)		jaracU	inapplicable
Nonfinal Pre-Yer Lengthening (44)		inapplicable	ja:rUca
Yer Deletion (12)		jarac	ja:rca

Many additional examples of this pattern can be found in Matešić 1970. There appear to be lexically marked exceptions to postcyclic Nonfinal Pre-Yer Lengthening (44), such as *prosac* 'suitor, nom. sg.', *prosca* 'gen. sg.', in which the genitive singular does not show lengthening.

In (46), we show derivations of the surface forms of the nominative singular, genitive singular, and genitive plural of the Serbo-Croatian masculine noun *orao* 'eagle'. (*PYL* = Pre-Yer Lengthening; *IR* = intermediate representation)

(46)	*Nom. sg.*	*Gen. sg.*	*Gen. pl.*
First cycle			
UR	[orUl + o] + U	[orUl + o] + a	[orUl + U] + U
Yer Lowering (35)	inapplicable	inapplicable	[oral + U] + U
PYL (24)	inapplicable	inapplicable	[ora:l + U] + U
Vowel Truncation (5a)	inapplicable	inapplicable	inapplicable
Second cycle			
IR	[orUl + o + U]	[orUl + o + a]	[ora:l + U + U]
Yer Lowering (35)	inapplicable	inapplicable	[ora:l + a + U]
PYL (24)	orUl + o: + a	inapplicable	[ora:l + a: + U]
Vowel Truncation (5a)	[orUl + Ø + U]	[orUl + Ø + a]	exception (see (39a))
Postcyclic block			
IR	orUlU	orUla	ora:la:U
Yer Lowering (35)	oralU	inapplicable	inapplicable
Nonfinal PYL (44)	inapplicable	o:rUla	inapplicable
Yer Deletion (12)	oral	o:rla	ora:la:
Coda *l*-vocalization	orao	inapplicable	inapplicable
	[orao]	[o:rla]	[ora:la:]

As a result of (41), the same rules yield lengthening of the stem-initial vowel in the genitive singular, lengthening of the stem-final vowel in the genitive plural, and lengthening of neither stem-internal vowel in the nominative singular. (46) shows the result that root-internal interactions occur only in the postcyclic block (as in the genitive singular).

In the above account of genitive plural forms, the fact that these forms are systematic exceptions to Vowel Truncation (5a) plays a crucial role. By a coincidence that is close to miraculous, the historical record of this development has been preserved. In discussing the evolution of the Serbo-Croatian genitive plural, Leskien reports that the genitive plural form with long /a:/ became dominant in the sixteenth century, but can be documented already in the fourteenth century. In his words: "The traditional Church Slavonic orthography of the older records writes all genitive forms with -*I*, [single yer] even where *a* was already likely to have been pronounced. *In the fourteenth century, people began to write in place of the single -*I*, the double -*II*; e.g., pastirII, človekII, selII, rabotII" (Leskien 1914:434; emphasis added). On the plausible assumption that these spellings represent the pronunciation of an archaic (or archaizing) dialect without Yer Lowering and Yer Deletion, we have here a written record of the fact that in the fourteenth century, Serbo-Croatian genitive plural forms became exceptions to the rule of Vowel Truncation (5a) (see (34)), and these forms surfaced with sequences of two yers.

This was not Leskien's view. Since Leskien's theory of phonology and morphology did not view the phonetic surface form as the result of the application of ordered rules to abstract underlying representations, it would have been all but impossible for Leskien to analyze these forms as special exceptions to Vowel Truncation (5a). He therefore assumed that the spellings with two yers did not reflect the actual phonetics of these forms, but were a roundabout way of representing a long [a:]. He wrote, "That in fact -a was pronounced here is shown by spellings of that time such as *župa, zemalja*, which are already found regularly in the fifteenth century. The phonetic output form [Gesamtlautgestalt] of the genitive plural is here already that of present-day Štokavian" (Leskien 1914:434).

We see no reason to suppose that the two different spellings—the yer sequence ⟨II⟩ and ⟨a⟩—reflect the same phonetic event. If the genitive plural ending had been pronounced as [a] in the fourteenth century, this would have been so recorded by the scribes, since both *a* and yer were letters in their alphabet. The fact that the letter *a* does not appear in genitive plural endings until a century later indicates that [a] was not pronounced here in the fourteenth century and that the written sequence of two yers represents the actual pronunciation of as a sequence of two central vowels.

Our account of the intricate facts of both Czech and Serbo-Croatian is based on our assumption that rules are not only subject to ordering, but also assigned to different blocks (cyclic vs. noncyclic), and that particular constituents of the word may be systematic exceptions to the rules of the cyclic block. Our account of the phonology of Russian, Czech, and Serbo-Croatian has relied on aspects of ordering to account for facts that would otherwise require complications of the rules. We believe this exploitation of various aspects of rule ordering afforded by our theory is a general property of the phonology of all languages. To the extent that we have succeeded in presenting a correct account of the facts, we have also provided empirical evidence to support the theory that underpins our account. We have developed a theory that sticks to well-motivated phonological rules and derives divergent surface results through different ways of applying these rules: namely, by their order of application.

An important question that deserves further thought and study concerns the nature and function of theme vowels. Oltra-Massuet (1999) proposes that in Catalan, every functional head requires that a theme vowel adjoin to it postsyntactically. She cites examples such as *agudidzari∅az* 'sharpen, cond.', with three theme vowels: between stem and mood, between mood and tense, and between tense and agreement. Theme vowels have no syntactic or semantic function, as they occur not only in verbs and nouns but also in adjectives. We would like to tentatively suggest that theme vowels serve a parsing purpose, functioning as boundary markers between contentful morphemes that assist the hearer in recovering the constituency of the linear phonetic string.

A point worth emphasis concerns the positing of underlying representations containing yers. The inclusion of a yer in the memorized form of a morpheme or word attributes considerable theoretical sophistication to each fluent speaker of the languages discussed here. As we have shown, however, this abstract nature of the underlying representations allows simple accounts of a great variety of surface facts. For example, the obvious fact that the yer is a vowel leads to the correct conclusion that it triggers Vowel Truncation. It also implies correctly that this vowel will trigger or undergo Yer Lowering, and, in Czech and Serbo-Croatian, that it will trigger Pre-Yer Lengthening. Traditional and recent accounts of these facts that have excluded yers on a priori grounds have been forced to employ considerably more complex and less perspicuous solutions than the handful of rules presented above.

Notes

We thank Pavel Caha, Chuck Cairns, Markéta Ceplová, Bill Idsardi, Jay Jasanoff, Ivona Kučerová, Horace Lunt, Nikola Predolac, Eric Raimy, Tobias Scheer, Donca Steriade, and Markéta Ziková for helpful discussions during the course of this research.

1. Bermúdez-Otero (2007) has recently argued for a synchronic rule of heteromorphemic vowel deletion in Spanish that is strikingly similar and perhaps suggestive of a broader phenomenon at hand.

2. One possible explanation might be that /u/ is a complex morpheme that signals both present tense and first person singular agreement. The /-z/ suffix in English verb forms such as *plays* has such composite structure: it simultaneously signals present tense and third person singular agreement. But in English it is common for a suffix to signal both tense and agreement. For Russian, this analysis would be attributing composite structure to some suffixes and not to others, and this would require special stipulations in the syntax-morphology interface of Russian. A second explanation might posit two phonetic realizations of the present tense: /-e-/ in some (most) person forms of the verb, and zero elsewhere. Again, a parallel could be cited from English, where the present tense forms of all verbs other than those of the third person singular take such a zero suffix. (This is shown by the fact that *Do* Support is triggered by the negative verb forms, both those that take the suffix /-z/, as in *she doe + s not play*, and those that take the zero suffix, as in *we do + ∅ not play*.) If this proposal were to be adopted for Russian, it would again require some complications in the morphology; at a minimum, we would have to posit a ∅ present tense morpheme, which appears only in first person singular forms, while /-e-/ appears elsewhere.

Neither of these accounts is to be rejected on a priori grounds; as noted above, the proposals are very similar to what is actually found in English. But in Russian they are essentially ad hoc accounts, with nothing to support them beyond their limited descriptive adequacy, and in missing the generalization about vowel deletion, they are to be dispreferred to an account like the one in the text.

3. The distinction between underlying and surface representations was explicitly made also in a celebrated paper by Edward Sapir, "The Psychological Reality of Phonemes," which first appeared in 1933, the same year as Bloomfield's *Language*, in a French translation in *Journal de Psychologie Normale et Pathologique* (30:247–265). Trubetzkoy drew Jakobson's attention to Sapir's paper in a letter of 10 July 1933; see Jakobson 1975:279.

4. In Jakobson's formulation, morphemes ending with nasals were included in (5b), however, Jakobson was mistaken about nasals deleting before consonants, as noted first in Kayne 1967.

5. The stem *laja* is composed of /laj + a/, that is, a verbal root plus theme vowel, while *lez* is "athematic," having a zero theme vowel. We omit zero morphemes here for expository ease.

6. For instructive discussions of the yer facts in Polish, which differ only little from those considered below, see Gussmann 1980 and Szpyra 1995.

7. Both nouns in (13) contain the underlying theme vowel -*o*-, as can be seen in the instrumental singulars *parkom* and *turkom*. This theme vowel deletes in (13) because of Vowel Truncation (5a); we omit it in the example to maintain focus on the application of Yer Lowering (11) and Yer Deletion (12).

8. Additional rules of Russian phonology also apply to this form, including a rule that turns stressed *e* into *o* before an unpatalalized consonant. We omit the theme vowels in (16) as they will be deleted by Vowel Truncation (5a) and our focus in (16) is on cyclic Yer Lowering (11).

9. The change of *k* to *č* in the first of two diminutive suffixes is due to a rule that we leave aside here.

10. Further research may reveal that the postcyclic character of Slavic prefixes may be due to their syntactic status. For recent discussion, see Arsenijević 2005 and Svenonius 2005.

11. That the prefix /sU/ contains a yer may be shown by examining the feminine past tense *sožgla*, where the yer of the prefix lowers because of the application of a postcyclic version of

Yer Lowering. We motivate the existence of this application of Yer Lowering in section 18.4. As (18) shows, /sU/ creates a postcyclic constituent and hence does not undergo cyclic lowering on the [prefix + root] cycle.

12. An additional class represented by *kuř* 'chicken' (neut.) behaves identically to *mař* in the singular and *mEst* in the plural; we omit explicit mention of this class from further discussion. Everything said about the singular forms of *mař* applies to the singular forms of *kuř*, and everything said about the plural forms of *mEst* applies to the plural forms of *kuř*.

13. The relevance of Czech vowel length alternations for a phonological model employing underlying yers and rule ordering was first brought to our attention by Ivona Kučerová. Kučerová 2004 provided inspiration for the current analysis.

14. We do not treat the vocative case in this chapter.

15. For discussion of Pre-Yer Lengthening in Slovak, which is similar in many respects to the rule in Czech, see Rubach 1993:168ff. The formulation in (24) is shorthand for a representation in which vowel length is the result of an extra timing slot, and thus for a representation in which length is reflected by skeletal structure and not a subsegmental feature. See Clements and Keyser 1983 for an extended discussion of such a model.

16. This rule is fully regular in inflectional suffixes but subject to some variation with respect to stem-internal vowels when they are [−back, −round]; thus, *mli:ko* and *mle:ko* 'milk, nom. sg.' are in variation for many speakers.

17. Ivona Kučerová suggests that this readjustment rule is due to a phonotactic constraint against the sequence *ux* in Czech, a sequence that is apparently unattested.

18. Additional evidence that the [root + theme] constituent is postcyclic may be found in the behavior of roots ending in a vowel, such as *kaka-o* 'cocoa', whose genitive plural *kaka-i:*, based on the underlying form [[kaka + e] + U], parallels the derivation of *ru:ži:*, but crucially does not show application of Vowel Truncation (5a) on the postcyclic innermost constituent [kaka + e]. We thank Pavel Caha and Markéta Ziková for pointing out the relevance of this example.

19. Among the case endings, the reader will notice the extremely widespread distribution of *-u* and *-i*, whose appearance may be reduced to an underspecified [+high] elsewhere item. A full morphological analysis of Czech syncretism should capture the regularities of their appearance; see Caha and Ziková 2005 for discussion.

20. In the orthography of Serbo-Croatian, the stress-bearing syllable is marked with an accent only in words with initial stress. In such words, the initial syllable is marked with a "falling" accent, of which there are two: the "long falling" accent in words of the form $\#C_0\hat{V}$: . . . and the "short falling" accent in words of the form $\#C_0\grave{V}$. . . . Words with stress on a noninitial syllable mark the syllable before the stress, and the marked syllables are said to have "rising" accent. There are two "rising" accents: a "long rising" accent in words of the form . . . $C_0\hat{V}$:$C_0'V$ . . . and a "short rising" accent in words of the form . . . $C_0\grave{V}C_0'V$. . . .

21. In Leskien's notation, an acute accent marks a long vowel with a rising tone.

References

Arsenijević, Boban. 2005. Slavic verb prefixes are resultative. To appear in *Cahiers Chronos*, a selection of papers from Chronos 6, Geneva 2004.

Bailyn, John, and Andrew Nevins. 2008. Russian genitive plurals are impostors. In *Inflectional identity*, ed. by Asaf Bachrach and Andrew Nevins, 237–270. Oxford: Oxford University Press.

Bermúdez-Otero, Ricardo. 2007. Morphological structure and phonological domains in Spanish denominal derivation. In *Optimality-theoretic studies in Spanish phonology*, ed. by Sonia Colina and Fernando Martínez-Gil, 278–311. Amsterdam: John Benjamins.

Bloomfield, Leonard. 1933. *Language*. New York: Henry Holt.

Caha, Pavel, and Markéta Ziková. 2005. Czech syncretism. Paper presented at Formal Description of Slavic Languages, 2005.

Chomsky, Noam, Morris Halle, and Fred Lukoff. 1956. On accent and juncture in English. In *For Roman Jakobson*, ed. by Morris Halle, Horace G. Lunt, and Hugh McLean, 65–80. The Hague: Mouton.

Clements, G. N., and Samuel Jay Keyser. 1983. *CV phonology: A generative theory of the syllable*. Cambridge, Mass.: MIT Press.

Gussmann, Edward. 1980. *Studies in abstract phonology*. Cambridge, Mass.: MIT Press.

Halle, Morris. 1994. The Russian declension: An illustration of the theory of Distributed Morphology. In *Perspectives in phonology*, ed. by Jennifer Cole and Charles Kisseberth, 29–60. Stanford, Calif.: CSLI Publications.

Halle, Morris, and Ora Matushansky. 2006. The morphophonology of Russian adjectival inflection. *Linguistic Inquiry* 37:351–404.

Halle, Morris, and K. P. Mohanan. 1985. Segmental phonology of Modern English. *Linguistic Inquiry* 16:57–116.

Halle, Morris, and Jean-Roger Vergnaud. 1987. *An essay on stress*. Cambridge, Mass.: MIT Press.

Havránek, Bohuslav, and Alois Jedlička. 1981. *Česká mluvnice*. Prague: Státní pedagogické nakladatelství.

Jakobson, Roman. 1948. Russian conjugation. *Word* 4:155–167.

Jakobson, Roman. 1975. *N. S. Trubetzkoy's letters and notes*. The Hague: Mouton.

Kayne, Richard. 1967. Against a cyclic analysis of Russian segmental phonology. Generals paper, MIT.

Kenstowicz, Michael. 1994. *Phonology in generative grammar*. Oxford: Blackwell.

Kučerová, Ivona. 2004. On the Czech declension. Ms., MIT.

Leskien, August. 1914. *Grammatik der serbo-kroatischen Sprache*. Heidelberg: Universitätsverlag C. Winter.

Lightner, Theodore. 1972. *Problems in theory of phonology*. Vol. 1, *Russian phonology and Turkish phonology*. Edmonton-Champaign: Linguistic Research, Inc.

Mascaró, Joan. 1976. Catalan phonology and the phonological cycle. Doctoral dissertation, MIT.

Matešić, Josip. 1970. *Der Wortakzent in der serbokroatischen Schriftsprache*. Heidelberg: Universitätsverlag C. Winter.

Oltra-Massuet, Isabel. 1999. On the notion of theme vowel: A new approach to Catalan verbal morphology. Master's thesis, MIT.

Rubach, Jerzy. 1993. *The Lexical Phonology of Slovak*. Oxford: Oxford University Press.

Sapir, Edward. 1933. The psychological reality of phonemes. In *Edward Sapir: Selected writings in language, culture and personality*, ed. by David G. Mandelbaum, 46–60. Berkeley and Los Angeles: University of California Press, 1949.

Scheer, Tobias. 2002. How yers made Lightner, Gussmann, Rubach, and Spencer & Co invent CVCV. Paper presented at Generative Linguistics in Poland 3.

Svenonius, Peter. 2005. Russian prefixes are phrasal. Paper presented at Formal Description of Slavic Languages 5.

Szpyra, Jolanta. 1995. *Three tiers in Polish and English phonology*. Lublin: Wydawnictwo Uniwersytetu Marii Curie-Skłodowskiej.

Townsend, Charles, and Laura Janda. 1996. *Common and comparative Slavic: Phonology and inflection*. Columbus, Ohio: Slavica.

19 Deriving Reduplicative Templates in a Modular Fashion

Eric Raimy

19.1 Introduction

This chapter argues that reduplicative templates can be straightforwardly derived from general principles regarding the modular organization of grammar, computation in phonology, and language acquisition. These three areas act as organic constraints on all proposed formal systems of reduplication. Once these organic restrictions are understood, it is clear that Precedence-Based Phonology (PBP; see, e.g., Raimy 1999, 2000a,b) provides an explanatorily adequate account of reduplicative templates. Comparing PBP with surface-prosody-based analyses such as Prosodic Morphology (PM; e.g., McCarthy and Prince 1996/1986, 2001/1993) demonstrates that the PBP model of reduplication naturally incorporates the advantages of the organic constraints identified in this chapter while PM-based models must be modified in incongruent ways that create redundancies.

Section 19.2 discusses the role that the formal representation of reduplication plays in accounting for reduplicative templates and illustrates the distinctions between a PM and a PBP approach. Section 19.3 demonstrates how a modular approach to morphology and phonology immediately derives the surface appearance of prosodic templates without positing prosodic templates as theoretical entities in their own right. Section 19.4 further shows that commonly held assumptions about possible (and impossible) computations in the phonology component further constrain possible reduplication patterns. Section 19.5 discusses the relevance of language acquisition to sharpening our understanding of common versus uncommon reduplication patterns. The result of these observations is that the minimalist theoretical machinery in PBP can economically and insightfully account for patterns of reduplication with little to no redundancy. On the other hand, each section highlights the redundancies in a PM account of reduplication. Consequently, currently popular surface-oriented, prosody-based accounts of reduplication should be abandoned.

19.2   Formal Underpinnings of a Theory of Reduplication

Any theory of reduplication must make specific claims about the formal nature of reduplication. For the purposes of this chapter, we need only to compare two distinct classes of formal proposals on this issue. The first is surface-oriented, prosody-based approaches; these assume that reduplication results from a phonologically underspecified affix whose full surface phonological specification results from the interaction of prosodic demands on the surface representation. This view is best exemplified by contemporary Optimality Theory (OT; Prince and Smolensky 2004) approaches to reduplication, based on proposals in McCarthy and Prince 1995. This approach posits an abstract RED morpheme whose surface phonological content is determined through constraint interaction.

Early forms of this model, such as McCarthy and Prince's (2001/1993), posited direct templatic constraints on RED at the surface (e.g., RED = $\sigma_{\mu\mu}$ 'heavy syllable'). Most contemporary approaches (e.g., atemplatic reduplication (Spaelti 1997, Gafos 1998, Hendricks 1999) or generalized templates (Urbanczyk 1996, 2006)) derive the surface form of reduplicative templates primarily from constraint interaction. The common theme is that these approaches posit mechanisms that directly restrict the surface prosodic shape of the abstract morpheme RED. Templatic, atemplatic, and generalized template approaches differ in the content of this constraining mechanism; they vary in how explicitly the surface prosodic category of the reduplicant is specified. They all assume that possible reduplicative templates are constrained by the vocabulary of prosodic categories and by the constraints that encode the RED morpheme in a rather direct fashion. The creation and the interpretation of RED are conflated in this approach.

PBP separates the creation and interpretation of reduplicated structures. All PBP models of reduplication (Raimy 1999, 2000a,b, Halle 2001, 2005, Frampton 2004) assume that the morphology builds the reduplicated structure, which the phonology then interprets. Although all these models benefit from this separation (despite their fundamental differences), in this chapter I will concentrate on explicating the model developed in Raimy 1999, 2000a,b.

(1) presents reduplication data from Pangasinan (all drawn from Benton 1971). The most important aspect of the data is the rich diversity of reduplication patterns found in this single language.

(1) *Reduplication in Pangasinan*
   a. *Total reduplication – nominal affixation (p. 103)*

toó	'man'	tóo-tóo	'figure of a man'
ogáw	'child'	ogáw-ogáw	'figure of a child'
abóng	'house'	abóñg-ábong	'toy house'

man-bása	'(will) read'	man-bása-bása	'reading anything and everything'
man-pasiár	'(will) go around'	man-pasiár-pasiár	'going around all over the place ...'

b. *Initial (C)VCV (p. 101)*
   Noun plurals

tamuró	'forefinger'	tamu-tamuró
pañgánsi	'ring finger'	pañgá-pañgánsi
lusór	'cup'	lusó-lusór
otót	'mouse, rat'	otó-otót

c. *Initial (C)VC reduplication*
   Noun plurals (pp. 100–101)

báley	'town'	bal-báley
balíta	'news'	bal-balíta
paltóg	'gun'	pal-paltóg
lúpa	'face'	lup-lúpa
áteñg	'parent'	at-áteñg

   Numerals of limitation (p. 151)

sakéy	'one'	sak-sakéy	'one only'
taló	'three'	tal-taló-ra	'three only'
+apát	'four'	a-pat-pátíra	'four only' INFIX

d. *Initial (C)V reduplication*
   Noun plurals (pp. 99–100)

kanáyon	'relative'	ka-kanáyon	'relatives'
dalikán	'clay stove'	da-ralikán	'clay stoves'
báso	'glass'	ba-báso	'glasses'
+amígo	'friend'	a-mi-mígo	'friends' INFIX

   Verbs (p. 120)

likét	'be happy'	maí-li-likét	'always happy'
ermén	'be sorrowful'	maí-e-ermén	'sentimental'
akís	'cry'	maí-a-akís	'crybabyish'

Pangasinan has at least four distinct reduplication patterns: total reduplication (1a), (C)VCV reduplication (1b), initial (C)VC reduplication (1c), and initial (C)V reduplication (1d). I say "at least" because of the two additional subpatterns of reduplication indicated by the forms in (1c) and (1d) with a "+" symbol. These two patterns show the infixing of the repeated sequence of phonemes as opposed to the strictly prefixing pattern found in all the other examples.

(2) shows the phonological representations built by the morphology that will account for the four main reduplication patterns in Pangasinan. The representations

are based on proposals in Raimy 1999, 2000a,b. The arrows indicate precedence relations, and the different reduplication patterns result because in each case different
phonemes are "inside" or "outside" of the "loop." See note 4 of Raimy, this volume,
for the purely expository nature of loops.

(2) *Precedence-Based Phonology representations for Pangasinan*
   a. *Total reduplication*

$$\# \to o \to g \to a \to w \to \% \qquad\qquad > \text{ogaw-ogaw}$$

   b. *(C)VCV reduplication*

$$\# \to t \to a \to m \to u \to r \to o \to \% \qquad > \text{tamu-tamuro}$$

   c. *(C)VC reduplication*

$$\# \to b \to a \to l \to e \to y \to \% \qquad\qquad > \text{bal-baley}$$

   d. *(C)V reduplication* $> \text{mai-a-akis}$

$$m \to a \to i$$
$$\# \to a \to k \to i \to s \to \%$$

The main thing to note about the examples in (2) is that segments that are inside
the loop end up being reduplicated, while segments outside the loop do not. Thus, in
(2a) total reduplication occurs because all the segments are "inside the loop," while
in (2b) (C)VCV reduplication occurs because only the first CVCV of the root is
"inside the loop." Reduplication occurs when there is a loop in a phonological
representation because of a linearization process that ensures that phonological
representations are interpretable by the phonetics-phonology interface. (See Raimy
1999, 2000a for discussion of the nature of linearization.) Linearization is not a
reduplication-specific device, because all phonological forms are linearized.

The representations in (2) also demonstrate how different reduplication patterns
are encoded in PBP. Different loops are created depending on how the begin and
end points of the precedence link that creates a given loop are described. (3) specifies
the begin and end points for the reduplication patterns in (2).

(3) *Descriptions of Pangasinan reduplication patterns*

Pattern	Begin	End
a. total	"last segment"	"first segment"
b. (C)VCV	"second vowel"	"first segment"
c. (C)VC	"after first vowel"	"first segment"
d. (C)V	"first vowel"	"first segment"

(3a) provides the general description for total reduplication. It specifies the begin point of the precedence link (the tail of an arrow) as "last segment" and the end of the precedence link (the head of the arrow) as "first segment." The combination of these two anchor points defines a new precedence link that causes an entire word to be within a loop, resulting in the surface effect of total reduplication. The descriptions of the anchor points are specific and deterministic (e.g., every word has a first segment) but variable (e.g., the distance between the first and last segment varies, depending on specific lexical items), thereby succinctly encoding the surface-variable total reduplication pattern. One noteworthy aspect of the descriptions in (3) is that the end setting for all the precedence links is the same. This uniformity in the end settings in (3) captures the generalization that all of these reduplication patterns are prefixing. Any partial repetition will appear before the entire lexical item because of this anchor point setting. The differences between the reduplication patterns are then encoded as differences in the begin anchor point. (3b) is distinct from (3a) in that the added precedence relation anchors to the "second vowel" which produces the surface effect of repeating the lexical item up to the second vowel. (3c) encodes an even smaller region of repetition, creating a loop from the segment "after the first vowel" to the "first segment." Finally, (3d) creates the smallest loop by anchoring to the "first vowel."

The fundamental difference between the PBP and PM models of reduplicative templates lies in the description of reduplication patterns. In PBP, there is no formal, necessary connection between the specifications for the begin and end anchor points that describe a reduplicative template. PM models describe reduplication patterns primarily through units of prosody such as mora, syllable, foot, or prosodic word. PBP does not deny the existence of any of these prosodic categories; it merely denies the primacy of their utility in describing reduplication patterns.

The PBP approach to reduplicative templates has two important consequences. First, the PBP approach can be considered truly atemplatic (McCarthy and Prince 1994) in that it involves no matching to a prosodic target. Second, this truly atemplatic aspect of PBP has the apparent liability that there is no constraint on the formal system to produce only reduplication patterns that coincide with a prosodic pattern. This disconnect between the anchor point system and prosody has been criticized by Downing (2001), Nevins (2002), and Lieber (2004). As the following sections demonstrate, however, this concern is unfounded.

To summarize this section: The fundamental formal distinction between the PM and PBP approaches to reduplicative templates is based on how different reduplication patterns are described. PM describes reduplication patterns either explicitly by using prosodic templates or implicitly by deriving a particular prosodic template from the interaction of surface-based prosodic constraints in language-specific configurations.

In contrast, PBP describes reduplication patterns by specifying how a precedence link is attached in terms of its anchor points. The PM approach appears more constrained than the PBP approach because of PM's limitation to only "legitimate prosodic categories"; we will see, however, that this restriction is actually a redundancy that can be eliminated.

19.3   Organic Constraint I: Grammatical Architecture

One question that must be answered when developing a model of reduplication is, What is the relationship between morphology and phonology?—more generally, What is the overall architecture of the grammar? Although examples where a morphological process is sensitive to a phonological distinction (e.g., expletive infixation and stress; McCarthy 1982) are easy to find, they do not require the conclusion that morphology and phonology are equally mixed. Answering the question about the relationship between morphology and phonology is another place where PM and PBP differ.

The PBP model generally adopts Distributed Morphology (Halle and Marantz 1993, 1994) as the model of grammatical architecture. Distributed Morphology is a modular approach to grammar in which the morphological and phonological modules are distinct. Furthermore, the phonology module follows the morphology module; this arrangement constrains the surface effects of any morphological operation to be in line with the general prosody of the language in question. In other words, the modular organization of Distributed Morphology ensures that the phonology acts as a filter on morphological processes. This is important because it derives the connection between occurring reduplication patterns and language-specific prosodic structures.

Let us consider the import of adopting this architecture by investigating some aspects of reduplication in Pangasinan. As the data in (1) show, Pangasinan has a (C)VC reduplication pattern. The fact that Pangasinan allows codas licenses the existence of this reduplication pattern. If word-internal codas were not licensed in Pangasinan, it would not be possible for a model of reduplication that assumed a modular relationship between morphology and phonology to force a CVC reduplication pattern. Consider the example derivation in (4).

(4) *Impossible CVC reduplication*
    a. *Morphophonology*
        $\# \rightarrow t \rightarrow a \rightarrow b \rightarrow u \rightarrow \%$

b. *Linearization and resyllabification*

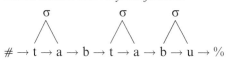

$\# \rightarrow t \rightarrow a \rightarrow b \rightarrow t \rightarrow a \rightarrow b \rightarrow u \rightarrow \%$

c. *Deletion*

$\ast \# \rightarrow t \rightarrow a \rightarrow b \rightarrow t \rightarrow a \rightarrow b \rightarrow u \rightarrow \% \quad \# \rightarrow t \rightarrow a \rightarrow t \rightarrow a \rightarrow b \rightarrow u \rightarrow \%$

The constraint on CVC reduplication in a strictly CV language is derived from this organization of grammar. If we allow the morphology to create a CVC reduplication structure as in (4a), it will be linearized and resyllabified as in (4b). The potential coda consonant in (4b) will be targeted for repair because it is not syllabified according to the general syllabification of the language in question. Consequently, as indicated in (4c), the offending coda consonant will be deleted. The point to note here is that the morphology can potentially generate structures that do not follow the surface prosodic patterns of the language and yet still not overgenerate because the phonology will repair and constrain this type of overgeneration. No match need be stipulated between the structures that the morphology generates and the surface prosody. This result is predicted by and obtained from the derivationally ordered modular structure of Distributed Morphology.

PBP combined with Distributed Morphology predicts a stronger connection between reduplication patterns and syllable structure than do PM approaches to reduplication. To see this, consider a variety of PM instantiated within an OT model of grammar that adopts a strictly templatic approach to reduplicative templates, which are evaluated at the surface. Within such a model, a CVC reduplication pattern could be specified and, depending on where the constraint that specifies the CVC template is ranked, the templatic requirement could override the general prosodic pattern of the language in question. Consider the tableau in (6) with the constraints listed in (5).

(5) *Constraints for pathological templates*
    a. MAX-STEM
        All segments of the stem in the input must appear in the output.
    b. MAX-BR
        All segments in the base must occur in the reduplicant.
    c. NOCODA
        Don't have codas.
    d. $\text{RED} = \sigma_{\mu\mu}$
        The reduplicant must have a branching rhyme.
    e. *LONGV
        Don't have long vowels.

(6) *Pathological templates*

/RED + tabu/	RED = $\sigma_{\mu\mu}$	MAX-BR	NOCODA	*LONGV	MAX-STEM
☞ a. tab-tabu		*	*		
b. taa-tabu		**!		*	
c. ta-tabu	*!	**			
d. tabu-tabu	*!				

The constraints in (5) are generic versions of commonly used constraints and are only informally defined. If we rank these constraints as shown in tableau (6), we can see that a CVC reduplicant, (6a), can be produced in a language that does not allow for codas. Note that the constraint requiring a branching coda (RED = $\sigma_{\mu\mu}$) is undominated, while MAX-STEM is dominated by NOCODA. This encodes the necessity that the reduplicant have a coda (the presence of the coda as opposed to vowel lengthening can also be derived from a MAX-BR effect) but that codas are not allowed in stems. We thus derive the emergence of the marked. The candidates in (6b–d) are all less harmonic because they violate undominated RED = $\sigma_{\mu\mu}$.

OT approaches to reduplicative templates do not necessarily produce the pathological effect in (6), and readers familiar with contemporary OT analyses of reduplication will immediately see the flaw—namely, the constraints that determine the size of the reduplicant, RED = $\sigma_{\mu\mu}$ and MAX-BR, are ranked above the general MAX-STEM constraint. This type of constraint ranking is generally eschewed for the simple reason that it can produce the types of pathological effects demonstrated in (6). Rejecting (6) as a possible grammar is a reasonable move, and it produces the correct type of constraint on reduplicative templates. However, this result has nothing to do with whether the reduplication pattern is specified via prosodic units or not. Rather, it is produced by a stipulated metaranking that prevents RED-specific constraints from dominating general Faithfulness constraints. In other words, it is a brute force prediction and does not flow organically from the architecture of the theory as it does in PBP approaches.

At first blush, atemplatic approaches to reduplication in OT would appear not to need the metaconstraint approach to rule out an analysis similar to (6) because the offending RED = $\sigma_{\mu\mu}$ is not available. This is not the case, though, at least for atemplatic approaches to reduplication based on proposals by Spaelti (1997) and Hendricks (1999). Both of these approaches use constraint interaction to derive limits on the size of reduplicants. Tableau (7) demonstrates an approach in this spirit where a heavy syllable is the target for reduplication. The constraints in (7) are the same as those in (6) except that the templatic constraint RED = $\sigma_{\mu\mu}$ has been removed. Instead, total reduplication is limited to a single syllable by the constraint *σ ("Don't have syllables"), in that if we assume that the RED morpheme must have some sort of surface exponent (see Gafos 1998 and Walker 2000 for proposals along these lines), then ranking MAX-BR beneath *σ will produce a reduplicant one syllable in size.

(7) *Pathological atemplatic approaches*

/RED + tabu/	*σ	MAX-BR	NoCODA	*LONGV	MAX-STEM
☞ a. tab-tabu	***	*	*		
b. taa-tabu	***	**!		*	
c. ta-tabu	***	**!			
d. tabu-tabu	****!				

Candidate (7a) is the most harmonic because it copies as much material from the base into the reduplicant as is allowed in a single syllable. The fact that MAX-BR is ranked above NoCODA (just as in (6)) causes the reduplicant to have a coda. Although some might object to the ranking in (7) because the general MAX-STEM constraint is dominated by *σ—a ranking that may be interpreted as suggesting that there are no syllables in the language, this objection is based on assuming the containment model of OT (Prince and Smolensky 2004) where segments occurred at the surface only if they were prosodically licensed (e.g., parsed into syllables; Ito 1986). The correspondence theory model of OT (McCarthy and Prince 1995) supplanted the containment model, and this has had the effect of dissociating the insertion and deletion of segments from whether they are prosodically licensed or not. Raimy and Idsardi (1997) use this aspect of syllabification in correspondence theory in analyzing reduplication in Bella Coola, which is notorious for its unsyllabified segments (Bagemihl 1991). Consequently, we must come to the same conclusion for atemplatic models as we did for templatic models: a metaconstraint that prevents RED-specific constraints from being ranked above general Faithfulness constraints is the source of the isomorphy between a language's prosodic structures and possible reduplication patterns.

The presence of this very useful metaconstraint on possible rankings makes any additional formal mechanisms constraining reduplicative templates completely redundant. This is where the PBP and PM approaches converge in the analysis of reduplication. It is the general architecture of particular theories that serves as a constraint on the shape of possible reduplication patterns; PBP invokes a modular approach of morphology first, whereas PM invokes a metaranking on reduplication-specific constraints. Neither theoretical approach requires additional restrictions on reduplication based on authentic units of prosody. Consequently, the PBP approach to reduplicative templates is not less constrained on this particular front even though there is no necessary connection between a prosodic category and the definition of a precedence link.

To summarize this section, the observation that reduplicative templates never violate language-specific surface prosody is the result of the architecture of grammar in both the PBP and PM approaches. In the PBP approach, modularity—with the morphology preceding the phonology—derives this effect. In the PM approach, a meta-constraint prevents constraint rankings that would produce pathological grammars. Neither theory requires any other mechanism to capture this generalization about the relationship between surface prosody and possible reduplicative templates. It follows that the additional constraints on reduplicative templates assumed in the PM approach are superfluous. In turn, it follows that PBP approaches show more promise of achieving explanatory adequacy than do PM approaches.

19.4   Organic Constraint II: Phonological Computation

The constraint on reduplication patterns derived from general grammatical architecture developed in section 19.3 does not fully constrain possible reduplication patterns. There are other conceivable patterns that would have legitimate prosodic structure but are nevertheless unattested in natural human language and are considered to be impossible. Downing (2001:448–449) suggests that PBP reduplication is unconstrained on this front because it could express the generalization "Copy up to the first three vowels," among others. Downing's question here is actually a recycled version of a question that McCarthy and Prince (1996/1986:2) asked: why there aren't any reduplication patterns of the type "Reduplicate the first three segments."

The general answer to this question is that phonology is only capable of certain calculations and has a limited stock of representations. All theories are equally constrained (or unconstrained) on this front. One way of demonstrating this point is to modify the above question and ask it about moras and syllables instead of segments or vowels. Why aren't there reduplication patterns that reduplicate the first three moras? Why aren't there reduplication patterns that reduplicate the first three syllables? The answer has nothing to do with whether the target of counting (moras vs. syllables vs. segments vs. vowels) is an authentic unit of prosody. The answer is based on the nature of the counting involved. Phonology only robustly supports binary counting (see Idsardi, this volume, for a different view; but note that admitting ternary counting to phonology does not help any particular model of reduplication), so any pattern that requires counting beyond two will be ruled out. Note that invoking the prosodic category "foot" or "syllable" to derive the counting-to-two restriction does not adequately explain why phonology doesn't count to three. This type of

response only shifts the question to a different domain: why do feet not consist
of three syllables, or syllables of three moras? PM and PBP have the same source of
constraints on possible reduplication patterns: that is, they are based on our general
knowledge of the "counting abilities" of phonology. This constraint on counting
ability is an organic property of both approaches, and in neither approach is it inherently connected to the notion "authentic units of prosody." So PM still faces the
question, how does the constraint that restricts reduplicative templates to authentic
units of prosody add to our understanding of reduplication? PBP faces an analogous
question: what constrains how precedence links can be defined?

Although in many cases different theories are equivalent when provided identical
resources, there are still questions about what patterns a theory can and cannot produce. In Raimy 1999, 2000a,b, the set of anchor points that describe possible reduplication patterns is not explicitly delineated, and this is a major source of confusion
with respect to PBP. Anchor point theory (Raimy 2005) remedies this omission and
subsumes proposals by Yu (2003) about where infixation can occur. The set of anchor points that describe where a precedence relation can be concatenated to a representation is delimited by the parameters in (8).

(8) *Parameters for an anchor point*
    Placement: {at/before/after}
    Edge: {first/last}
    Plane: {x-tier/metrical/syllable/consonantal}
    Target: {plain/stressed(head)/consonant}

Each parameter expresses a variable regarding how phonological representations
can be searched. Phonology must search (Reiss 2007) each representation as part of
any process or constraint evaluation because representations are directed graphs
(Raimy 2004). The placement parameter, (8a), refers to whether the element that is
being searched for is the target of the process, or whether the element immediately
before or after it is. The edge parameter, (8b), indicates whether the search is, informally speaking, left to right (first) or right to left (last). More formally, the edge parameter indicates whether a strictly left-to-right search terminates as soon as a target
is found (first) or whether the search continues all the way to the end of the representation and the last target found is used. The plane parameter, (8c), indicates which
representation in 3-D phonology (Halle 1985) is the locus of the calculation. Finally,
the target parameter, (8d), can narrow the locus of the search to subcategories of
stressed elements or consonants, creating cross-planar calculations (Archangeli and
Pulleyblank 1994) such as "the onset of the stressed syllable" or (as we'll see in a moment) "the segment after the first vowel."

In Raimy 2005, I argue that the parameters in (8) are sufficient to capture all documented reduplication and infixation patterns, but demonstrating the validity of these

claims is beyond the scope of this chapter. Instead, I will illustrate my proposals by formalizing the informal descriptions of the anchor points for the patterns of reduplication in Pangasinan proposed in (3). These generalizations have the formal parameter settings shown in (9).

(9) *Formal settings of the anchor point descriptions in (3)*
    a. "first segment" = {at, first, x-tier, plain}
    b. "last segment" = {at, last, x-tier, plain}
    c. "first vowel" = {at, first, metrical, plain}
    d. "second vowel" = {after, first, metrical, plain}
    e. "after first vowel" = {after, first, metrical, consonant}

The parameter settings for "first segment" and "last segment," (9a) and (9b), respectively, are straightforward in that the search operates on the x-tier. It thus scans every segment and ends when either the first or the last segment is reached. The "first vowel" anchor point, (9c), is produced by limiting the search to elements on the metrical tier alone (i.e., vowels) via the plane parameter and thus differs from the "first segment" anchor point in (9a) by only one parameter setting. The "second vowel" anchor point, (9d), is derived by again changing a single parameter, but this time it is the placement parameter. Changing the placement parameter setting from "at" in (9c) to "after" in (9d) allows the second vowel to be identified and produces the surface appearance of a foot being reduplicated. Finally, the "after first vowel" anchor point, (9e), differs from the "second vowel" anchor point, (9d), only in that if the target parameter is changed to "consonant," the search on the metrical tier to find the first vowel switches to the x-tier and selects the following segment (a consonant). See Raimy 2005 for a full discussion of the empirical adequacy of anchor point theory.

While the parameters in (8) are capable of producing all documented reduplication patterns, they are still restricted in that they cannot produce all hypothetical patterns. Consider the hypothetical XXX pattern presented in (10), discussed by McCarthy and Prince (1996/1986:2).

(10) *Hypothetical XXX reduplication*
    a. badupi   >   bad-badupi
    b. bladupi >   bla-bladupi
    c. adupi   >   adu-adupi

The PBP model cannot produce all three forms in (10) from a single generalization, because the surface patterns of reduplication for each of the three examples are distinct. If we view the three patterns in (10) in light of the analysis of Pangasinan in (3) and (9), then (10a) is (C)VC reduplication as in (3c), (10b) is (C)V reduplication as in (3d), and (10c) is (C)VCV reduplication as in (3b). Each of these reduplication patterns has a distinct begin setting as listed in (3) and formalized in (9). Therefore, PBP correctly predicts that the three forms in (10) do not create a coherent reduplication pattern.

The main point to take away from this demonstration is that the PBP model of reduplication is distinct from previous derivational models of reduplication (e.g., Marantz 1982, Mester 1988, Steriade 1988). It follows that arguments that have been lodged against these specific models of reduplication do not hold against the PBP approach. This observation does not give the PBP and PM models of reduplication a free pass, though, because both models have new sources of potential overgeneration that must be confronted. A specific example is Lieber's (2004) question about how the PBP model rules out the hypothetical last-vowel-to-first-vowel (LVTFV) reduplication pattern in (11).

(11) *Last-vowel-to-first-vowel reduplication pattern (Lieber 2004:199)*

    babab   babaabab

    dait   daiait

    balabat   balabaalabat

Lieber is correct in suggesting that the frequent occurrence of the anchor points "first vowel" and "last vowel" raises the question why we don't find them paired to create a "no coda and no onset" reduplication pattern. However, Lieber's discussion misses two points. The first is that this particular aberrant overgeneration is shared by all existing models of reduplication, as the following data from Korean onomatopoeic and mimetic reduplication illustrate:

(12) *Onomatopoeic and mimetic reduplication in Korean (Jun 2006)*

	Base	*Total reduplication*	*V-initial reduplication*
a.	pulkɨt	pulkɨt-pulkɨt	ulkɨt-pulkɨt
b.	pollok	pollok-pollok	ollok-pollok
c.	pulluk	pulluk-pulluk	ulluk-pulluk
d.	pulthuŋ	pulthuŋ-pulthuŋ	ulthuŋ-pulthuŋ
e.	təmpəŋ	təmpəŋ-təmpəŋ	əmpəŋ-təmpəŋ
f.	c'ukɨl	c'ukɨl-c'ukɨl	ukɨl-c'ukɨl

These data present a total reduplication pattern and a V-initial reduplication pattern. The importance of the V-initial reduplication pattern is twofold: first, how would a PM-based model of reduplication account for a reduplicant that must delete an initial onset, and second, once we have a mechanism that can produce this "no onset" effect, why doesn't it occur with a "no coda" ranking? Again, we can see that there are more parallels between PM and PBP once we begin to investigate where and how reduplicative templates are constrained.

It is also incorrect to suggest, as Lieber (2004:199) does, that the formal mechanisms of a theory are the only source of constraints. The inaccuracy of this view is clear from the current discussion and section 19.3. Lieber's question cannot be rejected, though, because it can be generalized to one that asks why all possible operations in reduplication (i.e., onset effects, no coda effects, no onset effects, complex onset effects, etc.) do not appear in all possible combinations and in all templatic patterns. Answers already exist for some parts of this question (see Raimy 2000a:163–177 for discussion), but not for the LVTFV pattern in (11). Another way of posing Lieber's question is to ask what other sources of organic constraints there can be beyond architectural and computational aspects.

19.5   Organic Constraint III: Language Acquisition

The final organic constraint on reduplicative templates that we will investigate is language acquisition. The general view of language acquisition that will be adopted here is presented in Yang 2002. Yang argues that language acquisition is the result of both Universal Grammar (UG; Chomsky 1980) and statistical learning. UG's role is to constrain the hypothesis space within which statistical learning occurs. For the purposes of reduplication, UG provides the formalisms of a particular theory. For our purposes, UG is a PBP-based model of reduplication along with anchor point theory (see section 19.4). Under this view, the formal system described by PBP delimits the hypothesis space and nothing more. The explanation for how a child arrives at particular places in the hypothesis space should result from a combination of particular proposals about statistical learning and the environment.

At this point, we must recognize that there is a distinction between the lack of a particular pattern and children's inability to learn the pattern. Lieber (2004) conflates these two options when she suggests that because LVTFV reduplication is not attested, it must therefore be impossible in UG, and thus unlearnable. I suggest that this is too hasty a conclusion. We first must determine whether children can or cannot learn this pattern if presented with appropriate data. One way of investigating this question is experimental. Marcus et al. (1999) have demonstrated that 7-month-olds can learn reduplication patterns sufficiently to distinguish between ABA (e.g., *wo-fe-wo*) and ABB (e.g., *wo-fe-fe*) patterns and between AAB (e.g., *wo-wo-fe*) and ABB (e.g., *wo-fe-fe*) patterns. The particular relevance of this finding is that 7-month-old infants with very limited exposure (2-minute speech sample) can process reduplication patterns well enough to distinguish between two reduplication patterns. While Marcus et al.'s results do not answer our particular question, they do provide the template for experiments that would potentially determine whether we should treat the LVTFV reduplication pattern as a gap or an impossible pattern.

Another useful avenue of inquiry into LVTFV reduplication is formal in nature. What is the starting state of the learner? Exactly what pattern of forms is needed to induce a LVTFV generalization? Both of these questions have been investigated by Iba and Nevins (2004), who developed a computational model of a selectionist learner (Yang 2002) for reduplication, called the *reduplicator*, based on general PBP proposals. As part of the selectionist learner implementation, the reduplicator returns multiple working solutions for reduplication patterns that are ambiguous with respect to description via anchor points. Given the possibility of ambiguous patterns, it is very likely that UG provides biases toward particular solutions over others. These biases can be encoded as the likelihood of when particular anchor point pairings are selected as hypotheses to compare input data with in a selectionist learner. (13) presents two general biases that will guide learning of reduplication patterns.

(13) *Biases for reduplicative learning*
    a. *Be conservative:* favor anchor points with more general parameter settings.
       Placement: at   >   before/after
       Plane: x-tier >   metrical/syllable/consonantal
       Target: plain   >   stressed(head)/consonant
    b. *Be different:* if the anchor points, X and Y, that define a precedence link are not identical (X = Y), then favor pairs of anchor points that are distinct with respect to (a).

The biases in (13) reflect general aspects of language acquisition and do not appear to be unique to reduplication. (13a), "Be conservative," is the general idea that learners move to more specific hypotheses only when positive evidence forces them to. For each parameter in (8), there is a most general setting that contains the others. Consequently, (13a) can also be viewed as the application of the Elsewhere Condition (Kiparsky 1973) as a metric over parameter settings. Note that there is no representational way to determine whether "first" or "last" is more general for the placement parameter of an anchor point, so it has been omitted from (13a). The "Be different" bias in (13b) can be understood as some sort of knowledge similar to the Obligatory Contour Principle, where the learner knows that sequences of extremely similar but not identical elements are generally disfavored.

The interaction of the biases in (13) creates a dynamic ranking of hypotheses that depends on the particular reduplicated form being considered. For reasons of space, I cannot fully investigate these ideas here, but the general shape of their impact is clear from (14).

(14) *Acquisition biases for total reduplication pattern*
    a. $\# \to t \to a \to g \to o \to \%$ Anchor point descriptors for /t/
                                   "first segment"
                                   "first consonant"
                                   "before first vowel"
                                   Anchor point descriptors for /o/
                                   "last segment"
                                   "last vowel"
                                   "after last consonant"

b. *Hypotheses*
  i. "last segment" → "first segment"   Least marked hypothesis
                                                                    Next level of markedness

  ii. "last segment" → "first consonant"
  iii. "last vowel" → "first segment"

                                                                    Next level of markedness

  iv. "last vowel" → "first consonant"
  v. "last segment" → "before first vowel"
  vi. "after last consonant" → "first segment"

                                                                    Most marked hypotheses

  vii. "last vowel" → "before first vowel"
  viii. "after last consonant" → "first
        consonant"
  ix. "after last consonant" → "before
       first vowel"

(14a) presents the hypothetical reduplicated form *tago-tago*, which in a vacuum would generally be interpreted as a case of total reduplication. The point of (14) is to demonstrate that this form is actually multiply ambiguous. The ambiguity can be seen by considering the anchor points that can describe the reduplicative precedence link. The /t/ at the head of the precedence link can be described as "first segment," "first consonant," or "before the first vowel," and the /o/ at the foot of the precedence link can be described as "last segment," "last vowel," or "after the last consonant." When these two sets of anchor points are freely combined, we get the nine hypotheses about what this reduplication pattern could be.

The biases in (13) allow us to rank these nine hypotheses as in (14b). The least marked hypothesis about the pattern in (14a) is (14bi): "the last segment precedes the first segment." This is the least marked hypothesis because when we interpret the element informally called "segment" in terms of specific anchor point parameter settings from (8), it results from the least marked setting for placement ("at"), plane ("x-tier"), and target ("plain"). Because "segment" is the most general hypothesis that works for both anchor points, this analysis will be favored by the learner. All the other solutions that also work are more specific along some dimension of (13a) and are thus less favored by the learner. (14bii) and (14biii) each take one step toward the more specific by altering the setting for the plane parameter. (14bii), "first consonant," changes the plane setting to "consonantal," and (14biii), "last vowel," changes the plane setting to "metrical" (producing "vowel"). The remaining hypotheses about the reduplication pattern in (14a) are all more specific than the one in (14bi).

The biases in (13) do not eliminate more specific hypotheses from consideration, but they do make their adoption less likely for the learner. This view of the biases has two immediate benefits. The first is that this type of bias can be modeled very easily in selectionist learning (Yang 2002) by adding probabilities to particular hypotheses based on the biases instead of selecting a hypothesis purely at random to test against the data. Hypotheses favored by the biases in (13) will be chosen to test at a higher frequency than disfavored hypotheses. The result is that some learners will adopt a surface-ambiguous but disfavored hypothesis (see Lightner 1972:50–51 for discussion of this idea) as their solution to a particular reduplication pattern. This possibility might provide insight into language change or variation.

Fitzpatrick and Nevins (2004) demonstrate the usefulness of surface-form ambiguity in their discussion of a dialectal difference in Tigrinya, based on two reduplication patterns for quadriliteral forms documented by Rose (2003). Fitzpatrick and Nevins argue that the two distinct patterns for quadriliteral forms are directly explained by the ambiguity of how to describe the reduplication pattern on triliteral forms. Consider the data in (15).

(15) *Tigrinya frequentive forms*
   a. Triliteral: $\sqrt{grf}$ 'whip'   graf > gərarəf
   b. "First reduplicate C_2 to achieve quadriliteral status, then infix /a/ between C_2 and C_3."

   $\# \rightarrow g \rightarrow r \rightarrow f \rightarrow \%$ *linearize*

   $\# \rightarrow g \rightarrow r \rightarrow r \rightarrow f \rightarrow \%$ *linearize* $\# \rightarrow g \rightarrow r \rightarrow a \rightarrow r \rightarrow f \rightarrow \%$

   a

   c. "Ca reduplication on penult C"
   $\# \rightarrow g \rightarrow r \rightarrow f \rightarrow \%$ *linearize* $\# \rightarrow g \rightarrow r \rightarrow a \rightarrow r \rightarrow f \rightarrow \%$

   a

   d. Quadriliteral: $\sqrt{glbt}$ 'turn over'
   $\# \rightarrow g \rightarrow l \rightarrow b \rightarrow t \rightarrow \%$
   i. glabt > gəlabət
   ii. glbabt > gələba:bət

(15a) presents the triliteral root $\sqrt{grf}$ 'whip' and its frequentive form [gərarəf] (note that all schwas in (15) are epenthetic and thus have been left out in some representations). (15b) and (15c) demonstrate that there are at least two distinct ways of producing the intermediate form /grarf/. (15b) reduplicates the medial consonant in order to produce a quadriliteral form of the base through linearization, and then infixes /a/ between C_2 ("consonant after the first consonant") and C_3 ("consonant before the last consonant") in the now quadriliteral form. (15c) shows that the same surface form can be created through what Fitzpatrick and Nevins call *Ca* reduplication, where the infix /a/ uses the same anchor point, "consonant before the last consonant," for beginning and end. (15d) then demonstrates that both analyses are attested as a dialectal difference in how the frequentive is formed on true quadriliteral forms in Tigrinya. (15di) is based on the derivation in (15b), and (15dii) is based on the derivation in (15c).

From an acquisition point of view, we must allow learners of Tigrinya to base their learning primarily on triliteral forms (presumably occurring much more frequently than quadriliteral forms) and then assume that they choose a specific hypothesis (either (15b) or (15c)) in the face of multiple possible solutions. Once learners make a decision based on the dominant triliteral forms, it can be the locus of language change (see Calabrese, this volume, and Kaisse, this volume, for discussion of this point) because the quadriliteral forms will now distinguish possible hypotheses for triliteral roots. For this particular case, learners must choose a single solution to the ambiguity of triliteral roots. This general theme of explaining variation through ambiguity is also found in Nevins and Vaux 2007.

To return to Lieber's challenge, we have now arrived at an explanation for the lack of attested LVTFV reduplication patterns. It is not that this pattern is ruled out by UG; instead, the acquisition aspect of reduplication very much disfavors it. In essence, the LVTFV generalization violates both biases in (13): the informal "vowel" anchor point requires the more specific plane parameter (i.e., metrical) setting, which violates (13a), and then reuses this marked identical anchor point setting, now violating (13b). Other surface-ambiguous hypotheses that fare better on the biases in (13) will serve as better acquisition targets, thus hindering the learner from settling on the LVTFV pattern. Consider the forms in (16), which add likely bases and corresponding LVTFV reduplication patterns to the ones suggested by Lieber.

(16) *Additional last-vowel-to-first-vowel forms*

	Base	*Reduplicated*	*Favored hypothesis*
a.	abo	abo-abo	"last segment to first segment"
b.	abot	abo-abot	"last vowel to first segment"
c.	dabo	dabo-abo	"last segment to first vowel"
d.	ba	ba-a	"first vowel to first vowel"

These forms are all implied by the forms that Lieber chose and are based primarily on what is known about the typology of syllables. First, in order for the LVTFV pattern to exist at all, vowel hiatus must be tolerated by the language, which implies that there can be onsetless syllables. Consequently, forms like (16a) and (16b) should occur in the language, with (16a) suggesting to the learner that total reduplication is an option and (16b) suggesting that total reduplication with a "no coda" effect is an option. Second, since syllables without codas are universal, (16c) and (16d) should appear in the language. Both of these forms obscure the identification of the "last vowel" anchor point. (16c) will pull the learner toward a "last segment" hypothesis, and (16d) suggests a "first vowel lengthening" process. When these forms are added to the learning environment, it becomes clear that the LVTFV hypothesis is a very difficult one for a learner to grab onto. This observation is sufficient to explain why the LVTFV pattern is not attested, yet it leaves the question of whether humans can learn this pattern an empirical matter. This is the most appropriate state of affairs regarding this pattern.

To summarize this section, the final constraining mechanism on reduplicative templates is a theory of language acquisition. A theory of language acquisition cannot be viewed as an ad hoc mechanism that exists only to artificially constrain an overly powerful formal mechanism. Instead, a theory of language acquisition should be considered a core component of any formal proposal. Consequently, contrary to Lieber's (2004:199) suggestion that the PBP model is not constrained enough to further our understanding of reduplication, the model in fact provides the right amount of constrained formalism in that it creates a hypothesis space in which a learner could use proposed acquisition devices such as selectionist learning (Yang 2002) or other statistical models of language acquisition (see the 2006 *Trends in Cognitive Science* special issue on probabilistic learning). The hypothesis space for reduplication patterns created by PBP is empirically adequate in that it contains all attested reduplication patterns. Because this hypothesis space is not "flat," not all patterns of reduplication are equally likely. The remaining question for the PBP approach is how much of the warping of the hypothesis space can be derived from general linguistic resources and/or general cognitive resources.

19.6   Conclusions

The purpose of this chapter has been to demonstrate that independently needed theories of grammatical architecture, computation, and acquisition all serve as organic constraints on possible reduplication patterns. All formal theories of reduplication are obliged to explain how these components of human cognition interact with the proposed formal system accounting for reduplication. The main claim of this chapter has been that once the role of these other components of human cognition is fleshed out with respect to reduplication, the claim that reduplicative templates are constrained by surface prosodic considerations as suggested by Prosodic Morphology becomes vacuous. The strongest aspect of the arguments in this chapter against PM approaches to reduplication is that all of the advances and insights provided by the Precedence-Based Phonology model require the PM model to be modified in ad hoc ways to mimic the PBP model. The fact that the insights from the PBP model of reduplication can be used to improve the PM model clearly suggests that these insights are not theory-internal to PBP but instead are actual improvements in our understanding of the nature of reduplication. Because the prosodic constraints proposed by PM add no explanatory force to analyses of reduplication, and because it appears that all other things are equal between PM and PBP models of reduplication (e.g., weak generative capacity appears to be the same), Occam's razor suggests that the PBP model of reduplication patterns should replace the PM approach.

Note

I would like to thank the participants and audience at the CUNY Phonology Forum Symposium on Architecture and Representation in Phonology for discussion of these issues. Further discussion occurred with Bill Idsardi, and Chuck Cairns has spent a large amount of time helping sift these ideas. All errors of fact and interpretation that remain are mine.

References

Archangeli, Diana, and Douglas Pulleyblank. 1994. *Grounded Phonology*. Cambridge, Mass.: MIT Press.

Bagemihl, Bruce. 1991. Syllable structure in Bella Coola. *Linguistic Inquiry* 22:589–646.

Benton, Richard. 1971. *Pangasinan reference grammar*. Honolulu: University of Hawaii Press.

Chomsky, Noam. 1980. *Rules and representations*. New York: Columbia University Press.

Downing, Laura. 2001. Review of Eric Raimy (2000) *The phonology and morphology of reduplication. Phonology* 18:445–451.

Fitzpatrick, Justin, and Andrew Nevins. 2004. Linearizing nested and overlapping precedence in multiple reduplication. In *Proceedings of the 27th Annual Penn Linguistics Colloquium*, ed. by Sudha Arunachalam and Tatjana Scheffler, 75–88. Penn Working Papers in Linguistics 10.1. Philadelphia: University of Pennsylvania, Penn Linguistics Club.

Frampton, John. 2004. Distributed reduplication. Ms., Northeastern University. http://www.math.neu.edu/ling/DR/dr.html.

Gafos, Diamandis [Adamantios]. 1998. A-templatic reduplication. *Linguistic Inquiry* 29:515–527.

Halle, Morris. 2001. Infixation versus onset metathesis in Tagalog, Chamorro, and Toba Batak. In *Ken Hale: A life in language*, ed. by Michael Kenstowicz, 153–168. Cambridge, Mass.: MIT Press.

Halle, Morris. 1985. Speculations about the representations of words in memory. In *Phonetic linguistics: Essays in honor of Peter Ladefoged*, ed. by Victoria Fromkin, 101–114. Orlando, Fla.: Academic Press. Reprinted in *From memory to speech and back: Papers on phonetics and phonology 1954–2002*, 122–136. Berlin: Mouton de Gruyter, 2002.

Halle, Morris. 2005. Reduplication. Ms., MIT.

Halle, Morris, and Alec Marantz. 1993. Distributive Morphology and the pieces of inflection. In *The view from Building 20: Essays in linguistics in honor of Sylvain Bromberger*, ed. by Kenneth Hale and Samuel Jay Keyser, 111–176. Cambridge, Mass.: MIT Press.

Halle, Morris, and Alec Marantz. 1994. Some key features of Distributed Morphology. In *Papers on phonology and morphology*, ed. by Andrew Carnie and Heidi Harley, 275–288. MIT Working Papers in Linguistics 21. Cambridge, Mass.: MIT, MIT Working Papers in Linguistics.

Hendricks, Sean. 1999. Reduplication without template constraints: A study in bare-consonant reduplication. Doctoral dissertation, University of Arizona.

Iba, Aaron, and Andrew Nevins. 2004. A selectionist learner for parametrically ambiguous reduplicants. Paper presented at the 78th annual meeting of the Linguistic Society of America.

Ito, Junko. 1986. Syllable theory in prosodic phonology. Doctoral dissertation, University of Massachusetts, Amherst.

Jun, Jongho. 2006. Variable affix position in Korean partial reduplication. Paper presented at the 80th annual meeting of the Linguistic Society of America, Albuquerque.

Kiparsky, Paul. 1973. "Elsewhere" in phonology. In *A festschrift for Morris Halle*, ed. by Stephen R. Anderson and Paul Kiparsky, 277–314. New York: Academic Press.

Lieber, Rochelle. 2004. Review of *The phonology and morphology of reduplication* by Eric Raimy. *General Linguistics* 42 (1–4): 195–200.

Lightner, Theodore. 1972. *Problems in the theory of phonology*. Edmonton, Alberta: Linguistic Research, Inc.

Marantz, Alec. 1982. Re reduplication. *Linguistic Inquiry* 13:435–482.

Marcus, G. F., S. Vijayan, S. Bandi Rao, and P. M. Viston. 1999. Rule learning by seven-month-old infants. *Science* 283:77–80.

McCarthy, John J. 1982. Prosodic structure and expletive infixation. *Language* 58:574–590.

McCarthy, John J., and Alan Prince. 1994. Two lectures on Prosodic Morphology (Utrecht, 1994). Part I, Template form in Prosodic Morphology. Part II, Faithfulness and reduplicative identity. Ms., University of Massachusetts, Amherst, and Rutgers University. Rutgers Optimality Archive ROA-59. http://roa.rutgers.edu.

McCarthy, John J., and Alan Prince. 1995. Faithfulness and reduplicative identity. In *Papers in Optimality Theory*, ed. by Jill Beckman, Suzanne Urbanczyk, and Laura Walsh Dickey, 249–384. University of Massachusetts Occasional Papers in Linguistics 18. Amherst: University of Massachusetts, Graduate Linguistic Student Association. Rutgers Optimality Archive ROA-60. http://roa.rutgers.edu.

McCarthy, John J., and Alan Prince. 1996/1986. Prosodic morphology 1986. Ms., University of Massachusetts, Amherst, and Rutgers University. RuCCS Technical Report 32.

McCarthy, John J., and Alan Prince. 2001/1993. Prosodic Morphology: Constraint interaction and satisfaction. Ms., University of Massachusetts, Amherst, and Rutgers University. Rutgers Optimality Archive ROA 482. http://roa.rutgers.edu.

Mester, Armin. 1988. *Studies in tier structure*. New York: Garland.

Nevins, Andrew. 2002. Review of *The phonology and morphology of reduplication* by Eric Raimy. *Language* 78:770–773.

Nevins, Andrew, and Bert Vaux. 2007. Metalinguistic, shmetalinguistic: The phonology of shm-reduplication. In *CLS 39-1: The Main Session*, ed. by Jon Cihlar, Amy Franklin, Dave

Kaiser, and Irene Kimbara, 702–721. Chicago: University of Chicago, Chicago Linguistic Society. http://ling.auf.net/lingBuzz/000319.

Prince, Alan, and Paul Smolensky. 2004. *Optimality Theory: Constraint interaction in generative grammar*. Malden, Mass.: Blackwell.

Raimy, Eric. 1999. Representing reduplication. Doctoral dissertation, University of Delaware.

Raimy, Eric. 2000a. *The phonology and morphology of reduplication*. Berlin: Mouton de Gruyter.

Raimy, Eric. 2000b. Remarks on backcopying. *Linguistic Inquiry* 31:541–552.

Raimy, Eric. 2004. Primitives of affixation. Paper presented at the Third North American Phonology Conference, Concordia University.

Raimy, Eric. 2005. Prosodic residue in an a-templatic world. Paper presented at University of Delaware Linguistic Colloquium Series, Newark.

Raimy, Eric, and William J. Idsardi. 1997. A minimalist approach to reduplication in Optimality Theory. In *Proceedings of North East Linguistic Society (NELS) 27*, ed. by Kiyomi Kusumoto, 369–382. Amherst: University of Massachusetts, Graduate Linguistic Student Association.

Reiss, Charles. 2007. Adjacency as a long-distance relation. Paper presented at the CUNY Conference on Precedence Relations. http://www.cunyphonologyforum.net/forum.php.

Rose, Sharon. 2003. Triple take: Tigre and the case of internal reduplication. In *San Diego linguistic papers* 1, 109–128. La Jolla, Calif.: University of California, San Diego, Department of Linguistics.

Spaelti, Phillip. 1997. Dimensions of variation in multi-pattern reduplication. Doctoral dissertation, University of California, Santa Cruz.

Steriade, Donca. 1988. Reduplication and syllable transfer in Sanskrit and elsewhere. *Phonology* 5:73–155.

Urbanczyk, Suzanne. 1996. Patterns of reduplication in Lushootseed. Doctoral dissertation, University of Massachusetts, Amherst.

Urbanczyk, Suzanne. 2006. Reduplicative form and the root-affix asymmetry. *Natural Language and Linguistic Theory* 24:179–240.

Walker, Rachel. 2000. Nasal reduplication in Mbe affixation. *Phonology* 17:65–115.

Yang, Charles. 2002. *Knowledge and learning in natural language*. Oxford: Oxford University Press.

Yu, Alan C. L. 2003. The morphology and phonology of infixation. Doctoral dissertation, University of California, Berkeley.

Index

Current Studies in Linguistics
Samuel Jay Keyser, general editor